Microsoft®
OUTLOOK® 2013

COMPLETE

Steven M. Freund
Corinne L. Hoisington

CENGAGE
Learning®

SHELLY
CASHMAN
SERIES®

Australia • Brazil • Japan • Korea • Mexico • Singapore • Spain • United Kingdom • United States

CENGAGE
Learning®

Microsoft® Outlook® 2013: Complete
Steven M. Freund and Corinne L. Hoisington

Executive Editor: Kathleen McMahon

Product Manager: Caitlin Womersley

Associate Product Manager: Crystal Parenteau

Editorial Assistant: Sarah Ryan

Print Buyer: Julio Esperas

Director of Production: Patty Stephan

Content Project Manager: Matthew Hutchinson

Development Editor: Lisa Ruffalo

Senior Brand Manager: Elinor Gregory

Market Development Manager: Kristie Clark

Market Development Manager:
Gretchen Swann

Marketing Coordinator: Amy McGregor

QA Manuscript Reviewers: Jeffrey Schwartz, John Freitas, Serge Palladino, Susan Pedicini, Danielle Shaw, Susan Whalen

Art Director: GEX Publishing Services, Inc.

Text Design: Joel Sadagursky

Cover Design: Lisa Kuhn, Curio Press, LLC

Cover Photo: Tom Kates Photography

Compositor: PreMediaGlobal

Copyeditor: Michael Beckett

Proofreader: Christine Clark

Indexer: Alexandra Nickerson

For product information and technology assistance, contact us at
Cengage Learning Customer & Sales Support, 1-800-354-9706

For permission to use material from this text or product, submit all requests online at **cengage.com/permissions**
Further permissions questions can be emailed to
permissionrequest@cengage.com

Library of Congress Control Number: 2013941389

ISBN-13: 978-1-285-16887-6
ISBN-10: 1-285-16887-9

Cengage Learning
20 Channel Center Street
Boston, MA 02210
USA

Cengage Learning is a leading provider of customized learning solutions with office locations around the globe, including Singapore, the United Kingdom, Australia, Mexico, Brazil, and Japan. Locate your local office at:
international.cengage.com/region

Cengage Learning products are represented in Canada by Nelson Education, Ltd.

To learn more about Cengage Learning, visit **www.cengage.com**

Purchase any of our products at your local college bookstore or at our preferred online store at **www.cengagebrain.com**

Printed in the United States of America
1 2 3 4 5 6 7 18 17 16 15 14

Microsoft® OUTLOOK® 2013
COMPLETE

Contents

Microsoft **Office 365**

Office 365 Essentials

Microsoft **Outlook 2013**

CHAPTER ONE
Managing Email Messages with Outlook

CHAPTER TWO
Managing Calendars with Outlook

Preface

The Shelly Cashman Series® offers the finest textbooks in computer education. We are proud that since Microsoft® Office 4.3, our series of Microsoft Office textbooks have been the most widely used books in education. With each new edition of our Office books, we make significant improvements based on the software and comments made by instructors and students. Microsoft® Outlook® 2013 text, the Shelly Cashman Series development team carefully reviewed our pedagogy and analyzed its effectiveness in teaching today's Office student. Students today read less, but need to retain more. They need not only to be able to perform skills, but to retain those skills and know how to apply them to different settings. Today's students need to be continually engaged and challenged to retain what they're learning.

With this Microsoft Outlook 2013 text, we continue our commitment to focusing on the users and how they learn best.

Objectives of This Textbook

Microsoft Outlook 2013: Complete is intended for a six- to nine-week period in a course that teaches Outlook 2013 in conjunction with another application or computer concepts. No experience with a computer is assumed, and no mathematics beyond the high school freshman level is required. The objectives of this book are:

- To offer an in-depth presentation of Microsoft Outlook 2013

- To expose students to practical examples of the computer as a useful tool

- To acquaint students with the proper procedures to create email and calendars suitable for coursework, professional purposes, and personal use

- To help students discover the underlying functionality of Outlook 2013 so they can become more productive

- To develop an exercise-oriented approach that allows learning by doing

The Shelly Cashman Approach

A Proven Pedagogy with an Emphasis on Project Planning

Each chapter presents a practical problem to be solved within a project planning framework. The project orientation is strengthened by the use of the Roadmap, which provides a visual framework for the project. Step-by-step instructions with supporting screens guide students through the steps. Instructional steps are supported by the Q&A, Experimental Step, and BTW features.

A Visually Engaging Book that Maintains Student Interest

The step-by-step tasks, with supporting figures, provide a rich visual experience for the student. Call-outs on the screens that present both explanatory and navigational information provide students with information they need when they need to know it.

Supporting Reference Materials (Quick Reference)

With the Quick Reference, students can quickly look up information about a single task, such as keyboard shortcuts, and find page references to where in the book the task is illustrated.

Integration of the World Wide Web

The World Wide Web is integrated into the Outlook 2013 learning experience with (1) BTW annotations; (2) BTW, Q&A, and Quick Reference Summary Web pages; and (3) the Learn Online resources for each chapter.

End-of-Chapter Student Activities

Extensive end-of-chapter activities provide a variety of reinforcement opportunities for students to apply and expand their skills through individual and group work. To complete some of these assignments, you will be required to use the Data Files for Students. Visit www.cengage.com/ct/studentdownload for detailed access instructions or contact your instructor for information about accessing the required files.

New to this Edition

Enhanced Coverage of Critical Thinking Skills

A new Consider This element poses thought-provoking questions throughout each chapter, providing an increased emphasis on critical thinking and problem-solving skills. Also, every task in the project now includes a reason *why* the students are performing the task and *why* the task is necessary.

Enhanced Retention and Transference

A new Roadmap element provides a visual framework for each project, showing students where they are in the process of creating each project, and reinforcing the context of smaller tasks by showing how they fit into the larger project.

Integration of Office with Cloud and Web Technologies

A new Lab focuses entirely on integrating cloud and web technologies with Outlook 2013, using technologies like blogs, social networks, and SkyDrive.

More Personalization

Each chapter project includes an optional instruction for the student to personalize his or her solution, if required by an instructor, making each student's solution unique.

More Collaboration

A new Research and Collaboration project has been added to the Consider This: Your Turn assignment at the end of each chapter.

Instructor Resources

The Instructor Resources include both teaching and testing aids and can be accessed via CD-ROM or at www.cengage.com/login.

Instructor's Manual Includes lecture notes summarizing the chapter sections, figures and boxed elements found in every chapter, teacher tips, classroom activities, lab activities, and quick quizzes in Microsoft Word files.

Syllabus Easily customizable sample syllabi that cover policies, assignments, exams, and other course information.

Figure Files Illustrations for every figure in the textbook in electronic form.

Powerpoint Presentations A multimedia lecture presentation system that provides slides for each chapter. Presentations are based on chapter objectives.

Solutions to Exercises Includes solutions for all end-of-chapter and chapter reinforcement exercises.

Test Bank & Test Engine Test banks include 112 questions for every chapter, featuring objective-based and critical thinking question types, and including page number references and figure references, when appropriate. Also included is the test engine, ExamView, the ultimate tool for your objective-based testing needs.

Data Files for Students Includes all the files that are required by students to complete the exercises.

Additional Activities for Students Consists of Chapter Reinforcement Exercises, which are true/false, multiple-choice, and short answer questions that help students gain confidence in the material learned.

Learn Online

CengageBrain.com is the premier destination for purchasing or renting Cengage Learning textbooks, eBooks, eChapters, and study tools at a significant discount (eBooks up to 50% off Print). In addition, CengageBrain.com provides direct access to all digital products, including eBooks, eChapters, and digital solutions, such as CourseMate and SAM, regardless of where purchased. The following are some examples of what is available for this product on www.cengagebrain.com.

Student Companion Site The Student Companion Site reinforces chapter terms and concepts using true/false questions, multiple choice questions, short answer questions, flash cards, practice tests, and learning games, all available for no additional cost at www.cengagebrain.com.

SAM: Skills Assessment Manager Get your students workplace-ready with SAM, the market-leading proficiency-based assessment and training solution for Microsoft Office! SAM's active, hands-on environment helps students master Microsoft Office skills and computer concepts that are essential to academic and career success, delivering the most comprehensive online learning solution for your course!

Through skill-based assessments, interactive trainings, business-centric projects, and comprehensive remediation, SAM engages students in mastering the latest Microsoft Office programs on their own, giving instructors more time to focus on teaching. Computer concepts labs supplement instruction of important technology-related topics and issues through engaging simulations and interactive, auto-graded assessments. With enhancements including streamlined course setup, more robust grading and reporting features, and the integration of fully interactive MindTap Readers containing Cengage Learning's premier textbook content, SAM provides the best teaching and learning solution for your course.

MindLinks MindLinks is a new Cengage Learning Service designed to provide the best possible user experience and facilitate the highest levels of learning retention and outcomes, enabled through a deep integration of Cengage Learning's digital suite into an instructor's Learning Management System (LMS). MindLinks works on any LMS that supports the IMS Basic LTI open standard. Advanced features, including gradebook exchange, are the result of active, enhanced LTI collaborations with industry-leading LMS partners to drive the evolving technology standards forward.

CourseNotes

Cengage Learning's CourseNotes are six-panel quick reference cards that reinforce the most important and widely used features of a software application in a visual and user-friendly format. CourseNotes serve as a great reference tool during and after the course. CourseNotes are available for software applications, such as Microsoft Office 2013. There are also topic-based CourseNotes available for Best Practices in Social Networking, Hot Topics in Technology, and Web 2.0. Visit www.cengagebrain.com to learn more!

Certification Prep Tool

This textbook was developed to instruct on the Microsoft® Office 2013 certification objectives. Microsoft Corporation has developed a set of standardized, performance-based examinations that you can take to demonstrate your overall expertise with Microsoft Office 2013 programs. Microsoft Office 2013 certification provides a number of benefits for you:

- Differentiate yourself in the employment marketplace from those who are not Microsoft Office Specialist or Expert certified.
- Prove skills and expertise when using Microsoft Office 2013.
- Perform at a higher skill level in your job.
- Work at a higher professional level than those who are not certified.
- Broaden your employment opportunities and advance your career more rapidly.

For more information about Microsoft Office 2013 certification, including a complete list of certification objectives, visit the Microsoft web site, http://www.microsoft.com/learning. To see which Microsoft Office 2013 certification objectives are addressed by the contents of this text and where each is included in the text, visit the Certification resource on the Student Companion Site located on www.cengagebrain.com. For detailed instructions about accessing available resources, visit www.cengage.com/ct/studentdownload or contact your instructor for information about accessing the required files.

About Our Covers

The Shelly Cashman Series is continually updating our approach and content to reflect the way today's students learn and experience new technology. This focus on student success is reflected on our covers, which feature real students from The University of Rhode Island using the Shelly Cashman Series in their courses, and reflect the varied ages and backgrounds of the students learning with our books. When you use the Shelly Cashman Series, you can be assured that you are learning computer skills using the most effective courseware available.

Textbook Walk-Through

The Shelly Cashman Series Pedagogy: Project-Based — Step-by-Step — Variety of Assessments

Roadmaps provide a visual framework for each project, showing the students where they are in the process of creating each project.

Step-by-step instructions provide a context beyond the point-and-click. Each step provides information on why students are performing each task and what will occur as a result.

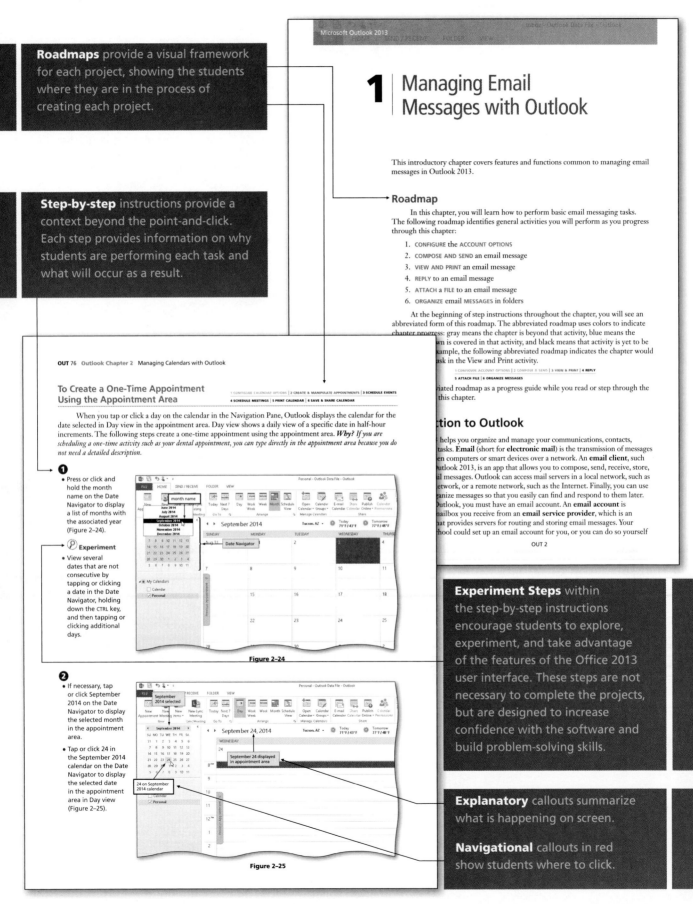

Microsoft Outlook 2013

1 Managing Email Messages with Outlook

This introductory chapter covers features and functions common to managing email messages in Outlook 2013.

Roadmap

In this chapter, you will learn how to perform basic email messaging tasks. The following roadmap identifies general activities you will perform as you progress through this chapter:

1. CONFIGURE the ACCOUNT OPTIONS
2. COMPOSE AND SEND an email message
3. VIEW AND PRINT an email message
4. REPLY to an email message
5. ATTACH a FILE to an email message
6. ORGANIZE email MESSAGES in folders

At the beginning of step instructions throughout the chapter, you will see an abbreviated form of this roadmap. The abbreviated roadmap uses colors to indicate chapter progress: gray means the chapter is beyond that activity, blue means the ___own is covered in that activity, and black means that activity is yet to be ___ample, the following abbreviated roadmap indicates the chapter would ___ask in the View and Print activity.

1 CONFIGURE ACCOUNT OPTIONS | 2 COMPOSE & SEND | 3 VIEW & PRINT | 4 REPLY
5 ATTACH FILE | 6 ORGANIZE MESSAGES

___viated roadmap as a progress guide while you read or step through the ___ this chapter.

___ction to Outlook

___ helps you organize and manage your communications, contacts, ___ tasks. **Email** (short for **electronic mail**) is the transmission of messages ___en computers or smart devices over a network. An **email client**, such ___utlook 2013, is an app that allows you to compose, send, receive, store, ___il messages. Outlook can access mail servers in a local network, such as ___etwork, or a remote network, such as the Internet. Finally, you can use ___anize messages so that you easily can find and respond to them later. ___utlook, you must have an email account. An **email account** is ___ailbox you receive from an **email service provider**, which is an ___at provides servers for routing and storing email messages. Your ___chool could set up an email account for you, or you can do so yourself

OUT 2

OUT 76 Outlook Chapter 2 Managing Calendars with Outlook

To Create a One-Time Appointment Using the Appointment Area

1 CONFIGURE CALENDAR OPTIONS | 2 CREATE & MANIPULATE APPOINTMENTS | 3 SCHEDULE EVENTS
4 SCHEDULE MEETINGS | 5 PRINT CALENDAR | 6 SAVE & SHARE CALENDAR

When you tap or click a day on the calendar in the Navigation Pane, Outlook displays the calendar for the date selected in Day view in the appointment area. Day view shows a daily view of a specific date in half-hour increments. The following steps create a one-time appointment using the appointment area. *Why? If you are scheduling a one-time activity such as your dental appointment, you can type directly in the appointment area because you do not need a detailed description.*

1
- Press or click and hold the month name on the Date Navigator to display a list of months with the associated year (Figure 2–24).

Experiment
- View several dates that are not consecutive by tapping or clicking a date in the Date Navigator, holding down the CTRL key, and then tapping or clicking additional days.

Figure 2–24

2
- If necessary, tap or click September 2014 on the Date Navigator to display the selected month in the appointment area.
- Tap or click 24 in the September 2014 calendar on the Date Navigator to display the selected date in the appointment area in Day view (Figure 2–25).

Figure 2–25

Experiment Steps within the step-by-step instructions encourage students to explore, experiment, and take advantage of the features of the Office 2013 user interface. These steps are not necessary to complete the projects, but are designed to increase confidence with the software and build problem-solving skills.

Explanatory callouts summarize what is happening on screen.

Navigational callouts in red show students where to click.

Q&A boxes anticipate questions students may have when working through the steps and provide additional information about what they are doing right where they need it.

4
• In the My Calendars pane, tap or click Personal to insert a check mark in the check box, so that both the default Calendar and the Personal calendars are selected and displayed in the appointment area of the Outlook window (Figure 2–6).

Q&A Why is the default calendar displayed in a different color from the Personal calendar?
Outlook automatically assigns a different color to each new calendar you create to make it easier to distinguish one calendar from the other. Your calendar colors might be different from those shown in Figure 2–6.

Can I select a color for the calendar?
Yes. Tap or click the VIEW tab, tap or click the Color button (VIEW tab | Color group), and then select a color from the Color gallery.

Figure 2–6

5
• Tap or click Calendar in the My Calendars pane to remove the check mark from the Calendar check box so that the default calendar no longer is displayed in the appointment area (Figure 2–7).

Q&A Why does my view look different from what is shown?
Figure 2–7 shows Month view, which is the default view for Calendar. If this is not the current view, tap or click the Month button (HOME tab | Arrange group).

What is the purpose of the colored tabs on each side of the appointment area?
The tabs provide navigation to the previous and next appointments.

Figure 2–7

---

a meeting request arrive in the Inbox of the meeting organizer. To create a meeting request, you use the Untitled – Meeting request window, which is similar to the Untitled – Appointment window with a few exceptions. The meeting request window includes the To text box, where you enter an email address for **attendees**, who are people invited to the meeting, and the Send button, which sends the invitation for the meeting to the attendees. When a meeting request arrives in the attendee's Inbox, it displays an icon different from an email message icon.

Before you invite others to a meeting, confirm that the meeting date and time are available. Your school or business may have shared calendars that can be downloaded to your Outlook calendar. This shared calendar may be an iCalendar with an .ics file extension. An **iCalendar** represents a universal calendar format used by several email and calendar programs, including Microsoft Outlook, Google Calendar, and Apple iCal. The iCalendar format enables users to publish and share calendar information on the Web and by email.

Before you send out a meeting request, how can you set the groundwork for an effective meeting?

• Import other calendars to compare everyone's schedule.

• Prepare an agenda stating the purpose of the meeting.

• Be sure you include everyone who needs to attend the meeting. Invite only those people whose attendance is absolutely necessary to ensure that all of the agenda items can be addressed at the meeting.

• Confirm that the location of the meeting is available and that the room is the appropriate size for the number of people invited. Also, make sure the room can accommodate any multimedia equipment that might be needed for the meeting, such as a projector or telephone.

CONSIDER THIS

To Import an iCalendar File

1 CONFIGURE CALENDAR OPTIONS | 2 CREATE & MANIPULATE APPOINTMENTS | 3 SCHEDULE EVENTS
4 SCHEDULE MEETINGS | 5 PRINT CALENDAR | 6 SAVE & SHARE CALENDAR

Before scheduling a meeting, you can open your school's calendar to view your availability. Your school has a shared calendar in the iCalendar format that contains the school's master schedule. The following steps import an iCalendar file into Outlook. *Why? By importing another calendar, you can compare available dates for a meeting.*

1
• Tap or click the FILE tab on the ribbon to open the Backstage view.

• Tap or click Open & Export to display the Open gallery (Figure 2–71).

Figure 2–71

Consider This boxes pose thought-provoking questions with answers throughout each chapter, promoting critical thought along with immediate feedback.

Textbook Walk-Through

Chapter Summary A listing of the tasks completed within the chapter, grouped into major task categories in an outline format.

Consider This: Plan Ahead box presents a single master planning guide that students can use as they create documents on their own.

BTW
Certification
The Microsoft Office Specialist (MOS) program provides an opportunity for you to obtain a valuable industry credential — proof that you have the Outlook 2013 skills required by employers. For more information, visit the Certification resource on the Student Companion Site located on www.cengagebrain.com. For detailed instructions about accessing available resources, visit www.cengage.com/ct/studentdownload or contact your instructor for information about accessing the required files.

To Exit Outlook

This project now is complete. The following steps exit Outlook. For a detailed example of the procedure summarized below, refer to the Office 2013 and Windows 8 chapter at the beginning of this book.

1 If you have an email message open, tap or click the Close button on the right side of the title bar to close the message window.

2 Tap or click the Close button on the right side of the title bar to exit Outlook.

Chapter Summary

In this chapter, you have learned how to use Outlook to create a personal schedule by entering appointments, creating recurring appointments, moving appointments to new dates, and scheduling events. You also learned how to invite attendees to a meeting, accept a meeting request, and change the time of a meeting. To review your schedule, you learned to view and print your calendar in different views and print styles. Finally, you learned how to save your calendar and share your schedule with others. The items listed below include all the new Outlook skills you have learned in this chapter with the tasks grouped by activity.

Configuring the Outlook Calendar
Create a Personal Calendar Folder (OUT 64)
Add a City to the Calendar Weather Bar (OUT 67)
Go to a Specific Date (OUT 68)
Display the Calendar in Work Week View (OUT 69)
Display the Calendar in Week View (OUT 70)
Display the Calendar in Month View (OUT 71)
Display the Calendar in Schedule View (OUT 71)
Add Holidays to the Default Calendar (OUT 73)

Creating and Editing Appointments
Create a One-Time Appointment Using the Appointment Area (OUT 76)
Add Color Categories (OUT 78)
Assign a Color Category to an Appointment (OUT 80)
Create an Appointment Using the Appointment Window (OUT 81)
Set a Reminder for an Appointment (OUT 85)
Set Recurrence Options for an Appointment (OUT 87)
Save an Appointment (OUT 90)
Create an Appointment Date and Time Using Natural Language Phrases (OUT 92)
Move an Appointment to a Different Time on the Same Day (OUT 94)
Move an Appointment to a Different Date (OUT 94)
Delete a Single Occurrence of a Recurring Appointment (OUT 95)

Scheduling Events
Create a One-Time Event in the Appointment Window (OUT 97)
Delete a One-Time Event (OUT 99)
Create a Recurring Event Using the Appointment Window (OUT 99)
Move a Recurring Event to a Different Day (OUT 101)

Scheduling Meetings
Import an iCalendar File (OUT 104)
View Calendars in the Overlay Mode (OUT 106)
View and Dock the Peek Calendar (OUT 107)
Create and Send a Meeting Request (OUT 108)
Change the Time of a Meeting and Send an Update (OUT 110)
Reply to a Meeting Request (OUT 111)
Propose a New Meeting Time (OUT 112)
Cancel a Meeting (OUT 112)

Printing Calendars in Different Views
Print the Calendar in Weekly Calendar Style (OUT 112)
Change the Calendar View to List View (OUT 114)
Print the Calendar in List View (OUT 115)

Saving and Sharing the Calendar
Save a Calendar as an iCalendar File (OUT 116)
Share a Calendar (OUT 117)

BTW
Quick Reference
For a table that lists how to complete the tasks covered in this book using touch gestures, the mouse, ribbon, shortcut menu, and keyboard, see the Quick Reference Summary at the back of this book, or visit the Quick Reference resource on the Student Companion Site located on www.cengagebrain.com. For detailed instructions about accessing available resources, visit www.cengage.com/ct/studentdownload or contact your instructor for information about accessing the required files.

CONSIDER THIS

Consider This: Plan Ahead
What decisions will you need to make when composing and respondin[g]
Outlook folders in the future?

A. Set Up Outlook:
   1. Determine the language preferences and sensitivity level.
   2. Decide on the sensitivity level.
B. Compose the Email Message:
   1. Plan the content of your email message based on a formal
   2. Select an appropriate theme.
C. Open Incoming Email Messages:
   1. Determine your preference for displaying messages.
   2. Save the attachment to the appropriate folder.
D. Respond to Messages:
   1. Plan your response to the incoming message.
   2. Correct errors and revise as necessary.
   3. Establish which file you will attach to your email message.
   4. Determine the importance level of the message.
E. Organize Your Outlook Folders:
   1. Establish your folder names.
   2. Plan where each email message should be stored.

CONSIDER THIS

How should you submit solutions to questions in the assignments identified with a ⊛ symbol?
Every assignment in this book contains one or more questions identified with a ⊛ symbol. These questions require you to think beyond the assigned file. Present your solutions to the questions in the format required by your instructor. Possible formats may include one or more of these options: write the answer; create a document that contains the answer; present your answer to the class; discuss your answer in a group; record the answer as audio or video using a webcam, smartphone, or portable media player; or post answers on a blog, wiki, or website.

BTW
Certification
The Microsoft Office Specialist (MOS) program provides an opportunity for you to obtain a valuable industry credential — proof that you have the Outlook 2013 skills required by employers. For more information, visit the Certification resource on the Student Companion Site located on www.cengagebrain.com. For detailed instructions about accessing available resources, visit www.cengage.com/ct/studentdownload or contact your instructor for information about accessing the required files.

Apply Your Knowledge

Reinforce the skills and apply the concepts you learned in this chapter.

Creating an Email with an Attachment
Note: To complete this assignment, you will be required to use the Data Files for Students. Visit www.cengage.com/ct/studentdownload for detailed instructions or contact your instructor for information about accessing the required files.

Instructions: You are to send an email message addressed to the director of the Chamber of Commerce, who is assisting in marketing an Earth Day Run. You also attach a file named Apply 1-1 Earth Day Flyer from the Data Files for Students.

Apply Your Knowledge This exercise usually requires students to open and manipulate a file that parallels the activities learned in the chapter.

Extend Your Knowledge

Extend the skills you learned in this chapter and experiment with new skills. You will use Help to complete the assignment.

Organizing Email Messages

Note: To complete this assignment, you will be required to use the Data Files for Students. Visit www.cengage.com/ct/studentdownload for detailed instructions or contact your instructor for information about accessing the required files.

Instructions: You are organizing a river rafting trip for you and your friends. In the Extend 1-1.pst mailbox file, you will create two folders, add a folder in the Favorites section, and then move messages into the appropriate folders. You also will apply a follow-up flag for the messages in one of the folders. Use Outlook Help to learn about how to duplicate a folder in the Favorites section, how to add a flag to a message for follow-up, and how to create an Outlook Data File (.pst file).

Perform the following tasks:

1. Run Outlook.

2. Open the Outlook Data File Extend 1-1.pst mailbox file.

3. Create two new folders within the Inbox folder. Name the first folder River Rafting and the second folder Camping. Move the messages into the appropriate folders. Make sure that only mail items are contained in the new folders.

4. The Favorites section is at the top of the Folder Pane on the left. Display a duplicate of the River Rafting folder in the Favorites section.

5. To the message regarding the Riverfront Campground, assign a flag for follow-up for tomorrow.

6. Based on the message headers and content of the email messages in the Extend 1-1 mailbox, move each message to the appropriate folders you created. Figure 1–78 shows the mailbox with the messages moved to the new folders.

7. Export the Inbox mailbox to an Outlook Data File (.pst). Navigate to the Outlook folder in the Documents library, save the document using the file name Extend 1-1 River Rafting.pst, and then submit it in the format specified by your instructor.

8. Exit Outlook.

9. Saving your mailbox as a .pst file provides a backup copy of your email messages to submit to your instructor. What are other reasons for sav

Figure 1–

Extend Your Knowledge projects at the end of each chapter allow students to extend and expand on the skills learned within the chapter. Students use critical thinking to experiment with new skills to complete each project.

Analyze, Correct, Improve projects call on the students to analyze a file, discover errors in it, fix the errors, and then improve upon the file using the skills they learned in the chapter.

Analyze, Correct, Improve

Analyze an email message, correct all errors, and improve the design.

Correcting Errors and Changing the Format of an Email Message

Note: To complete this assignment, you will be required to use the Data Files for Students. Visit www.cengage.com/ct/studentdownload for detailed instructions or contact your instructor for information about accessing the required files.

Instructions: In a folder window, double-tap or double-click the message file, Analyze 1-1, to open the file from the Data Files for Students. Outlook starts and opens the message. The lawn care business referral message contains spelling errors. If red wavy lines do not appear below some words, tap or click at the end of the message and then press the SPACEBAR. The email message was sent using the HTML message format. If you received the message as Plain Text, change the message format to HTML.

Perform the following tasks:

1. Correct Recheck the spelling and grammar errors by tapping or clicking the FILE tab on the ribbon to open the Backstage view, and then tap or click Options to display the Outlook Options dialog box. Click the Mail category, if necessary. In the Compose messages section, tap or click the Editor Options button to display the Editor Options dialog box. Tap or click Proofing in the left pane (Editor Options dialog box). In the 'When correcting spelling in Outlook' section, ensure the 'Check spelling as you type' check box contains a check mark. Tap or click the Recheck E-mail button and then tap or click Yes. Tap or click the OK button two times. Correct the errors in the message. Change the email address of the recipient and then change the greeting to address the new recipient. The corrected message is displayed in Figure 1–79.

2. Improve Change the message importance to High Importance. If requested by your instructor, change the name in signature line 1 to the name of your father or uncle. Navigate to the Outlook folder in the Documents library, save the document using the file name Analyze 1-1 Lawn Care Referrals, and then submit it in the format specified by your instructor.

3. Think about the reason you use email communication. In the case of the lawn care referral message, why would you use email instead of a phone call, Facebook posting, Twitter message, or text message?

Figure 1–79

Textbook Walk-Through

> **In the Lab** Three in-depth assignments in each chapter that require students to apply the chapter concepts and techniques to solve problems. One Lab is devoted entirely to Cloud and Web 2.0 integration.

In the Labs

Use the guidelines, concepts, and skills presented in this chapter to increase your knowledge of Outlook. Labs 1 and 2, which increase in difficulty, require you to create solutions based on what you learned in the chapter; Lab 3 requires you to create a solution, which uses cloud and web technologies, by learning and investigating on your own from general guidance.

Lab 1: Composing an Email Message with an Attachment

Note: To complete this assignment, you will be required to use the Data Files for Students. Visit www.cengage.com/ct/studentdownload for detailed instructions or contact your instructor for information about accessing the required files.

Problem: Your grandparents would like you to share photos from your recent trip to Yellowstone National Park using email, because they are not on Facebook. Compose an email message to your grandparents as shown in Figure 1–80 with the three picture attachments of Yellowstone.

Instructions: Perform the following tasks:
1. Compose a new email message. Address the message to yourself with a courtesy copy to your instructor.
2. Enter the subject, message text, and signature shown in Figure 1–80. Insert blank lines where they are shown in the figure. If Outlook flags any misspelled words as you type, check their spelling and correct them.
3. Change the theme of the email message to the Wisp theme.
4. If requested by your instructor, change the city and state from Goldstream, CA, to the city and state of your birth. Also change the signature to your name.
5. Attach the three image files named Lab 1-1 Park1, Lab 1-1 Park2, and Lab 1-1 Park3 from the Data Files for Students to the email message.

3. Attach the Lab 1-3 Avoid Texting While Driving file (PowerPoint file) from the Data Files for Students to the email message.
4. Send the email message with high importance.
5. Open your Microsoft account at outlook.com. Open the email message that you sent from Outlook, and then tap or click View online to view the PowerPoint file attachment.
6. Tap or click Edit in Browser to edit the PowerPoint presentation in the Microsoft PowerPoint web app.
7. If requested by your instructor, change the name on the first slide to your name on the first line and the name of your hometown on the second line.
8. Add a fourth slide to the PowerPoint presentation with a statistic about the dangers of texting while driving. (*Hint:* Research this statistic on the web.)
9. Tap or click the INSERT tab, and then add a clip art image about texting to the fourth slide.
10. Tap or click the FILE tab, and then tap or click Share to share the PowerPoint file.
11. Tap or click 'Share with other people', and then type your instructor's email address and a short message describing how sharing a file by sending a link to your SkyDrive can be easier than sending an attachment. Include your name at the end of the message.
12. Tap or click the Share button to send the shared link of the completed PowerPoint file to your instructor.
13. Exit the PowerPoint web app, and then exit Outlook.
14. ⊕ In this lab, you sent an email from the Outlook client to your web-based email service provider at outlook.com. What are the advantages of using a Microsoft account with Outlook on your personal computer and checking the same email address at outlook.com when you are on a public computer?

Figure 1–80

⊛ Consider This: Your Turn

Apply your creative thinking and problem solving skills to design and implement a solution.

1: Composing an Email Message about your Favorite Music and Attaching a File
Personal

Part 1: You are taking a Music Appreciation class. During the first class, your instructor requests that you send an email message with your favorite song as an attachment. The email message should be addressed to yourself and your instructor. Insert an appropriate subject line based on the content of your message. Explain why the attached song is your favorite in a paragraph within the email message. Apply a theme other than the Office theme. You can use your own digital music file as an attachment. Use the concepts and techniques presented in this chapter to create this email message. Be sure to check spelling and grammar before you send the message. Submit your assignment in the format specified by your instructor.

Part 2: ⊛ You made several decisions while creating the email message in this assignment. When you decide on the subject of an email message, what considerations should you make? Why is it important that the email subject be eye-catching and informative? Why should you not use the following subject lines: FYI, Hi, or Open This?

2: Composing an Email in Response to a Job Opening and Attaching a File
Professional

Note: To complete this assignment, you will be required to use the Data Files for Students. Visit www.cengage.com/ct/studentdownload for detailed instructions or contact your instructor for information about accessing the required files.

Continued >

> **Consider This: Your Turn** exercises call on students to apply creative thinking and problem solving skills to design and implement a solution.

Office 2013 and Windows 8: Essential Concepts and Skills

Microsoft product screen shots used with permission from Microsoft Corporation.

Objectives

You will have mastered the material in this chapter when you can:

- Use a touch screen
- Perform basic mouse operations
- Start Windows and sign in to an account
- Identify the objects in the Windows 8 desktop
- Identify the apps in and versions of Microsoft Office 2013
- Run an app
- Identify the components of the Microsoft Office ribbon

- Create folders
- Save files
- Change screen resolution
- Perform basic tasks in Microsoft Office apps
- Manage files
- Use Microsoft Office Help and Windows Help

Office 2013 and Windows 8: Essential Concepts and Skills

This introductory chapter covers features and functions common to Office 2013 apps, as well as the basics of Windows 8.

Roadmap

In this chapter, you will learn how to perform basic tasks in Windows and the Office apps. The following roadmap identifies general activities you will perform as you progress through this chapter:

1. SIGN IN to an account
2. USE WINDOWS
3. USE Office APPS
4. FILE and Folder MANAGEMENT
5. SWITCH between APPS
6. SAVE and Manage FILES
7. CHANGE SCREEN RESOLUTION
8. EXIT Office APPS
9. USE ADDITIONAL Office APPS
10. USE Office and Windows HELP

At the beginning of the step instructions throughout the chapter, you will see an abbreviated form of this roadmap. The abbreviated roadmap uses colors to indicate chapter progress: gray means the chapter is beyond that activity, blue means the task being shown is covered in that activity, and black means that activity is yet to be covered. For example, the following abbreviated roadmap indicates the chapter would be showing a task in the Use Apps activity.

1 SIGN IN | 2 USE WINDOWS | 3 USE APPS | 4 FILE MANAGEMENT | 5 SWITCH APPS | 6 SAVE FILES
7 CHANGE SCREEN RESOLUTION | 8 EXIT APPS | 9 USE ADDITIONAL APPS | 10 USE HELP

Use the abbreviated roadmap as a progress guide while you read or step through the instructions in this chapter.

Introduction to the Windows 8 Operating System

Windows 8 is the newest version of Microsoft Windows, which is a popular and widely used operating system. An **operating system** is a computer program (set of computer instructions) that coordinates all the activities of computer hardware, such as memory, storage devices, and printers, and provides the capability for you to communicate with the computer.

The Windows operating system simplifies the process of working with documents and apps by organizing the manner in which you interact with the computer. Windows is used to run apps. An **app** (short for application) consists of programs designed to make users more productive and/or assist them with personal tasks, such as word processing or browsing the web.

The Windows 8 interface begins with the **Start screen**, which shows tiles (Figure 1). A **tile** is a shortcut to an app or other content. The tiles on the Start screen include installed apps that you use regularly. From the Start screen, you can choose which apps to run using a touch screen, mouse, or other input device.

Figure 1

Using a Touch Screen and a Mouse

Windows users who have computers or devices with touch screen capability can interact with the screen using gestures. A **gesture** is a motion you make on a touch screen with the tip of one or more fingers or your hand. Touch screens are convenient because they do not require a separate device for input. Table 1 on the next page presents common ways to interact with a touch screen.

If you are using your finger on a touch screen and are having difficulty completing the steps in this chapter, consider using a stylus. Many people find it easier to be precise with a stylus than with a finger. In addition, with a stylus you see the pointer. If you still are having trouble completing the steps with a stylus, try using a mouse.

Table 1 Touch Screen Gestures

Motion	Description	Common Uses
Tap	Quickly touch and release one finger one time.	Activate a link (built-in connection) Press a button Run a program or an app
Double-tap	Quickly touch and release one finger two times.	Run a program or an app Zoom in (show a smaller area on the screen, so that contents appear larger) at the location of the double-tap
Press and hold	Press and hold one finger to cause an action to occur, or until an action occurs.	Display a shortcut menu (immediate access to allowable actions) Activate a mode enabling you to move an item with one finger to a new location
Drag, or slide	Press and hold one finger on an object and then move the finger to the new location.	Move an item around the screen Scroll
Swipe	Press and hold one finger and then move the finger horizontally or vertically on the screen.	Select an object Swipe from edge to display a bar such as the Charms bar, Apps bar, and Navigation bar (all discussed later)
Stretch	Move two fingers apart.	Zoom in (show a smaller area on the screen, so that contents appear larger)
Pinch	Move two fingers together.	Zoom out (show a larger area on the screen, so that contents appear smaller)

© 2014 Cengage Learning

BTW

BTWs

For a complete list of the BTWs found in the margins of this book, visit the BTW resource on the Student Companion Site located on www.cengagebrain.com. For detailed instructions about accessing available resources, visit www.cengage.com/ct/studentdownload or contact your instructor for information about accessing the required files.

BTW

Touch Screen Differences

The Office and Windows interfaces may vary if you are using a touch screen. For this reason, you might notice that the function or appearance of your touch screen differs slightly from this chapter's presentation.

CONSIDER THIS

Will your screen look different if you are using a touch screen?
The Windows and Microsoft Office interface varies slightly if you are using a touch screen. For this reason, you might notice that your screen looks slightly different from the screens in this chapter.

Windows users who do not have touch screen capabilities typically work with a mouse that has at least two buttons. For a right-handed user, the left button usually is the primary mouse button, and the right mouse button is the secondary mouse button. Left-handed people, however, can reverse the function of these buttons.

Table 2 explains how to perform a variety of mouse operations. Some apps also use keys in combination with the mouse to perform certain actions. For example, when you hold down the CTRL key while rolling the mouse wheel, text on the screen may become larger or smaller based on the direction you roll the wheel. The function of the mouse buttons and the wheel varies depending on the app.

Table 2 Mouse Operations

Operation	Mouse Action	Example*
Point	Move the mouse until the pointer on the desktop is positioned on the item of choice.	Position the pointer on the screen.
Click	Press and release the primary mouse button, which usually is the left mouse button.	Select or deselect items on the screen or run an app or app feature.
Right-click	Press and release the secondary mouse button, which usually is the right mouse button.	Display a shortcut menu.
Double-click	Quickly press and release the primary mouse button twice without moving the mouse.	Run an app or app feature.
Triple-click	Quickly press and release the primary mouse button three times without moving the mouse.	Select a paragraph.
Drag	Point to an item, hold down the primary mouse button, move the item to the desired location on the screen, and then release the mouse button.	Move an object from one location to another or draw pictures.
Right-drag	Point to an item, hold down the right mouse button, move the item to the desired location on the screen, and then release the right mouse button.	Display a shortcut menu after moving an object from one location to another.
Rotate wheel	Roll the wheel forward or backward.	Scroll vertically (up and down).
Free-spin wheel	Whirl the wheel forward or backward so that it spins freely on its own.	Scroll through many pages in seconds.
Press wheel	Press the wheel button while moving the mouse.	Scroll continuously.
Tilt wheel	Press the wheel toward the right or left.	Scroll horizontally (left and right).
Press thumb button	Press the button on the side of the mouse with your thumb.	Move forward or backward through webpages and/or control media, games, etc.

*Note: The examples presented in this column are discussed as they are demonstrated in this chapter.

© 2014 Cengage Learning

Scrolling

A **scroll bar** is a horizontal or vertical bar that appears when the contents of an area may not be visible completely on the screen (Figure 2). A scroll bar contains **scroll arrows** and a **scroll box** that enable you to view areas that currently cannot be seen on the screen. Tapping or clicking the up and down scroll arrows moves the screen content up or down one line. You also can tap or click above or below the scroll box to move up or down a section, or drag the scroll box up or down to move to a specific location.

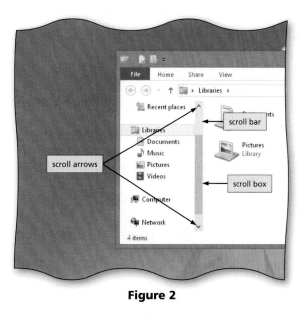

Figure 2

BTW

Pointer

If you are using a touch screen, the pointer may not appear on the screen as you perform touch gestures. The pointer will reappear when you begin using the mouse.

BTW

Minimize Wrist Injury

Computer users frequently switch between the keyboard and the mouse during a word processing session; such switching strains the wrist. To help prevent wrist injury, minimize switching. For instance, if your fingers already are on the keyboard, use keyboard keys to scroll. If your hand already is on the mouse, use the mouse to scroll. If your hand is on the touch screen, use touch gestures to scroll.

What should you do if you are running Windows 7 instead of Windows 8?

Although Windows 8 includes several user interface and feature enhancements, many of the steps in this chapter work in both Windows 7 and Windows 8. If you have any questions about differences between the two operating systems or how to perform tasks in an earlier version of Windows, contact your instructor.

CONSIDER THIS

Keyboard Shortcuts

In many cases, you can use the keyboard instead of the mouse to accomplish a task. To perform tasks using the keyboard, you press one or more keyboard keys, sometimes identified as a **keyboard shortcut**. Some keyboard shortcuts consist of a single key, such as the F1 key. For example, to obtain help in many apps, you can press the F1 key. Other keyboard shortcuts consist of multiple keys, in which case a plus sign separates the key names, such as CTRL+ESC. This notation means to press and hold down the first key listed, press one or more additional keys, and then release all keys. For example, to display the Start screen, press CTRL+ESC; that is, hold down the CTRL key, press the ESC key, and then release both keys.

Starting Windows

It is not unusual for multiple people to use the same computer in a work, educational, recreational, or home setting. Windows enables each user to establish a **user account**, which identifies to Windows the resources, such as apps and storage locations, a user can access when working with the computer.

Each user account has a user name and may have a password and an icon, as well. A **user name** is a unique combination of letters or numbers that identifies a specific user to Windows. A **password** is a private combination of letters, numbers, and special characters associated with the user name that allows access to a user's account resources. An icon is a small image that represents an object, thus a **user icon** is a picture associated with a user name.

When you turn on a computer, Windows starts and displays a **lock screen** consisting of the time and date (Figure 3a). To unlock the screen, swipe up or click the lock screen. Depending on your computer's settings, Windows may or may not display a sign-in screen that shows the user names and user icons for users who have accounts on the computer (Figure 3b). This **sign-in screen** enables you to sign in to your user account and makes the computer available for use. Tapping or clicking the user icon begins the process of signing in, also called logging on, to your user account.

At the bottom of the sign-in screen is the 'Ease of access' button and a Shut down button. Tapping or clicking the 'Ease of access' button displays the Ease of access menu, which provides tools to optimize a computer to accommodate the needs of the mobility-, hearing- and vision-impaired users. Tapping or clicking the Shut down

Figure 3a

SC Series user icon

Note: To help you locate screen elements that are referenced in the step instructions, such as buttons and commands, this book uses red boxes to point to these screen elements.

Figure 3b

button displays a menu containing commands related to restarting the computer, putting it in a low-power state, and shutting it down. The commands available on your computer may differ.

- The Sleep command saves your work, turns off the computer fans and hard disk, and places the computer in a lower-power state. To wake the computer from sleep mode, press the power button or lift a laptop's cover, and sign in to your account.
- The Shut down command exits running apps, shuts down Windows, and then turns off the computer.
- The Restart command exits running apps, shuts down Windows, and then restarts Windows.

BTW

Q&As
For a complete list of the Q&As found in many of the step-by-step sequences in this book, visit the Q&A resource on the Student Companion Site located on www.cengagebrain.com. For detailed instructions about accessing available resources, visit www.cengage.com/ct/studentdownload or contact your instructor for information about accessing the required files.

To Sign In to an Account

1 SIGN IN | 2 USE WINDOWS | 3 USE APPS | 4 FILE MANAGEMENT | 5 SWITCH APPS | 6 SAVE FILES
7 CHANGE SCREEN RESOLUTION | 8 EXIT APPS | 9 USE ADDITIONAL APPS | 10 USE HELP

The following steps, which use SC Series as the user name, sign in to an account based on a typical Windows installation. *Why? After starting Windows, you might be required to sign in to an account to access the computer's resources.* You may need to ask your instructor how to sign in to your account. If you are using Windows 7, skip these steps and instead perform the steps in the yellow box that immediately follows these Windows 8 steps.

1

- Swipe up or click the lock screen (shown in Figure 3a) to display a sign-in screen (shown in Figure 3b).

- Tap or click the user icon (for SC Series, in this case) on the sign-in screen, which, depending on settings, either will display a second sign-in screen that contains a Password text box (Figure 4) or will display the Windows Start screen (shown in Figure 5 on the next page).

Q&A
Why do I not see a user icon?
Your computer may require you to type a user name instead of tapping or clicking an icon.

What is a text box?
A text box is a rectangular box in which you type text.

Why does my screen not show a Password text box?
Your account does not require a password.

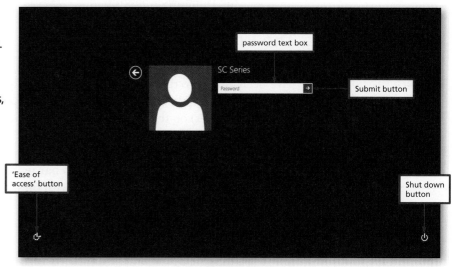

password text box

SC Series

Password

Submit button

'Ease of access' button

Shut down button

Figure 4

- If Windows displays a sign-in screen with a Password text box, type your password in the text box.

2

- Tap or click the Submit button (shown in Figure 4 on the previous page) to sign in to your account and display the Windows Start screen (Figure 5).

Q&A

Why does my Start screen look different from the one in Figure 5? The Windows Start screen is customizable, and your school or employer may have modified the screen to meet its needs. Also, your screen resolution, which affects the size of the elements on the screen, may differ from the screen resolution used in this book. Later in this chapter, you learn how to change screen resolution.

How do I type if my tablet has no keyboard?
You can use your fingers to press keys on a keyboard that appears on the screen, called an on-screen keyboard, or you can purchase a separate physical keyboard that attaches to or wirelessly communicates with the tablet.

Figure 5

To Sign In to an Account Using Windows 7

If you are using Windows 7, perform these steps to sign in to an account instead of the previous steps that use Windows 8.

1. Click the user icon on the Welcome screen; depending on settings, this either will display a password text box or will sign in to the account and display the Windows 7 desktop.
2. If Windows 7 displays a password text box, type your password in the text box and then click the arrow button to sign in to the account and display the Windows 7 desktop.

The Windows Start Screen

BTW
Modern UI
The new Windows 8 user interface also is referred to as the Modern UI (user interface).

The Windows Start screen provides a scrollable space for you to access apps that have been pinned to the Start screen (shown in Figure 5). Pinned apps appear as tiles on the Start screen. In addition to running apps, you can perform tasks such as pinning apps (placing tiles) on the Start screen, moving the tiles around the Start screen, and unpinning apps (removing tiles) from the Start screen.

If you swipe up from the bottom of or right-click an open space on the Start screen, the App bar will appear. The **App bar** includes a button that enables you to display all of your apps. When working with tiles, the App bar also provides options for manipulating the tiles, such as resizing them.

CONSIDER THIS

How do you pin apps, move tiles, and unpin apps?

- To pin an app, swipe up from the bottom of the Start screen or right-click an open space on the Start screen to display the App bar, tap or click the All apps button on the App bar to display the Apps list, swipe down on or right-click the app you want to pin, and then tap or click the 'Pin to Start' button on the App bar. One way to return to the Start screen is to swipe up from the bottom or right-click an open space in the Apps list and then tap or click the All apps button again.

- To move a tile, drag the tile to the desired location.

- To unpin an app, swipe down on or right-click the app to display the App bar and then tap or click the 'Unpin from Start' button on the App bar.

Introduction to Microsoft Office 2013

Microsoft Office 2013 is the newest version of Microsoft Office, offering features that provide users with better functionality and easier ways to work with the various files they create. These features include enhanced design tools, such as improved picture formatting tools and new themes, shared notebooks for working in groups, mobile versions of Office apps, broadcast presentations for the web, and a digital notebook for managing and sharing multimedia information.

Microsoft Office 2013 Apps

Microsoft Office 2013 includes a wide variety of apps such as Word, PowerPoint, Excel, Access, Outlook, Publisher, OneNote, InfoPath, SharePoint Workspace, and Lync:

- **Microsoft Word 2013**, or Word, is a full-featured word processing app that allows you to create professional-looking documents and revise them easily.

- **Microsoft PowerPoint 2013**, or PowerPoint, is a complete presentation app that enables you to produce professional-looking presentations and then deliver them to an audience.

- **Microsoft Excel 2013**, or Excel, is a powerful spreadsheet app that allows you to organize data, complete calculations, make decisions, graph data, develop professional-looking reports, publish organized data to the web, and access real-time data from websites.

- **Microsoft Access 2013**, or Access, is a database management system that enables you to create a database; add, change, and delete data in the database; ask questions concerning the data in the database; and create forms and reports using the data in the database.

- **Microsoft Outlook 2013**, or Outlook, is a communications and scheduling app that allows you to manage email accounts, calendars, contacts, and access to other Internet content.

- **Microsoft Publisher 2013**, or Publisher, is a desktop publishing app that helps you create professional-quality publications and marketing materials that can be shared easily.

- **Microsoft OneNote 2013**, or OneNote, is a note-taking app that allows you to store and share information in notebooks with other people.

- **Microsoft InfoPath Designer 2013**, or InfoPath, is a form development app that helps you create forms for use on the web and gather data from these forms.

- **Microsoft SharePoint Workspace 2013**, or SharePoint, is a collaboration app that allows you to access and revise files stored on your computer from other locations.

- **Microsoft Lync 2013** is a communications app that allows you to use various modes of communications such as instant messaging, videoconferencing, and sharing files and apps.

Microsoft Office 2013 Suites

A **suite** is a collection of individual apps available together as a unit. Microsoft offers a variety of Office suites, including a stand-alone desktop app (boxed software), Microsoft Office 365, and Microsoft Office Web Apps. **Microsoft Office 365**, or Office 365, provides plans that allow organizations to use Office in a mobile setting while also being able to communicate and share files, depending on the type of plan selected by the organization. **Microsoft Office Web Apps**, or Web Apps, are apps that allow you to edit and share files on the web using the familiar Office interface. Table 3 on the next page outlines the differences among these Office suites.

Table 3 Office Suites

Apps/ Licenses	Office 365 Home Premium	Office 365 Small Business Premium	Office Home & Student	Office Home & Business	Office Professional
Word	✔	✔	✔	✔	✔
PowerPoint	✔	✔	✔	✔	✔
Excel	✔	✔	✔	✔	✔
Access	✔	✔			✔
Outlook	✔	✔		✔	✔
Publisher	✔	✔			✔
Lync		✔			
OneNote			✔	✔	✔
InfoPath		✔			
Licenses	5	5	1	1	1

© 2014 Cengage Learning

During the Office 365 installation, you select a plan, and depending on your plan, you receive different apps and services. Office Web Apps do not require a local installation and are accessed through SkyDrive and your browser. **SkyDrive** is a cloud storage service that provides storage and other services, such as Office Web Apps, to computer users.

CONSIDER THIS

How do you sign up for a SkyDrive account?

• Use your browser to navigate to skydrive.live.com.

• Create a Microsoft account by tapping or clicking the 'Sign up now' link and then entering your information to create the account.

• Sign in to SkyDrive using your new account or use it in Office to save your files on SkyDrive.

Apps in a suite, such as Microsoft Office, typically use a similar interface and share features. Once you are comfortable working with the elements and the interface and performing tasks in one app, the similarity can help you apply the knowledge and skills you have learned to another app(s) in the suite. For example, the process for saving a file in Word is the same in PowerPoint, Excel, and the other Office apps. While briefly showing how to use several Office apps, this chapter illustrates some of the common functions across the apps and identifies the characteristics unique to these apps.

Running and Using an App

To use an app, you must instruct the operating system to run the app. Windows provides many different ways to run an app, one of which is presented in this section (other ways to run an app are presented throughout this chapter). After an app is running, you can use it to perform a variety of tasks. The following pages use Word to discuss some elements of the Office interface and to perform tasks that are common to other Office apps.

Word

Word is a full-featured word processing app that allows you to create many types of personal and business documents, including flyers, letters, memos, resumes, reports, fax cover sheets, mailing labels, and newsletters. Word also provides tools that enable you to create webpages and save these webpages directly on a web server. Word has many features designed to simplify the production of documents and add visual appeal. Using Word, you easily can change the shape, size, and color of text. You also can include borders, shading, tables, images, pictures, charts, and web addresses in documents.

To Run an App from the Start Screen

The Start screen contains tiles that allow you to run apps, some of which may be stored on your computer. *Why? When you install an app, for example, tiles are added to the Start screen for the various Office apps included in the suite.* The following steps, which assume Windows is running, use the Start screen to run an Office app based on a typical installation. You may need to ask your instructor how to run an Office app on your computer. Although the steps illustrate running the Word app, the steps to run any Office app are similar. If you are using Windows 7, skip these steps and instead perform the steps in the yellow box that immediately follows these Windows 8 steps.

1

- If necessary, scroll to display the Word tile on the Start screen (Figure 6).

Q&A

Why does my Start screen look different?

It may look different because of your computer's configuration. The Start screen may be customized for several reasons, such as usage requirements or security restrictions.

What if the app I want to run is not on the Start screen?

You can display all installed apps by swiping up from the bottom of the Start screen or right-clicking an open space on the Start screen and then tapping or clicking the All apps button on the App bar.

How do I scroll on a touch screen?

Use the slide gesture; that is, press and hold your finger on the screen and then move your finger in the direction you wish to scroll.

Figure 6

2

- Tap or click the Word 2013 tile to run the Word app and display the Word start screen (Figure 7).

Figure 7

3

- Tap or click the Blank document thumbnail on the Word start screen to create a blank Word document in the Word window (Figure 8).

Q&A What happens when you run an app?

Some apps provide a means for you to create a blank document, as shown in Figure 7 on the previous page; others immediately display a blank document in an app window, such as the Word window shown in Figure 8. A **window** is a rectangular area that displays data and information. The top of a window has a **title bar**, which is a horizontal space that contains the window's name.

Figure 8

Other Ways

1. Tap or click Search charm on Charms bar, type app name in search box, tap or click app name in results list
2. Double-tap or double-click file created in app you want to run

TO RUN AN APP USING THE START MENU USING WINDOWS 7

BTW

Touch Keyboard
To display the on-screen touch keyboard, tap the Touch Keyboard button on the Windows taskbar. When finished using the touch keyboard, tap the X button on the touch keyboard to close the keyboard.

If you are using Windows 7, perform these steps to run an app using the Start menu instead of the previous steps that use Windows 8.

1. Click the Start button on the Windows 7 taskbar to display the Start menu.
2. Click All Programs at the bottom of the left pane on the Start menu to display the All Programs list.
3. If the app you wish to start is located in a folder, click, or scroll to and then click, the folder in the All Programs list to display a list of the folder's contents.
4. Click, or scroll to and then click, the app name in the list to run the selected app.

Windows Desktop

When you run an app in Windows, it may appear in an on-screen work area app, called the **desktop** (shown in Figure 8). You can perform tasks such as placing objects in the desktop, moving the objects around the desktop, and removing items from the desktop.

Some icons also may be displayed in the desktop. For instance, the icon for the **Recycle Bin**, the location of files that have been deleted, appears in the desktop by default. A **file** is a named unit of storage. Files can contain text, images, audio, and video. You can customize your desktop so that icons representing apps and files you use often appear in the desktop.

To Switch between an App and the Start Screen

1 SIGN IN | 2 USE WINDOWS | 3 USE APPS | 4 FILE MANAGEMENT | 5 SWITCH APPS | 6 SAVE FILES
7 CHANGE SCREEN RESOLUTION | 8 EXIT APPS | 9 USE ADDITIONAL APPS | 10 USE HELP

While working with an app or in the desktop, you easily can return to the Start screen. The following steps switch from the desktop to the Start screen. *Why? Returning to the Start screen allows you to run any of your other apps.* If you are using Windows 7, read these steps without performing them because Windows 7 does not have a Start screen.

1

- Swipe in from the left edge of the screen, and then back to the left, or point to the lower-left corner of the desktop to display a thumbnail of the Start screen (Figure 9).

thumbnail of Start screen

PAGE 1 OF 1   0 WORDS

Start

Figure 9

2

- Tap or click the thumbnail of the Start screen to display the Start screen (Figure 10).

3

- Tap or click the Desktop tile to redisplay the desktop (shown in Figure 8).

Start screen displayed

Start

Mail | Calendar | Store | Internet Explorer | Bing

People | Photos | Maps | SkyDrive | Travel

Desktop tile

Messaging | Weather | Sports | Games | Ca

Desktop | Finance | News | Music

Figure 10

Other Ways

1. Press WINDOWS key to display Start screen

To Maximize a Window

Sometimes content is not visible completely in a window. One method of displaying the entire contents of a window is to **maximize** it, or enlarge the window so that it fills the entire screen. The following step maximizes the Word window; however, any Office app's window can be maximized using this step. *Why?* *A maximized window provides the most space available for using the app.*

1

- If the app window is not maximized already, tap or click the Maximize button (shown in Figure 8 on page OFF 12) next to the Close button on the window's title bar (the Word window title bar, in this case) to maximize the window (Figure 11).

Q&A

What happened to the Maximize button?

It changed to a Restore Down button, which you can use to return a window to its size and location before you maximized it.

How do I know whether a window is maximized?

A window is maximized if it fills the entire display area and the Restore Down button is displayed on the title bar.

Figure 11

Other Ways

1. Double-tap or double-click title bar   2. Drag title bar to top of screen

Word Document Window, Ribbon, and Elements Common to Office Apps

The Word window consists of a variety of components to make your work more efficient and documents more professional. These include the document window, ribbon, mini toolbar, shortcut menus, Quick Access Toolbar, and Microsoft Account area. Most of these components are common to other Microsoft Office apps; others are unique to Word.

You view a portion of a document on the screen through a **document window** (Figure 12). The default (preset) view is **Print Layout view**, which shows the document on a mock sheet of paper in the document window.

Scroll Bars   You use a scroll bar to display different portions of a document in the document window. At the right edge of the document window is a vertical scroll bar. If a document is too wide to fit in the document window, a horizontal scroll bar also appears at the bottom of the document window. On a scroll bar, the position of the scroll box reflects the location of the portion of the document that is displayed in the document window.

Status Bar   The **status bar**, located at the bottom of the document window above the Windows taskbar, presents information about the document, the progress of current tasks, and the status of certain commands and keys; it also provides controls for viewing the document. As you type text or perform certain tasks, various indicators and buttons may appear on the status bar.

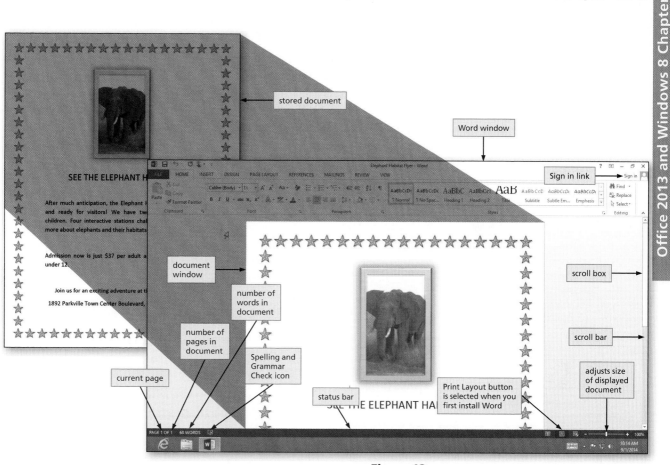

Figure 12

The left side of the status bar in Figure 12 shows the current page followed by the total number of pages in the document, the number of words in the document, and an icon to check spelling and grammar. The right side of the status bar includes buttons and controls you can use to change the view of a document and adjust the size of the displayed document.

Ribbon   The ribbon, located near the top of the window below the title bar, is the control center in Word and other Office apps (Figure 13). The ribbon provides easy, central access to the tasks you perform while creating a document. The ribbon consists of tabs, groups, and commands. Each **tab** contains a collection of groups, and each **group** contains related commands. When you run an Office app, such as Word, it initially displays several main tabs, also called default or top-level tabs. All Office apps have a HOME tab, which contains the more frequently used commands.

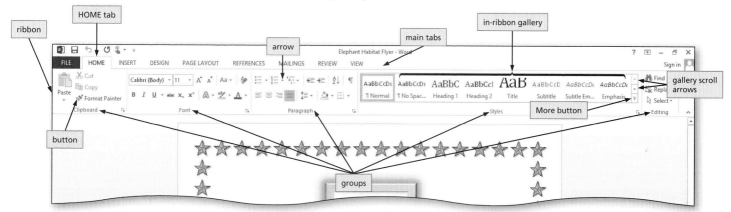

Figure 13

In addition to the main tabs, the Office apps display **tool tabs**, also called contextual tabs (Figure 14), when you perform certain tasks or work with objects such as pictures or tables. If you insert a picture in a Word document, for example, the PICTURE TOOLS tab and its related subordinate FORMAT tab appear, collectively referred to as the PICTURE TOOLS FORMAT tab. When you are finished working with the picture, the PICTURE TOOLS FORMAT tab disappears from the ribbon. Word and other Office apps determine when tool tabs should appear and disappear based on tasks you perform. Some tool tabs, such as the TABLE TOOLS tab, have more than one related subordinate tab.

Figure 14

Items on the ribbon include buttons, boxes, and galleries (shown in Figure 13 on the previous page). A **gallery** is a set of choices, often graphical, arranged in a grid or in a list. You can scroll through choices in an in-ribbon gallery by tapping or clicking the gallery's scroll arrows. Or, you can tap or click a gallery's More button to view more gallery options on the screen at a time.

Some buttons and boxes have arrows that, when tapped or clicked, also display a gallery; others always cause a gallery to be displayed when tapped or clicked. Most galleries support **live preview**, which is a feature that allows you to point to a gallery choice and see its effect in the document — without actually selecting the choice (Figure 15). Live preview works only if you are using a mouse; if you are using a touch screen, you will not be able to view live previews.

PICTURE TOOLS FORMAT tab is one of many tool tabs that appear automatically depending on the task you perform

as you move pointer from one gallery option to next, Word shows live preview of style in document, so that you can see effect of option in document before selecting it

picture changes to Snip Diagonal Corner, White as you point to that style in gallery

SEE THE ELEPHANT HABITAT

Figure 15

Some commands on the ribbon display an image to help you remember their function. When you point to a command on the ribbon, all or part of the command glows in a shade of blue, and a ScreenTip appears on the screen. A **ScreenTip** is an on-screen note that provides the name of the command, available keyboard shortcut(s), a description of the command, and sometimes instructions for how to obtain help about the command (Figure 16).

Quick Access Toolbar

Touch/Mouse Mode button

Paste {Ctrl+V}
Pick a paste option, such as keeping formatting or pasting only content.

ScreenTip for Paste arrow

pointer on Paste arrow

Figure 16

Some groups on the ribbon have a small arrow in the lower-right corner, called a **Dialog Box Launcher**, that when tapped or clicked, displays a dialog box or a task pane with additional options for the group (Figure 17). When presented with a dialog box, you make selections and must close the dialog box before returning to the document. A **task pane**, in contrast to a dialog box, is a window that can remain open and visible while you work in the document.

BTW
Touch Mode
The Office and Windows interfaces may vary if you are using Touch mode. For this reason, you might notice that the function or appearance of your touch screen differs slightly from this chapter's presentation.

Figure 17

Mini Toolbar The **mini toolbar**, which appears automatically based on tasks you perform, contains commands related to changing the appearance of text in a document (Figure 18). If you do not use the mini toolbar, it disappears from the screen. The buttons, arrows, and boxes on the mini toolbar vary, depending on whether you are using Touch mode versus Mouse mode. If you press and hold or right-click an item in the document window, Word displays both the mini toolbar and a shortcut menu, which is discussed in a later section in this chapter.

All commands on the mini toolbar also exist on the ribbon. The purpose of the mini toolbar is to minimize hand or mouse movement.

Figure 18

Quick Access Toolbar The **Quick Access Toolbar**, located initially (by default) above the ribbon at the left edge of the title bar, provides convenient, one-tap or one-click access to frequently used commands (shown in Figure 16). The commands on the Quick Access Toolbar always are available, regardless of the task you are performing. The Touch/Mouse Mode button on the Quick Access Toolbar allows you to switch between Touch mode and Mouse mode. If you primarily are using touch gestures, Touch mode will add more space between commands in menus and on the ribbon so that they are easier to tap. While touch gestures are convenient ways to interact with Office apps, not all features are supported when you are using Touch mode. If you are using a mouse, Mouse mode will not add the extra space between buttons and commands. The Quick Access Toolbar is discussed in more depth later in the chapter.

KeyTips If you prefer using the keyboard instead of the mouse, you can press the ALT key on the keyboard to display **KeyTips**, or keyboard code icons, for certain commands (Figure 19). To select a command using the keyboard, press the letter or number displayed in the KeyTip, which may cause additional KeyTips related to the selected command to appear. To remove KeyTips from the screen, press the ALT key or the ESC key until all KeyTips disappear, or tap or click anywhere in the app window.

Microsoft Account Area In this area, you can use the Sign in link to sign in to your Microsoft account. Once signed in, you will see your account information as well as a picture if you have included one in your Microsoft account.

Figure 19

To Display a Different Tab on the Ribbon

1 SIGN IN | 2 USE WINDOWS | 3 USE APPS | 4 FILE MANAGEMENT | 5 SWITCH APPS | 6 SAVE FILES
7 CHANGE SCREEN RESOLUTION | 8 EXIT APPS | 9 USE ADDITIONAL APPS | 10 USE HELP

When you run Word, the ribbon displays nine main tabs: FILE, HOME, INSERT, DESIGN, PAGE LAYOUT, REFERENCES, MAILINGS, REVIEW, and VIEW. The tab currently displayed is called the **active tab**.

The following step displays the INSERT tab; that is, makes it the active tab. *Why? When working with an Office app, you may need to switch tabs to access other options for working with a document.*

1
- Tap or click INSERT on the ribbon to display the INSERT tab (Figure 20).

Experiment
- Tap or click the other tabs on the ribbon to view their contents. When you are finished, tap or click INSERT on the ribbon to redisplay the INSERT tab.

Q&A | If I am working in a different Office app, such as PowerPoint or Access, how do I display a different tab on the ribbon?
Follow this same procedure; that is, tap or click the desired tab on the ribbon.

Figure 20

To Collapse and Expand the Ribbon and Use Full Screen Mode

1 SIGN IN | 2 USE WINDOWS | 3 USE APPS | 4 FILE MANAGEMENT | 5 SWITCH APPS | 6 SAVE FILES
7 CHANGE SCREEN RESOLUTION | 8 EXIT APPS | 9 USE ADDITIONAL APPS | 10 USE HELP

To display more of a document or other item in the window of an Office app, some users prefer to collapse the ribbon, which hides the groups on the ribbon and displays only the main tabs, or to use **Full Screen mode**, which hides all the commands and just displays the document. Each time you run an Office app, the ribbon appears the same way it did the last time you used that Office app. The chapters in this book, however, begin with the ribbon appearing as it did at the initial installation of the software.

The following steps collapse, expand, and restore the ribbon in an Office app and then switch to Full Screen mode. *Why? If you need more space on the screen to work with your document, you may consider collapsing the ribbon or switching to Full Screen mode to gain additional workspace.*

1

- Tap or click the 'Collapse the Ribbon' button on the ribbon (shown in Figure 20) to collapse the ribbon (Figure 21).

Q&A What happened to the groups on the ribbon?
When you collapse the ribbon, the groups disappear so that the ribbon does not take up as much space on the screen.

What happened to the 'Collapse the Ribbon' button?
The 'Pin the ribbon' button replaces the 'Collapse the Ribbon' button when the ribbon is collapsed. You will see the 'Pin the ribbon' button only when you expand a ribbon by tapping or clicking a tab.

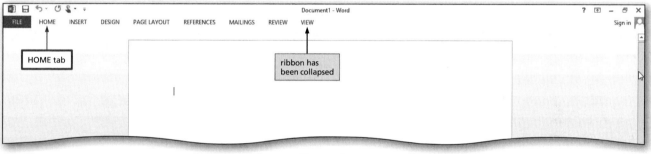

Figure 21

2

- Tap or click HOME on the ribbon to expand the HOME tab (Figure 22).

Q&A Why would I click the HOME tab?
If you want to use a command on a collapsed ribbon, tap or click the main tab to display the groups for that tab. After you select a command on the ribbon, the groups will be collapsed once again. If you decide not to use a command on the ribbon, you can collapse the groups by tapping or clicking the same main tab or tapping or clicking in the app window.

Experiment

- Tap or click HOME on the ribbon to collapse the groups again. Tap or click HOME on the ribbon to expand the HOME tab.

Figure 22

3

- Tap or click the 'Pin the ribbon' button on the expanded HOME tab to restore the ribbon.
- Tap or click the 'Ribbon Display Options' button to display the Ribbon Display Options menu (Figure 23).

Figure 23

4

- Tap or click Auto-hide Ribbon to hide all the commands from the screen (Figure 24).
- Tap or click the ellipsis to temporarily display the ribbon.
- Tap or click the 'Ribbon Display Options' button to display the Ribbon Display Options menu (shown in Figure 23).
- Tap or click 'Show Tabs and Commands' to exit Full Screen mode.

Figure 24

Other Ways

1. Double-tap or double-click a main tab on the ribbon   2. Press CTRL+F1

To Use a Shortcut Menu to Relocate the Quick Access Toolbar

1 SIGN IN | 2 USE WINDOWS | 3 USE APPS | 4 FILE MANAGEMENT | 5 SWITCH APPS | 6 SAVE FILES
7 CHANGE SCREEN RESOLUTION | 8 EXIT APPS | 9 USE ADDITIONAL APPS | 10 USE HELP

When you press and hold or right-click certain areas of the Word and other Office app windows, a shortcut menu will appear. A **shortcut menu** is a list of frequently used commands that relate to an object. *Why? You can use shortcut menus to access common commands quickly.* When you press and hold or right-click the status bar, for example, a shortcut menu appears with commands related to the status bar. When you press and hold or right-click the Quick Access Toolbar, a shortcut menu appears with commands related to the Quick Access Toolbar. The following steps use a shortcut menu to move the Quick Access Toolbar, which by default is located on the title bar.

1

- Press and hold or right-click the Quick Access Toolbar to display a shortcut menu that presents a list of commands related to the Quick Access Toolbar (Figure 25).

Q&A What if I cannot make the shortcut menu appear using the touch instruction?

When you use the press and hold technique, be sure to release your finger when the circle appears on the screen to display the shortcut menu. If the technique still does not work, you might need to add more space around objects on the screen, making it easier for you to press or tap them. Click the 'Customize Quick Access Toolbar' button and then click Touch/Mouse Mode on the menu.

Figure 25

2

- Tap or click 'Show Quick Access Toolbar Below the Ribbon' on the shortcut menu to display the Quick Access Toolbar below the ribbon (Figure 26).

Figure 26

3

- Press and hold or right-click the Quick Access Toolbar to display a shortcut menu (Figure 27).

4

- Tap or click 'Show Quick Access Toolbar Above the Ribbon' on the shortcut menu to return the Quick Access Toolbar to its original position (shown in Figure 25).

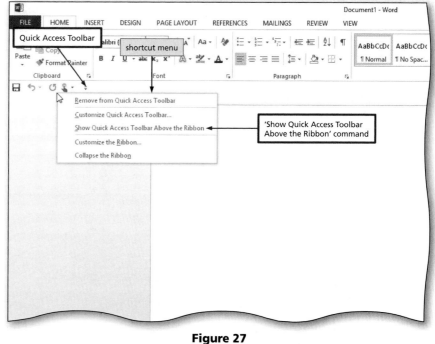

Figure 27

Other Ways

1. Tap or click 'Customize Quick Access Toolbar' button on Quick Access Toolbar, tap or click 'Show Below the Ribbon' or 'Show Above the Ribbon'

To Customize the Quick Access Toolbar

The Quick Access Toolbar provides easy access to some of the more frequently used commands in the Office apps. By default, the Quick Access Toolbar contains buttons for the Save, Undo, and Redo commands. You can customize the Quick Access Toolbar by changing its location in the window, as shown in the previous steps, and by adding more buttons to reflect commands you would like to access easily. The following steps add the Quick Print button to the Quick Access Toolbar. *Why? Adding the Quick Print button to the Quick Access Toolbar speeds up the process of printing.*

1

- Tap or click the 'Customize Quick Access Toolbar' button to display the Customize Quick Access Toolbar menu (Figure 28).

Q&A

Which commands are listed on the Customize Quick Access Toolbar menu?
It lists commands that commonly are added to the Quick Access Toolbar.

What do the check marks next to some commands signify?
Check marks appear next to commands that already are on the Quick Access Toolbar. When you add a button to the Quick Access Toolbar, a check mark will be displayed next to its command name.

2

- Tap or click Quick Print on the Customize Quick Access Toolbar menu to add the Quick Print button to the Quick Access Toolbar (Figure 29).

Q&A

How would I remove a button from the Quick Access Toolbar?
You would press and hold or right-click the button you wish to remove and then tap or click 'Remove from Quick Access Toolbar' on the shortcut menu or tap or click the 'Customize Quick Access Toolbar' button on the Quick Access Toolbar and then click the button name in the Customize Quick Access Toolbar menu to remove the check mark.

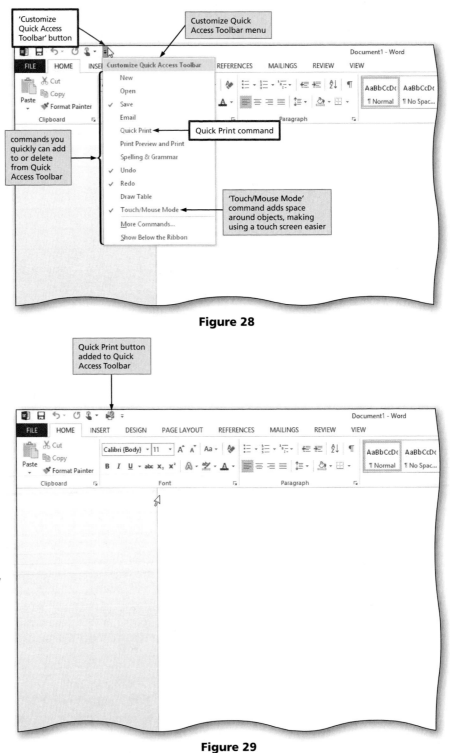

Figure 28

Figure 29

To Enter Text in a Document

The first step in creating a document is to enter its text by typing on the keyboard. By default, Word positions text at the left margin as you type. The following steps type this first line of a flyer. *Why? To begin creating a flyer, for example, you type the headline in the document window.*

1

- Type **SEE THE ELEPHANT HABITAT** as the text (Figure 30).

Q&A What is the blinking vertical bar to the right of the text?
The blinking bar is the insertion point, which indicates where text, graphics, and other items will be inserted in the document. As you type, the insertion point moves to the right, and when you reach the end of a line, it moves down to the beginning of the next line.

What if I make an error while typing?
You can press the BACKSPACE key until you have deleted the text in error and then retype the text correctly.

Why does a circle appear below the insertion point?
If you are using a touch screen, a selection handle (small circle) appears below the text so that you can format the text easily.

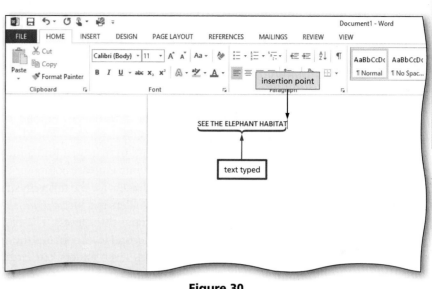

Figure 30

2

- Press the ENTER key to move the insertion point to the beginning of the next line (Figure 31).

Q&A Why did blank space appear between the entered text and the insertion point?
Each time you press the ENTER key, Word creates a new paragraph and inserts blank space between the two paragraphs. Depending on your settings, Office may or may not insert a blank space between the two paragraphs.

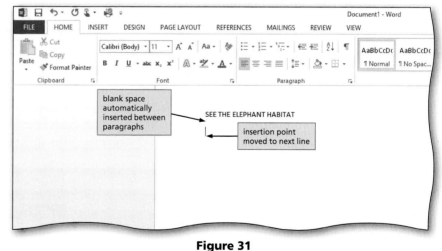

Figure 31

Saving and Organizing Files

While you are creating a document, the computer stores it in memory. When you save a document, the computer places it on a storage medium such as a hard disk, solid state drive (SSD), USB flash drive, or optical disc. The storage medium can be permanent in your computer, may be portable where you remove it from your computer, or may be on a web server you access through a network or the Internet.

BTW
File Type
Depending on your Windows settings, the file type .docx may be displayed immediately to the right of the file name after you save the file. The file type .docx is a Word 2013 document.

A saved document is referred to as a file. A **file name** is the name assigned to a file when it is saved. When saving files, you should organize them so that you easily can find them later. Windows provides tools to help you organize files.

How often should you save a document?

It is important to save a document frequently for the following reasons:

• The document in memory might be lost if the computer is turned off or you lose electrical power while an app is running.

• If you run out of time before completing a project, you may finish it at a future time without starting over.

Organizing Files and Folders

A file contains data. This data can range from a research paper to an accounting spreadsheet to an electronic math quiz. You should organize and store files in folders to avoid misplacing a file and to help you find a file quickly.

If you are taking an introductory computer class (CIS 101, for example), you may want to design a series of folders for the different subjects covered in the class. To accomplish this, you can arrange the folders in a hierarchy for the class, as shown in Figure 32.

The hierarchy contains three levels. The first level contains the storage medium, such as a hard disk. The second level contains the class folder (CIS 101, in this case), and the third level contains seven folders, one each for a different Office app that will be covered in the class (Word, PowerPoint, Excel, Access, Outlook, Publisher, and OneNote).

When the hierarchy in Figure 32 is created, the storage medium is said to contain the CIS 101 folder, and the CIS 101 folder is said to contain the separate Office folders (i.e., Word, PowerPoint, Excel, etc.). In addition, this hierarchy easily can be expanded to include folders from other classes taken during additional semesters.

The vertical and horizontal lines in Figure 32 form a pathway that allows you to navigate to a drive or folder on a computer or network. A **path** consists of a drive letter (preceded by a drive name when necessary) and colon, to identify the storage device, and one or more folder names. A hard disk typically has a drive letter of C. Each drive or folder in the hierarchy has a corresponding path.

By default, Windows saves documents in the Documents library, music in the Music library, photos in the Pictures library, and videos in the Videos library. A **library** helps you manage multiple folders stored in various locations on a computer and devices. It does not store the folder contents; rather, it keeps track of their locations so that you can access the folders and their contents quickly. For example, you can save pictures from a digital camera in any folder on any storage location on a computer. Normally, this would make organizing the different folders difficult. If you add

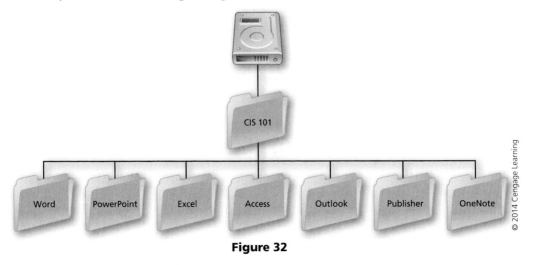

Figure 32

the folders to a library, however, you can access all the pictures from one location regardless of where they are stored.

The following pages illustrate the steps to organize the folders for this class and save a file in one of those folders:

1. Create the folder identifying your class.

2. Create the Word folder in the folder identifying your class.

3. Create the remaining folders in the folder identifying your class (one each for PowerPoint, Excel, Access, Outlook, Publisher, and OneNote).

4. Save a file in the Word folder.

5. Verify the location of the saved file.

To Create a Folder

1 SIGN IN | 2 USE WINDOWS | 3 USE APPS | 4 FILE MANAGEMENT | 5 SWITCH APPS | 6 SAVE FILES
7 CHANGE SCREEN RESOLUTION | 8 EXIT APPS | 9 USE ADDITIONAL APPS | 10 USE HELP

When you create a folder, such as the CIS 101 folder shown in Figure 32, you must name the folder. A folder name should describe the folder and its contents. A folder name can contain spaces and any uppercase or lowercase characters, except a backslash (\), slash (/), colon (:), asterisk (*), question mark (?), quotation marks ("), less than symbol (<), greater than symbol (>), or vertical bar (I). Folder names cannot be CON, AUX, COM1, COM2, COM3, COM4, LPT1, LPT2, LPT3, PRN, or NUL. The same rules for naming folders also apply to naming files.

The following steps create a class folder (CIS 101, in this case) in the Documents library. *Why? When storing files, you should organize the files so that it will be easier to find them later.* If you are using Windows 7, skip these steps and instead perform the steps in the yellow box that immediately follows these Windows 8 steps.

①

● Tap or click the File Explorer app button on the taskbar to run the File Explorer app (Figure 33).

◄ | Why does the title bar say Libraries?
Q&A ◯ | File Explorer, by default, displays the name of the selected library or folder on the title bar.

Figure 33

2

- Tap or click the Documents library in the navigation pane to display the contents of the Documents library in the file list (Figure 34).

Q&A
What if my screen does not show the Documents, Music, Pictures, and Videos libraries?
Double-tap or double-click Libraries in the navigation pane to expand the list.

Figure 34

3

- Tap or click the New folder button on the Quick Access Toolbar to create a new folder with the name, New folder, selected in a text box (Figure 35).

Q&A
Why is the folder icon displayed differently on my computer?
Windows might be configured to display contents differently on your computer.

Figure 35

4

- Type CIS 101 (or your class code) in the text box as the new folder name.

  If requested by your instructor, add your last name to the end of the folder name.

- Press the ENTER key to change the folder name from New folder to a folder name identifying your class (Figure 36).

Q&A
What happens when I press the ENTER key?
The class folder (CIS 101, in this case) is displayed in the file list, which contains the folder name, date modified, type, and size.

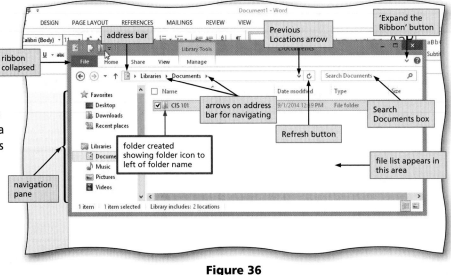

Figure 36

Other Ways

1. Press CTRL+SHIFT+N   2. Tap or click the New folder button (Home tab | New group)

TO CREATE A FOLDER USING WINDOWS 7

If you are using Windows 7, perform these steps to create a folder instead of the previous steps that use Windows 8.

1. Click the Windows Explorer button on the taskbar to run Windows Explorer.
2. Click the Documents library in the navigation pane to display the contents of the Documents library in the file list.
3. Click the New folder button on the toolbar to display a new folder icon with the name, New folder, selected in a text box.
4. Type **CIS 101** (or your class code) in the text box to name the folder.
5. Press the ENTER key to create the folder.

Folder Windows

The Documents window (shown in Figure 36) is called a folder window. Recall that a folder is a specific named location on a storage medium that contains related files. Most users rely on **folder windows** for finding, viewing, and managing information on their computers. Folder windows have common design elements, including the following (shown in Figure 36).

- The **address bar** provides quick navigation options. The arrows on the address bar allow you to visit different locations on the computer.
- The buttons to the left of the address bar allow you to navigate the contents of the navigation pane and view recent pages.
- The **Previous Locations arrow** displays the locations you have visited.
- The **Refresh button** on the right side of the address bar refreshes the contents of the folder list.
- The **search box** contains the dimmed words, Search Documents. You can type a term in the search box for a list of files, folders, shortcuts, and elements containing that term within the location you are searching. A **shortcut** is an icon on the desktop that provides a user with immediate access to an app or file.
- The **ribbon** contains five tabs used to accomplish various tasks on the computer related to organizing and managing the contents of the open window. This ribbon works similarly to the ribbon in the Office apps.
- The **navigation pane** on the left contains the Favorites area, Libraries area, Homegroup area, Computer area, and Network area.
- The **Favorites area** shows your favorite locations. By default, this list contains only links to your Desktop, Downloads, and Recent places.
- The **Libraries area** shows folders included in a library.

To Create a Folder within a Folder

1 SIGN IN | 2 USE WINDOWS | 3 USE APPS | 4 FILE MANAGEMENT | 5 SWITCH APPS | 6 SAVE FILES
7 CHANGE SCREEN RESOLUTION | 8 EXIT APPS | 9 USE ADDITIONAL APPS | 10 USE HELP

With the class folder created, you can create folders that will store the files you create using each Office app. The following steps create a Word folder in the CIS 101 folder (or the folder identifying your class). *Why?* *To be able to organize your files, you should create a folder structure.* If you are using Windows 7, skip these steps and instead perform the steps in the yellow box that immediately follows these Windows 8 steps.

1

- Double-tap or double-click the icon or folder name for the CIS 101 folder (or the folder identifying your class) in the file list to open the folder (Figure 37).

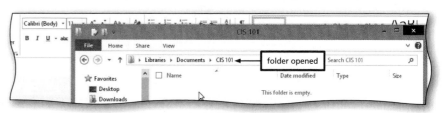

Figure 37

2

- Tap or click the New folder button on the Quick Access Toolbar to create a new folder with the name, New folder, selected in a text box folder.

- Type `Word` in the text box as the new folder name.

- Press the ENTER key to rename the folder (Figure 38).

Figure 38

Other Ways

1. Press CTRL+SHIFT+N	2. Tap or click the New folder button (Home tab | New group)

TO CREATE A FOLDER WITHIN A FOLDER USING WINDOWS 7

If you are using Windows 7, perform these steps to create a folder within a folder instead of the previous steps that use Windows 8.

1. Double-click the icon or folder name for the CIS 101 folder (or the folder identifying your class) in the file list to open the folder.
2. Click the New folder button on the toolbar to display a new folder icon and text box for the folder.
3. Type `Word` in the text box to name the folder.
4. Press the ENTER key to create the folder.

To Create the Remaining Folders

The following steps create the remaining folders in the folder identifying your class (in this case, CIS 101). If you are using Windows 7, skip these steps and instead perform the steps in the yellow box that immediately follows these Windows 8 steps.

1 Tap or click the New folder button on the Quick Access Toolbar to create a new folder with the name, New folder, selected in a text box.

2 Type `PowerPoint` in the text box as the new folder name.

3 Press the ENTER key to rename the folder.

4 Repeat Steps 1 through 3 to create each of the remaining folders, using Excel, Access, Outlook, Publisher, and OneNote as the folder names (Figure 39).

Figure 39

To Create the Remaining Folders Using Windows 7

If you are using Windows 7, perform these steps to create the remaining folders instead of the previous steps that use Windows 8.

1. Click the New folder button on the toolbar to create a new folder with the name, New folder, selected in a text box.

2. Type **PowerPoint** in the text box as the new folder name.

3. Press the ENTER key to rename the folder.

4. Repeat Steps 1 through 3 to create each of the remaining folders, using Excel, Access, Outlook, Publisher, and OneNote as the folder names.

To Expand a Folder, Scroll through Folder Contents, and Collapse a Folder

1 SIGN IN | 2 USE WINDOWS | 3 USE APPS | **4 FILE MANAGEMENT** | **5 SWITCH APPS** | **6 SAVE FILES**
7 CHANGE SCREEN RESOLUTION | **8 EXIT APPS** | **9 USE ADDITIONAL APPS** | **10 USE HELP**

Folder windows display the hierarchy of items and the contents of drives and folders in the file list. You might want to expand a library or folder in the navigation pane to view its contents, slide or scroll through its contents, and collapse it when you are finished viewing its contents. *Why? When a folder is expanded, you can see all the folders it contains. By contrast, a collapsed folder hides the folders it contains.* The following steps expand, slide or scroll through, and then collapse the folder identifying your class (CIS 101, in this case).

①

- Double-tap or double-click the Documents library in the navigation pane, which expands the library to display its contents and displays a black arrow to the left of the Documents library icon (Figure 40).

Figure 40

②

- Double-tap or double-click the My Documents folder, which expands the folder to display its contents and displays a black arrow to the left of the My Documents folder icon.

Q&A What is the My Documents folder? When you save files on your hard disk, the My Documents folder is the default save location.

- Double-tap or double-click the CIS 101 folder, which expands the folder to display its contents and displays a black arrow to the left of the folder icon (Figure 41).

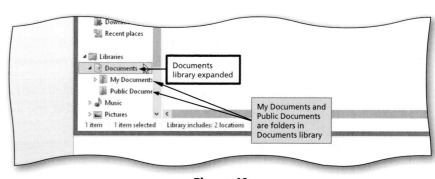

Figure 41

🔎 **Experiment**

- Slide the scroll bar down or click the down scroll arrow on the vertical scroll bar to display additional folders at the bottom of the navigation pane. Slide the scroll bar up or click the scroll bar above the scroll box to move the scroll box to the top of the navigation pane. Drag the scroll box down the scroll bar until the scroll box is halfway down the scroll bar.

3

- Double-tap or double-click the folder identifying your class (CIS 101, in this case) to collapse the folder (Figure 42).

Q&A

Why are some folders indented below others?

A folder contains the indented folders below it.

Figure 42

Other Ways

1. Point to display arrows in navigation pane, tap or click white arrow to expand or tap or click black arrow to collapse

2. Select folder to expand or collapse using arrow keys, press RIGHT ARROW to expand; press LEFT ARROW to collapse.

To Switch from One App to Another

1 SIGN IN | 2 USE WINDOWS | 3 USE APPS | 4 FILE MANAGEMENT | 5 SWITCH APPS | 6 SAVE FILES
7 CHANGE SCREEN RESOLUTION | 8 EXIT APPS | 9 USE ADDITIONAL APPS | 10 USE HELP

The next step is to save the Word file containing the headline you typed earlier. Word, however, currently is not the active window. You can use the app button on the taskbar and live preview to switch to Word and then save the document in the Word document window.

Why? *By clicking the appropriate app button on the taskbar, you can switch to the open app you want to use.* The steps below switch to the Word window; however, the steps are the same for any active Office app currently displayed as an app button on the taskbar.

1

- If you are using a mouse, point to the Word app button on the taskbar to see a live preview of the open document(s) or the window title(s) of the open document(s), depending on your computer's configuration (Figure 43).

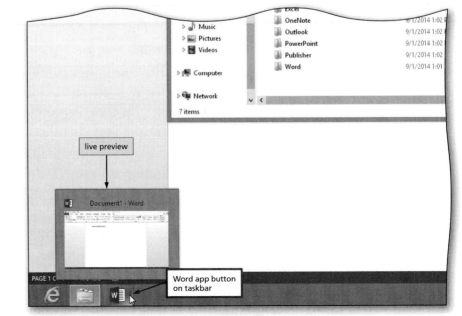

Figure 43

2

- Tap or click the app button or the live preview to make the app associated with the app button the active window (Figure 44).

Q&A What if multiple documents are open in an app?
Tap or click the desired live preview to switch to the window you want to use.

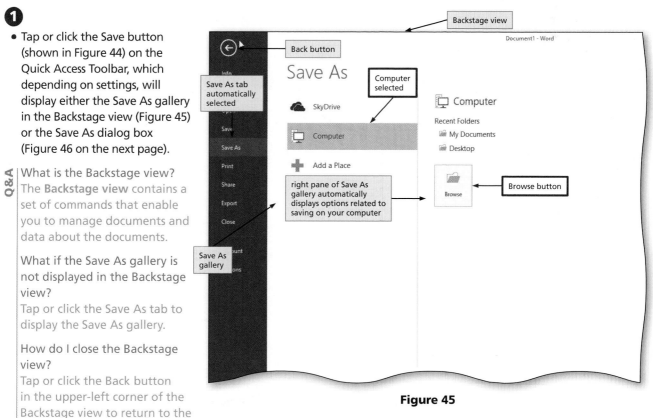

Figure 44

To Save a File in a Folder

1 SIGN IN | 2 USE WINDOWS | 3 USE APPS | 4 FILE MANAGEMENT | 5 SWITCH APPS | 6 SAVE FILES
7 CHANGE SCREEN RESOLUTION | 8 EXIT APPS | 9 USE ADDITIONAL APPS | 10 USE HELP

With the folders for storing your files created, you can save the Word document. *Why? Without saving a file, you may lose all the work you have done and will be unable to reuse or share it with others later.* The following steps save a file in the Word folder contained in your class folder (CIS 101, in this case) using the file name, Elephant Habitat.

1

- Tap or click the Save button (shown in Figure 44) on the Quick Access Toolbar, which depending on settings, will display either the Save As gallery in the Backstage view (Figure 45) or the Save As dialog box (Figure 46 on the next page).

Q&A What is the Backstage view?
The **Backstage view** contains a set of commands that enable you to manage documents and data about the documents.

What if the Save As gallery is not displayed in the Backstage view?
Tap or click the Save As tab to display the Save As gallery.

How do I close the Backstage view?
Tap or click the Back button in the upper-left corner of the Backstage view to return to the app window.

Figure 45

2

- If your screen displays the Backstage view, tap or click Computer, if necessary, to display options in the right pane related to saving on your computer; if your screen already displays the Save As dialog box, proceed to Step 3.

Q&A What if I wanted to save on SkyDrive instead?
You would tap or click SkyDrive. Saving on SkyDrive is discussed in a later section in this chapter.

- Tap or click the Browse button in the right pane to display the Save As dialog box (Figure 46).

Q&A Why does a file name already appear in the File name box?
Word automatically suggests a file name the first time you save a document. The file name normally consists of the first few words contained in the document. Because the suggested file name is selected, you do not need to delete it; as soon as you begin typing, the new file name replaces the selected text.

Figure 46

3

- Type **Elephant Habitat** in the File name box (Save As dialog box) to change the file name. Do not press the ENTER key after typing the file name because you do not want to close the dialog box at this time (Figure 47).

Q&A What characters can I use in a file name?
The only invalid characters are the backslash (\), slash (/), colon (:), asterisk (*), question mark (?), quotation mark ("), less than symbol (<), greater than symbol (>), and vertical bar (|).

Figure 47

4

- Navigate to the desired save location (in this case, the Word folder in the CIS 101 folder [or your class folder] in the My Documents folder in the Documents library) by performing the tasks in Steps 4a and 4b.

4a

- If the Documents library is not displayed in the navigation pane, slide to scroll or drag the scroll bar in the navigation pane until Documents appears.

- If the Documents library is not expanded in the navigation pane, double-tap or double-click Documents to display its folders in the navigation pane.

- If the My Documents folder is not expanded in the navigation pane, double-tap or double-click My Documents to display its folders in the navigation pane.

- If your class folder (CIS 101, in this case) is not expanded, double-tap or double-click the CIS 101 folder to select the folder and display its contents in the navigation pane (Figure 48).

Figure 48

Q&A

What if I do not want to save in a folder?

Although storing files in folders is an effective technique for organizing files, some users prefer not to store files in folders. If you prefer not to save this file in a folder, select the storage device on which you wish to save the file and then proceed to Step 5.

4b

- Tap or click the Word folder in the navigation pane to select it as the new save location and display its contents in the file list (Figure 49).

Figure 49

❺
- Tap or click the Save button (Save As dialog box) to save the document in the selected folder in the selected location with the entered file name (Figure 50).

Q&A | How do I know that the file is saved?
While an Office app is saving a file, it briefly displays a message on the status bar indicating the amount of the file saved. In addition, the file name appears on the title bar.

Figure 50

Other Ways

1. Tap or click FILE on ribbon, tap or click Save As in Backstage view, tap or click Computer, tap or click Browse button, type file name (Save As dialog box), navigate to desired save location, tap or click Save button

2. Press F12, type file name (Save As dialog box), navigate to desired save location, tap or click Save button

Navigating in Dialog Boxes

Navigating is the process of finding a location on a storage device. While saving the Elephant Habitat file, for example, Steps 4a and 4b on the previous page navigated to the Word folder located in the CIS 101 folder in the My Documents folder in the Documents library. When performing certain functions in Windows apps, such as saving a file, opening a file, or inserting a picture in an existing document, you most likely will have to navigate to the location where you want to save the file or to the folder containing the file you want to open or insert. Most dialog boxes in Windows apps requiring navigation follow a similar procedure; that is, the way you navigate to a folder in one dialog box, such as the Save As dialog box, is similar to how you might navigate in another dialog box, such as the Open dialog box. If you chose to navigate to a specific location in a dialog box, you would follow the instructions in Steps 4a and 4b.

To Minimize and Restore a Window

1 SIGN IN | **2 USE WINDOWS** | 3 USE APPS | 4 FILE MANAGEMENT | 5 SWITCH APPS | 6 SAVE FILES
7 CHANGE SCREEN RESOLUTION | 8 EXIT APPS | 9 USE ADDITIONAL APPS | 10 USE HELP

Before continuing, you can verify that the Word file was saved properly. To do this, you will minimize the Word window and then open the CIS 101 window so that you can verify the file is stored in the CIS 101 folder on the hard disk. A **minimized window** is an open window that is hidden from view but can be displayed quickly by clicking the window's app button on the taskbar.

In the following example, Word is used to illustrate minimizing and restoring windows; however, you would follow the same steps regardless of the Office app you are using. **Why?** *Before closing an app, you should make sure your file saved correctly so that you can find it later.*

The following steps minimize the Word window, verify that the file is saved, and then restore the minimized window. If you are using Windows 7, skip these steps and instead perform the steps in the yellow box that immediately follows these Windows 8 steps.

1

- Tap or click the Minimize button on the app's title bar (shown in Figure 50) to minimize the window (Figure 51).

Q&A Is the minimized window still available?
The minimized window, Word in this case, remains available but no longer is the active window. It is minimized as an app button on the taskbar.

- If the File Explorer window is not open on the screen, tap or click the File Explorer app button on the taskbar to make the File folder window the active window.

Figure 51

2

- Double-tap or double-click the Word folder in the file list to select the folder and display its contents (Figure 52).

Q&A Why does the File Explorer app button on the taskbar change?
A selected app button indicates that the app is active on the screen. When the button is not selected, the app is running but not active.

3

- After viewing the contents of the selected folder, tap or click the Word app button on the taskbar to restore the minimized window (as shown in Figure 50).

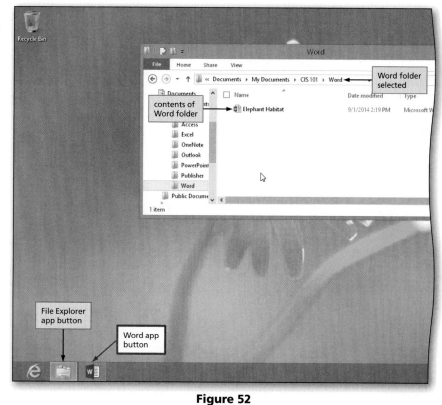

Figure 52

Other Ways

1. Press and hold or right-click title bar, tap or click Minimize on shortcut menu, tap or click taskbar button in taskbar button area

2. Press WINDOWS+M, press WINDOWS+SHIFT+M

TO MINIMIZE AND RESTORE A WINDOW USING WINDOWS 7

If you are using Windows 7, perform these steps to minimize and restore a window instead of the previous steps that use Windows 8.

1. Click the Minimize button on the app's title bar to minimize the window.
2. If the Windows Explorer window is not open on the screen, click the Windows Explorer button on the taskbar to make the Windows Explorer window the active window.
3. Double-click the Word folder in the file list to select the folder and display its contents.
4. After viewing the contents of the selected folder, click the Word button on the taskbar to restore the minimized window.

To Save a File on SkyDrive

1 SIGN IN | 2 USE WINDOWS | 3 USE APPS | 4 FILE MANAGEMENT | 5 SWITCH APPS | **6 SAVE FILES**
7 CHANGE SCREEN RESOLUTION | 8 EXIT APPS | 9 USE ADDITIONAL APPS | 10 USE HELP

One of the features of Office is the capability to save files on SkyDrive so that you can use the files on multiple computers without having to use external storage devices such as a USB flash drive. Storing files on SkyDrive also enables you to share files more efficiently with others, such as when using Office Web Apps and Office 365.

In the following example, Word is used to save a file to SkyDrive. *Why? Storing files on SkyDrive provides more portability options than are available from storing files in the Documents library.*

You can save files directly to SkyDrive from within Word, PowerPoint, and Excel. The following steps save the current Word file to the SkyDrive. These steps require that you have a Microsoft account and an Internet connection.

1

- Tap or click FILE on the ribbon to open the Backstage view (Figure 53).

Q&A | What is the purpose of the FILE tab?
The FILE tab opens the Backstage view for each Office app.

Figure 53

②

- Tap or click the Save As tab in the Backstage view to display the Save As gallery.

- Tap or click SkyDrive to display SkyDrive saving options or a Sign In button, if you are not signed in already to your Microsoft account (Figure 54).

Q&A What if my Save As gallery does not display SkyDrive as a save location?
Tap or click 'Add a Place' and proceed to Step 3.

Figure 54

③

- If your screen displays a Sign In button, tap or click it to display the Sign in dialog box (Figure 55).

Q&A What if the Sign In button does not appear?
If you already are signed into your Microsoft account, the Sign In button will not be displayed. In this case, proceed to Step 5.

Figure 55

4

- Type your Microsoft account user name and password in the text boxes and then tap or click the Sign in button (Sign in dialog box) to sign in to SkyDrive.

5

- Tap or click your SkyDrive to select your SkyDrive as the storage location (Figure 56).

Figure 56

6

- Tap or click the Browse button to contact the SkyDrive server (which may take some time, depending on the speed of your Internet connection) and then display the Save As dialog box (Figure 57).

Q&A Why does the path in the address bar contain various letters and numbers?
The letters and numbers in the address bar uniquely identify the location of your SkyDrive files and folders.

7

- Tap or click the Save button (Save As dialog box) to save the file on SkyDrive.

Figure 57

To Sign Out of a Microsoft Account

If you are using a public computer or otherwise wish to sign out of your Microsoft account, you should sign out of the account from the Accounts gallery in the Backstage view. Signing out of the account is the safest way to make sure that nobody else can access online files or settings stored in your Microsoft account. *Why? For security reasons, you should sign out of your Microsoft account when you are finished using a public or shared computer. Staying signed in to your Microsoft account might enable others to access your files.*

The following steps sign out of a Microsoft account from Word. You would use the same steps in any Office app. If you do not wish to sign out of your Microsoft account, read these steps without performing them.

1 Tap or click FILE on the ribbon to open the Backstage view.

2 Tap or click the Account tab to display the Account gallery (Figure 58).

3 Tap or click the Sign out link, which displays the Remove Account dialog box. If a Can't remove Windows accounts dialog box appears instead of the Remove Account dialog box, click the OK button and skip the remaining steps.

Q&A Why does a Can't remove Windows accounts dialog box appear?
If you signed in to Windows using your Microsoft account, then you also must sign out from Windows, rather than signing out from within Word. When you are finished using Windows, be sure to sign out at that time.

4 Tap or click the Yes button (Remove Account dialog box) to sign out of your Microsoft account on this computer.

Q&A Should I sign out of Windows after removing my Microsoft account?
When you are finished using the computer, you should sign out of Windows for maximum security.

5 Tap or click the Back button in the upper-left corner of the Backstage view to return to the document.

Figure 58

Screen Resolution

Screen resolution indicates the number of pixels (dots) that the computer uses to display the letters, numbers, graphics, and background you see on the screen. When you increase the screen resolution, Windows displays more information on the screen, but the information decreases in size. The reverse also is true: as you decrease the screen resolution, Windows displays less information on the screen, but the information increases in size.

Screen resolution usually is stated as the product of two numbers, such as 1366×768 (pronounced "thirteen sixty-six by seven sixty-eight"). A 1366×768 screen resolution results in a display of 1366 distinct pixels on each of 768 lines, or about 1,050,624 pixels. Changing the screen resolution affects how the ribbon appears in Office apps and some Windows dialog boxes. Figure 59 shows the Word ribbon at screen resolutions of 1366 × 768 and 1024 × 768. All of the same commands are available regardless of screen resolution. The app (Word, in this case), however, makes changes to the groups and the buttons within the groups to accommodate the various screen resolutions. The result is that certain commands may need to be accessed differently depending on the resolution chosen. A command that is visible on the ribbon and available by tapping or clicking a button at one resolution may not be visible and may need to be accessed using its Dialog Box Launcher at a different resolution.

Comparing the two ribbons in Figure 59, notice the changes in content and layout of the groups and galleries. In some cases, the content of a group is the same in each resolution, but the layout of the group differs. For example, the same gallery and buttons appear in the Styles groups in the two resolutions, but the layouts differ. In other cases, the content and layout are the same across the resolution, but the level of detail differs with the resolution.

Figure 59a

Figure 59b

1 SIGN IN | 2 USE WINDOWS | 3 USE APPS | 4 FILE MANAGEMENT | 5 SWITCH APPS | 6 SAVE FILES
7 CHANGE SCREEN RESOLUTION | 8 EXIT APPS | 9 USE ADDITIONAL APPS | 10 USE HELP

To Change the Screen Resolution

If you are using a computer to step through the chapters in this book and you want your screen to match the figures, you may need to change your screen's resolution. **Why?** *The figures in this book use a screen resolution of 1366 × 768.* The following steps change the screen resolution to 1366 × 768. Your computer already may be set to 1366 × 768. Keep in mind that many computer labs prevent users from changing the screen resolution; in that case, read the following steps for illustration purposes.

1

• Tap or click the Show desktop button, which is located at the far-right edge of the taskbar, to display the Windows desktop.

Q&A I cannot see the Show desktop button. Why not?
When you point to the far-right edge of the taskbar, a small outline appears to mark the Show desktop button.

• Press and hold or right-click an empty area on the Windows desktop to display a shortcut menu that contains a list of commands related to the desktop (Figure 60).

Q&A Why does my shortcut menu display different commands?
Depending on your computer's hardware and configuration, different commands might appear on the shortcut menu.

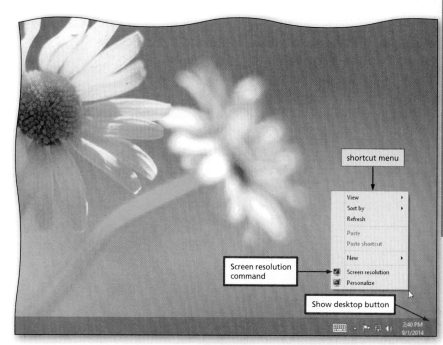

Figure 60

2

• Tap or click Screen resolution on the shortcut menu to open the Screen Resolution window (Figure 61).

3

• Tap or click the Resolution button in the Screen Resolution window to display the resolution slider.

Figure 61

4

- If necessary, drag the resolution slider until the desired screen resolution (in this case, 1366 × 768) is selected (Figure 62).

Q&A What if my computer does not support the 1366 × 768 resolution?

Some computers do not support the 1366 ×768 resolution. In this case, select a resolution that is close to the 1366 × 768 resolution.

What is a slider?

A **slider** is an object that allows users to choose from multiple predetermined options. In most cases, these options represent some type of numeric value. In most cases, one end of the slider (usually the left or bottom) represents the lowest of available values, and the opposite end (usually the right or top) represents the highest available value.

Figure 62

5

- Tap or click an empty area of the Screen Resolution window to close the resolution slider.

- Tap or click the OK button to change the screen resolution and display the Display Settings dialog box (Figure 63).

- Tap or click the Keep changes button (Display Settings dialog box) to accept the new screen resolution.

Q&A Why does a message display stating that the image quality can be improved?

Some computer monitors or screens are designed to display contents better at a certain screen resolution, sometimes referred to as an optimal resolution.

Figure 63

To Exit an Office App with One Document Open

1 SIGN IN | 2 USE WINDOWS | 3 USE APPS | 4 FILE MANAGEMENT | 5 SWITCH APPS | 6 SAVE FILES
7 CHANGE SCREEN RESOLUTION | 8 EXIT APPS | 9 USE ADDITIONAL APPS | 10 USE HELP

When you exit an Office app, such as Word, if you have made changes to a file since the last time the file was saved, the Office app displays a dialog box asking if you want to save the changes you made to the file before it closes the app window. ***Why?*** *The dialog box contains three buttons with these resulting actions: the Save button saves the changes and then exits the Office app, the Don't Save button exits the Office app without saving changes, and the Cancel button closes the dialog box and redisplays the file without saving the changes.*

If no changes have been made to an open document since the last time the file was saved, the Office app will close the window without displaying a dialog box.

The following steps exit an Office app. In the following example, Word is used to illustrate exiting an Office app; however, you would follow the same steps regardless of the Office app you were using.

①

- If necessary, tap or click the Word app button on the taskbar to display the Word window on the desktop.

- If you are using a mouse, point to the Close button on the right side of the app's title bar, Word in this case (Figure 64).

Figure 64

②

- Tap or click the Close button to close the document and exit Word.

Q&A What if I have more than one document open in an Office app?
You could click the Close button for each open document. When you click the last open document's Close button, you also exit the Office app. As an alternative that is more efficient, you could press and hold or right-click the app button on the taskbar and then tap or click 'Close all windows' on the shortcut menu, or press ALT+F4 to close all open documents and exit the Office app.

③

- If a Microsoft Word dialog box appears, tap or click the Save button to save any changes made to the document since the last save.

Other Ways

1. Press and hold or right-click the Office app button on Windows taskbar, click Close window on shortcut menu   2. Press ALT + F4

To Copy a Folder to a USB Flash Drive

1 SIGN IN | 2 USE WINDOWS | 3 USE APPS | 4 FILE MANAGEMENT | 5 SWITCH APPS | 6 SAVE FILES
7 CHANGE SCREEN RESOLUTION | 8 EXIT APPS | 9 USE ADDITIONAL APPS | 10 USE HELP

To store files and folders on a USB flash drive, you must connect the USB flash drive to an available USB port on a computer. The following steps copy your CIS 101 folder to a USB flash drive. *Why? It often is good practice to have a backup of your files. Besides SkyDrive, you can save files to a portable storage device, such as a USB flash drive.* If you are using Windows 7, skip these steps and instead perform the steps in the yellow box that immediately follows these Windows 8 steps.

①

- Insert a USB flash drive in an available USB port on the computer to connect the USB flash drive.

Q&A How can I ensure the USB flash drive is connected?
In File Explorer, you can use the navigation bar to find the USB flash drive. If it is not showing, then it is not connected properly.

②

- Tap or click the File Explorer app button on the taskbar to make the folder window the active window.

- If necessary, navigate to the CIS 101 folder in the File Explorer window (see Step 4a on page OFF 33 for instructions about navigating to a folder location).

Figure 65

- Press and hold or right-click the CIS 101 folder to display a shortcut menu (Figure 65).

❸

- Tap or point to Send to, which causes a submenu to appear (Figure 66).

Figure 66

❹

- Tap or click the USB flash drive to copy the folder to the USB flash drive (Figure 67).

Q&A Why does the drive letter of my USB flash drive differ?

Windows assigns the next available drive letter to your USB flash drive when you connect it. The next available drive letter may vary by computer, depending on the number of storage devices that currently are connected.

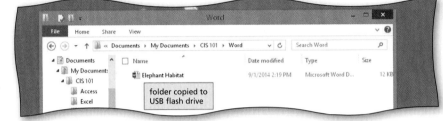

Figure 67

TO COPY A FOLDER TO A USB FLASH DRIVE USING WINDOWS 7

If you are using Windows 7, perform these steps to copy a folder to a USB flash drive instead of the previous steps that use Windows 8.

1. Insert a USB flash drive in an available USB port on the computer to open the AutoPlay window.
2. Click the 'Open folder to view files' link in the AutoPlay window to open the Windows Explorer window.
3. Navigate to the Documents library.
4. Right-click the CIS 101 folder to display a shortcut menu.
5. Point to Send to, which causes a submenu to appear.
6. Click the USB flash drive to copy the folder to the USB flash drive.

Break Point: If you wish to take a break, this is a good place to do so. To resume at a later time, continue to follow the steps from this location forward.

Additional Microsoft Office Apps

The previous section used Word to illustrate common features of Office and some basic elements unique to Word. The following sections present elements unique to PowerPoint, Excel, and Access, as well as illustrate additional common features of Office. In the following pages, you will learn how to do the following:

1. Run an Office app (PowerPoint) using the search box.
2. Create two small documents in the same Office app (PowerPoint).
3. Close one of the documents.
4. Reopen the document just closed.
5. Create a document in a different Office app (Excel).
6. Save the document with a new file name.
7. Create a file in a different Office app (Access).
8. Close the file and then open the file.

PowerPoint

PowerPoint is a full-featured presentation app that allows you to produce compelling presentations to deliver and share with an audience (Figure 68). A PowerPoint **presentation** also is called a **slide show**. PowerPoint contains many features to design, develop, and organize slides, including formatting text, adding and editing video and audio clips, creating tables and charts, applying artistic effects to pictures, animating graphics, and collaborating with friends and colleagues. You then can turn your presentation into a video, broadcast your slide show on the web, or create a photo album.

Figure 68

(a) Slide 1 (Title)

Product Listing

Hand Blown Glass

Sea Shell Sculptures

Custom Jewelry

Rustic Wood Art

(b) Slide 2 (Text and Diagram)

Delivery Options

(c) Slide 3 (Text and Picture)

Figure 68 (Continued)

To Run an App Using the Search Box

1 SIGN IN | 2 USE WINDOWS | 3 USE APPS | 4 FILE MANAGEMENT | 5 SWITCH APPS | 6 SAVE FILES
7 CHANGE SCREEN RESOLUTION | 8 EXIT APPS | 9 USE ADDITIONAL APPS | **10 USE HELP**

The following steps, which assume Windows is running, use the search box to run the PowerPoint app based on a typical installation; however, you would follow similar steps to run any Office app. *Why? Sometimes an app does not appear on the Start screen, so you can find it quickly by searching.* You may need to ask your instructor how to run apps for your computer. If you are using Windows 7, skip these steps and instead perform the steps in the yellow box that immediately follows these Windows 8 steps.

1
- Swipe in from the right edge of the screen or point to the upper-right corner of the screen to display the Charms bar (Figure 69).

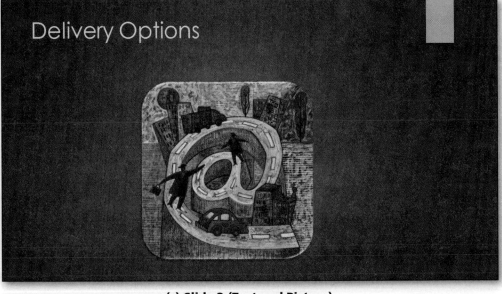

Figure 69

2

- Tap or click the Search charm on the Charms bar to display the Search menu (Figure 70).

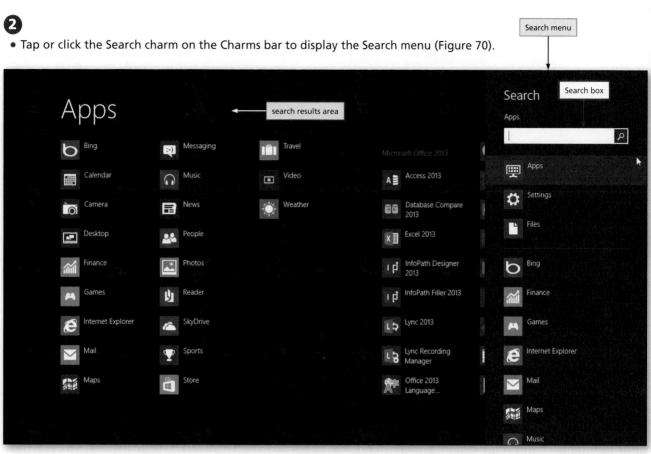

Figure 70

3

- Type **PowerPoint 2013** as the search text in the Search box and watch the search results appear in the Apps list (Figure 71).

Q&A Do I need to type the complete app name or use correct capitalization?

No, you need to type just enough characters of the app name for it to appear in the Apps list. For example, you may be able to type PowerPoint or powerpoint, instead of PowerPoint 2013.

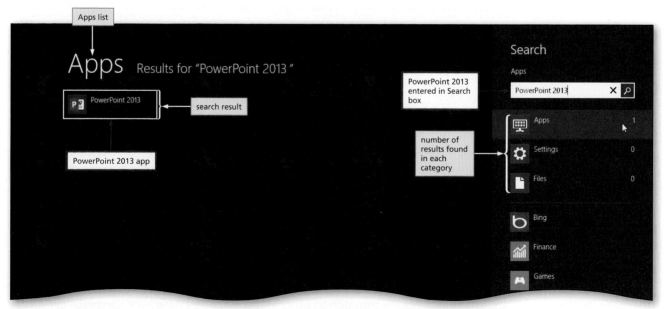

Figure 71

4

- Tap or click the app name, PowerPoint 2013 in this case, in the search results to run PowerPoint.

- Tap or click the Blank Presentation thumbnail to create a blank presentation and display it in the PowerPoint window.

- If the app window is not maximized, tap or click the Maximize button on its title bar to maximize the window (Figure 72).

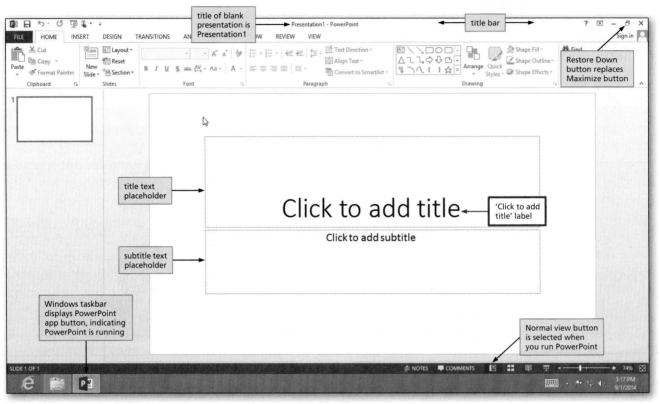

Figure 72

TO RUN AN APP USING THE SEARCH BOX USING WINDOWS 7

If you are using Windows 7, perform these steps to run an app using the search box instead of the previous steps that use Windows 8.

1. Click the Start button on the Windows 7 taskbar to display the Start menu.

2. Type **PowerPoint 2013** as the search text in the 'Search programs and files' text box and watch the search results appear on the Start menu.

3. Click the app name, PowerPoint 2013 in this case, in the search results on the Start menu to run PowerPoint.

4. Click the Blank Presentation thumbnail to create a blank presentation and display it in the PowerPoint window.

5. If the app window is not maximized, click the Maximize button on its title bar to maximize the window.

The PowerPoint Window and Ribbon

The PowerPoint window consists of a variety of components to make your work more efficient and documents more professional: the window, ribbon, mini toolbar, shortcut menus, Quick Access Toolbar, and Microsoft Account area. Many of these components are common to other Office apps and have been discussed earlier in this chapter. Other components, discussed in the following paragraphs and later in subsequent chapters, are unique to PowerPoint.

The basic unit of a PowerPoint presentation is a **slide**. A slide may contain text and objects, such as graphics, tables, charts, and drawings. **Layouts** are used to position this content on the slide. When you create a new presentation, the default **Title Slide** layout appears (shown in Figure 72). The purpose of this layout is to introduce the presentation to the audience. PowerPoint includes several other built-in standard layouts.

The default slide layouts are set up in **landscape orientation**, where the slide width is greater than its height. In landscape orientation, the slide size is preset to 10 inches wide and 7.5 inches high when printed on a standard sheet of paper measuring 11 inches wide and 8.5 inches high.

Placeholders **Placeholders** are boxes with dashed or solid borders that are displayed when you create a new slide. All layouts except the Blank slide layout contain placeholders. Depending on the particular slide layout selected, title and subtitle placeholders are displayed for the slide title and subtitle; a content placeholder is displayed for text or a table, chart, picture, graphic, or movie. The title slide in Figure 73 has two text placeholders for the main heading, or title, and the subtitle.

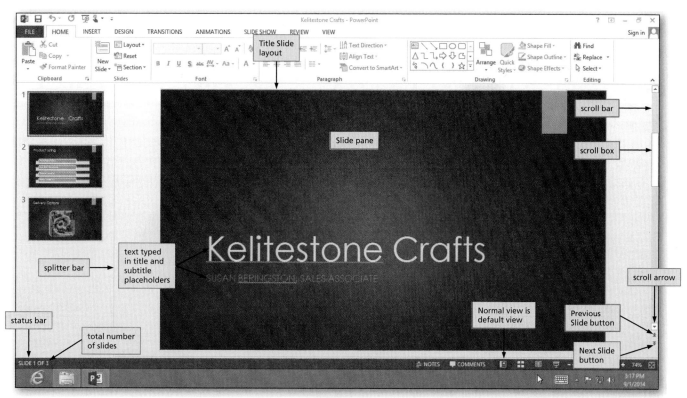

Figure 73

Ribbon The ribbon in PowerPoint is similar to the one in Word and the other Microsoft Office apps. When you run PowerPoint, the ribbon displays nine main tabs: FILE, HOME, INSERT, DESIGN, TRANSITIONS, ANIMATIONS, SLIDE SHOW, REVIEW, and VIEW.

To Enter Content in a Title Slide

1 SIGN IN | 2 USE WINDOWS | 3 USE APPS | 4 FILE MANAGEMENT | 5 SWITCH APPS | 6 SAVE FILES
7 CHANGE SCREEN RESOLUTION | 8 EXIT APPS | 9 USE ADDITIONAL APPS | 10 USE HELP

With the exception of a blank slide, PowerPoint assumes every new slide has a title. Many of PowerPoint's layouts have both a title text placeholder and at least one content placeholder. To make creating a presentation easier, any text you type after a new slide appears becomes title text in the title text placeholder. As you begin typing text in the title text placeholder, the title text also is displayed in the Slide 1 thumbnail in the Thumbnail pane. The title for this presentation is Kelitestone Crafts. The steps on the next page enter a presentation title on the title slide. *Why? In general, every presentation should have a title to describe what the presentation will be covering.*

1

- Tap or click the 'Click to add title' label located inside the title text placeholder (shown in Figure 72 on page OFF 48) to select the placeholder (Figure 74).

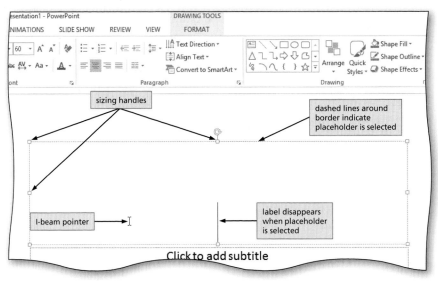

Figure 74

Q&A

What are the white squares that appear around the title text placeholder as I type the presentation title?

The white squares are sizing handles, which you can drag to change the size of the title text placeholder. Sizing handles also can be found around other placeholders and objects within an Office app.

2

- Type **Kelitestone Crafts** in the title text placeholder. Do not press the ENTER key because you do not want to create a new line of text (Figure 75).

Figure 75

To Save a File in a Folder

The following steps save the presentation in the PowerPoint folder in the class folder (CIS 101, in this case) in the My Documents folder in the Documents library using the file name, Kelitestone Crafts.

1 Tap or click the Save button on the Quick Access Toolbar (shown in Figure 75), which, depending on settings, will display either the Save As gallery in the Backstage view or the Save As dialog box.

2 If your screen displays the Backstage view, tap or click Computer, if necessary, to display options in the right pane related to saving on your computer; if your screen already displays the Save As dialog box, proceed to Step 4.

3 Tap or click the Browse button in the right pane to display the Save As dialog box.

4 If necessary, type **Kelitestone Crafts** in the File name box (Save As dialog box) to change the file name. Do not press the ENTER key after typing the file name because you do not want to close the dialog box at this time.

5 Navigate to the desired save location (in this case, the PowerPoint folder in the CIS 101 folder [or your class folder] in the My Documents folder in the Documents library). For specific instructions, perform the tasks in Steps 5a through 5e.

5a If the Documents library is not displayed in the navigation pane, slide to scroll or drag the scroll bar in the navigation pane until Documents appears.

5b If the Documents library is not expanded in the navigation pane, double-tap or double-click Documents to display its folders in the navigation pane.

5c If the My Documents folder is not expanded in the navigation pane, double-tap or double-click My Documents to display its folders in the navigation pane.

5d If your class folder (CIS 101, in this case) is not expanded, double-tap or double-click the CIS 101 folder to select the folder and display its contents in the navigation pane.

5e Tap or click the PowerPoint folder in the navigation pane to select it as the new save location and display its contents in the file list.

6 Tap or click the Save button (Save As dialog box) to save the presentation in the selected folder in the selected location with the entered file name.

To Create a New Office Document from the Backstage View

1 SIGN IN | 2 USE WINDOWS | 3 USE APPS | 4 FILE MANAGEMENT | 5 SWITCH APPS | 6 SAVE FILES
7 CHANGE SCREEN RESOLUTION | 8 EXIT APPS | 9 USE ADDITIONAL APPS | **10 USE HELP**

As discussed earlier, the Backstage view contains a set of commands that enable you to manage documents and data about the documents. *Why? From the Backstage view in PowerPoint, for example, you can create, open, print, and save presentations. You also can share documents, manage versions, set permissions, and modify document properties. In other Office 2013 apps, the Backstage view may contain features specific to those apps.* The following steps create a file, a blank presentation in this case, from the Backstage view.

1

• Tap or click FILE on the ribbon to open the Backstage view (Figure 76).

Q&A | What is the purpose of the Info tab in the Backstage view?
The Info tab, which is selected by default when you click FILE on the ribbon, allows you to protect your document, inspect your document, and manage versions of your document as well as view all the file properties such as when the file was created.

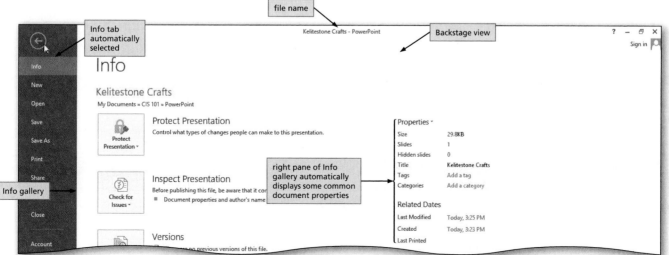

Figure 76

2

- Tap or click the New tab in the Backstage view to display the New gallery (Figure 77).

Q&A Can I create documents through the Backstage view in other Office apps?

Yes. If the Office app has a New tab in the Backstage view, the New gallery displays various options for creating a new file.

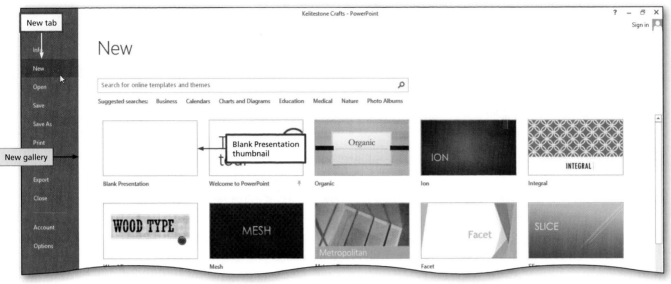

Figure 77

3

- Tap or click the Blank Presentation thumbnail in the New gallery to create a new presentation (Figure 78).

Figure 78

Other Ways

1. Press CTRL+N

To Enter Content in a Title Slide of a Second PowerPoint Presentation

The presentation title for this presentation is Elephant Habitat Opening. The following steps enter a presentation title on the title slide.

1 Tap or click the title text placeholder (shown in Figure 78) to select it.

2 Type **Elephant Habitat Opening** in the title text placeholder. Do not press the ENTER key (Figure 79).

Figure 79

To Save a File in a Folder

The following steps save the second presentation in the PowerPoint folder in the class folder (CIS 101, in this case) in the My Documents folder in the Documents library using the file name, Elephant Habitat Opening.

1 Tap or click the Save button on the Quick Access Toolbar (shown in Figure 79), which, depending on settings, will display either the Save As gallery in the Backstage view or the Save As dialog box.

2 If your screen displays the Backstage view, tap or click Computer, if necessary, to display options in the right pane related to saving on your computer; if your screen already displays the Save As dialog box, proceed to Step 4.

3 Tap or click the Browse button in the right pane to display the Save As dialog box.

4 If necessary, type **Elephant Habitat Opening** in the File name box (Save As dialog box) to change the file name. Do not press the ENTER key after typing the file name because you do not want to close the dialog box at this time.

5 If necessary, navigate to the desired save location (in this case, the PowerPoint folder in the CIS 101 folder [or your class folder] in the My Documents folder in the Documents library). For specific instructions, perform the tasks in Steps 5a through 5e on page OFF 51.

6 Tap or click the Save button (Save As dialog box) to save the presentation in the selected folder on the selected drive with the entered file name.

To Close an Office File Using the Backstage View

Sometimes, you may want to close an Office file, such as a PowerPoint presentation, entirely and start over with a new file. *Why else would I close a file? You also may want to close a file when you are finished working with it so that you can begin a new file.* The following steps close the current active Office file; that is, the Elephant Habitat Opening presentation, without exiting the active app (PowerPoint, in this case).

1

• Tap or click FILE on the ribbon (shown in Figure 79 on the previous page) to open the Backstage view (Figure 80).

2

• Tap or click Close in the Backstage view to close the open file (Elephant Habitat Opening, in this case) without exiting the active app.

Q&A

What if the Office app displays a dialog box about saving?

Tap or click the Save button if you want to save the changes, tap or click the Don't Save button if you want to ignore the changes since the last time you saved, and tap or click the Cancel button if you do not want to close the document.

Can I use the Backstage view to close an open file in other Office apps, such as Word and Excel?
Yes.

Figure 80

Other Ways

1. Press CTRL+F4

To Open a Recent Office File Using the Backstage View

You sometimes need to open a file that you recently modified. *Why? You may have more changes to make such as adding more content or correcting errors.* The Backstage view allows you to access recent files easily. The following steps reopen the Elephant Habitat Opening file just closed.

1

• Tap or click FILE on the ribbon to open the Backstage view.

• Tap or click the Open tab in the Backstage view to display the Open gallery (Figure 81).

2

• Tap or click the desired file name in the Recent Presentations list, Elephant Habitat Opening in this case, to open the file (shown in Figure 79 on the previous page).

Q&A

Can I use the Backstage view to open a recent file in other Office apps, such as Word and Excel?
Yes, as long as the file name appears in the list of recent files.

Figure 81

Other Ways

1. Tap or click FILE on ribbon, tap or click Open in Backstage view, tap or click Computer, tap or click Browse, navigate to file (Open dialog box), tap or click Open button

To Exit an Office App

You are finished using PowerPoint. Thus, you should exit this Office app. The following steps exit PowerPoint.

1 If you have one Office document open, tap or click the Close button on the right side of the title bar to close the document and exit the Office app; or if you have multiple Office documents open, press and hold or right-click the app button on the taskbar and then tap or click 'Close all windows' on the shortcut menu, or press ALT+F4 to close all open documents and exit the Office app.

Q&A If I am using a touch screen, could I press and hold the Close button until all windows close and the app exits?
Yes.

2 If a dialog box appears, tap or click the Save button to save any changes made to the document since the last save.

Excel

Excel is a powerful spreadsheet app that allows users to organize data, complete calculations, make decisions, graph data, develop professional-looking reports (Figure 82), publish organized data to the web, and access real-time data from websites. The four major parts of Excel are:

- **Workbooks and Worksheets:** A **workbook** is like a notebook. Inside the workbook are sheets, each of which is called a **worksheet**. Thus, a workbook is a collection of worksheets. Worksheets allow users to enter, calculate, manipulate, and analyze data such as numbers and text. The terms worksheet and spreadsheet are interchangeable.

- **Charts:** Excel can draw a variety of charts such as column charts and pie charts.

- **Tables:** Tables organize and store data within worksheets. For example, once a user enters data into a worksheet, an Excel table can sort the data, search for specific data, and select data that satisfies defined criteria.

• **Web Support:** Web support allows users to save Excel worksheets or parts of a worksheet in a format that a user can view in a browser, so that a user can view and manipulate the worksheet using a browser. Excel web support also provides access to real-time data, such as stock quotes, using web queries.

Figure 82

To Create a New Blank Office Document from File Explorer

1 SIGN IN | 2 USE WINDOWS | 3 USE APPS | 4 FILE MANAGEMENT | 5 SWITCH APPS | 6 SAVE FILES
7 CHANGE SCREEN RESOLUTION | 8 EXIT APPS | 9 USE ADDITIONAL APPS | 10 USE HELP

File Explorer provides a means to create a blank Office document without running an Office app. The following steps use File Explorer to create a blank Excel document. *Why? Sometimes you might need to create a blank document and then return to it later for editing.* If you are using Windows 7, skip these steps and instead perform the steps in the yellow box that immediately follows these Windows 8 steps.

1

• If necessary, double-tap or double-click the File Explorer app button on the taskbar to make the folder window the active window.

• If necessary, double-tap or double-click the Documents library in the navigation pane to expand the Documents library.

• If necessary, double-tap or double-click the My Documents folder in the navigation pane to expand the My Documents folder.

• If necessary, double-tap or double-click your class folder (CIS 101, in this case) in the navigation pane to expand the folder.

• Tap or click the Excel folder in the navigation pane to display its contents in the file list.

• With the Excel folder selected, press and hold or right-click an open area in the file list to display a shortcut menu.

• Tap or point to New on the shortcut menu to display the New submenu (Figure 83).

Figure 83

2

• Tap or click 'Microsoft Excel Worksheet' on the New submenu to display an icon and text box for a new file in the current folder window with the file name, New Microsoft Excel Worksheet, selected (Figure 84).

Figure 84

3

• Type **Iverstonit Electronics** in the text box and then press the ENTER key to assign a new name to the new file in the current folder (Figure 85).

Figure 85

TO CREATE A NEW BLANK OFFICE DOCUMENT FROM WINDOWS EXPLORER USING WINDOWS 7

If you are using Windows 7, perform these steps to create a new blank Office document from Windows Explorer instead of the previous steps that use Windows 8.

1. If necessary, click the Windows Explorer button on the taskbar to make the folder window the active window.

2. If necessary, double-click the Documents library in the navigation pane to expand the Documents library.

3. If necessary, double-click the My Documents folder in the navigation pane to expand the My Documents folder.

4. If necessary, double-click your class folder (CIS 101, in this case) in the navigation pane to expand the folder.

5. Click the Excel folder in the navigation pane to display its contents in the file list.

6. With the Excel folder selected, right-click an open area in the file list to display a shortcut menu.

7. Point to New on the shortcut menu to display the New submenu.

8. Click 'Microsoft Excel Worksheet' on the New submenu to display an icon and text box for a new file in the current folder window with the name, New Microsoft Excel Worksheet, selected.

9. Type **Iverstonit Electronics** in the text box and then press the ENTER key to assign a new name to the new file in the current folder.

To Run an App from File Explorer and Open a File

1 SIGN IN | 2 USE WINDOWS | 3 USE APPS | 4 FILE MANAGEMENT | 5 SWITCH APPS | 6 SAVE FILES
7 CHANGE SCREEN RESOLUTION | 8 EXIT APPS | 9 USE ADDITIONAL APPS | 10 USE HELP

Previously, you learned how to run an Office app using the Start screen and the Search charm. The steps on the next page, which assume Windows is running, use File Explorer to run the Excel app based on a typical installation. *Why? Another way to run an Office app is to open an existing file from File Explorer, which causes the app in which the file was created to run and then open the selected file.* You may need to ask your instructor how to run Office apps for your computer. If you are using Windows 7, follow the steps in the yellow box that immediately follows these Windows 8 steps.

1

- If necessary, display the file to open in the folder window in File Explorer (shown in Figure 85 on the previous page).

- Press and hold or right-click the file icon or file name (Iverstonit Electronics, in this case) to display a shortcut menu (Figure 86).

Figure 86

2

- Tap or click Open on the shortcut menu to open the selected file in the app used to create the file, Excel in this case (Figure 87).

- If the app window is not maximized, tap or click the Maximize button on the title bar to maximize the window.

Q&A Instead of using File Explorer, can I run Excel using the same method shown previously for Word and PowerPoint?
Yes, you can use any method of running an Office app to run Excel.

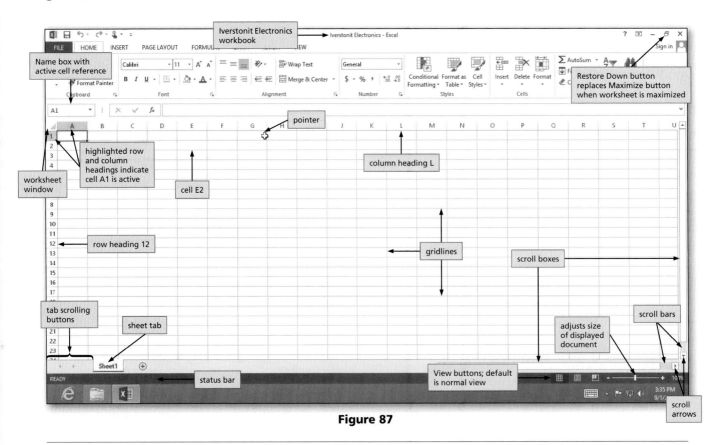

Figure 87

TO RUN AN APP FROM WINDOWS EXPLORER AND OPEN A FILE USING WINDOWS 7

If you are using Windows 7, perform these steps to run an app from Windows Explorer and open a file instead of the previous steps that use Windows 8.

1. Display the file to open in the folder window in Windows Explorer.

2. Right-click the file icon or file name (Iverstonit Electronics, in this case) to display a shortcut menu.

3. Click Open on the shortcut menu to open the selected file in the app used to create the file, Excel in this case.

4. If the app window is not maximized, click the Maximize button on the title bar to maximize the window.

Unique Features of Excel

The Excel window consists of a variety of components to make your work more efficient and worksheets more professional. These include the document window, ribbon, mini toolbar and shortcut menus, Quick Access Toolbar, and Microsoft Account area. Some of these components are common to other Office apps; others are unique to Excel.

Excel opens a new workbook with one worksheet. If necessary, you can add additional worksheets as long as your computer has enough memory to accommodate them.

Each worksheet has a sheet name that appears on a **sheet tab** at the bottom of the workbook. For example, Sheet1 is the name of the active worksheet displayed in the Iverstonit Electronics workbook. You can add more sheets to the workbook by clicking the New sheet button.

The Worksheet The worksheet is organized into a rectangular grid containing vertical columns and horizontal rows. A column letter above the grid, also called the **column heading**, identifies each column. A row number on the left side of the grid, also called the **row heading**, identifies each row. With the screen resolution set to 1366 × 768 and the Excel window maximized, Excel displays 20 columns (A through T) and 23 rows (1 through 23) of the worksheet on the screen, as shown in Figure 87.

The intersection of each column and row is a cell. A **cell** is the basic unit of a worksheet into which you enter data. Each worksheet in a workbook has 16,384 columns and 1,048,576 rows for a total of 17,179,869,180 cells. Only a small fraction of the active worksheet appears on the screen at one time.

A cell is referred to by its unique address, or **cell reference**, which is the coordinates of the intersection of a column and a row. To identify a cell, specify the column letter first, followed by the row number. For example, cell reference E2 refers to the cell located at the intersection of column E and row 2 (Figure 87).

One cell on the worksheet, designated the **active cell**, is the one into which you can enter data. The active cell in Figure 87 is A1. The active cell is identified in three ways. First, a heavy border surrounds the cell; second, the active cell reference shows immediately above column A in the Name box; and third, the column heading A and row heading 1 are highlighted so that it is easy to see which cell is active (Figure 87).

The horizontal and vertical lines on the worksheet itself are called **gridlines**. Gridlines make it easier to see and identify each cell in the worksheet. If desired, you can turn the gridlines off so that they do not show on the worksheet. While learning Excel, gridlines help you to understand the structure of the worksheet.

BTW

The Worksheet Size and Window
The 16,384 columns and 1,048,576 rows in Excel make for a huge worksheet that — if you could imagine — takes up the entire side of a building to display in its entirety. Your computer screen, by comparison, is a small window that allows you to view only a minute area of the worksheet at one time. While you cannot see the entire worksheet, you can move the window over the worksheet to view any part of it.

BTW

Customizing the Ribbon
In addition to customizing the Quick Access Toolbar, you can add items to and remove items from the ribbon. To customize the ribbon, click FILE on the ribbon to open the Backstage view, click Options in the Backstage view, and then click Customize Ribbon in the left pane of the Options dialog box. More information about customizing the ribbon is presented in a later chapter.

The pointer in Figure 87 on page OFF 58 has the shape of a block plus sign. The pointer appears as a block plus sign whenever it is located in a cell on the worksheet. Another common shape of the pointer is the block arrow. The pointer turns into the block arrow when you move it outside the worksheet or when you drag cell contents between rows or columns. The other pointer shapes are described when they appear on the screen.

Ribbon   When you run Excel, the ribbon displays eight main tabs: FILE, HOME, INSERT, PAGE LAYOUT, FORMULAS, DATA, REVIEW, and VIEW. The FORMULAS and DATA tabs are specific to Excel. The FORMULAS tab allows you to work with Excel formulas, and the DATA tab allows you to work with data processing features such as importing and sorting data.

Formula Bar   As you type, Excel displays the entry in the **formula bar**, which appears below the ribbon (Figure 88). You can make the formula bar larger by dragging the sizing handle at the bottom of the formula bar or tapping or clicking the expand button to the right of the formula bar. Excel also displays the active cell reference in the **Name box** on the left side of the formula bar.

Figure 88

To Enter a Worksheet Title

1 SIGN IN | 2 USE WINDOWS | 3 USE APPS | 4 FILE MANAGEMENT | 5 SWITCH APPS | 6 SAVE FILES
7 CHANGE SCREEN RESOLUTION | 8 EXIT APPS | 9 USE ADDITIONAL APPS | 10 USE HELP

To enter data into a cell, you first must select it. The easiest way to select a cell (make it active) is to tap the cell or use the mouse to move the block plus sign pointer to the cell and then click. An alternative method is to use the arrow keys that are located just to the right of the typewriter keys on the keyboard. An arrow key selects the cell adjacent to the active cell in the direction of the arrow on the key.

In Excel, any set of characters containing a letter, hyphen (as in a telephone number), or space is considered text. **Text** is used to place titles, such as worksheet titles, column titles, and row titles, on the worksheet. The following steps enter the worksheet title in cell A1. *Why? A title informs others as to the contents of the worksheet, such as information regarding a company.*

1

- If it is not already the active cell, tap or click cell A1 to make it the active cell (Figure 89).

Figure 89

2

- Type **Iverstonit Electronics** in cell A1 (Figure 90).

Q&A Why did the appearance of the formula bar change?
Excel displays the title in the formula bar and in cell A1. When you begin typing a cell entry, Excel displays two additional boxes in the formula bar: the Cancel box and the Enter box. Tapping or clicking the Enter box completes an entry. Tapping or clicking the Cancel box cancels an entry.

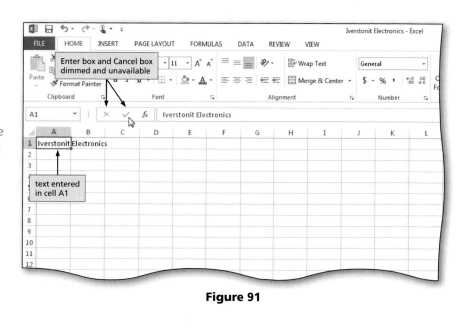

Figure 90

3

- Tap or click the Enter box to complete the entry and enter the worksheet title in cell A1 (Figure 91).

Q&A Why do some commands on the ribbon appear dimmed?
Excel dims the commands that are unavailable for use at the current time.

Figure 91

Other Ways

1. To complete entry, tap or click any cell other than active cell

2. To complete entry, press ENTER, HOME, PAGE UP, PAGE DOWN, END, UP ARROW, DOWN ARROW, LEFT ARROW, or RIGHT ARROW

To Save an Existing Office File with the Same File Name

1 SIGN IN | 2 USE WINDOWS | 3 USE APPS | 4 FILE MANAGEMENT | 5 SWITCH APPS | 6 SAVE FILES
7 CHANGE SCREEN RESOLUTION | 8 EXIT APPS | 9 USE ADDITIONAL APPS | 10 USE HELP

Saving frequently cannot be overemphasized. *Why? You have made modifications to the file (spreadsheet) since you created it. Thus, you should save again. Similarly, you should continue saving files frequently so that you do not lose the changes you have made since the time you last saved the file.* You can use the same file name, such as Iverstonit Electronics, to save the changes made to the document. The step on the next page saves a file again with the same file name.

1

- Tap or click the Save button on the Quick Access Toolbar to overwrite the previously saved file (Iverstonit Electronics, in this case) in the Excel folder (Figure 92).

Save button

Excel saved workbook with same file name, Iverstonit Electronics

Iverstonit Electronics - Excel

FILE tab

Inverstonit Electronics

	A	B	C	D	E	F	G	H	I	J	K	L
1	Iverstonit	Electronics										
2												
3												
4												
5												

Figure 92

Other Ways

1. Press CTRL+S or press SHIFT+F12

To Save a File with a New File Name

You might want to save a file with a different name or to a different location. For example, you might start a homework assignment with a data file and then save it with a final file name for submission to your instructor, saving it to a location designated by your instructor. The following steps save a file with a different file name.

1 Tap or click the FILE tab to open the Backstage view.

2 Tap or click the Save As tab to display the Save As gallery.

3 If necessary, tap or click Computer to display options in the right pane related to saving on your computer.

4 Tap or click the Browse button in the right pane to display the Save As dialog box.

5 Type **Iverstonit Electronics Rental Summary** in the File name box (Save As dialog box) to change the file name. Do not press the ENTER key after typing the file name because you do not want to close the dialog box at this time.

6 If necessary, navigate to the desired save location (in this case, the Excel folder in the CIS 101 folder [or your class folder] in the My Documents folder in the Documents library). For specific instructions, perform the tasks in Steps 5a through 5e on page OFF 51, replacing the PowerPoint folder with the Excel folder.

7 Tap or click the Save button (Save As dialog box) to save the worksheet in the selected folder on the selected drive with the entered file name.

To Exit an Office App

You are finished using Excel. The following steps exit Excel.

1 If you have one Office document open, tap or click the Close button on the right side of the title bar to close the document and exit the Office app; or if you have multiple Office documents open, press and hold or right-click the app button on the taskbar and then tap or click 'Close all windows' on the shortcut menu, or press ALT+F4 to close all open documents and exit the Office app.

2 If a dialog box appears, tap or click the Save button to save any changes made to the file since the last save.

Access

The term **database** describes a collection of data organized in a manner that allows access, retrieval, and use of that data. **Access** is a database management system. A **database management system** is software that allows you to use a computer to create a database; add, change, and delete data in the database; create queries that allow you to ask questions concerning the data in the database; and create forms and reports using the data in the database.

To Run an App

The following steps, which assume Windows is running, run the Access app based on a typical installation. You may need to ask your instructor how to run apps for your computer. If you are using Windows 7, skip these steps and instead perform the steps in the yellow box that immediately follows these Windows 8 steps.

 Swipe in from the right edge of the screen or point to the upper-right corner of the screen to display the Charms bar.

 Tap or click the Search charm on the Charms bar to display the Search menu.

 Type **Access 2013** as the search text in the Search box and watch the search results appear in the Apps list.

 Tap or click the app name, Access 2013 in this case, in the search results to run Access.

 If the app window is not maximized, tap or click the Maximize button on its title bar to maximize the window (Figure 93).

Figure 93

Q&A
Do I have to run Access using these steps?
No. You can use any previously discussed method of running an Office app to run Access.

To Run an App Using Windows 7

If you are using Windows 7, perform these steps to run an app instead of the previous steps that use Windows 8.

1. Click the Start button on the Windows 7 taskbar to display the Start menu.

2. Type **Access 2013** as the search text in the 'Search programs and files' text box and watch the search results appear on the Start menu.

3. Click the app name, Access 2013 in this case, in the search results on the Start menu to run Access.

4. If the app window is not maximized, click the Maximize button on its title bar to maximize the window.

Unique Elements in Access

You work on objects such as tables, forms, and reports in the **Access work area**. Figure 94 shows a work area with multiple objects open. **Object tabs** for the open objects appear at the top of the work area. You select an open object by tapping or clicking its tab. In the figure, the Asset List table is the selected object. To the left of the work area is the Navigation Pane, which contains a list of all the objects in the database. You use this pane to open an object. You also can customize the way objects are displayed in the Navigation Pane.

Because the Navigation Pane can take up space in the window, you may not have as much open space for working as you would with Word or Excel. You can use the 'Shutter Bar Open/Close Button' to minimize the Navigation Pane when you are not using it, which allows more space to work with tables, forms, reports, and other database elements.

Figure 94

Ribbon When you run Access, the ribbon displays five main tabs: FILE, HOME, CREATE, EXTERNAL DATA, and DATABASE TOOLS. Access has unique groupings such as Sort & Filter and Records that are designed specifically for working with databases. Many of the formatting options are reserved for the tool tabs that appear when you are working with forms and reports.

To Create an Access Database

1 SIGN IN | 2 USE WINDOWS | 3 USE APPS | 4 FILE MANAGEMENT | 5 SWITCH APPS | 6 SAVE FILES
7 CHANGE SCREEN RESOLUTION | 8 EXIT APPS | 9 USE ADDITIONAL APPS | 10 USE HELP

Unlike the other Office apps, Access saves a database when you first create it. When working in Access, you will add data to an Access database. As you add data to a database, Access automatically saves your changes rather than waiting until you manually save the database or exit Access. Recall that in Word and Excel, you entered the data first and then saved it.

Because Access automatically saves the database as you add and change data, you do not always have to click the Save button on the Quick Access Toolbar. Instead, the Save button in Access is used for saving the objects (including tables, queries, forms, reports, and other database objects) a database contains. You can use either the 'Blank desktop database' option or a template to create a new database. If you already know the organization of your database, you would use the 'Blank desktop database' option. If not, you can use a template. Templates can guide you by suggesting some commonly used database organizations.

The following steps use the 'Blank desktop database' option to create a database named Rimitoein Construction in the Access folder in the class folder (CIS 101, in this case) in the Documents library. *Why? You have decided to use Microsoft Access to maintain large amounts of data.*

- Tap or click the 'Blank desktop database' thumbnail (shown in Figure 93 on page OFF 63) to select the database type.

- Type **Rimitoein Construction** in the File Name box to enter the new file name. Do not press the ENTER key after typing the file name because you do not want to create the database at this time (Figure 95).

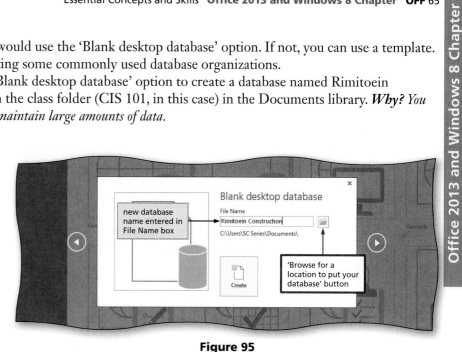

Figure 95

2

- Tap or click the 'Browse for a location to put your database' button to display the File New Database dialog box.

- Navigate to the location for the database; that is, the Documents library, the My Documents folder, then to the folder identifying your class (CIS 101, in this case), and then to the Access folder (Figure 96). For specific instructions, perform the tasks in Steps 5a through 5e on page OFF 51, replacing the PowerPoint folder with the Access folder.

Q&A Why does the 'Save as type' box say Microsoft Access 2007 - 2013 Databases?

Microsoft Access database formats change with some new versions of Microsoft Access. The most recent format is the Microsoft Access 2007 - 2013 Databases format, which was released with Access 2007 and Access 2013.

Figure 96

3

- Tap or click the OK button (File New Database dialog box) to select the Access folder as the location for the database and close the dialog box (Figure 97).

Figure 97

4

- Tap or click the Create button to create the database on the selected drive in the selected folder with the file name, Rimitoein Construction (Figure 98).

Q&A How do I know that the Rimitoein Construction database is created?
The file name of the database appears on the title bar.

Figure 98

To Close an Office File

Assume you need to close the Access database and return to it later. The following step closes an Office file.

1 Tap or click FILE on the ribbon to open the Backstage view and then tap or click Close in the Backstage view to close the open file (Rimitoein Construction, in this case) without exiting the active app.

Q&A Why is Access still on the screen?
When you close a database, the app remains running.

1 SIGN IN | 2 USE WINDOWS | 3 USE APPS | 4 FILE MANAGEMENT | 5 SWITCH APPS | 6 SAVE FILES
7 CHANGE SCREEN RESOLUTION | 8 EXIT APPS | 9 USE ADDITIONAL APPS | 10 USE HELP

To Open an Existing Office File

Assume you wish to continue working on an existing file; that is, a file you previously saved. Earlier in this chapter, you learned how to open a recently used file through the Backstage view. The following step opens a database, specifically the Rimitoein Construction database, that recently was saved. **Why?** *Because the file has been created already, you just need to reopen it.*

1

- Tap or click FILE on the ribbon to open the Backstage view and then tap or click Open in the Backstage view to display the Open gallery in the Backstage view.

- Tap or click Computer to display recent folders accessed on your computer.

- Tap or click the Browse button to display the Open dialog box.

- If necessary, navigate to the location of the file to open.

- Tap or click the file to open, Rimitoein Construction in this case, to select the file.

- Tap or click the Open button (Open dialog box) to open the file. If necessary, tap or click the Enable Content button (Figure 99).

Q&A
Why did the Security Warning appear?
The Security Warning appears when you open an Office file that might contain harmful content. The files you create in this chapter are not harmful, but you should be cautious when opening files from other people.

Figure 99

Other Ways

1. Press CTRL+O   2. Navigate to file in File Explorer window, double-tap or double-click file

To Exit an Office App

You are finished using Access. The following step exits Access.

1 Tap or click the Close button on the right side of the title bar to close the file and exit the Office app.

Other Office Apps

In addition to the Office apps discussed thus far, three other apps are useful when collaborating and communicating with others: Outlook, Publisher, and OneNote.

Outlook

Outlook is a powerful communications and scheduling app that helps you communicate with others, keep track of contacts, and organize your calendar. Apps such as Outlook provide a way for individuals and workgroups to organize, find, view, and share information easily. Outlook allows you to send and receive email messages and provides a means to organize contacts. Users can track email messages, meetings, and notes related to a particular contact. Outlook's Calendar, People, Tasks, and Notes components aid in this organization. Contact information readily is available from the Outlook Calendar, Mail, People, and Task components by accessing the Search Contacts feature.

Email is the transmission of messages and files over a computer network. Email has become an important means of exchanging information and files between business associates, classmates and instructors, friends, and family. Businesses find that using email to send documents electronically saves both time and money. Parents with students away at college or relatives who live across the country find that communicating by email is an inexpensive and easy way to stay in touch with their family members. Exchanging email messages is a widely used service of the Internet.

The Outlook Window Figure 100 shows an Outlook window, which is divided into three panes: the Folder pane, the Inbox message pane to the left of center, and the Reading Pane to the right of center.

When an email message is open in Outlook, it is displayed in a Message window (Figure 101). When you open a message, the Message tab on the ribbon appears, which contains the more frequently used commands.

Figure 100

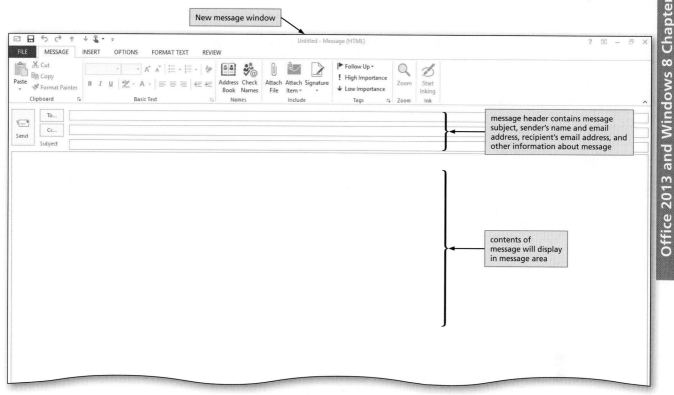

Figure 101

Publisher

Publisher is a powerful desktop publishing (DTP) app that assists you in designing and producing professional-quality documents that combine text, graphics, illustrations, and photos. DTP software provides additional tools beyond those typically found in word processing apps, including design templates, graphic manipulation tools, color schemes or libraries, advanced layout and printing tools, and web components. For large jobs, businesses use DTP software to design publications that are camera ready, which means the files are suitable for outside commercial printing. In addition, DTP software can be used to create webpages and interactive web forms.

Publisher is used by people who regularly produce high-quality color publications, such as newsletters, brochures, flyers, logos, signs, catalogs, cards, and business forms. Saving publications as webpages or complete websites is a powerful component of Publisher. All publications can be saved in a format that easily is viewed and manipulated using a browser.

Publisher has many features designed to simplify production and make publications visually appealing. Using Publisher, you easily can change the shape, size, and color of text and graphics. You can include many kinds of graphical objects, including mastheads, borders, tables, images, pictures, charts, and web objects in publications, as well as integrate spreadsheets and databases.

The Publisher Window   Publisher initially displays a list of publication types. **Publication types** are typical publications used by desktop publishers. The more popular types are displayed in the center of the window.

Once you select a publication type, a dialog box is displayed to allow you to create the publication (Figure 102 on the next page). Some templates are installed with Publisher, and others are available online. In Figure 102, the Brochure publication dialog box is displayed.

BTW

Running Publisher
When you first run Publisher, the New templates gallery usually is displayed in the Backstage view. If it is not displayed, click FILE on the ribbon, click Options in the Backstage view, click General (Publisher Options dialog box), and then click 'Show the New template gallery when starting Publisher' to select the check box in the right pane.

Figure 102

When you click the template, Publisher creates the document and sets it up for you to edit. Figure 103 shows the Brochure document that Publisher creates when default options are selected.

Figure 103

OneNote

OneNote is a note taking app that assists you in entering, saving, organizing, searching, and using notes. It enables you to create pages, which are organized in sections, just as in a physical notebook. In OneNote, you can type notes anywhere on a page and then easily move the notes around on the page. You can create lists and outlines, use handwriting to enter notes, and create drawings. If you use a tablet to add handwritten notes to a document, OneNote can convert the handwriting to text. It also can perform searches on the handwritten entries. Pictures and data from other apps easily are incorporated in your notes.

In addition to typing and handwriting, you can take audio notes. For example, you could record conversations during a meeting or lecture. As you record, you can take additional notes. When you play back the audio notes, you can synchronize the additional notes you took; that is, OneNote will show you during playback the exact points at which you added the notes. A variety of note flags, which are symbols that call your attention to notes on a page, enable you to flag notes as being important. You then can use the Note Flags summary to view the flagged notes, which can be sorted in a variety of ways.

OneNote includes tools to assist you with organizing a notebook and navigating its contents. It also includes a search feature, making it easy to find the specific notes in which you are interested. For short notes that you always want to have available readily, you can use Side Notes, which are used much like the sticky notes that you might use in a physical notebook.

OneNote Window   All activity in OneNote takes place in the **notebook** (Figure 104). Like a physical notebook, the OneNote notebook consists of notes that are placed on **pages**. The pages are grouped into **sections**, which can be further grouped into **folders**. (No folders are shown in the notebook in the figure.) You can use the Search box to search for specific text in your notes.

You can add pages to the notebook using the Add Page button in the Page Tabs pane. If Page Tabs are displayed, you can switch to a page by tapping or clicking its tab. Figure 104 shows the Quick Notes page being displayed for the notebook.

Figure 104

Break Point: If you wish to take a break, this is a good place to do so. To resume at a later time, continue to follow the steps from this location forward.

Renaming, Moving, and Deleting Files

Earlier in this chapter, you learned how to organize files in folders, which is part of a process known as **file management**. The following sections cover additional file management topics including renaming, moving, and deleting files.

1 SIGN IN | 2 USE WINDOWS | 3 USE APPS | **4 FILE MANAGEMENT** | 5 SWITCH APPS | 6 SAVE FILES
7 CHANGE SCREEN RESOLUTION | 8 EXIT APPS | 9 USE ADDITIONAL APPS | **10 USE HELP**

To Rename a File

In some circumstances, you may want to change the name of, or rename, a file or a folder. *Why? You may want to distinguish a file in one folder or drive from a copy of a similar file, or you may decide to rename a file to better identify its contents.* The Word folder shown in Figure 67 on page OFF 44 contains the Word document, Elephant Habitat. The following steps change the name of the Elephant Habitat file in the Word folder to Elephant Habitat Flyer. If you are using Windows 7, skip these steps and instead perform the steps in the yellow box that immediately follows these Windows 8 steps.

- If necessary, tap or click the File Explorer app button on the taskbar to make the folder window the active window.

- Navigate to the location of the file to be renamed (in this case, the Word folder in the CIS 101 [or your class folder] folder in the My Documents folder in the Documents library) to display the file(s) it contains in the file list.

- Press and hold or right-click the Elephant Habitat icon or file name in the file list to select the Elephant Habitat file and display a shortcut menu that presents a list of commands related to files (Figure 105).

Figure 105

- Tap or click Rename on the shortcut menu to place the current file name in a text box.

- Type **Elephant Habitat Flyer** in the text box and then press the ENTER key (Figure 106).

Q&A
Are any risks involved in renaming files that are located on a hard disk?
If you inadvertently rename a file that is associated with certain apps, the apps may not be able to find the file and, therefore, may not run properly. Always use caution when renaming files.

Can I rename a file when it is open?
No, a file must be closed to change the file name.

Figure 106

Other Ways

1. Select file, press F2, type new file name, press ENTER   2. Select file, tap or click Rename (Home tab | Organize group), type new file name, press ENTER

TO RENAME A FILE USING WINDOWS 7

If you are using Windows 7, perform these steps to rename a file instead of the previous steps that use Windows 8.

1. If necessary, click the Windows Explorer app button on the taskbar to make the folder window the active window.

2. Navigate to the location of the file to be renamed (in this case, the Word folder in the CIS 101 [or your class folder] folder in the My Documents folder in the Documents library) to display the file(s) it contains in the file list.

3. Right-click the Elephant Habitat icon or file name in the file list to select the Elephant Habitat file and display a shortcut menu that presents a list of commands related to files.

4. Click Rename on the shortcut menu to place the current file name in a text box.

5. Type **Elephant Habitat Flyer** in the text box and then press the ENTER key.

To Move a File

1 SIGN IN | 2 USE WINDOWS | 3 USE APPS | **4 FILE MANAGEMENT** | 5 SWITCH APPS | 6 SAVE FILES
7 CHANGE SCREEN RESOLUTION | 8 EXIT APPS | 9 USE ADDITIONAL APPS | **10 USE HELP**

Why? *At some time, you may want to move a file from one folder, called the source folder, to another, called the destination folder.* When you move a file, it no longer appears in the original folder. If the destination and the source folders are on the same media, you can move a file by dragging it. If the folders are on different media, then you will need to press and hold and then drag, or right-drag the file, and then click Move here on the shortcut menu. The following step moves the Iverstonit Electronics Rental Summary file from the Excel folder to the OneNote folder. If you are using Windows 7, skip these steps and instead perform the steps in the yellow box that immediately follows these Windows 8 steps.

1

- In File Explorer, navigate to the location of the file to be moved (in this case, the Excel folder in the CIS 101 folder [or your class folder] in the Documents library).

- Tap or click the Excel folder in the navigation pane to display the files it contains in the right pane (Figure 107).

- Drag the Iverstonit Electronics Rental Summary file in the right pane to the OneNote folder in the navigation pane.

Experiment

- Click the OneNote folder in the navigation pane to verify that the file was moved.

Figure 107

Other Ways

1. Press and hold or right-click file to move, tap or click Cut on shortcut menu, press and hold or right-click destination folder, tap or click Paste on shortcut menu

2. Select file to move, press CTRL+X, select destination folder, press CTRL+V

TO MOVE A FILE USING WINDOWS 7

If you are using Windows 7, perform these steps to move a file instead of the previous steps that use Windows 8.

1. In Windows Explorer, navigate to the location of the file to be moved (in this case, the Excel folder in the CIS 101 folder [or your class folder] in the Documents library).

2. Click the Excel folder in the navigation pane to display the files it contains in the right pane.

3. Drag the Iverstonit Electronics Rental Summary file in the right pane to the OneNote folder in the navigation pane.

To Delete a File

1 SIGN IN | 2 USE WINDOWS | 3 USE APPS | **4 FILE MANAGEMENT** | 5 SWITCH APPS | 6 SAVE FILES
7 CHANGE SCREEN RESOLUTION | 8 EXIT APPS | 9 USE ADDITIONAL APPS | **10 USE HELP**

A final task you may want to perform is to delete a file. Exercise extreme caution when deleting a file or files. When you delete a file from a hard disk, the deleted file is stored in the Recycle Bin where you can recover it until you empty the Recycle Bin. If you delete a file from removable media, such as a USB flash drive, the file is deleted permanently. The next steps delete the Elephant Habitat Opening file from the PowerPoint folder. *Why? When a file no longer is needed, you can delete it to conserve space in your storage location.* If you are using Windows 7, skip these steps and instead perform the steps in the yellow box that immediately follows these Windows 8 steps.

1

- In File Explorer, navigate to the location of the file to be deleted (in this case, the PowerPoint folder in the CIS 101 folder [or your class folder] in the Documents library).

- Press and hold or right-click the Elephant Habitat Opening icon or file name in the right pane to select the file and display a shortcut menu (Figure 108).

2

- Tap or click Delete on the shortcut menu to delete the file.

- If a dialog box appears, tap or click the Yes button to delete the file.

Q&A | Can I use this same technique to delete a folder?
Yes. Right-click the folder and then click Delete on the shortcut menu. When you delete a folder, all of the files and folders contained in the folder you are deleting, together with any files and folders on lower hierarchical levels, are deleted as well.

Figure 108

Other Ways

1. Select icon, press DELETE

To Delete a File Using Windows 7

If you are using Windows 7, perform these steps to delete a file instead of the previous steps that use Windows 8.

1. In Windows Explorer, navigate to the location of the file to be deleted (in this case, the PowerPoint folder in the CIS 101 folder [or your class folder] in the Documents library).
2. Right-click the Elephant Habitat Opening icon or file name in the right pane to select the file and display a shortcut menu.
3. Click Delete on the shortcut menu to delete the file.
4. If a dialog box appears, click the Yes button to delete the file.

Microsoft Office and Windows Help

At any time while you are using one of the Office apps, you can use Office Help to display information about all topics associated with the app. To illustrate the use of Office Help, this section uses Word. Help in other Office apps operates in a similar fashion.

In Office, Help is presented in a window that has browser-style navigation buttons. Each Office app has its own Help home page, which is the starting Help page that is displayed in the Help window. If your computer is connected to the Internet, the contents of the Help page reflect both the local help files installed on the computer and material from Microsoft's website.

To Open the Help Window in an Office App

1 SIGN IN | 2 USE WINDOWS | 3 USE APPS | **4 FILE MANAGEMENT** | 5 SWITCH APPS | 6 SAVE FILES
7 CHANGE SCREEN RESOLUTION | 8 EXIT APPS | 9 USE ADDITIONAL APPS | **10 USE HELP**

The following step opens the Word Help window. *Why? You might not understand how certain commands or operations work in Word, so you can obtain the necessary information using help.*

1

- Run an Office app, in this case Word.

- Tap or click the Office app's Help button near the upper-right corner of the app window (the 'Microsoft Word Help' button, in this case) to open the app's Help window (Figure 109).

Figure 109

Other Ways

1. Press F1

Moving and Resizing Windows

At times, it is useful, or even necessary, to have more than one window open and visible on the screen at the same time. You can resize and move these open windows so that you can view different areas of and elements in the window. In the case of the Help window, for example, it could be covering document text in the Word window that you need to see.

To Move a Window by Dragging

You can move any open window that is not maximized to another location on the desktop by dragging the title bar of the window. *Why? You might want to have a better view of what is behind the window or just want to move the window so that you can see it better.* The following step drags the Word Help window to the upper-left corner of the desktop.

1

- Drag the window title bar (the Word Help window title bar, in this case) so that the window moves to the upper-left corner of the desktop, as shown in Figure 110.

Figure 110

To Resize a Window by Dragging

A method used to change the size of the window is to drag the window borders. The following step changes the size of the Word Help window by dragging its borders. *Why? Sometimes, information is not visible completely in a window, and you want to increase the size of the window.*

1

- If you are using a mouse, point to the lower-right corner of the window (the Word Help window, in this case) until the pointer changes to a two-headed arrow.

- Drag the bottom border downward to display more of the active window (Figure 111).

Q&A

Can I drag other borders on the window to enlarge or shrink the window?
Yes, you can drag the left, right, and top borders and any window corner to resize a window.

Will Windows remember the new size of the window after I close it?
Yes. When you reopen the window, Windows will display it at the same size it was when you closed it.

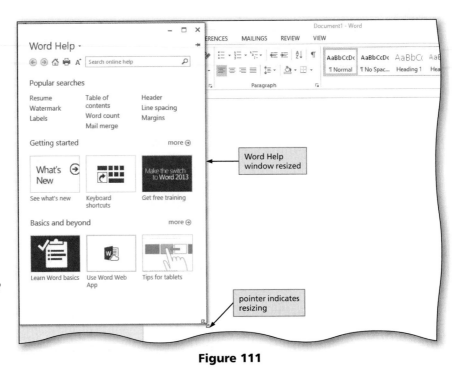

Figure 111

Using Office Help

Once an Office app's Help window is open, several methods exist for navigating Help. You can search for help by using any of the three following methods from the Help window:

1. Enter search text in the 'Search online help' text box.
2. Click the links in the Help window.
3. Use the Table of Contents.

To Obtain Help Using the 'Search online help' Text Box

1 SIGN IN | 2 USE WINDOWS | 3 USE APPS | 4 FILE MANAGEMENT | 5 SWITCH APPS | 6 SAVE FILES
7 CHANGE SCREEN RESOLUTION | 8 EXIT APPS | 9 USE ADDITIONAL APPS | 10 USE HELP

Assume for the following example that you want to know more about fonts. The following steps use the 'Search online help' text box to obtain useful information about fonts by entering the word, fonts, as search text. **Why?** *You may not know the exact help topic you are looking to find, so using keywords can help narrow your search.*

1

- Type **fonts** in the 'Search online help' text box at the top of the Word Help window to enter the search text.

- Tap or click the 'Search online help' button to display the search results (Figure 112).

Q&A Why do my search results differ?
If you do not have an Internet connection, your results will reflect only the content of the Help files on your computer. When searching for help online, results also can change as material is added, deleted, and updated on the online Help webpages maintained by Microsoft.

Why were my search results not very helpful?
When initiating a search, be sure to check the spelling of the search text; also, keep your search specific to return the most accurate results.

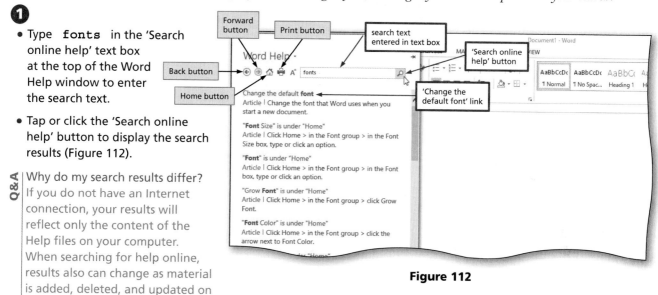

Figure 112

2

- Tap or click the 'Change the default font' link to display the Help information associated with the selected topic (Figure 113).

Figure 113

3

• Tap or click the Home button in the Help window to clear the search results and redisplay the Help home page (Figure 114).

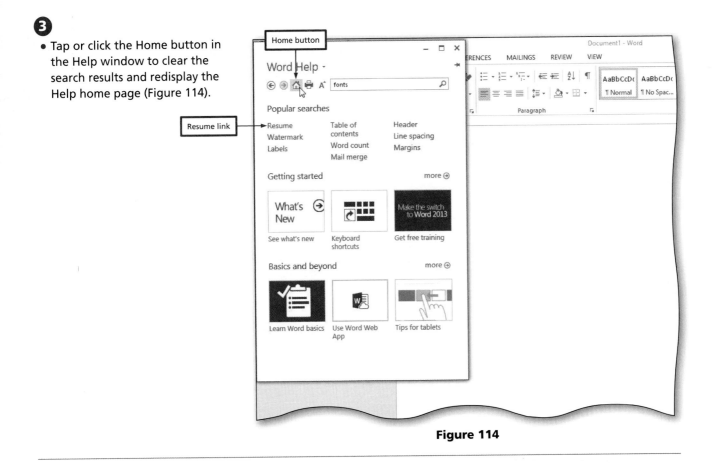

Figure 114

1 SIGN IN | 2 USE WINDOWS | 3 USE APPS | 4 FILE MANAGEMENT | 5 SWITCH APPS | 6 SAVE FILES
7 CHANGE SCREEN RESOLUTION | 8 EXIT APPS | 9 USE ADDITIONAL APPS | 10 USE HELP

To Obtain Help Using Help Links

If your topic of interest is listed in the Help window, you can click the link to begin browsing the Help categories instead of entering search text. *Why? You browse Help just as you would browse a website. If you know which category contains your Help information, you may wish to use these links.* The following step finds the Resume information using the Resume link from the Word Help home page.

1

• Tap or click the Resume link on the Help home page (shown in Figure 114) to display the Resume help links (Figure 115).

2

• After reviewing the page, tap or click the Close button to close the Help window.

• Tap or click the Office app's Close button (Word, in this case) to exit the Office app.

Figure 115

Obtaining Help while Working in an Office App

Help in the Office apps provides you with the ability to obtain help directly, without opening the Help window and initiating a search. For example, you may be unsure about how a particular command works, or you may be presented with a dialog box that you are not sure how to use.

Figure 116 shows one option for obtaining help while working in an Office app. If you want to learn more about a command, point to its button and wait for the ScreenTip to appear. If the Help icon appears in the ScreenTip, press the F1 key while pointing to the button to open the Help window associated with that command.

Figure 117 shows a dialog box that contains a Help button. Pressing the F1 key while the dialog box is displayed opens a Help window. The Help window contains help about that dialog box, if available. If no help file is available for that particular dialog box, then the main Help window opens.

Figure 116

Figure 117

Using Windows Help and Support

One of the more powerful Windows features is Windows Help and Support. **Windows Help and Support** is available when using Windows or when using any Microsoft app running in Windows. The same methods used for searching Microsoft Office Help can be used in Windows Help and Support. The difference is that Windows Help and Support displays help for Windows, instead of for Microsoft Office.

To Use Windows Help and Support

The following steps use Windows Help and Support and open the Windows Help and Support window, which contains links to more information about Windows. *Why? This feature is designed to assist you in using Windows or the various apps.* If you are using Windows 7, skip these steps and instead perform the steps in the yellow box that immediately follows these Windows 8 steps.

1

- Swipe in from the right edge of the screen or point to the upper-right corner of the screen to display the Charms bar (Figure 118).

Figure 118

2

- Tap or click the Settings charm on the Charms bar to display the Settings menu (Figure 119).

Figure 119

- Tap or click Help to open the Windows Help and Support window (Figure 120).

④

- After reviewing the Windows Help and Support window, tap or click the Close button to close the Windows Help and Support window.

Figure 120

Other Ways

1. Press WINDOWS + F1

TO USE WINDOWS HELP AND SUPPORT WITH WINDOWS 7

If you are using Windows 7, perform these steps to start Windows Help and Support instead of the previous steps that use Windows 8.

1. Click the Start button on the taskbar to display the Start menu.

2. Click Help and Support on the Start menu to open the Windows Help and Support window.

3. After reviewing the Windows Help and Support window, click the Close button to exit Windows Help and Support.

Chapter Summary

In this chapter, you learned how to use the Windows interface, several touch screen and mouse operations, file and folder management, some basic features of some Microsoft Office apps, including Word, PowerPoint, Excel, and Access, and discovered the common elements that exist among these different Office apps, and additional Office apps, including Office, Publisher, and OneNote. The items listed on the next page include all of the new Windows and Office apps skills you have learned in this chapter, with the tasks grouped by activity.

BTW
Certification
The Microsoft Office Specialist (MOS) program provides an opportunity for you to obtain a valuable industry credential — proof that you have the Microsoft Office 2013 skills required by employers. For more information, visit the Certification resource on the Student Companion Site located on www.cengagebrain.com. For detailed instructions about accessing available resources, visit www.cengage .com/ct/studentdownload or contact your instructor for information about accessing the required files.

BTW
Quick Reference
For a table that lists how to complete the tasks covered in this book using touch gestures, the mouse, ribbon, shortcut menu, and keyboard, see the Quick Reference Summary at the back of this book, or visit the Quick Reference resource on the Student Companion Site located on www.cengagebrain.com. For detailed instructions about accessing available resources, visit www.cengage .com/ct/studentdownload or contact your instructor for information about accessing the required files.

CONSIDER THIS: PLAN AHEAD

What guidelines should you follow to plan your projects?

The process of communicating specific information is a learned, rational skill. Computers and software, especially Microsoft Office 2013, can help you develop ideas and present detailed information to a particular audience and minimize much of the laborious work of drafting and revising projects. No matter what method you use to plan a project, it is beneficial to follow some specific guidelines from the onset to arrive at a final product that is informative, relevant, and effective. Use some aspects of these guidelines every time you undertake a project, and others as needed in specific instances.

1. Determine the project's purpose.
    a) Clearly define why you are undertaking this assignment.
    b) Begin to draft ideas of how best to communicate information by handwriting ideas on paper; composing directly on a laptop, tablet, or mobile device; or developing a strategy that fits your particular thinking and writing style.

2. Analyze your audience.
    a) Learn about the people who will read, analyze, or view your work.
    b) Determine their interests and needs so that you can present the information they need to know and omit the information they already possess.
    c) Form a mental picture of these people or find photos of people who fit this profile so that you can develop a project with the audience in mind.

3. Gather possible content.
    a) Locate existing information that may reside in spreadsheets, databases, or other files.
    b) Conduct a web search to find relevant websites.
    c) Read pamphlets, magazine and newspaper articles, and books to gain insights of how others have approached your topic.
    d) Conduct personal interviews to obtain perspectives not available by any other means.
    e) Consider video and audio clips as potential sources for material that might complement or support the factual data you uncover.

4. Determine what content to present to your audience.

   a) Write three or four major ideas you want an audience member to remember after reading or viewing your project.

   b) Envision your project's endpoint, the key fact you wish to emphasize, so that all project elements lead to this final element.

   c) Determine relevant time factors, such as the length of time to develop the project, how long readers will spend reviewing your project, or the amount of time allocated for your speaking engagement.

   d) Decide whether a graph, photo, or artistic element can express or enhance a particular concept.

   e) Be mindful of the order in which you plan to present the content, and place the most important material at the top or bottom of the page, because readers and audience members generally remember the first and last pieces of information they see and hear.

How should you submit solutions to questions in the assignments identified with a ✳ symbol?

Every assignment in this book contains one or more questions identified with a ✳ symbol. These questions require you to think beyond the assigned file. Present your solutions to the questions in the format required by your instructor. Possible formats may include one or more of these options: write the answer; create a document that contains the answer; present your answer to the class; discuss your answer in a group; record the answer as audio or video using a webcam, smartphone, or portable media player; or post answers on a blog, wiki, or website.

CONSIDER THIS

Apply Your Knowledge

Reinforce the skills and apply the concepts you learned in this chapter.

Creating a Folder and a Document

Instructions: You will create a Word folder and then create a Word document and save it in the folder.

Perform the following tasks:

1. Open the File Explorer window and then double-tap or double-click to open the Documents library.

2. Tap or click the New folder button on the Quick Access Toolbar to display a new folder icon and text box for the folder name.

3. Type `Word` in the text box to name the folder. Press the ENTER key to create the folder in the Documents library.

4. Run Word.

5. Enter the text shown in Figure 121 in a new blank document.

6. Tap or click the Save button on the Quick Access Toolbar. Navigate to the Word folder in the Documents library and then save the document using the file name, Apply 1 Class List.

7. If your Quick Access Toolbar does not show the Quick Print button, add the Quick Print button to the Quick Access Toolbar. Print the document using the Quick Print button on the Quick Access Toolbar. When you are finished printing, remove the Quick Print button from the Quick Access Toolbar.

8. Submit the printout to your instructor.

9. Exit Word.

10. ✳ What other commands might you find useful to include on the Quick Access Toolbar?

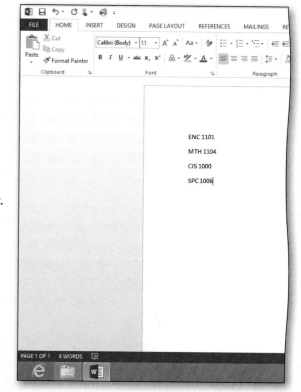

Figure 121

Extend Your Knowledge

Extend the skills you learned in this chapter and experiment with new skills. You will use Help to complete the assignment.

Using Help

Instructions: Use Office Help to perform the following tasks.

Perform the following tasks:

1. Run Word.
2. Tap or click the Microsoft Word Help button to open the Word Help window (Figure 122).
3. Search Word Help to answer the following questions.
   a.   What are the steps to add a new group to the ribbon?
   b.   What are Quick Parts?
4. With the Word app still running, run PowerPoint.
5. Tap or click the Microsoft PowerPoint Help button on the title bar to open the PowerPoint Help window.
6. Search PowerPoint Help to answer the following questions.
   a.   What is a slide master?
   b.   How do you copy slides from another presentation into the existing presentation?
7. Exit PowerPoint.

Figure 122

8. Run Excel.
9. Tap or click the Microsoft Excel Help button to open the Excel Help window.
10. Search Excel Help to answer the following questions.
    a.   What are three different functions available in Excel?
    b.   What are sparklines?
11. Exit Excel.
12. Run Access.
13. Tap or click the Microsoft Access Help button to open the Access Help window.
14. Search Access Help to answer the following questions.
    a.   What is SQL?
    b.   What is a data macro?
15. Exit Access.
16. Type the answers from your searches in a new blank Word document. Save the document with a new file name and then submit it in the format specified by your instructor.
17. Exit Word.
18. ✸ What search text did you use to perform the searches above? Did it take multiple attempts to search and locate the exact information for which you were searching?

Analyze, Correct, Improve

Analyze a file structure, correct all errors, and improve the design.

Organizing Vacation Photos

Note: To complete this assignment, you will be required to use the Data Files for Students. Visit www.cengage.com/ct/studentdownload for detailed instructions or contact your instructor for information about accessing the required files.

Instructions: Traditionally, you have stored photos from past vacations together in one folder. The photos are becoming difficult to manage, and you now want to store them in appropriate folders. You will create the folder structure shown in Figure 123. You then will move the photos to the folders so that they will be organized properly.

1. Correct Create the folder structure in Figure 123 so that you are able to store the photos in an organized manner.

2. Improve View each photo and drag it to the appropriate folder to improve the organization.

3. ✸ Think about the files you have stored on your computer. What folder hierarchy would be best to manage your files?

Figure 123

In the Labs

Use the guidelines, concepts, and skills presented in this chapter to increase your knowledge of Windows 8 and Office 2013. Labs 1 and 2, which increase in difficulty, require you to create solutions based on what you learned in the chapter; Lab 3 requires you to create a solution, which uses cloud and web technologies, by learning and investigating on your own from general guidance.

Lab 1: Creating Folders for a Video Store

Problem: Your friend works for Ebaird Video. He would like to organize his files in relation to the types of videos available in the store. He has six main categories: drama, action, romance, foreign, biographical, and comedy. You are to create a folder structure similar to Figure 124 on the next page.

Instructions: Perform the following tasks:
1. Insert a USB flash drive in an available USB port and then open the USB flash drive window.
2. Create the main folder for Ebaird Video.
3. Navigate to the Ebaird Video folder.
4. Within the Ebaird Video folder, create a folder for each of the following: Drama, Action, Romance, Foreign, Biographical, and Comedy.
5. Within the Action folder, create two additional folders, one for Science Fiction and the second for Western.
6. Submit the assignment in the format specified by your instructor.
7. ✸ Think about how you use your computer for various tasks (consider personal, professional, and academic reasons). What folders do you think will be required on your computer to store the files you save?

Continued >

In the Labs *continued*

Figure 124

Lab 2: **Saving Files in Folders**

Creating Office Documents

Problem: You are taking a class that requires you to create a Word, PowerPoint, Excel, and Access file. You will save these files to folders named for four different Office apps (Figure 125).

Instructions: Create the folders shown in Figure 125. Then, using the respective Office app, create a small file to save in each folder (i.e., create a Word document to save in the Word folder, a PowerPoint presentation to save in the PowerPoint folder, and so on).

1. Create a Word document containing the text, First Word Assignment.

2. In the Backstage view, tap or click Save As and then tap or click Computer.

3. Tap or click the Browse button to display the Save As dialog box.

4. Tap or click Documents to open the Documents library. Next, create the folder structure shown in Figure 125 using the New folder button.

5. Navigate to the Word folder and then save the file in the Word folder.

6. Create a PowerPoint presentation with one slide containing the title text, Sample PowerPoint Presentation, and then save it in the PowerPoint folder.

7. Create an Excel spreadsheet containing the text, My First Budget Excel Spreadsheet, in cell A1 and then save it in the Excel folder.

8. Save an Access database named, My Music Database, in the Access folder.

9. Submit the assignment in the format specified by your instructor.

10. ✻ Based on your current knowledge of Word, PowerPoint, Excel, and Access, which app do you think you will use most frequently? Why?

Figure 125

Lab 3: Expand Your World: Cloud and Web Technologies
Creating Office Web App Documents

Problem: You are taking a class that requires you to create a file in Word, PowerPoint, and Excel. You will save these files to folders named for three different Office Web apps (Figure 126).

Instructions: Create the folders shown in Figure 126. Then, using the respective Office Web app, create a small file to save in each folder (i.e., create a Word document to save in the Word folder, a PowerPoint presentation to save in the PowerPoint folder, and so on).

1. Sign in to SkyDrive in your browser.
2. Use the Create button to create the folder structure shown in Figure 126.
3. In the Word folder, use the Create button to create a Word document with the file name, Notes, and containing the text, Important Test on Tuesday.
4. Save the document and then exit the app.
5. Navigate to the PowerPoint folder.
6. Create a PowerPoint presentation called Kirek Sales with one slide containing the title text, Online Presentation, and then exit the app.
7. Navigate to the Excel folder.
8. Create an Excel spreadsheet, called Kirek Sales Analysis, containing the text, Sales Cost Analysis, in cell A1, and then exit the app.
9. Submit the assignment in the format specified by your instructor.
10. ✳ Based on your current knowledge of SkyDrive, do you think you will use it? What about the Web apps?

© 2014 Cengage Learning

Figure 126

✳ Consider This: Your Turn

Apply your creative thinking and problem solving skills to design and implement a solution.

1: Creating Beginning Files for Classes
Personal

You are taking the following classes: Introduction to Sociology, Chemistry, Calculus, and Marketing. Create folders for each of the classes. Create a folder structure that will store the documents for each of these classes. Use Word to create a Word document with the name of each class and the class meeting locations and times. Use PowerPoint to begin creating a simple lab presentation for your chemistry class. It should begin with a title slide containing the text, Chemical Reactions. Create and save a database named Companies for your marketing class. The database does not need to contain any data. In the Calculus folder, create an Excel spreadsheet with the text, Excel Formulas, in cell A1. Use the concepts and techniques presented in this chapter to create the folders and files, and store the files in their respective locations. Submit your assignment in the format specified by your instructor.

✳ You made several decisions while determining the folder structure in this assignment. What was the rationale behind these decisions? Are there any other decisions that also might have worked?

Continued >

Consider This: Your Turn *continued*

2: Creating Folders

Professional

Your boss at the music store where you work part-time has asked for help with organizing his files. After looking through the files, you decided on a file structure for her to use, including the following folders: CDs, DVDs, and general merchandise. Think about the different types of CDs, DVDs, and general merchandise that might be sold at your store, and create a folder structure that will be used to store information about the three types of items (CDs, DVDs, and general merchandise), and also can organize the different types of each item. For example, general merchandise might include items such as clothing, portable media players, and accessories. Use the concepts and techniques presented in this chapter to create the folders. Submit your assignment in the format specified by your instructor.

✻ You made several decisions while determining the folder structure in this assignment. What was the rationale behind these decisions? Justify why you feel this folder structure will help your boss organize her files.

3: Using Help

Research and Collaboration

You have just installed a new computer with the Windows operating system and want to be sure that it is protected from the threat of viruses, so you ask two of your friends to help research computer viruses, virus prevention, and virus removal. In a team of three people, each person should choose a topic (computer viruses, virus prevention, and virus removal) to research. Use the concepts and techniques presented in this chapter to use Help to find information regarding these topics. Create a Word document that contains steps to properly safeguard a computer from viruses, ways to prevent viruses, as well as the different ways to remove a virus should your computer become infected. Submit your assignment in the format specified by your instructor.

✻ You made several decisions while searching Windows Help and Support for this assignment. What decisions did you make? What was the rationale behind these decisions? How did you locate the required information about viruses in help?

Learn Online

Reinforce what you learned in this chapter with games, exercises, training, and many other online activities and resources.

Student Companion Site   Reinforcement activities and resources are available at no additional cost on www.cengagebrain.com. Visit www.cengage.com/ct/studentdownload for detailed instructions about accessing the resources available at the Student Companion Site.

SAM   Put your skills into practice with SAM Projects! If you have a SAM account, go to www.cengage.com/sam2013 to access SAM assignments for this chapter.

Office 365 Essentials

Objectives

You will have mastered the material in this chapter when you can:

- Describe the components of Office 365

- Compare Office 2013 to Office 365 subscription plans

- Understand the productivity tools of Office 365

- Sync multiple devices using Office 365

- Describe how business teams collaborate using SharePoint

- Describe how to use a SharePoint template to design a public website

- Describe how to conduct an online meeting with Lync

Explore Office 365

Introduction to Office 365

Microsoft Office 365 uses the cloud to deliver a subscription-based service offering the newest Office suite and much more. The Microsoft cloud provides Office software and information stored on remote servers all over the world. Your documents are located online or on the cloud, which provides you access to your information anywhere using a PC, Mac, tablet, mobile phone, or other device with an Internet connection. For businesses and students alike, Office 365 offers significant cost savings compared to the traditional cost of purchasing Microsoft Office 2013. In addition to the core desktop Office suite, Office 365 provides access to email, calendars, conferencing, file sharing, and website design, which sync across multiple devices.

Cloud Computing

Cloud computing refers to a collection of computer servers that house resources users access through the Internet (Figure 1). These resources include email messages, schedules, music, photos, videos, games, websites, programs, apps, servers, storage, and more. Instead of accessing these resources on your computer or mobile device, you access them on the cloud.

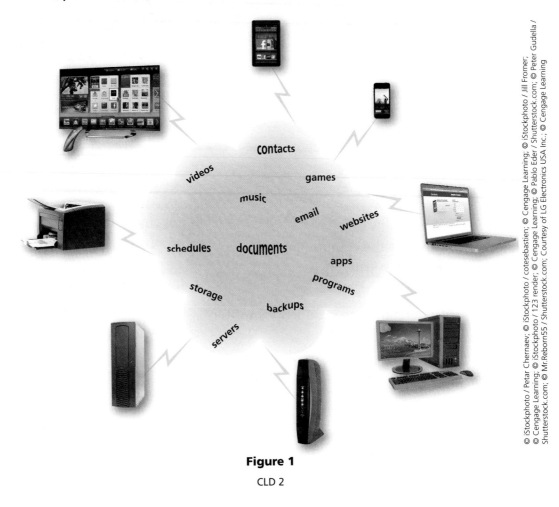

videos   contacts   games   music   email   websites   schedules   documents   apps   programs   storage   backups   servers

Figure 1

Cloud computing can help businesses be more efficient and save them money by shifting usage and the consumption of resources, such as servers and programs, from a local environment to the Internet. For example, an employee working during the day in California could use computing resources located in an office in London that is closed for the evening. When the company in California uses the computing resources, it pays a fee that is based on the amount of computing time and other resources it consumes, much in the same way that consumers pay utility companies for the amount of electricity they use.

Cloud computing is changing how users access and pay for software applications. Fading fast are the days when software packages were sold in boxes at a physical store location with a one-time purchase software license fee. Instead, the new pricing structure is a subscription-based model, where users pay a monthly or annual fee for the software that you can use on multiple devices. The cloud-based Office 365 offers the Office suite with added features that allow you to communicate and collaborate with others in real time.

When you create a free Microsoft account, do you get free cloud storage space?
Yes, when you create a free Microsoft account at Outlook.com, you have access to 7 GB of cloud storage for any type of files.

CONSIDER THIS

What Is Office 365?

Office 365 (Office365.com) is a collection of programs and services, which includes the Microsoft Office 2013 suite, file storage, online collaboration, and file synchronization, as shown in Figure 2 on the next page. You can access these services using your computer, browser, or supported mobile device. For example, a business has two options for providing Office to their employees. A business could purchase Office 2013 and install the software on company computers and servers; however, this traditional Office 2013 package with perpetual licensing does not include the communication and collaboration tools. Employees could not access the Office software if they were not using their work computers. In contrast, if the business purchases a monthly subscription to Office 365, each employee has access to the Office suite on up to five different computers, whether at home or work; company-wide email; web conferencing; website creation capabilities; cloud storage; and shared files. For a lower price, Office 365 provides many more features. In addition, a business may prefer a subscription plan with predictable monthly costs and no up-front infrastructure costs.

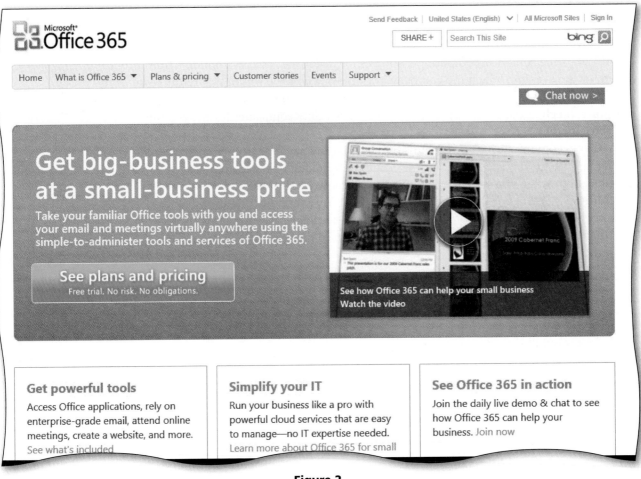

Figure 2

Office 2013 and Office 365 Features Comparison

Office 2013 is the name of the perpetual software package that includes individual applications that can be installed on a single computer. An Office 365 subscription comes with a license to install the software on multiple PCs or Macs at the same time, giving you more flexibility to use your Office products in your home, school, or workplace, whether on a computer or a mobile device. Office 365 provides the Office 2013 programs as part of a subscription service that includes online storage, sharing, and syncing via Microsoft cloud services as shown in Table 1.

Office 365 is available in business, consumer, education, and government editions. Office 365 combines the full version of the Microsoft Office desktop suite with cloud-based versions of Microsoft's communications and collaboration services. The subscription package includes:

- Microsoft Exchange online for shared email and calendars
- Microsoft SharePoint Online for shared file access and public website creation
- Microsoft Office Web apps for browser viewing
- Microsoft Lync Online for communication services

Table 1 Office 2013 and Office 365 Feature Comparison	
Office 2013 Professional (Installed on a single device)	**Office 365 Subscription (Installed on 2 to 5 devices)**
Microsoft Word	Microsoft Word
Microsoft Excel	Microsoft Excel
Microsoft PowerPoint	Microsoft PowerPoint
Microsoft Access	Microsoft Access
Microsoft Outlook	Microsoft Outlook
Microsoft Publisher	Microsoft Publisher
Microsoft OneNote	Microsoft OneNote
	email and calendars (Exchange Online)
	file sharing (SharePoint Online)
	public website design and publishing (SharePoint Online)
	browser-based Office Web Apps
	instant messaging (Lync Online)
	audio and video web conferencing (Lync Online)
	screen sharing with shared control (Lync Online)
	technical support

© 2014 Cengage Learning

Subscription-Based Office 365 Plans

Microsoft provides various subscription plans for Office 365 with different benefits for each individual or organization. Subscription plans include Office 365 Home Premium for home users, Office 365 University for students, Office 365 Small Business, Office 365 Small Business Premium, Office 365 Midsize Business, and Office 365 Enterprise and Government. During the Office 365 sign-up process, you create a Microsoft email address and password to use on your multiple devices. A single subscription to an Office 365 Home Premium account can cover an entire household. The Office 365 Home Premium subscription allows up to five concurrent installations by using the same email address and password combination. This means that your mother could be on the main family computer while you use your tablet and smartphone at the same time. You each can sign in with your individual Microsoft accounts using your settings and accessing your own documents using a single Office 365 subscription.

The Office 365 University subscription plan is designed for higher-education full-time and part-time students, faculty, and staff. By submitting the proper credentials, such as a school email address, students and faculty can purchase Office 365 University, including Word, PowerPoint, Excel, Access, Outlook, Publisher, and OneNote. A one-time payment covers a four-year subscription. In addition, Office 365 University provides users with 27 GB of SkyDrive cloud storage rather than the free 7 GB provided by a Microsoft account, and 60 Skype world minutes per month for videoconferencing. Students have the option of renewing for another four years, for a total of eight years. The Office 365 University edition is limited to two computers (PC or Mac).

The Microsoft Office 365 Business Plans can provide full support for employees to work from any location, whether they are in their traditional business office, commuting to and from work across the country, or working from a home office. Office 365 small business plans (Small Business and Small Business Premium) are best for companies with up to 10 employees, but can accommodate up to 25 users. Office 365 Midsize Business accommodates from 11 to 300 users. Office 365 Enterprise Plan fits organizations ranging in size from a single employee to 50,000-plus users. Each employee can install Microsoft Office 365 on five different computers.

First Look at Office 365

Microsoft Office 365 subscription plans offer all the same applications that are available in the Microsoft Office Professional 2013 suite in addition to multiple communication and collaboration tools. With Office 365 you can retrieve, edit, and save Office documents on the Office 365 cloud, coauthor documents in real time with others, and quickly initiate computer-based calls, instant messages, and web conferences with others.

Productivity Tools

Whether you are inserting audio and video into a Word document to create a high-impact business plan proposal or utilizing the visualization tools in Excel to chart the return on investment of a new mobile marketing program, Office 365 premium plans deliver the full Office product with the same features as the latest version of Microsoft Office. Office 365 uses a quick-start installation technology, called **Click-to-Run**, that downloads and installs the basics within minutes, so that users are able to start working almost immediately. It also includes **Office on Demand**, which streams Office to Windows 7- and Windows 8-based PCs for work performed on public computers. The single-use copy that is installed temporarily on the Windows computer does not count toward the device limit. No installation is necessary when using Office on Demand, and the applications disappear from the computer once you are finished using them. If you have a document on a USB drive or on SkyDrive that you need to edit on another PC, you can use Office on Demand to get the full version of Word in just a few minutes.

In effect, the Office 365 subscription provides access to the full Office applications wherever you are working. When you access your Office 365 account management panel, three choices are listed: 32- and 64-bit versions of Office 2013, and Office for Mac. Selecting the third option will initiate a download of an installer that must be run in the standard OS X fashion. When you install Office 365 on a Mac, the most current Mac version of Office is installed.

CONSIDER THIS

Unlike Google, which offers online documents, spreadsheets, and presentations called Google Docs, Microsoft Office 365 installs locally on your computer in addition to being available online. Google Docs is entirely browser based, which means if you are not connected to the Internet, you cannot access your Google Docs files.

Email and Calendars

In business, sharing information is essential to meeting the needs of your customers and staff. Office 365 offers shared access to business email, calendars, and contacts using **Exchange Online** from a computer, tablet, phone, and browser. The cloud-based Exchange Online enables business people to access Outlook information from anywhere at any time, while eliminating the cost of purchasing and maintaining servers to store data. If you need to meet with a colleague about a new project, you can compare calendars to view availability, confirm conference room availability, share project contacts, search email messages related to the project, and send email invitations to the project meeting. Exchange Online also allows you to search and access your company's address list.

Online Meetings

When you are working with a team on a project that requires interaction, email and text communications can slow the communications process. Microsoft Lync connects you with others by facilitating real-time, interactive presentations and meetings over the Internet using both video and audio calling. As shown in Figure 3, you can conduct an online meeting with a team member or customer that includes an instant messaging conversation, audio, high-definition video, virtual whiteboards, and screen sharing. If the customer does not have an Office 365 subscription, they still can join the meeting through the invitation link, which runs the Lync Web App.

Skype is another tool in the Office 365 subscription, which enables users to place video calls to computers and smartphones and voice calls to landlines. Skype also supports instant message and file sharing to computers and mobile devices. While Skype may be adequate for simple communication, Lync provides for more robust, comprehensive communications. These robust features include high-definition (HD) videoconferencing capabilities, a whiteboard, and a larger audience. Using Lync, meeting attendees simultaneously can view up to five participants' video, identify the active speaker, and associate names with faces. Lync supports up to 250 attendees per meeting. Unlike Skype, Lync meetings can be recorded for replaying at a later time. This enables businesses and schools to schedule meetings or organize online classes using Lync capabilities.

File Sharing

Office 365 includes a team site, which is a password-protected portal that supports sharing of large, difficult-to-email files and provides a single location for the latest versions of documents. In business, for example, colleagues working on common projects can save valuable time by being able to access instantly the latest master copy of each document. Security can be managed through different

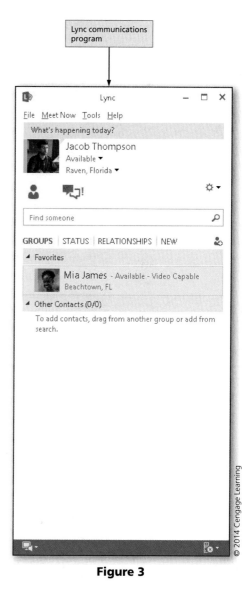

Lync communications program

Figure 3

© 2014 Cengage Learning

levels of user access so that users see only what they are supposed to see. Office 365 provides access to shared files using the cloud, making writing, editing, and sharing documents easier. If a construction company creates a commercial bid for a building project, the customers can be invited to view an Excel spreadsheet bid, construction timetable with a shared calendar, and an Access database of all the materials needed using the file sharing feature online.

Website Creation

Office 365 business plan subscriptions include a built-in hosted public website, where customers and clients can find an online storefront of a company. This public website, called the Website, can be customized to market a company by using various templates within the Office 365 cloud. The website creation tools include those for adding a theme, graphics, fonts, maps, directions, blogs, stock tickers, slide shows, PayPal, weather, and videos to interact with the website's visitors.

Synchronization

Office 365 subscription plans provide a central place to store and access your documents and business information. A feature of Office 365 ensures the original and backup computer files in two or more locations are identical through a process called **Active Directory Synchronization**. For example, if you open a PowerPoint presentation on your smartphone while you are riding a city bus and then add a new slide as you head to school, the PowerPoint presentation automatically is synced with Office 365. When you arrive on campus and open the PowerPoint presentation on a school computer, your new slide already is part of the finished slide show. By storing your files in Office 365, you can access your files on another computer if your home computer fails, with no loss of time or important information. When using your mobile phone's data plan, you do not need to search for a Wi-Fi hot spot to connect to the Office 365 cloud. Computer labs in schools can be configured to synchronize automatically all student files to Office 365 online.

Multiple Device Access to Office 365

With a single sign-in process, Office 365 provides access to multiple computers and mobile devices, including Android smartphones and tablets, Apple iPhones and iPads, Windows phones, and Blackberry phones. After you configure your devices' email settings, you can view your Microsoft account calendar, contacts, and email. Your personalized settings, preferences, and documents can be synchronized among all the different devices included in your Office 365 premium subscription. With the mobility of Office 365, students and employees can work anywhere, accessing information and responding to email requests immediately. If you lose your phone, Office 365 includes a feature that allows you to remotely wipe your phone clean of any data. By wiping your phone's data, you can prevent any unauthorized access to sensitive information, such as your banking information, passwords, and contacts, as well as discourage identity theft. Because your phone contacts and other information are stored on the Microsoft cloud, damaged or lost equipment is never a problem.

CONSIDER THIS

A thief can be quite resourceful if he or she steals your phone. Before you can alert your parents or spouse to the theft, they might receive a text from "you" asking for your ATM or credit card PIN number. Your parents or spouse might then reply with the PIN number. Your bank account could be emptied in minutes.

Teams Using Office 365 in Business

In the business world, rarely does an employee work in isolation. Companies need their employees to collaborate, whether they work in the same office or in locations around the world. Telecommuters working from home can communicate as if they were on-site by using a common team website and conferencing software. SharePoint Online and Lync Online provide seamless communication.

Small business subscription plans as low as $6.00 per user per month allow employees to create and store Word documents, Excel spreadsheets, and PowerPoint presentations online and communicate with one another via email, instant messaging, or video chat as they work on projects together. As shown in Figure 4, a team portal page is shown when you subscribe at https://portal.microsoftonline.com. Larger companies and those requiring more features can take advantage of the Office 365 business premium package, which, in addition to the features listed above, provides access to the Office 365 portal website and eliminates the effort and cost of the users maintaining their own costly computer servers.

Figure 4

Email Communication Using Exchange

Office 365 includes Exchange Online, an email-based collaborative communications server for business. Exchange enables employees to be more productive by effectively managing email across multiple devices and facilitating teamwork.

Collaboration Using SharePoint

SharePoint Online, a part of Office 365 subscription plans, allows employees to collaborate with one another, share documents, post announcements, and track tasks, as shown in Table 2.

Table 2 Office 365 SharePoint Features	
Team Site Feature	**Description**
Calendar	Track important dates
Shared Document Library	Store related documents according to topic; picture, report, and slide libraries often are included
Task List	Track team tasks according to who is responsible for completion
Team Discussion Board	Discuss the topics at hand in an open forum
Contacts List	Share contact lists of employees, customers, contractors, and suppliers

© 2014 Cengage Learning

Office 365 provides the tools to plan meetings. Users can share calendars side by side, view availability, and suggest meeting times from shared calendars. Typically, a SharePoint team administrator or website owner establishes a folder structure to share and manage documents. The team website is fully searchable online, making locating and sharing data more efficient than using a local server. With a team website, everyone on the team has a central location to store and find all the information for a project, client, or department, as shown in Figure 5.

Figure 5

Website Design Using SharePoint

SharePoint provides templates to create a professional looking, public website for an online presence to market your business. As shown in Figure 6, a local pet sitting business is setting up a business website by customizing a SharePoint template. SharePoint Public Website includes features within the Design Manager that you use to customize and design your website by adding your own images, forms, style sheets, maps, themes, and social networking tools. When you finish customizing your business site, you can apply your own domain name to the site. A **domain** is a unique web address that identifies where your website can be found. Office 365 SharePoint hosts your website as part of your subscription. Your customers easily can find your business online and learn about your services.

BTW

Creating SharePoint Intranet Sites
A SharePoint website also can be customized to serve as an internal company website for private communications within the company.

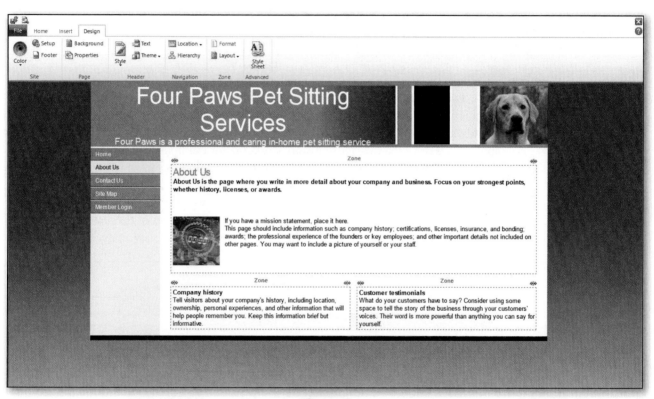

Figure 6

Real-Time Communications Using Lync

Lync Online is Microsoft's server platform for online team communications and comes bundled with Office 365 business subscriptions. As shown in Figure 7, Lync connects in real time to allow instant messaging, videoconferencing, and voice communications; it also integrates with email and Microsoft Office applications.

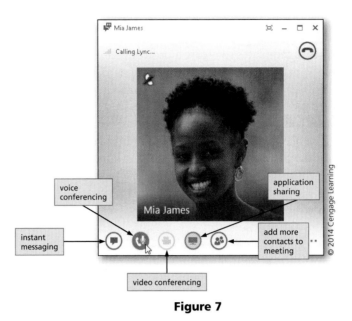

Figure 7

Lync allows you to connect with staff at remote locations using instant messaging capabilities, desktop sharing, videoconferencing, and shared agendas or documents. Lync is integrated into Office 365, which allows staff to start communicating from within the applications in which they currently are working. For example, while an employee is creating a PowerPoint presentation for a new product line, as shown in Figure 8, Lync enables him or her to collaborate with the entire team about the details of the product presentation. The team can view the presenter's screen displaying the PowerPoint presentation. The presenter can share control with any member of the team and can share his or her screen at any time during the Lync meeting.

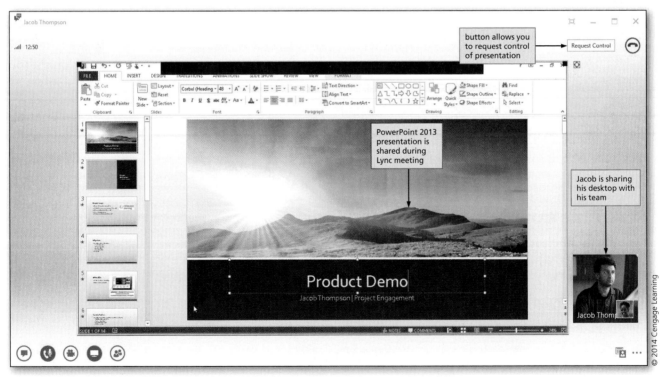

Figure 8

Users can send a Lync meeting request to schedule a team meeting, or an impromptu conversation can be started immediately using the Meet Now feature. Participants receive a Lync meeting request link via an email message, and when they click the meeting request link, Lync automatically connects them to the online conference. If the participant does not have Lync installed, the Lync Web App automatically connects to the Lync meeting through the user's PC or Mac OS X browser. If a participant is away from his or her computer, he or she still can participate using the Lync Mobile apps for Windows Phone, iOS, and Android. As shown in Figure 9, Lync utilizes **instant messaging** (IM), allowing two or more people to share text messages. They can communicate in real time, similar to a voice conversation. In addition to a simple instant message, Lync provides a feature called **persistent chat**, which allows end-users to participate in a working session of instant messages that is persistent or sustained over a specified amount of time in a moderated chat room. Consider having an instant messaging session with a group of colleagues in different parts of your organization, regardless of geographic region, where you all are working on the same project. Over the course of the project, different people post questions and concerns, and others are able to respond to all those who have subscribed to your topic or been admitted to the chat room. Instead of a long trail of email messages, a team can keep information in a controlled environment with a full history of the discussion in one location.

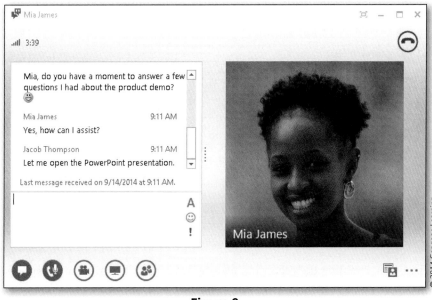

Figure 9

Lync also delivers support for full high-definition (HD) videoconferencing, so that a team can have a clear view of the participants, products, and demos. Before you join the video feed, you can preview your video feed to make sure your video camera is at the correct angle, your image is centered within the video frame, and that your room lighting provides for a clear image. The Lync preview option is important in creating a positive first impression over video. Your audio devices can be tested for clarity to make sure your headset, microphone, and speakers are functioning properly.

Lync provides a polling feature that presenters can use to ask the participants' opinions during a meeting (Figure 10). The poll question can consist of up to seven possible choices. The presenter has the option to view the results privately or share the results with the entire group.

Figure 10

Finally, by enabling the recording feature, Lync meetings and conversations can be captured for viewing at a later time. For instance, you can capture the audio, video, instant messaging (IM), screen sharing, Microsoft PowerPoint presentations, whiteboard, and polling portions of the Lync session and then play them back just as they transpired during the live Lync event. The meeting recordings can be made available to others so that they can view all or part of the Lync event. Instructors can record Lync online class sessions for students who were unable to attend the original presentation. The recording starts in Microsoft Lync; recordings then can be viewed within the Recording Manager feature.

Chapter Summary

In this chapter, you have learned how to subscribe to Office 365, which provides local and online access to Office applications, email, document sharing, web conferencing, and business websites. You also learned how a business can utilize Office 365 features on the cloud to facilitate teamwork. Finally, you learned about the features of SharePoint and Lync, which provide collaboration and communications for business teams using Office 365.

✳ Consider This: Your Turn

Apply your creative thinking and problem solving skills to design and implement a solution.

1: Comparing Office 365 Personal Plans

Personal

Part 1: You are a freshman in college living at home with your family. You are considering if it would be a better value to subscribe to Office 365 University or Office 365 Home Premium. Write a one-page document comparing the pros and cons of the two subscription plans. Research the different subscriptions in detail at Office365.com. Submit your assignment in the format specified by your instructor.

Part 2: ✳ Which type of computer and/or devices would you use with your Office 365 subscription? If you are at a friend's home that does not have Office 365, how could you access your Office files if you do not have your computer or mobile device with you?

2: Upgrading a Local Business to Office 365

Professional

Part 1: You are an employee at Impact Digital Marketing, a small marketing firm with 12 employees. The firm is setting up an Office 365 Small Business subscription next week, and you need to compose an email message with multiple paragraphs to explain the features of this new subscription plan to the members of your firm. Research the Office 365 Small Business subscription plan in detail at Office365.com, and compile your findings in an email message. Submit your assignment in the format specified by your instructor.

Part 2: ✳ Give three examples of how a marketing firm could use Lync. How could a marketing firm use the SharePoint Websites feature?

3: Conducting a Lync Meeting

Research and Collaboration

* Students need an Office 365 subscription to complete the following assignment.

Part 1: Using your Office 365 subscription, conduct a meeting using Lync. Working with a partner, use your Office 365 subscription to research how to use Lync. Then, conduct a 15-minute Lync meeting, including instant messaging, to discuss the features of Lync. Use the concepts and techniques presented in this chapter to create the Lync meeting. Submit your assignment in the format specified by your instructor.

Part 2: ✳ When using Lync in business, when would the video feature best be utilized?

1 Managing Email Messages with Outlook

Objectives

You will have mastered the material in this chapter when you can:

- Add a Microsoft account to Outlook
- Set language preferences and sensitivity levels
- Apply a theme
- Compose, address, and send an email message
- Open, read, print, and close an email message
- Preview and save a file attachment
- Display the People Pane

- Reply to an email message
- Check spelling as you type an email message
- Attach a file to an outgoing email message
- Forward an email message
- Copy another person when sending an email message
- Create and move messages into a folder
- Delete an email message
- View the mailbox size

1 | Managing Email Messages with Outlook

This introductory chapter covers features and functions common to managing email messages in Outlook 2013.

Roadmap

In this chapter, you will learn how to perform basic email messaging tasks. The following roadmap identifies general activities you will perform as you progress through this chapter:

1. CONFIGURE the ACCOUNT OPTIONS
2. COMPOSE AND SEND an email message
3. VIEW AND PRINT an email message
4. REPLY to an email message
5. ATTACH a FILE to an email message
6. ORGANIZE email MESSAGES in folders

At the beginning of step instructions throughout the chapter, you will see an abbreviated form of this roadmap. The abbreviated roadmap uses colors to indicate chapter progress: gray means the chapter is beyond that activity, blue means the task being shown is covered in that activity, and black means that activity is yet to be covered. For example, the following abbreviated roadmap indicates the chapter would be showing a task in the View and Print activity.

1 CONFIGURE ACCOUNT OPTIONS | 2 COMPOSE & SEND | 3 VIEW & PRINT | 4 REPLY
5 ATTACH FILE | 6 ORGANIZE MESSAGES

Use the abbreviated roadmap as a progress guide while you read or step through the instructions in this chapter.

Introduction to Outlook

Outlook 2013 helps you organize and manage your communications, contacts, schedules, and tasks. **Email** (short for **electronic mail**) is the transmission of messages and files between computers or smart devices over a network. An **email client**, such as Microsoft Outlook 2013, is an app that allows you to compose, send, receive, store, and delete email messages. Outlook can access mail servers in a local network, such as your school's network, or a remote network, such as the Internet. Finally, you can use Outlook to organize messages so that you easily can find and respond to them later.

To use Outlook, you must have an email account. An **email account** is an electronic mailbox you receive from an **email service provider**, which is an organization that provides servers for routing and storing email messages. Your employer or school could set up an email account for you, or you can do so yourself through your Internet service provider (ISP) or using a web application such as a Microsoft account, Google Gmail, Yahoo! Mail, or iCloud Mail. Outlook does not create or issue email accounts; it merely provides you with access to them. When you have an email account, you also have an **email address**, which identifies your email account on a network so you can send and receive email messages.

Project — Composing and Sending Email Messages

The project in this chapter follows the general guidelines for using Outlook to compose, open, and reply to email messages, as shown in Figure 1–1. To communicate with individuals and groups, you typically send or receive some kind of message. Phone calls, letters, texting, and email are examples of ways to communicate a message. Email is a convenient way to send information to multiple people at once.

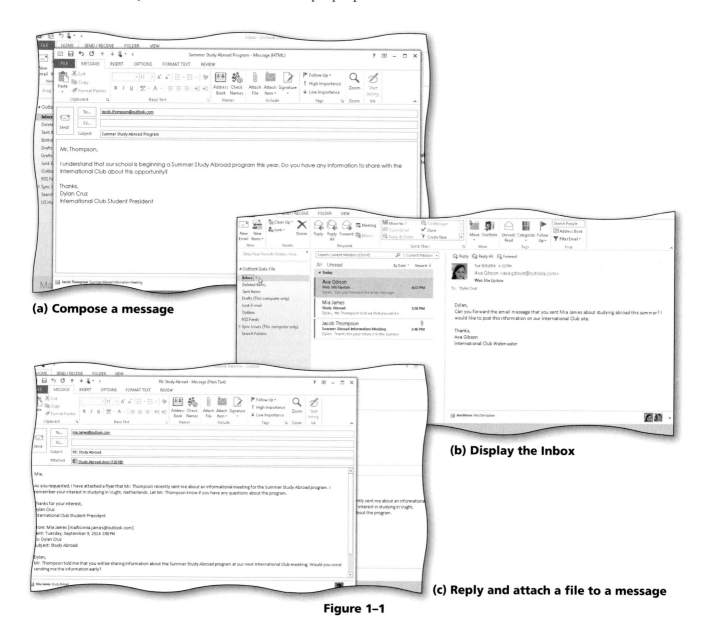

(a) Compose a message

(b) Display the Inbox

(c) Reply and attach a file to a message

Figure 1–1

BTW
The Outlook Window
The chapters in this book begin with the Outlook window appearing as it did at the initial installation of the software. Your Outlook window may look different depending on your screen resolution and other Outlook settings.

The International Club president, Dylan Cruz, a student at Raven College, uses Outlook to communicate with faculty and fellow students. This chapter uses Microsoft Outlook 2013 to compose, send, read, reply to, and forward email messages regarding an upcoming Summer Study Abroad program. As club president, Dylan's responsibilities include collecting information about the Summer Study Abroad program, coordinating the marketing of the informational meeting, and sharing information with students who are interested in studying abroad. Using Outlook, Dylan reads email messages from instructors and students regarding the Summer Study Abroad program. He replies to email messages and includes a document containing a flyer about the informational meeting. To organize messages, he also creates folders and then stores the messages in the folders.

Setting Up Outlook

BTW
BTWs
For a complete list of the BTWs found in the margins of this book, visit the BTW resource on the Student Companion Site located on www.cengagebrain.com. For detailed instructions about accessing available resources, visit www.cengage.com/ ct/studentdownload or contact your instructor for information about accessing the required files.

Many computer users have an email account from an online email service provider such as Outlook.com or Gmail.com and another email account at work or school. Instead of using a web app for your online email account and another app for your school account, you can use Outlook 2013 to access all of your email messages in a single location. When you access your email in Outlook 2013, you can take advantage of a full set of features that include social networking, translation services, and file management. You can read your downloaded messages offline and set options to organize your messages in a way that is logical and convenient for you.

The first time you start Outlook on a personal computer, the Auto Account Setup feature guides you to provide information that Outlook needs to send and receive email messages (Figure 1–2). First, the setup feature prompts you to provide your name, which will appear in email messages that you send to other people. Next, the setup feature requests your email address and a password.

What should you do if you do not have an email address?

- Use a browser such as Internet Explorer to go to the Outlook.com or Gmail.com website. Look for a Create an Account link or button, tap or click it, and then follow the instructions to create an account, which includes creating an email address.

Figure 1–2

Parts of an Email Address

An email address is divided into two parts. The first part contains a **user name**, which is a combination of characters, such as letters of the alphabet and numbers, that identifies a specific user. The last part is a **domain name**, which is the name associated with a specific Internet address and is assigned by your email service provider. A user name must be different from other user names in the same domain. For example, the outlook.com domain can have only one user named dylan.cruz. An email address contains an @ (pronounced *at*) symbol to separate the user name from the domain name. Figure 1–3 shows an email address for Dylan Cruz, which would be read as dylan dot cruz at outlook dot com.

Figure 1–3

© 2014 Cengage Learning

To Run Outlook

If you are using a computer to step through the project in this chapter and you want your screens to match the figures in this book, you should change your screen's resolution to 1366 × 768. For information about how to change a computer's resolution, refer to the Office and Windows chapter at the beginning of this book.

The following steps, which assume Windows 8 is running, use the Start screen or the search box to run Outlook based on a typical installation. You may need to ask your instructor how to run Outlook on your computer. For a detailed example of the procedure summarized below, refer to the Office and Windows chapter.

1 Scroll the Start screen for an Outlook 2013 tile. If your Start screen contains an Outlook 2013 tile, tap or click it to run Outlook and then proceed to Step 5; if the Start screen does not contain the Outlook 2013 tile, proceed to the next step to search for the Outlook app.

2 Swipe in from the right edge of the screen or point to the upper-right corner of the screen to display the Charms bar, and then tap or click the Search charm on the Charms bar to display the Search menu.

3 Type `Outlook` as the search text in the Search box and watch the search results appear in the Apps list.

4 Tap or click Outlook 2013 in the search results to run Outlook.

5 If the Outlook window is not maximized, tap or click the Maximize button on its title bar to maximize the window.

TO ADD AN EMAIL ACCOUNT

You can add one or more of your personal email accounts to Outlook. For most accounts, Outlook automatically detects and configures the account after you type your name, email address, and password. Add an email account to Outlook when you are working on your personal or home computer only. You do not want your personal

---

For an introduction to Windows and instruction about how to perform basic Windows tasks, read the Office and Windows chapter at the beginning of this book, where you can learn how to resize windows, change screen resolution, create folders, move and rename files, use Windows Help, and much more.

One of the few differences between Windows 7 and Windows 8 occur in the steps to run Outlook. If you are using Windows 7, click the Start button, type `Outlook` in the `Search programs and files' text box, click Outlook 2013, and then, if necessary, maximize the Outlook window. For detailed steps to run Outlook in Windows 7, refer to the Office and Windows chapter at the beginning of this book. For a summary of the steps, refer to the Quick Reference located at the back of this book.

BTW
**Touch Screen
Differences**
The Office and Windows
interfaces may vary if you are
using a touch screen. For this
reason, you might notice that
the function or appearance
of your touch screen differs
slightly from this chapter's
presentation.

information or email messages on a public computer. Although most people add an email account the first time Outlook runs, you can add email accounts at any time. This chapter assumes you already set up an email account in Outlook. If you choose to add an email account to Outlook, you would use the following steps.

1. If you started Outlook for the first time, tap or click the Next button to set up an email account. Otherwise, tap or click the FILE tab, and then tap or click Add Account.

2. Tap or click the Yes button to add an email account, and then tap or click the Next button to display the Add Account window.

3. Tap or click the Your Name text box, and then type your first and last name to associate your name with the account.

4. Tap or click the Email Address text box, and then type your full email address to associate your email address with the account.

5. Tap or click the Password text box, and then type your password to verify the password to your email account.

6. Tap or click the Retype Password text box, and then type your password again to confirm your password.

7. Tap or click the Next button to configure your account settings and sign in to your mail server.

8. Tap or click the Finish button to add your email account.

CONSIDER THIS

How do you remove an email account?

• To remove an email account in Outlook, tap or click the FILE tab on the ribbon.

• If necessary, tap or click the Info tab in the Backstage view.

• Tap or click the Account Settings button, and then tap or click Account Settings to display the Account Setting dialog box.

• Tap or click the account you want to remove, and then tap or click Remove.

• In the Account Settings dialog box, tap or click the Yes button.

BTW
The Ribbon and Screen Resolution
Outlook may change how the groups and buttons within the groups appear on the ribbon, depending on the computer's screen resolution. Thus, your ribbon may look different from the ones in this book if you are using a screen resolution other than 1366 x 768.

To Change the Navigation Bar Options

1 CONFIGURE ACCOUNT OPTIONS | 2 COMPOSE & SEND | 3 VIEW & PRINT | 4 REPLY
5 ATTACH FILE | 6 ORGANIZE MESSAGES

The first time you start Outlook, the lower-left corner of the screen provides compact navigation by default. To change the Navigation bar from displaying small icons representing Mail, Calendar, Contacts, and Task to a text view, you can disable the compact navigation setting on the Navigation bar. The following steps change the Navigation bar options. *Why? Instead of small icons, you can display the Mail, Calendar, Contacts, and Task text labels.*

1

- Tap or click the Navigation Options button (three dots) on the Navigation bar to display a list of Navigation bar options (Figure 1–4).

Q&A The left pane in my Outlook window is not expanded as it is in Figure 1-4. What should I do? Click the Expand the Folder Pane button, which is a small arrow button to the left of today's date in the Outlook window.

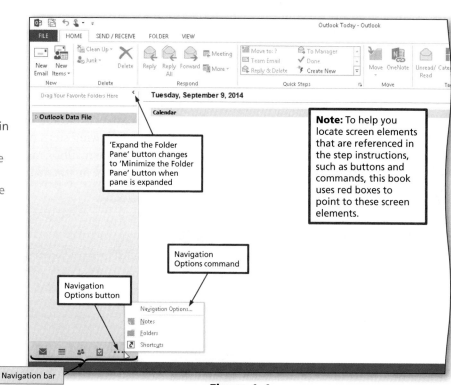

Note: To help you locate screen elements that are referenced in the step instructions, such as buttons and commands, this book uses red boxes to point to these screen elements.

'Expand the Folder Pane' button changes to 'Minimize the Folder Pane' button when pane is expanded

Navigation Options command

Navigation Options button

Navigation bar

Figure 1–4

2

- Tap or click Navigations Options to display the Navigation Options dialog box.

- If necessary, tap or click the Compact Navigation check box (Navigation Options dialog box) to remove the check mark and disable the compact navigation setting on the Navigation bar (Figure 1–5).

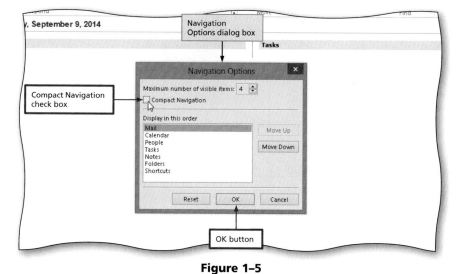

Navigation Options dialog box

Compact Navigation check box

OK button

Figure 1–5

3

- Tap or click the OK button to change the Navigation bar so it displays text labels instead of icons (Figure 1–6).

Navigation bar

Figure 1–6

To Open an Outlook Data File

Microsoft Outlook uses a special file format called a **personal storage table (.pst file)** to save your email files, calendar entries, and contacts. The email messages with which you work in this chapter are stored in a personal storage table file named Dylan.pst, which is an Outlook mailbox available on the Data Files for Students. To complete this chapter project, you will be required to use the Data Files for Students. Visit www.cengage.com/ct/studentdownload for detailed instructions or contact your instructor for information about accessing the required files. In this example, the Dylan mailbox is located in the Chapter 01 folder in the Outlook folder in the Data Files for Students folder. The following steps open the Dylan.pst file in Outlook, display the Inbox for the Dylan file, and then make your Dylan mailbox match the figures in this chapter. *Why? Importing a .pst file allows you to move your email and other Outlook information to another computer.*

1

- Tap or click FILE on the ribbon to open the Backstage view.

- Tap or click the Open & Export tab in the Backstage view to display the Open gallery (Figure 1–7).

For an introduction to Office and instruction about how to perform basic tasks in Office apps, read the Office and Windows chapter at the beginning of this book, where you can learn how to run an application, use the ribbon, save a file, open a file, exit an application, use Help, and much more.

Figure 1–7

2

- Tap or click Open Outlook Data File to display the Open Outlook Data File dialog box.

- Navigate to the mailbox location (in this case, the Chapter 01 folder in the Outlook folder in the Data Files for Students folder) (Figure 1–8).

Figure 1–8

❸

- Tap or click Dylan to select the file, and then tap or click the OK button (Open Outlook Data File dialog box) to open the Dylan mailbox in your Outlook window.

- If necessary, tap or click the white triangle next to the Outlook Data File mailbox in the Navigation Pane to expand the folders.

- Tap or click the Inbox folder below the Outlook Data File heading in the Navigation Pane to view Dylan's Inbox (Figure 1–9).

Q&A | What is the Navigation Pane?

The **Navigation Pane** is a pane along the left side of the Outlook window that contains shortcuts to your Outlook folders and gives you quick access to them. You use the Navigation Pane to browse all your Outlook folders using one of its views: Mail, Calendar, People, or Tasks.

What is the Inbox?

The **Inbox** is the Outlook folder that contains incoming email messages.

The contact photo shown in Figure 1–9 does not appear in my Outlook window. What should I do?

Outlook needs to synchronize the contact photos with the email addresses in the Dylan data file. Click the Close button to close Outlook, restart it, and then expand the Outlook Data File in the Navigation Pane to have the photos appear.

Figure 1–9

1 CONFIGURE ACCOUNT OPTIONS | 2 COMPOSE & SEND | 3 VIEW & PRINT | 4 REPLY
5 ATTACH FILE | 6 ORGANIZE MESSAGES

To Set Language Preferences

You can use the Outlook Options dialog box to set the Office Language Preferences. *Why? You can specify the editing and display languages, such as the languages used in the dictionaries, grammar checking, and sorting.* Usually, Outlook configures the language settings to match your operating system; however, if you want to change those settings, you can adjust the Language preferences. The following steps set the Language preferences.

1

- Tap or click FILE on the ribbon to open the Backstage view (Figure 1–10).

Q&A Why does my account information appear in the Backstage view?
If you have already set up an email account in Outlook, it appears on the Info tab in the Backstage view. Other options, such as Rules and Alerts, might also appear.

Figure 1–10

2

- Tap or click the Options tab in the Backstage view to display the Outlook Options dialog box.

- In the left pane, tap or click Language (Outlook Options dialog box) to display the Language options.

- Tap or click the '[Add additional editing languages]' arrow to display a list of editing languages that can be added to Outlook (Figure 1–11).

Q&A How do I set a default language?
After selecting an editing language that you want to use, tap or click the name of the language and then tap or click the 'Set as Default' button.

3

- If necessary, scroll the list and then tap or click English (United States) to set the default editing language. Otherwise, tap or click the '[Add additional editing languages]' arrow again to close the list.

Figure 1–11

To Set the Sensitivity Level for All New Messages

1 CONFIGURE ACCOUNT OPTIONS | 2 COMPOSE & SEND | 3 VIEW & PRINT | 4 REPLY
5 ATTACH FILE | 6 ORGANIZE MESSAGES

The **Sensitivity level** of a message advises the recipient on how to treat the contents of the message. Sensitivity levels are Normal, Personal, Private, and Confidential. Changing the Sensitivity setting in the Outlook Options dialog box changes the default Sensitivity level of all messages created afterward. *Why? For example, if you set the Sensitivity level of a message to Confidential, the information should not be disclosed to anyone except the recipient.* The following steps set the default Sensitivity level.

1

- In the left pane, tap or click Mail (Outlook Options dialog box) to display the Mail options.

- Drag the scroll bar to display the Send messages area (Figure 1–12).

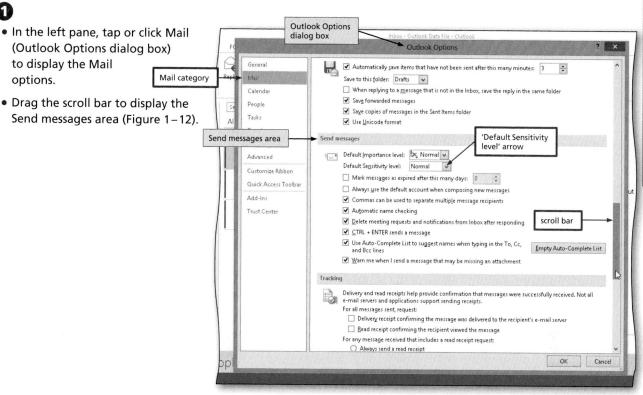

Figure 1–12

2

- Tap or click the 'Default Sensitivity level' arrow to display a list of Sensitivity levels (Figure 1–13).

Q&A Can I set one message to an individual Sensitivity level?
Yes, you can set the Sensitivity level for a single message using the More Options Dialog Box Launcher (OPTIONS tab | More Options group) to open the More Options dialog box.

3

- If necessary, tap or click Normal to set the default Sensitivity level of all new messages.

- Tap or click the OK button to close the Outlook Options dialog box.

Q&A What should I do if the ribbon does not stay open?
Tap or click the 'Pin the ribbon' button (thumbtack icon) on the lower-right corner of the ribbon to keep the ribbon open.

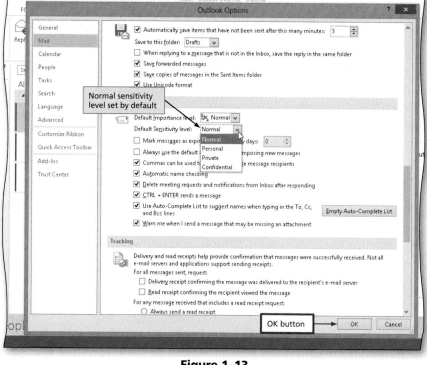

Figure 1–13

Composing and Sending Email messages

BTW

Inserting Hyperlinks
To insert a web address in an email message, tap or click where you want to insert the hyperlink, and then tap or click the Hyperlink button (INSERT tab | Links group) to display the Insert Hyperlink dialog box. In the Address text box, type the web address you want to insert as a hyperlink, and then tap or click the OK button to insert the hyperlink into the message body.

Composing an email message is the most frequent personal and business task you perform in Microsoft Outlook. Composing an email message consists of four basic steps: open a new message window, enter message header information, enter the message text, and add a signature. When composing an email message, it is best to keep your message text short and to the point.

An email message is organized into two areas: the message header and the message area. The information in the **message header** routes the message to its recipients and identifies the subject of the message. The message header identifies the primary recipient(s) in the To box. If you have multiple recipients in the To box, you can separate each email address with a semicolon. Recipients in the Cc (courtesy copy or carbon copy) and Bcc (blind courtesy copy) boxes, if displayed, also receive the message; however, the names of the recipients in the Bcc box are not visible to other recipients. The **subject line** states the purpose of the message.

The **message area**, where you type an email message, consists of a greeting line or salutation, the message text, an optional closing, and one or more signature lines as shown in Table 1–1.

Table 1–1 Message Area Parts

Part	Description
Greeting line or salutation	Sets the tone of the message and can be formal or informal, depending on the nature of the message. You can use a colon (:) or comma (,) at the end of the greeting line.
Message text	Informs the recipient or requests information.
Closing	Informs the recipient or requests information. A closing signals an end to the message using courtesy words such as *Thank you* or *Regards*. Because the closing is most appropriate for formal email messages, it is optional.
Signature line(s)	Identifies the sender and may contain additional information, such as a job title, business name, and phone number(s). In a signature, the name usually is provided on one line followed by other information listed on separate lines.

© 2014 Cengage Learning

To Compose an Email Message

1 CONFIGURE ACCOUNT OPTIONS | 2 COMPOSE & SEND | 3 VIEW & PRINT | 4 REPLY
5 ATTACH FILE | 6 ORGANIZE MESSAGES

An email message from Dylan Cruz, the International Club student president, requests information about the Summer Study Abroad program from an instructor named Jacob Thompson. The following steps compose a new email message. *Why? Composing email messages is a quick and efficient method to connect with personal and professional contacts.*

1

- Tap or click the New Email button (HOME tab | New group) to open the Untitled – Message (HTML) window (Figure 1–14).

Q&A
What does HTML mean in the title bar?
HTML is the format for the new email message. Outlook messages can use two other formats: Rich Text Format (RTF) and Plain Text. All of these formats are discussed later in this chapter.

Figure 1–14

2

- Type `jacob.thompson@outlook.com` (with no spaces) in the To text box to enter the email address of the recipient.

- Tap or click the Subject text box, and then type `Summer Study Abroad Program` to enter the subject line.

- Press the TAB key to move the insertion point into the message area (Figure 1–15).

Figure 1–15

3

- Type `Mr. Thompson,` as the greeting line.

- Press the ENTER key to move the insertion point to the beginning of the next line.

- Press the ENTER key again to insert a blank line between the greeting line and the message text (Figure 1–16).

Q&A What does it mean if I use all capital letters in my email message?
Writing in all capital letters is considered the same as shouting. Use proper capitalization as you compose your email.

Figure 1–16

4

- Type I understand that our school is beginning a Summer Study Abroad program this year. Do you have any information to share with the International Club about this opportunity? to enter the message text.

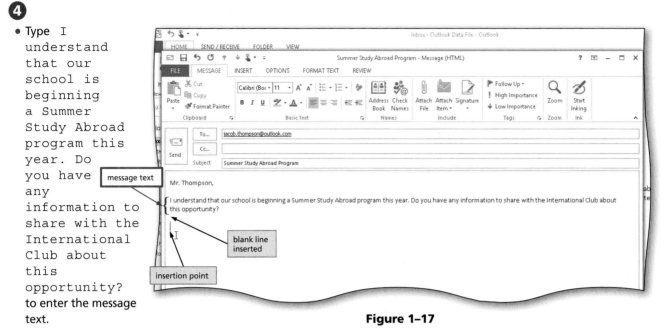

Figure 1–17

- Press the ENTER key two times to insert a blank line below the message text (Figure 1–17).

5

- Type Thanks, to enter the closing for the message.

- Press the ENTER key to move the insertion point to the next line.

- Type Dylan Cruz as the first line of the signature.

- Press the ENTER key to move the insertion point to the next line.

Figure 1–18

- Type International Club Student President as the second line of the signature (Figure 1–18).

Q&A

What if I make an error while typing an email message?
Press the BACKSPACE key until you have deleted the error and then retype the text correctly. You also can click the Undo button on the Quick Access Toolbar to undo your most recent action.

Do I always need to type my last name in the signature of an email message?
No. If you and your recipient know each other, you can type only your first name as the signature.

Other Ways

1. Tap or click Inbox folder, press CTRL+N

To Apply a Theme

An Outlook theme can give an email message instant style. Each theme provides a unique set of colors, fonts, and effects. *Why? Themes give your organization's communications a modern, professional look.* The following steps apply a theme to the message.

1

- Tap or click OPTIONS on the ribbon to display the OPTIONS tab.

- Tap or click the Themes button (OPTIONS tab | Themes group) to display the Themes gallery (Figure 1–19).

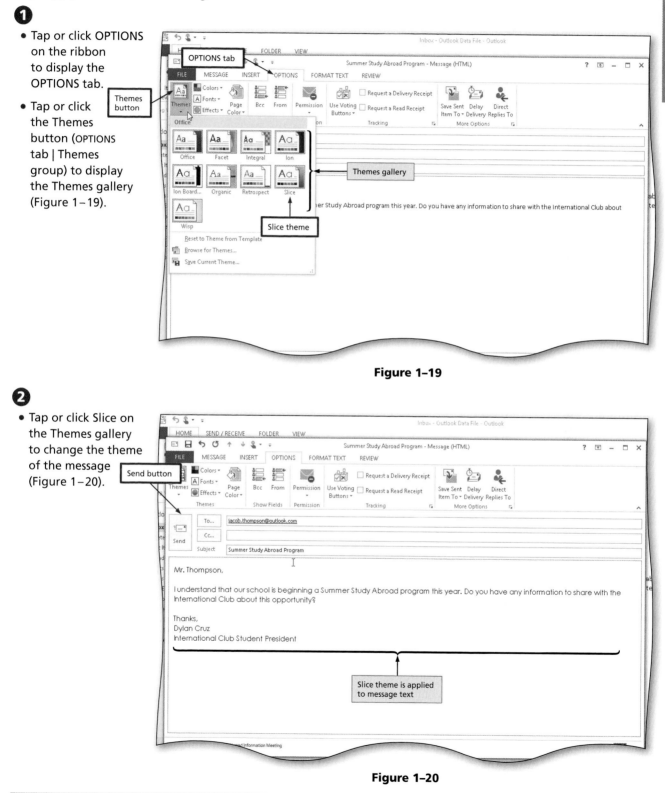

Figure 1–19

2

- Tap or click Slice on the Themes gallery to change the theme of the message (Figure 1–20).

Figure 1–20

CONSIDER THIS

How can you create your own theme for your messages?

• Format a message with a customized font, colors, and background.

• Tap or click the Themes button (OPTIONS tab | Themes group) to display the Themes gallery.

• Tap or click Save Current Theme to display the Save Current Theme dialog box.

• Type a name in the File name text box to name your new theme.

• Tap or click the Save button to save your new theme.

To Send an Email Message

Why? *After you complete a message, send it to the recipient, who typically receives the message in seconds.* The following step sends the completed email message to the recipient.

1

• Tap or click the Send button in the message header to send the email message and close the message window.

Q&A

What happened to the email message?

Outlook automatically sends email messages to their recipient(s) when you tap or click Send in a new message window if you have your own email account set up.

Why did I get an error message that stated that 'No valid email accounts are configured. Add an account to send email'?

If you do not have an email account set up in Outlook, you cannot connect to the Internet to send the email. Tap or click Cancel to close the message.

Other Ways

1. Tap or click Inbox folder, press ALT+S

How Email Messages Travel from Sender to Receiver

When you send someone an email message, it travels across the Internet to the computer at your email service provider that handles outgoing email messages. This computer, called the **outgoing email server**, examines the email address on your message, selects the best route for sending the message across the Internet, and then sends the email message. Many outgoing email servers use **SMTP (Simple Mail Transfer Protocol)**, which is a communications protocol, or set of rules for communicating with other computers. An email program such as Outlook contacts the outgoing email server and then transfers the email message(s) in its Outbox to that server. If the email program cannot contact the outgoing email server, the email message(s) remains in the Outbox until the program can connect to the server.

As an email message travels across the Internet, routers direct the email message to a computer at your recipient's email service provider that handles incoming email messages. A **router** is a device that forwards data on a network. The computer handling incoming email messages, called the incoming email server, stores the email message(s) until your recipient uses an email program such as Outlook to retrieve the email message(s). Some email servers use **POP3**, the latest version of **Post Office Protocol (POP)**, a communications protocol for incoming email. Figure 1–21 shows how an email message may travel from a sender to a receiver.

Figure 1–21

In most cases, the Auto Account Setup feature does not require you to enter the name of your POP or SMTP server, but many businesses require that you manually enter these server settings. You can verify these Internet email settings in the Change Account dialog box, which is displayed by tapping or clicking the FILE tab on the ribbon to open the Backstage view, tapping or clicking the Account Settings button in the Backstage view, tapping or clicking Account Settings to display the Account Settings dialog box, selecting your email address, and then tapping or clicking the Change button. Figure 1–22 shows the Change Account dialog box for Dylan Cruz. Notice that this account uses a mail server named blu-m.hotmail.com.

Figure 1–22

BTW
Know the Sender
If you receive an email
message from someone you
do not know, you should
not open it because it might
trigger a virus. Unsolicited
email messages, known
as **spam** or **junk email**,
are email messages sent
from an unknown sender
to many email accounts,
usually advertising a
product or service such
as low-cost medication,
low-interest loans, or free
credit reports. Do not tap or
click a hyperlink in an email
message from an unknown
sender. A **hyperlink** is a
word, phrase, symbol, or
picture in an email message
or on a webpage that, when
tapped or clicked, directs
you to another document or
website.

Working with Incoming Messages

When you receive email messages, Outlook directs them to your Inbox and displays them in the **message pane**, which lists the contents of the selected folder (Figure 1–23). The list of messages displayed in the message pane is called the **message list**. An unread (unopened) email message in the message list includes a blue vertical bar in front of the message and displays the subject text and time of arrival in a blue bold font. An open envelope icon indicates a previously read (opened) message. The blue number next to the Inbox folder shows how many unread messages are stored in the Inbox. The email messages on your computer may be different.

You can read incoming messages in three ways: in an open window, in the Reading Pane, or as a hard copy. A **hard copy** (**printout**) is information presented on a physical medium such as paper.

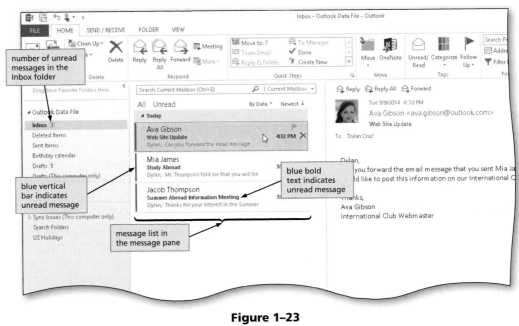

Figure 1–23

To View an Email Message in the Reading Pane

1 CONFIGURE ACCOUNT OPTIONS | 2 COMPOSE & SEND | 3 VIEW & PRINT | 4 REPLY
5 ATTACH FILE | 6 ORGANIZE MESSAGES

Why? You can preview messages in your Inbox without opening them by using the Reading Pane. The **Reading Pane** appears on the right side of the Outlook window by default and displays the contents of a message without requiring you to open the message. An advantage of viewing messages in the Reading Pane is that if a message includes content that could be harmful to your computer, such as a malicious script or an attachment containing a virus, the Reading Pane does not activate the harmful content. An **attachment** is a file such as a document or picture you send along with an email message. The instructor Jacob Thompson has sent a response to Dylan concerning the Summer Study Abroad program. The following step displays an email message from a sender.

1
- Tap or click the message header from Jacob Thompson in the Inbox message list to select the email message and display its contents in the Reading Pane (Figure 1–24).

Q&A | What happens to the message header when I select another message?
Outlook automatically marks messages as read after you preview the message in the Reading Pane and select another message to view. A read message is displayed in the message list without a vertical blue line or bold text.

Figure 1–24

To Open an Email Message in a Window

1 CONFIGURE ACCOUNT OPTIONS | 2 COMPOSE & SEND | 3 VIEW & PRINT | 4 REPLY
5 ATTACH FILE | 6 ORGANIZE MESSAGES

Why? *To fully evaluate an email message and use additional Outlook tools for working with messages, you display the email message in a window.* The following step displays an email message from a sender in a window.

1

- Double-tap or double-click the Jacob Thompson message in the message list to display the selected email message in its own window (Figure 1–25).

Q&A

Can I change the status of a message from read to unread without opening the message or displaying its contents in the Reading Pane?

Yes. Press and hold or right-click the message you want to change, and then tap or click Mark as Read on the shortcut menu.

Figure 1–25

Other Ways

1. Tap or click message header, press CTRL+O

To Open an Attachment

If you know the sender and you know the attachment is safe, you can open the attached file. The following steps open an attachment. *Why? By opening a Word attachment in Microsoft Word, you can edit the document with the full features of Word.*

1

- If necessary, tap or click the message header from Jacob Thompson in the Inbox message list to select the email message and display its contents in the Reading Pane.

- Double-tap or double-click the attachment in the Reading Pane to open the file attachment in Microsoft Word in Protected View (Figure 1–29).

Q&A | Why does the attachment open in Protected View in Microsoft Word?
File attachments can contain viruses, worms, or other kinds of malware, which can harm your computer. To help protect your computer, Microsoft Office apps open files from these potentially unsafe locations in Protected View. Tap or click the Enable Editing button if you trust the sender to edit the document.

2

- Tap or click the Close button to close the Word file.

Figure 1–29

Photo courtesy of Corinne Hoisington

To Print an Email Message

Occasionally, you may want to print the contents of an email message. *Why? A hard copy of an email message can serve as reference material if your storage medium becomes corrupted and you need to view the message when your computer is not readily available.* A printed copy of an email message also serves as a **backup**, which is an additional copy of a file or message that you store for safekeeping. You can print the contents of an email message from an open message window or directly from the Inbox window.

You would like to have a hard copy of Jacob Thompson's email message for reference at the next International Club meeting. The following steps print an email message.

1
- If necessary, tap or click HOME on the ribbon to display the HOME tab.
- In the message list, press and hold or right-click the Jacob Thompson message header to display a shortcut menu that presents a list of possible actions (Figure 1–30).

2
- Tap or click the Quick Print command on the shortcut menu to send the email message to the currently selected printer.

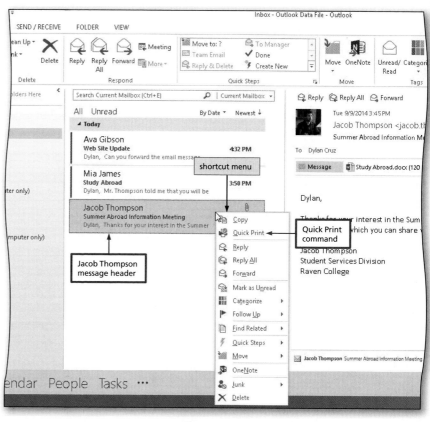

Figure 1–30

Other Ways

1. Press CTRL+P, tap or click Print button
2. Tap or click FILE tab, tap or click Print tab (Backstage view), tap or click Print button

---

Using the Outlook Social Connector

Outlook provides a means of communicating with the personal and business contacts in your social networks. The **Social Connector** is a feature designed to link Outlook to your social networks such as Facebook, LinkedIn, My Site (SharePoint), and other social networks, as shown in Figure 1–31. The Outlook Social Connector displays the communication you have had with someone from your social network, along with their photo. The **People Pane** accesses information that the Outlook Social Connector displays from social networks. If you enable these connections, the People Pane can display information such as Facebook status updates, tagged photos, and profile photos. For example, in the chapter project, the People Pane at the bottom of the Reading Pane displays the photos of the email sender and recipient. If you connect to your social networks, the People Pane, depending on a sender's privacy settings on their social network accounts, can display your friend's photos and contact information in one location.

Figure 1–31

To Change the View of the People Pane

By default, the People Pane is displayed in the Minimized view, so it appears as a one-line bar below an open email message and does not take up a lot of room in the Reading Pane or open message window. To view more details, you can change the People Pane view to Normal. *Why? When you are reading a message in Outlook, you can use the People Pane to view more information about the contacts associated with the message, such as the senders and receivers of the message.* The following steps change the view of the People Pane.

- Tap or click VIEW on the ribbon to display the VIEW tab.

- Tap or click the People Pane button (VIEW tab | People Pane group) to display the People Pane gallery (Figure 1–32).

Figure 1–32

If you are using your finger on a touch screen and are having difficulty completing the steps in this chapter, consider using a stylus. Many people find it easier to be precise with a stylus than with a finger. In addition, with a stylus you see the pointer. If you still are having trouble completing the steps with a stylus, try using a mouse.

2

- Tap or click Normal on the People Pane gallery to display the People Pane in Normal view below the email message in the Reading Pane (Figure 1–33).

🔍 Experiment

- Double-tap or double-click the first contact picture in the People Pane. A contact card opens that displays the contact information. When you are finished, tap or click the Close button to close the contact card.

Q&A When the People Pane expands to Normal view, should messages from this sender be listed below the sender's name?
Yes. Email messages appear in the People Pane if you have previously corresponded with the sender.

A yellow message appears below Jacob Thompson's name in the People Pane. How should I respond to the message?
Close the message by tapping or clicking its Close button.

Figure 1–33

3

- Tap or click the People Pane button (VIEW tab | People Pane group) to display the People Pane gallery.

- Tap or click Minimized on the People Pane gallery to collapse the People Pane into a single line below the Reading Pane (Figure 1–34).

Q&A Does the People Pane update contact information automatically?
The People Pane automatically updates information about your professional and social network contacts while Outlook is running.

Figure 1–34

Other Ways

1. Tap or click arrow to the right of the People Pane to expand or collapse pane

To Reposition the Reading Pane

By default, the Reading Pane is displayed on the right side of the Outlook window. You can change the position of the Reading Pane so it appears below the message list or you can hide the Reading Pane so it does not appear in the Outlook window. The following steps reposition the Reading Pane. *Why? In your work and personal life, you may spend a lot of time in Outlook, so create a layout that works best for your own needs.*

1

- Tap or click the Reading Pane button (VIEW tab | Layout group) to display the Reading Pane gallery (Figure 1–35).

Figure 1–35

2

- Tap or click Bottom on the Reading Pane gallery to display the Reading Pane below the message list for all mail folders (Figure 1–36).

Figure 1–36

❸

- Tap or click the Reading Pane button (VIEW tab | Layout group) to display the Reading Pane gallery.

- Tap or click Off on the Reading Pane gallery to hide the Reading Pane for all mail folders (Figure 1–37).

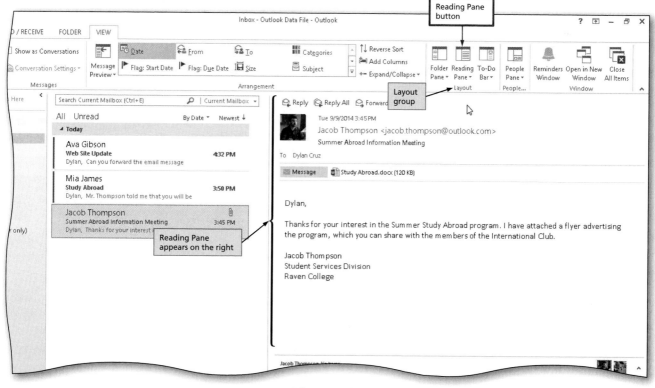

Figure 1–37

❹

- Tap or click the Reading Pane button (VIEW tab | Layout group) to display the Reading Pane gallery.

- Tap or click Right on the Reading Pane gallery to return the Reading Pane to the right side of the Outlook window for all mail folders (Figure 1–38).

Figure 1–38

Break Point: If you wish to take a break, this is a good place to do so. To resume at a later time, continue to follow the steps from this location forward.

Responding to Messages

When you receive a message, you can send a reply to the sender. You also have the option to forward the message to additional people.

How should a formal business response differ from a close friend's response?

- An email response you send to an instructor, coworker, or client should be more formal than the one you send to a close friend. For example, conversational language to a friend, such as "Can't wait to see you!" is not appropriate in professional email messages.

- A formal email message should be business-like and get to the point quickly. An informal email is more conversational and friendly.

- All standard grammar rules apply, such as punctuation, capitalization, and spelling, no matter the audience.

When responding to email messages, you have three options in Outlook: Reply, Reply All, or Forward. Table 1–2 lists the response options and their actions.

Table 1–2 Outlook Response Options	
Response Option	**Action**
Reply	Opens the RE: reply window and sends a reply to the person who sent the message.
Reply All	Opens the RE: reply window and sends a reply to everyone listed in the message header.
Forward	Opens the FW: message window and sends a copy of the selected message to additional people, if you want to share information with others. The original message text is included in the message window.

© 2014 Cengage Learning

You reply to messages you already have received. You can forward an email message to additional recipients to share information with others. Based on the situation, you should request permission from the sender before forwarding a message, in case the sender intended the original message to remain private. When forwarding, you send the message to someone other than the original sender of the message. A reply sends the message to the person who sent the message.

To Reply to an Email Message

1 CONFIGURE ACCOUNT OPTIONS | 2 COMPOSE & SEND | 3 VIEW & PRINT | **4 REPLY**
5 ATTACH FILE | 6 ORGANIZE MESSAGES

When you reply to an email message, the email address of the sender is inserted in the To box automatically. If you select Reply All, the To box automatically includes the sender and the other people who originally received the message (except for those who originally received a BCC message).

In an email message, a student named Mia James has requested that Dylan send her information about the Summer Study Abroad program. The following steps reply to an email message. *Why? When replying to a colleague, responding in a professional manner in an email message indicates how serious you are about your role and enhances your reputation within the organization.*

1

- Tap or click HOME on the ribbon to display the HOME tab.

- Tap or click the Mia James message header in the message list to select it and display its contents in the Reading Pane (Figure 1–39 on the next page).

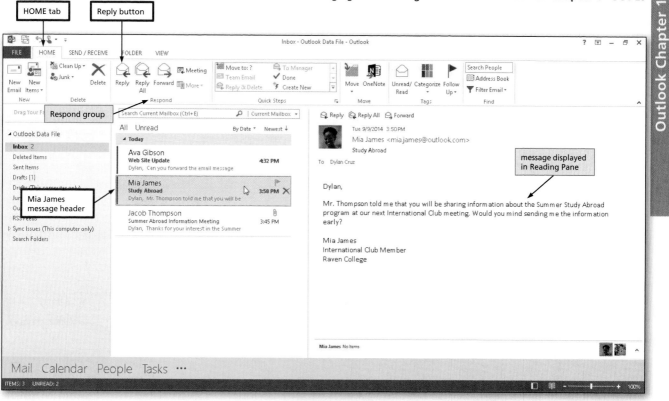

Figure 1–39

❷

• Tap or click the Reply button (HOME tab | Respond group) to reply to the message in the Reading Pane (Figure 1–40).

Figure 1–40

3

- Tap or click the Pop Out button to display the RE: Study Abroad – Message (HTML) window (Figure 1–41).

Q&A Why does RE: appear at the beginning of the subject line and in the title bar?
The RE: indicates this message is a reply to another message. The subject of the original message appears after the RE:.

RE: Study Abroad – Message (HTML) window

message header

From: Mia James [mailto:mia.james@outlook.com]
Sent: Tuesday, September 9, 2014 3:50 PM
To: Dylan Cruz
Subject: Study Abroad

Dylan,

Mr. Thompson told me that you will be sharing information about the Summer Study Abroad program at our next International Club meeting. Would you mind sending me the information early?

Figure 1–41

4

- If necessary, tap or click the message area below the message header to position the insertion point at the top of the message area.

- Type Mia, as the greeting line.

- Press the ENTER key two times to insert a blank line between the greeting line and the message text.

- Type As you requested, I have attached a flyer that Mr. Thompson recently sent me about an informational meeting for the Summer Study Abroad program. to enter the message text.

- Press the ENTER key two times to insert a blank line between the message text and the closing.

- Type Thanks for your interest, as the closing, and then press the ENTER key to move the insertion point to the next line.

- Type Dylan Cruz as signature line 1, and then press the ENTER key to move the insertion point to the next line.

- Type International Club Student President as signature line 2 (Figure 1–42).

Mia,

As you requested, I have attached a flyer that Mr. Thompson recently sent me about an informational meeting for the Summer Study Abroad program.

Thanks for your interest,
Dylan Cruz
International Club Student President

From: Mia James [mailto:mia.james@outlook.com]
Sent: Tuesday, September 9, 2014 3:50 PM
To: Dylan Cruz

line separates reply from original message

message text reply in blue font

Figure 1–42

Other Ways

1. Tap or click Reply or Reply All in Reading Pane
2. Tap and hold or right-click message header, click Reply
3. With message selected, press CTRL+R

Message Formats

As shown in Figure 1–42, Outlook's default (preset) message format is **HTML (Hypertext Markup Language)**, which is a format that allows you to view pictures and text formatted with color and various fonts and font sizes. **Formatting** refers to changing the appearance of text in a document such as the font (typeface), font size, color, and alignment of the text in a document.

Before you send an email message, reply to an email message, or forward an email message, consider which message format you want to use. A **message format** determines whether an email message can include pictures or formatted text, such as bold, italic, and colored fonts. Select a message format that is appropriate for your message and your recipient. Outlook offers three message formats: HTML, Plain Text, and Rich Text, as summarized in Table 1–3. If you select the HTML format, for example, the email program your recipient uses must be able to display formatted messages or pictures. If your recipient does not have high speed connectivity, a Plain Text format is displayed quickly, especially on a device such as a smartphone. Reading email in plain text offers important security benefits, reducing the possibility of a virus within the email.

Table 1–3 Message Formats

Message Format	Description
HTML	HTML is the default format for new messages in Outlook. HTML lets you include pictures and basic formatting, such as text formatting, numbering, bullets, and alignment. HTML is the recommended format for Internet mail because the more popular email programs use it.
Plain Text	Plain Text format is recognized by all email programs and is the most likely format to be allowed through a company's virus-filtering program. Plain Text does not support basic formatting, such as bold, italic, colored fonts, or other text formatting. It also does not support pictures displayed directly in the message.
Rich Text	Rich Text Format (RTF) is a Microsoft format that only the latest versions of **Microsoft Exchange** (a Microsoft message system that includes an email program and a mail server) and Outlook recognize. RTF supports more formats than HTML or Plain Text; it also supports hyperlinks. A hyperlink can be text, a picture or other object that is displayed in an email message.

© 2014 Cengage Learning

BTW
Using Plain Text Formatting to Guard Against Email Viruses
HTML-formatted messages can contain viruses. To minimize the risk of receiving a virus infected email message, change the format of messages you read. You can configure Outlook to format all opened messages in Plain Text. Tap or click FILE on the ribbon to open the Backstage view. Tap or click the Options tab. Tap or click the Trust Center option in the Outlook Options dialog box, and then tap or click the Trust Center Settings button to display the Trust Center dialog box. Tap or click E-mail Security (Trust Center dialog box), and in the Read as Plain Text section, tap or click the 'Read all standard mail in plain text' check box.

To Change the Message Format

1 CONFIGURE ACCOUNT OPTIONS | 2 COMPOSE & SEND | 3 VIEW & PRINT | 4 REPLY
5 ATTACH FILE | 6 ORGANIZE MESSAGES

Why? *You want to make sure that your reply message is not blocked by an antivirus program, so you will change the message format to Plain Text.* The following steps change the message format to Plain Text.

1

• Tap or click FORMAT TEXT on the ribbon in the message window to display the FORMAT TEXT tab (Figure 1–43).

Figure 1–43

2

- Tap or click the Plain Text button (FORMAT TEXT tab | Format group) to select the Plain Text message format, which removes all formatting in the message.

- When the Microsoft Outlook Compatibility Checker dialog box is displayed, tap or click the Continue button to change the formatted text to plain text (Figure 1–44).

Q&A

What happened to the line separating the existing message and the new message?

When Plain Text is selected as the message format, all formatting such as text color, font type, lines, themes, and size is removed.

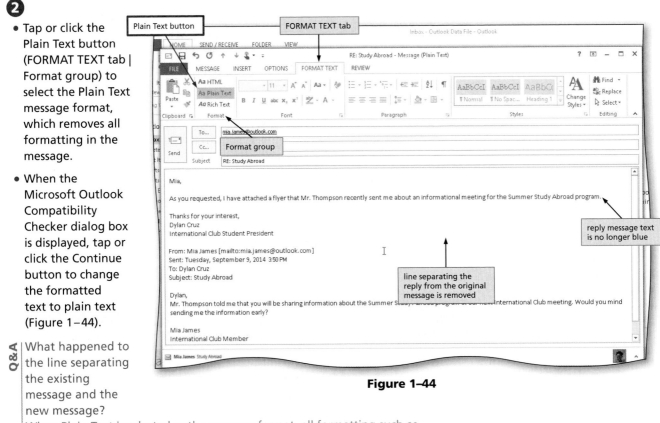

Figure 1–44

BTW

Removing the Original Message When Replying

Many email users prefer to reply to a message without including the original email message along with their response. To remove the original message from all email replies, tap or click FILE to open the Backstage view, and then tap or click the Options tab. Tap or click Mail to display the Mail options. In the Replies and forwards section, tap or click the 'When replying to a message box' arrow, select the 'Do not include original message' option, and then tap or click OK.

Checking Spelling and Grammar

Outlook checks your message for possible spelling and grammar errors as you type and flags any potential errors in the message text with a red, green, or blue wavy underline. A red wavy underline means the flagged text is not in Outlook's main dictionary because it is a proper name or misspelled. A green wavy underline indicates the text may be incorrect grammatically. A blue wavy underline indicates the text may contain a contextual spelling error such as the misuse of homophones (words that are pronounced the same but have different spellings or meanings, such as one and won). Although you can check the entire message for spelling and grammar errors at once, you also can check these flagged errors as they appear on the screen.

A flagged word is not necessarily misspelled. For example, many names, abbreviations, and specialized terms are not in Outlook's main dictionary. In these cases, you instruct Outlook to ignore the flagged word. As you type, Outlook also detects duplicate words while checking for spelling errors. For example, if your email message contains the phrase *to the the store*, Outlook places a red wavy underline below the second occurrence of the word, *the*.

1 CONFIGURE ACCOUNT OPTIONS | 2 COMPOSE & SEND | 3 VIEW & PRINT | 4 REPLY
5 ATTACH FILE | 6 ORGANIZE MESSAGES

To Check the Spelling of a Correctly Typed Word

Dylan adds one more sentence to his email document, recalling that Mia is interested in studying in a city named Vught in the Netherlands. In the email message, the city of Vught has a red wavy line below it even though it is spelled correctly, indicating the word is not in Outlook's main dictionary. The following steps ignore the error and remove the red wavy line. *Why? The main dictionary contains most common words, but does not include most proper names, technical terms, or acronyms that you use.*

1

- Tap or click after the first sentence in the email message to Mia to place the insertion point, and then press the SPACEBAR to insert a space.

- Type `I remember your interest in studying in Vught, Netherlands.` to enter a second sentence in the message text, and then click a blank spot in the window to have Outlook mark a spelling error (Figure 1–45).

Figure 1–45

Q&A | Why does a red wavy line appear below Vught even though the city name is spelled correctly?
Outlook places a red wavy line below any word that is not in its main dictionary.

2

- Press and hold or right-click the red wavy line below the proper name to display a shortcut menu that presents a list of suggested spelling corrections for the flagged word (in this case, the city name) (Figure 1–46).

Figure 1–46

Q&A | What if Outlook does not flag my spelling and grammar errors with wavy underlines?
To verify that the check spelling and grammar as you type features are enabled, tap or click the FILE tab on the ribbon to open the Backstage view and then tap or click Options to display the Outlook Options dialog box. Tap or click Mail (Outlook Options dialog box) and tap or click the Editor Options button to display the Editor Options dialog box. In the 'When correcting spelling in Outlook' section, ensure the 'Check spelling as you type' check box contains a check mark. Tap or click the OK button two times to close each open dialog box.

3

- Tap or click Ignore All on the shortcut menu to ignore this flagged error, close the shortcut menu, and remove the red wavy line beneath the proper name (Figure 1–47).

Figure 1–47

To Check the Spelling of Misspelled Text

In the following steps, the word *program* is misspelled intentionally as *profram* to illustrate Outlook's check spelling as you type feature. If you are performing the steps in this project, your email message may contain different misspelled words, depending on the accuracy of your typing. The following steps check the spelling of a misspelled word. *Why? The way that you present yourself in email messages contributes to the way you are perceived, so you should be sure to spell check and proofread all communications.*

1

- Tap or click after the second sentence in the email message to Mia to place the insertion point, and then press the SPACEBAR to insert a space.

Figure 1–48

- Type Let Mr. Thompson know if you have any questions about the profram. to complete the message text, and then press the SPACEBAR so that a red wavy line appears below the misspelled word (Figure 1–48).

2

- Press and hold or right-click the flagged word (profram, in this case) to display a shortcut menu that presents a list of suggested spelling corrections for the flagged word (Figure 1–49).

Figure 1–49

Q&A What should I do if the correction I want to use is not listed on the shortcut menu?
You can tap or click outside the shortcut menu to close it and then retype the correct word.

3

- Tap or click the correct spelling on the shortcut menu (in this case, program) to replace the misspelled word in the email message with the correctly spelled word (Figure 1–50).

Figure 1–50

Other Ways

1. Tap or click REVIEW tab (message window), tap or click Spelling & Grammar button (REVIEW tab | Proofing group) 2. Press F7

Saving and Closing an Email Message

Occasionally, you begin composing a message but cannot complete it. You may be waiting for information from someone else to include in the message, or you might prefer to rewrite the message later after you have time to evaluate its content. One option is to save the message, which stores the message in the Drafts folder for your email account until you are ready to send it. The Drafts folder is the default location for all saved messages. Later, you can reopen the message, finish writing it, and then send it.

To Save and Close an Email Message without Sending It

The Summer Study Abroad program information that Mia James requested has been drafted, but Dylan is not ready to send it yet. The following steps save a message in the Drafts folder for completion at a later time. *Why? If you are in the middle of composing a lengthy or important email and get called away, you can save your work so you can resume it later.*

1

- Tap or click the Save button on the Quick Access Toolbar to save the message in the Drafts folder (Figure 1–51).

Q&A

How does Outlook know where to store the saved message?
By default, Outlook stores saved messages in the Drafts folder for your email account.

Figure 1–51

Can I save the message to a location other than the Drafts folder?
To save the message to the Outlook student folder, tap or click the FILE tab on the ribbon to open the Backstage view, and then tap or click Save As in the Backstage view to display the Save As dialog box. Navigate to the Outlook student folder. In the File name text box, type the name of the message file and then tap or click the Save button. The message is saved with the extension .msg, which represents an Outlook message.

What should I do if Outlook did not save the message in the Drafts folder?
Click the FILE tab, click the Move to Folder button, click Other Folder, select the Drafts folder for the Outlook Data File, and then click the OK button.

2

- Tap or click the Close button on the title bar to close the RE: Study Abroad – Message (HTML) window (Figure 1–52).

Q&A

How do I know when a message is a draft rather than an incoming message?
The message appears in the message list with [Draft] displayed in red.

What happens if I tap or click the Close button without saving the message?
If you create a message and then tap or click the Close button, Outlook displays a dialog box asking if you want to save the changes. If you tap or click Yes, Outlook saves the file to the Drafts folder and closes the message window. If you tap or click No, Outlook discards the email message and closes the message window.

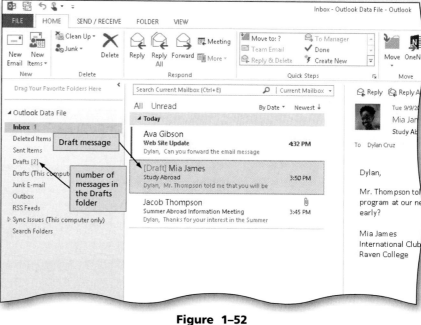

Figure 1–52

Other Ways

1. Tap or click Close button and tap or click Yes to keep saved draft of message   2. Press F12

To Open a Saved Email Message

The following steps open the message saved in the Drafts folder. *Why? By default, Outlook saves any email message in the Drafts folder every three minutes. You can also save a message and reopen it later.*

1

- Tap or click the Drafts folder in the Navigation Pane to display the message header for the Mia James email message in the message list (Figure 1–53).

Q&A What should I do if the message does not appear in my Drafts folder?
If the message does not appear in the Drafts folder, return to the Inbox, and then click the message header in the message pane.

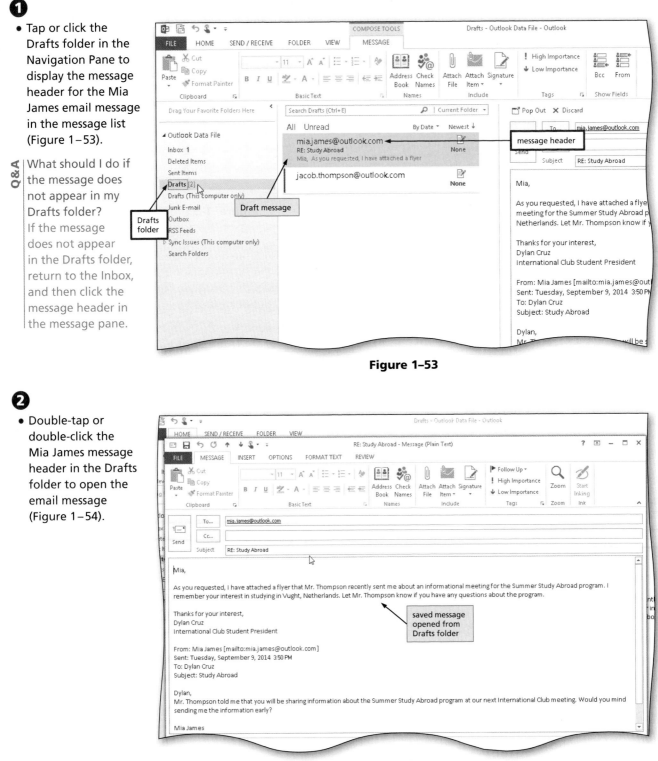

Figure 1–53

2

- Double-tap or double-click the Mia James message header in the Drafts folder to open the email message (Figure 1–54).

Figure 1–54

Other Ways

1. Press and hold or right-click message, and tap or click Open   2. With message selected, press CTRL+O

To Attach a File to an Email Message

To share a file such as a photo, announcement, or business document through email, you attach the file to an email message. Outlook does not have a predefined file size limit for attachments, but an email service provider may restrict the size of incoming attachments or the size of the email mailbox. Very large email attachments may be rejected by the recipient's email service provider and returned to the sender as undeliverable. Consider the size of a file before attaching it to an email message.

Before you send the email message to Mia, you need to attach a file of a flyer describing the informational meeting about the Study Abroad program. The following steps attach a file to an email message. *Why? Attaching a file to an email message provides additional information to a recipient.*

❶

- Tap or click the Attach File button (MESSAGE tab | Include group) to display the Insert File dialog box.

- If necessary, navigate to the folder containing the data files for this chapter (in this case, the Chapter 01 folder in the Outlook folder in the Data Files for Students folder) (Figure 1–55).

❷

- Tap or click Study Abroad (Word document) to select the file to attach (Figure 1–56).

Figure 1–55

Figure 1–56

3

• Tap or click the
Insert button (Insert
File dialog box) to
attach the selected
file to the email
message and close
the Insert File dialog
box (Figure 1–57).

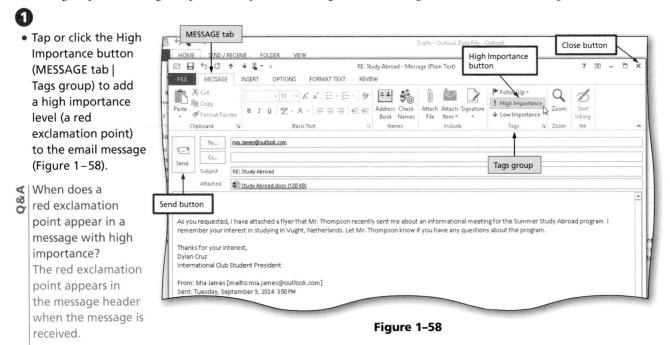

Figure 1–57

Other Ways

1. Tap or click INSERT tab, tap or click Attach File button (INSERT tab | Include group)
2. Drag file to message area
3. Press and hold or right-click file attachment, tap or click Copy, press and hold or right-click message area, tap or click Paste

To Set Message Importance and Send the Message

1 CONFIGURE ACCOUNT OPTIONS | 2 COMPOSE & SEND | 3 VIEW & PRINT | 4 REPLY
5 ATTACH FILE | 6 ORGANIZE MESSAGES

Why? When you have a message that requires urgent attention, you can send the message with a high importance level. Outlook provides the option to assign an **importance level** to a message, which indicates to the recipient the priority level of an email message. The default importance level for all new messages is normal importance, but you can change the importance level to high or low, depending on the priority level of the email message. A message sent with **high importance** displays a red exclamation point in the message header and indicates to the recipient that the message requires a higher priority than other messages he or she might have received. The **low importance** option displays a blue arrow and indicates to the recipient a low priority for the message. The following steps set the high importance option for a single email message and to send the message.

1

• Tap or click the High
Importance button
(MESSAGE tab |
Tags group) to add
a high importance
level (a red
exclamation point)
to the email message
(Figure 1–58).

Q&A When does a
red exclamation
point appear in a
message with high
importance?
The red exclamation
point appears in
the message header
when the message is
received.

How would I set a low importance to an email message?
Tap or click the Low Importance button (MESSAGE tab | Tags group).

Figure 1–58

②

- Tap or click the Send button in the message header to send the email message.

- If necessary, tap or click the Cancel button to close the Microsoft Outlook dialog box and then tap or click the Close button to close the message window.

Q&A A message appeared that states 'No valid email accounts are configured. Add an account to send email'. What does this mean?

The Dylan.pst data file is an Outlook Data File, which cannot send an email message. If you are using the Dylan.pst data file, the sent message remains in the Drafts folder unless you configure an email account. You can set up and configure your own email address in Outlook to send an email message.

What happens to the actual email message after I send it?

After Outlook closes the message window, it stores the email message reply in the Outbox folder while it sends the message to the recipient. You might not see the message in the Outbox because Outlook usually stores it there only briefly. Next, Outlook moves the message to the Sent Items folder. The original message in the message list now shows an envelope icon with a purple arrow to indicate a reply was sent.

Can you place a tag in an email message that requests the recipient to respond within a certain time period?

- If you are sending an email message that requires a timely response, you can click the Follow Up button (MESSAGE tab | Tags group) to insert a flag icon indicating that the recipient should respond within a specified period of time.

- Based on your expected response time, you can select the Follow Up flag for Today, Tomorrow, This Week, Next Week, No Date, or Custom.

CONSIDER THIS

To Forward an Email Message

1 CONFIGURE ACCOUNT OPTIONS | 2 COMPOSE & SEND | 3 VIEW & PRINT | 4 REPLY
5 ATTACH FILE | **6 ORGANIZE MESSAGES**

When you forward an email message, you resend a received or sent email message to another recipient. Ava Gibson, the student webmaster from the International Club, sent Dylan an email message requesting that he forward Mr. Thompson's email message about the Study Abroad program to post on the website. Dylan adds Mr. Thompson as a courtesy copy recipient to make him aware that Ava is receiving a copy of his email message. The following steps forward a previously received email message. **Why?** *Forwarding sends an email to someone who was not on the original recipient list.*

①

- Tap or click the Inbox folder to display the Inbox messages.

- Tap or click the Jacob Thompson message header in the message list to select the email message (Figure 1–59).

Q&A Why do my message headers show dates instead of times?

Outlook shows today's messages with times in the headers and messages prior to today with dates in the headers.

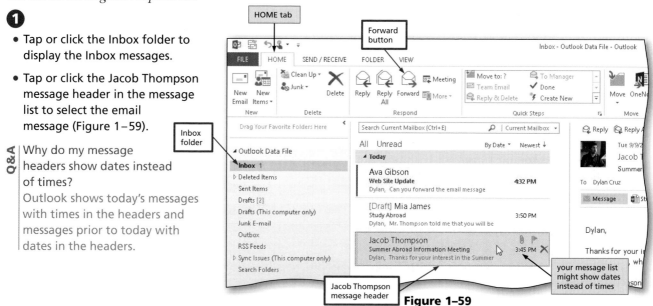

Figure 1–59

2

- Tap or click the Forward button (HOME tab | Respond group) to display the message in the Reading Pane (Figure 1–60).

Figure 1–60

3

- Tap or click the To text box, and then type `ava.gibson@outlook.com` (with no spaces) as the recipient's email address.

- Tap or click the Cc text box, and then type `jacob.thompson@outlook.com` (with no spaces) to send a courtesy copy to inform the original sender that you are forwarding his email message (Figure 1–61).

Experiment

- Tap or click the Bcc button (MESSAGE tab | Show Fields group) to display the Bcc (Blind carbon copy) text box. When you are finished, tap or click the Bcc button (MESSAGE tab | Show Fields group) again to hide the Bcc text box.

Q&A

Why does the original message appear in the message area of the window?

By default, Outlook displays the original message below the new message area for all message replies and forwards.

Figure 1–61

4

- Tap or click the message area above the original message text and then type `Ava,` as the greeting line.

- Press the ENTER key two times to enter a blank line before the message text.

- Type `Per your request, I am forwarding the email and informational meeting flyer from Mr. Thompson about the Study Abroad program.` to enter the message text.

- Press the ENTER key two times to place a blank line between the message text and the signature lines.

- Type `Dylan Cruz` as signature line 1, and then press the ENTER key to move the insertion point to the next line.

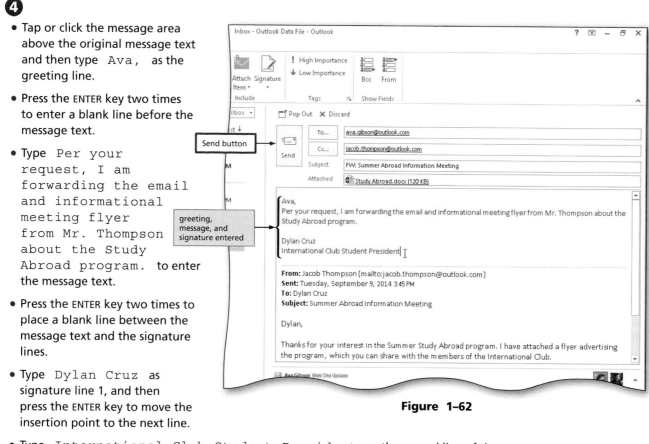

Figure 1–62

- Type `International Club Student President` as the second line of the signature to represent his title (Figure 1–62).

Q&A | Does Outlook automatically forward the attachment to the recipient?
Yes. Outlook automatically adds the attachment to the forwarded message unless you choose to remove it.

5

- Tap or click the Send button in the message header to forward the message.

- If necessary, tap or click the Cancel button to close the Microsoft Outlook dialog box.

Other Ways

1. Press and hold or right-click message header, tap or click Forward   2. Tap or click message header, press CTRL+F

Organizing Messages with Outlook Folders

To keep track of your email messages effectively, Outlook provides a basic set of **folders**, which are containers for storing Outlook items of a specific type, such as messages, appointments, or contacts. Email is supposed to help you be more efficient and save time, but if you do not manage it effectively, you can quickly become overloaded with messages. The Inbox is an email folder that stores your incoming email messages. Instead of leaving all of your incoming messages in the Inbox, you can create additional folders and then move messages to these new folders so you can organize and locate your messages easily.

To Create a New Folder in the Inbox Folder

By creating multiple folders within the Inbox folder, and then organizing messages in the new folders, you can find a specific email message easily. The following steps create a folder within the Inbox folder. *Why? Folders provide an efficient method for organizing your email.*

①

- If necessary, tap or click the Inbox folder to select it.

- Tap or click FOLDER on the ribbon to display the FOLDER tab.

- Tap or click the New Folder button (FOLDER tab | New group) to display the Create New Folder dialog box (Figure 1–63).

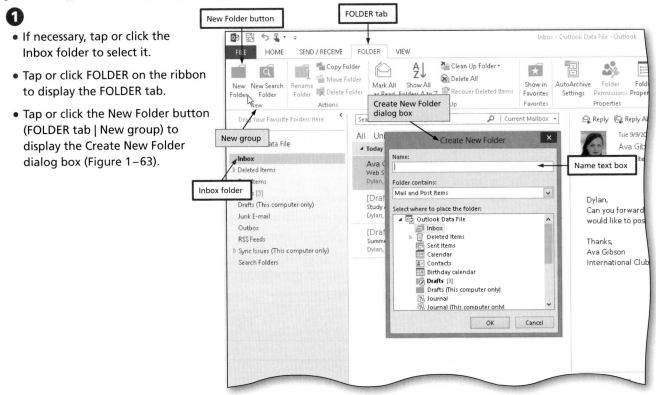

Figure 1–63

②

- Tap or click the Name text box, and then type `Study Abroad` to name the folder within the Inbox folder.

- If necessary, tap or click the Folder contains arrow, and then click 'Mail and Post Items' in the list to place only email messages in the new folder.

- If necessary, tap or click Inbox in the 'Select where to place the folder' list to place the new folder within the Inbox folder (Figure 1–64).

Figure 1–64

❸

- Tap or click the OK button to create the Study Abroad folder and close the Create New Folder dialog box (Figure 1–65).

Q&A

Why is the Study Abroad folder indented below the Inbox folder?
The Study Abroad folder is within the Inbox folder. Outlook indents the folder in the list to indicate that it is within the main folder.

Figure 1–65

Other Ways

1. Tap and hold or right-click folder in Folder pane, tap or click New Folder

To Move an Email Message to a Folder

1 CONFIGURE ACCOUNT OPTIONS | 2 COMPOSE & SEND | 3 VIEW & PRINT | 4 REPLY
5 ATTACH FILE | 6 ORGANIZE MESSAGES

Organizing important email messages about the Summer Study Abroad program into the Study Abroad folder saves time when you search through hundreds or thousands of email messages later. Specifically, you will move the message from Jacob Thompson from the Inbox folder to the Study Abroad folder. In this case, the Inbox folder is called the source folder, and the Study Abroad folder is called the destination folder. A **source folder** is the location of the document or message to be moved or copied. A **destination folder** is the location where you want to move or copy the file or message. The following steps move an email message into a folder. *Why? By organizing your emails into topical folders, you can access your messages easily.*

❶

- In the Inbox folder (source folder), tap or click the Jacob Thompson message header in the Inbox message list to select the email message.

- Tap or click HOME on the ribbon to display the HOME tab.

- Tap or click the Move button (HOME tab | Move group) to display the Move menu (Figure 1–66).

Figure 1–66

4

- In the Inbox folder, tap or click the Ava Gibson message header in the Inbox message list to select the email message.

- Tap or click Study Abroad in the Quick Steps gallery (HOME tab | Quick Steps group) to move the message to the Study Abroad folder.

- In the Navigation Pane, tap or click the Study Abroad folder to display its contents (Figure 1–71).

Figure 1–71

To Delete an Email Message

1 CONFIGURE ACCOUNT OPTIONS | 2 COMPOSE & SEND | 3 VIEW & PRINT | 4 REPLY
5 ATTACH FILE | 6 ORGANIZE MESSAGES

When you delete a message from a folder, Outlook removes the message from the folder and moves it to the Deleted Items folder. For example, Dylan no longer needs to keep the email message from Mia James in the Inbox and has decided to delete it. The following steps delete an email message. *Why? Delete messages you no longer need so you do not exceed the limits of your mailbox.*

1

- Tap or click the Inbox folder in the Navigation Pane to select the Inbox folder.

- Point to the Mia James message header in the message list to display the Delete icon (Figure 1–72).

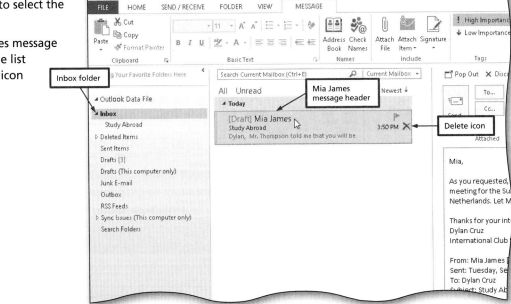

Figure 1–72

2

- Tap or click the Delete icon on the message header to move the email message from the Inbox folder to the Deleted Items folder.

- Tap or click the Deleted Items folder in the Navigation Pane to verify the location of the deleted message and display the Deleted Items message list in the message pane, which shows all deleted email messages (Figure 1–73).

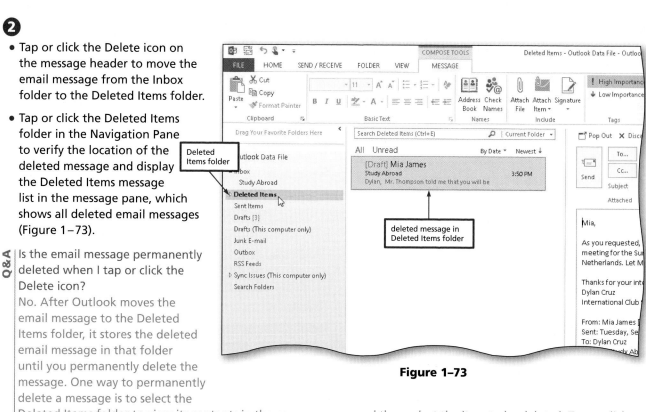

Figure 1–73

Q&A

Is the email message permanently deleted when I tap or click the Delete icon?

No. After Outlook moves the email message to the Deleted Items folder, it stores the deleted email message in that folder until you permanently delete the message. One way to permanently delete a message is to select the Deleted Items folder to view its contents in the message pane and then select the item to be deleted. Tap or click the Delete icon on the message header and then tap or click the Yes button in the Microsoft Outlook dialog box to permanently delete the selected item from Outlook.

Other Ways

1. Drag selected email message to Deleted Items folder   2. Tap or click email message, press DELETE   3. Tap or click email message, press CTRL+D

Working with the Mailbox

The system administrator who manages a company's or school's email system may set limits for the size of the Outlook mailbox due to limited space on the server. Some email service providers may not deliver new mail to a mailbox that exceeds the limit set by the system administrator. You can determine the total size of your mailbox and other details about individual folders.

BTW

Outlook Help

At any time while using Outlook, you can find answers to questions and display information about various topics through Outlook Help. Used properly, this form of assistance can increase your productivity and reduce your frustrations by minimizing the time you spend learning how to use Outlook. For instruction about Outlook Help and exercises that will help you gain confidence in using it, read the Office and Windows chapter at the beginning of this book.

To View Mailbox Size

1 CONFIGURE ACCOUNT OPTIONS | 2 COMPOSE & SEND | 3 VIEW & PRINT | 4 REPLY
5 ATTACH FILE | 6 ORGANIZE MESSAGES

The following steps view the amount of space available in the mailbox. *Why? You can determine if you are close to your mailbox size limit.*

1

- Tap or click Outlook Data File in the Navigation Pane to select the mailbox.

- Tap or click FOLDER on the ribbon to display the FOLDER tab (Figure 1–74).

Q&A What is the Outlook Data File in the Navigation Pane?
In this case, the Outlook Data File is the mailbox of Dylan Cruz.

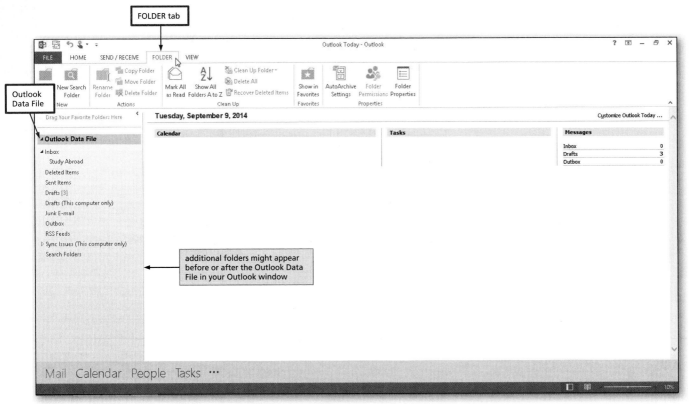

Figure 1–74

2

- Tap or click the Folder Properties button (FOLDER tab | Properties group) to display the Properties dialog box for the mailbox (Figure 1–75).

Figure 1–75

❸

- Tap or click the Folder Size button (mailbox Properties dialog box) to display the Folder Size dialog box (Figure 1–76).

❹

- After viewing the folder sizes, tap or click the Close button to close the Folder Size dialog box.

- Tap or click the OK button to close the mailbox Properties dialog box.

Figure 1–76

To Exit Outlook

This project now is complete. The following steps exit Outlook. For a detailed example of the procedure summarized below, refer to the Office and Windows chapter at the beginning of this book.

❶ If you have an email message open, tap or click the Close button on the right side of the title bar to close the message window.

❷ Tap or click the Close button on the right side of the title bar to exit Outlook.

BTW

Quick Reference
For a table that lists how to complete the tasks covered in this book using touch gestures, the mouse, ribbon, shortcut menu, and keyboard, see the Quick Reference Summary at the back of this book, or visit the Quick Reference resource on the Student Companion Site located on www.cengagebrain.com. For detailed instructions about accessing available resources, visit www.cengage.com/ct/studentdownload or contact your instructor for information about accessing the required files.

Chapter Summary

In this chapter, you learned how to use Outlook to set up your email account. You discovered how to compose, format, send, open, print, reply to, delete, save, and forward email messages. You viewed and saved file attachments and attached a file to an email message. You learned how to add a courtesy copy to an email message and set the sensitivity and importance of email messages. Finally, you created a folder in the Inbox and moved an email message to the new folder. The items listed below include all the new Outlook skills you have learned in this chapter, with the tasks grouped by activity.

Set Up Outlook
Change the Navigation Bar Options (OUT 6)
Open an Outlook Data File (OUT 8)
Set Language Preferences (OUT 9)
Set the Sensitivity Level for All New Messages (OUT 10)

Compose and Send Email Messages
Compose an Email Message (OUT 12)
Apply a Theme (OUT 15)
Send an Email Message (OUT 16)

Work with Incoming Messages
View an Email Message in the Reading Pane (OUT 18)
Open an Email Message in a Window (OUT 19)
Preview and Save an Attachment (OUT 20)
Open an Attachment (OUT 22)
Print an Email Message (OUT 22)
Change the View of the People Pane (OUT 24)
Reposition the Reading Pane (OUT 26)

Respond to Messages
Reply to an Email Message (OUT 28)
Change the Message Format (OUT 31)
Check the Spelling of a Correctly Typed Word (OUT 32)
Check the Spelling of Misspelled Text (OUT 34)
Save and Close an Email Message without Sending It (OUT 35)
Open a Saved Email Message (OUT 36)
Attach a File to an Email Message (OUT 37)
Set Message Importance and Send the Message (OUT 38)
Forward an Email Message (OUT 39)

Organize Messages with Outlook Folders
Create a New Folder in the Inbox Folder (OUT 42)
Move an Email Message to a Folder (OUT 43)
Move an Email Message Using Quick Steps (OUT 44)
Delete an Email Message (OUT 46)
View Mailbox Size (OUT 47)

Consider This: Plan Ahead

What decisions will you need to make when composing and responding to email messages, attaching files, and organizing your Outlook folders in the future?

A. Set Up Outlook:

    1. Determine the language preferences and sensitivity level.

    2. Decide on the sensitivity level.

B. Compose the Email Message:

    1. Plan the content of your email message based on a formal or informal tone.

    2. Select an appropriate theme.

C. Open Incoming Email Messages:

    1. Determine your preference for displaying messages.

    2. Save the attachment to the appropriate folder.

D. Respond to Messages:

    1. Plan your response to the incoming message.

    2. Correct errors and revise as necessary.

    3. Establish which file you will attach to your email message.

    4. Determine the importance level of the message.

E. Organize Your Outlook Folders:

    1. Establish your folder names.

    2. Plan where each email message should be stored.

How should you submit solutions to questions in the assignments identified with a ✹ symbol?

Every assignment in this book contains one or more questions identified with a ✹ symbol. These questions require you to think beyond the assigned file. Present your solutions to the questions in the format required by your instructor. Possible formats may include one or more of these options: write the answer; create a document that contains the answer; present your answer to the class; discuss your answer in a group; record the answer as audio or video using a webcam, smartphone, or portable media player; or post answers on a blog, wiki, or website.

BTW

Certification

The Microsoft Office Specialist (MOS) program provides an opportunity for you to obtain a valuable industry credential — proof that you have the Outlook 2013 skills required by employers. For more information, visit the Certification resource on the Student Companion Site located on www.cengagebrain.com. For detailed instructions about accessing available resources, visit www.cengage.com/ct/studentdownload or contact your instructor for information about accessing the required files.

Apply Your Knowledge

Reinforce the skills and apply the concepts you learned in this chapter.

Creating an Email with an Attachment

Note: To complete this assignment, you will be required to use the Data Files for Students. Visit www.cengage.com/ct/studentdownload for detailed instructions or contact your instructor for information about accessing the required files.

Instructions: You are to send an email message addressed to the director of the Chamber of Commerce, who is assisting in marketing an Earth Day Run. You also attach a file named Apply 1-1 Earth Day Flyer from the Data Files for Students.

Perform the following tasks:

1. Run Outlook.

2. Compose a new email message addressed to your instructor and add your own email address as a courtesy copy address.

3. Type `Earth Day Run` as the subject of the email message.

4. Type `Greetings,` as the greeting line. Check spelling as you type.

5. Enter the text shown in Figure 1–77 for the message text.

6. Type `Thanks,` as the closing line.

7. Enter your name as the first signature line.

8. Type `Ecology Club Publicity Manager` as the second signature line.

9. If requested by your instructor, type your personal cell phone number as the third signature line.

10. Attach the Apply 1-1 Earth Day Flyer file to the email message.

11. Tap or click the FILE tab, and then tap or click Save As. Navigate to the Outlook folder in the Documents library, and then save the message using the file name Apply 1-1 Earth Run.

12. Submit the email message in the format specified by your instructor.

13. Exit Outlook.

14. ✸ The communication in the email message to the Chamber of Commerce has a formal tone. What considerations should be made when composing a formal email message to a business or organization?

Figure 1–77

Extend Your Knowledge

Extend the skills you learned in this chapter and experiment with new skills. You will use Help to complete the assignment.

Organizing Email Messages

Note: To complete this assignment, you will be required to use the Data Files for Students. Visit www.cengage.com/ct/studentdownload for detailed instructions or contact your instructor for information about accessing the required files.

Instructions: You are organizing a river rafting trip for you and your friends. In the Extend 1-1.pst mailbox file, you will create two folders, add a folder in the Favorites section, and then move messages into the appropriate folders. You also will apply a follow-up flag for the messages in one of the folders. Use Outlook Help to learn about how to duplicate a folder in the Favorites section, how to add a flag to a message for follow-up, and how to create an Outlook Data File (.pst file).

Perform the following tasks:

1. Run Outlook.

2. Open the Outlook Data File Extend 1-1.pst mailbox file.

3. Create two new folders within the Inbox folder. Name the first folder River Rafting and the second folder Camping. Move the messages into the appropriate folders. Make sure that only mail items are contained in the new folders.

4. The Favorites section is at the top of the Folder Pane on the left. Display a duplicate of the River Rafting folder in the Favorites section.

5. To the message regarding the Riverfront Campground, assign a flag for follow-up for tomorrow.

6. Based on the message headers and content of the email messages in the Extend 1-1 mailbox, move each message to the appropriate folders you created. Figure 1–78 shows the mailbox with the messages moved to the new folders.

7. Export the Inbox mailbox to an Outlook Data File (.pst). Navigate to the Outlook folder in the Documents library, save the document using the file name Extend 1-1 River Rafting.pst, and then submit it in the format specified by your instructor.

8. Exit Outlook.

9. ✳ Saving your mailbox as a .pst file provides a backup copy of your email messages to submit to your instructor. What are other reasons for saving your mailbox as a .pst file?

Figure 1–78

Analyze, Correct, Improve

Analyze an email message, correct all errors, and improve the design.

Correcting Errors and Changing the Format of an Email Message

Note: To complete this assignment, you will be required to use the Data Files for Students. Visit www.cengage.com/ct/studentdownload for detailed instructions or contact your instructor for information about accessing the required files.

Instructions: In a folder window, double-tap or double-click the message file, Analyze 1-1, to open the file from the Data Files for Students. Outlook starts and opens the message. The lawn care business referral message contains spelling errors. If red wavy lines do not appear below some words, tap or click at the end of the message and then press the SPACEBAR. The email message was sent using the HTML message format. If you received the message as Plain Text, change the message format to HTML.

Perform the following tasks:

1. Correct Recheck the spelling and grammar errors by tapping or clicking the FILE tab on the ribbon to open the Backstage view, and then tap or click Options to display the Outlook Options dialog box. Click the Mail category, if necessary. In the Compose messages section, tap or click the Editor Options button to display the Editor Options dialog box. Tap or click Proofing in the left pane (Editor Options dialog box). In the 'When correcting spelling in Outlook' section, ensure the 'Check spelling as you type' check box contains a check mark. Tap or click the Recheck E-mail button and then tap or click Yes. Tap or click the OK button two times. Correct the errors in the message. Change the email address of the recipient and then change the greeting to address the new recipient. The corrected message is displayed in Figure 1–79.

2. Improve Change the message importance to High Importance. If requested by your instructor, change the name in signature line 1 to the name of your father or uncle. Navigate to the Outlook folder in the Documents library, save the document using the file name Analyze 1-1 Lawn Care Referrals, and then submit it in the format specified by your instructor.

3. ✺ Think about the reason you use email communication. In the case of the lawn care referral message, why would you use email instead of a phone call, Facebook posting, Twitter message, or text message?

Figure 1–79

In the Labs

Use the guidelines, concepts, and skills presented in this chapter to increase your knowledge of Outlook. Labs 1 and 2, which increase in difficulty, require you to create solutions based on what you learned in the chapter; Lab 3 requires you to create a solution, which uses cloud and web technologies, by learning and investigating on your own from general guidance.

Lab 1: Composing an Email Message with an Attachment

Note: To complete this assignment, you will be required to use the Data Files for Students. Visit www.cengage.com/ct/studentdownload for detailed instructions or contact your instructor for information about accessing the required files.

Problem: Your grandparents would like you to share photos from your recent trip to Yellowstone National Park using email, because they are not on Facebook. Compose an email message to your grandparents as shown in Figure 1–80 with the three picture attachments of Yellowstone.

Instructions: Perform the following tasks:

1. Compose a new email message. Address the message to yourself with a courtesy copy to your instructor.

2. Enter the subject, message text, and signature shown in Figure 1–80. Insert blank lines where they are shown in the figure. If Outlook flags any misspelled words as you type, check their spelling and correct them.

3. Change the theme of the email message to the Wisp theme.

4. If requested by your instructor, change the city and state from Goldstream, CA, to the city and state of your birth. Also change the signature to your name.

5. Attach the three image files named Lab 1-1 Park1, Lab 1-1 Park2, and Lab 1-1 Park3 from the Data Files for Students to the email message.

6. Send the email message.

7. When you receive the message, open it, navigate to the Outlook folder in the Documents library, and then save the message using the file name Lab 1-1 Yellowstone. Submit the file in the format specified by your instructor.

8. ✳ Using one of your own email service providers, determine the maximum allowed mailbox size. Report the name of your email service provider, the maximum size, and whether you feel that is enough.

Figure 1–80

Lab 2: Composing and Replying to an Email Message

Note: To complete this assignment, you will be required to use the Data Files for Students. Visit www.cengage.com/ct/studentdownload for detailed instructions or contact your instructor for information about accessing the required files.

Problem: You recently purchased headphones online from Rocktown Electronics. The headphones were not functioning properly and you would like to return them. Rocktown Electronics provided an email on their website. You need to send your electronic Excel receipt to request a full refund. First, you compose the email message shown in Figure 1–81a, and then you attach a file. Rocktown Electronics responds to your email as shown in Figure 1–81b.

Figure 1–81a

Instructions: Perform the following tasks:

1. Create a new email message. Address the message to your instructor with a courtesy copy to yourself.

2. Enter the subject, message text, and signature shown in Figure 1–81a. Check spelling and grammar.

3. If requested by your instructor, change the music group Nine Volt in the email message to your favorite musical artist/group.

4. Change the theme of the email message to the Ion theme.

5. Attach the Lab 1-2 Rocktown Electronics Receipt file (Excel file), from the Data Files for Students, to the email message.

6. Send the email message with high importance and use the HTML format for the message.

7. When you receive the email message, move it to a new folder in your Inbox named Purchases.

8. Open the message in the Purchases folder, and then compose the reply. Figure 1–81b shows the reply from Rocktown Electronics. Reply using the text in the email message shown in Figure 1–81b. If Outlook flags any misspelled words as you type, check their spelling and correct them.

9. If necessary, change the format of the email message to Plain Text, and then send the message to yourself.

10. When you receive the RE: Headphone Issue message, move it to the Purchases folder in your Inbox folder.

11. Navigate to the Outlook folder in the Documents library, and then save the message with the file name Lab 1-2 Headphones. Submit the file in the format specified by your instructor.

12. ✲ Some retail websites do not include a phone number. Why do you think that these business retail sites only include an email address for correspondence?

Continued >

Figure 1–81b

Lab 3: Expand Your World: Cloud and Web Technologies
Opening an Outlook.com Web-Based Email in the Outlook Client

Note: To complete this assignment, you will be required to use the Data Files for Students. Visit www.cengage.com/ct/studentdownload for detailed instructions or contact your instructor for information about accessing the required files.

Problem: In your Health class, you are presenting the topic, *Avoid Texting While Driving*. Using Outlook, you compose an email message shown in Figure 1–82 and include a PowerPoint file attachment. Save the attachment from your outlook.com account to your SkyDrive and edit the PowerPoint slides as a web app. Share the PowerPoint slides by providing a link to your SkyDrive. Sharing files in the cloud as links can eliminate large attachments and saves email storage space.

Instructions: Perform the following tasks:

1. If necessary, create a Microsoft account at outlook.com.

2. Compose a new email message from the client program, Outlook (not outlook.com). Address the email message to your Microsoft account with the message text shown in Figure 1–82. Replace the signature with your name and school name.

Figure 1–82

3. Attach the Lab 1-3 Avoid Texting While Driving file (PowerPoint file) from the Data Files for Students to the email message.

4. Send the email message with high importance.

5. Open your Microsoft account at outlook.com. Open the email message that you sent from Outlook, and then tap or click View online to view the PowerPoint file attachment.

6. Tap or click Edit in Browser to edit the PowerPoint presentation in the Microsoft PowerPoint web app.

7. If requested by your instructor, change the name on the first slide to your name on the first line and the name of your hometown on the second line.

8. Add a fourth slide to the PowerPoint presentation with a statistic about the dangers of texting while driving. (*Hint:* Research this statistic on the web.)

9. Tap or click the INSERT tab, and then add a clip art image about texting to the fourth slide.

10. Tap or click the FILE tab, and then tap or click Share to share the PowerPoint file.

11. Tap or click 'Share with other people', and then type your instructor's email address and a short message describing how sharing a file by sending a link to your SkyDrive can be easier than sending an attachment. Include your name at the end of the message.

12. Tap or click the Share button to send the shared link of the completed PowerPoint file to your instructor.

13. Exit the PowerPoint web app, and then exit Outlook.

14. ✺ In this lab, you sent an email from the Outlook client to your web-based email service provider at outlook.com. What are the advantages of using a Microsoft account with Outlook on your personal computer and checking the same email address at outlook.com when you are on a public computer?

✺ Consider This: Your Turn

Apply your creative thinking and problem solving skills to design and implement a solution.

1: Composing an Email Message about your Favorite Music and Attaching a File
Personal

Part 1:   You are taking a Music Appreciation class. During the first class, your instructor requests that you send an email message with your favorite song as an attachment. The email message should be addressed to yourself and your instructor. Insert an appropriate subject line based on the content of your message. Explain why the attached song is your favorite in a paragraph within the email message. Apply a theme other than the Office theme. You can use your own digital music file as an attachment. Use the concepts and techniques presented in this chapter to create this email message. Be sure to check spelling and grammar before you send the message. Submit your assignment in the format specified by your instructor.

Part 2:   ✺ You made several decisions while creating the email message in this assignment. When you decide on the subject of an email message, what considerations should you make? Why is it important that the email subject be eye-catching and informative? Why should you not use the following subject lines: FYI, Hi, or Open This?

2: Composing an Email Message in Response to a Job Opening and Attaching a File
Professional

Note: To complete this assignment, you will be required to use the Data Files for Students. Visit www.cengage.com/ct/studentdownload for detailed instructions or contact your instructor for information about accessing the required files.

Continued >

STUDENT ASSIGNMENTS

Consider This: Your Turn *continued*

Part 1: On the job search section of the LinkedIn website, you find a job listing in your dream city and in your field of study. Compose a professional email message that requests more information about the position. The email message should be addressed to yourself and your instructor. Insert an appropriate subject line based on the content of your message. Be sure to include your qualifications and the name of the position. Apply a theme other than the Office theme. Set the priority level of this email message as high importance. Use the concepts and techniques presented in this chapter to create the email message. Attach a resume to the message. The Data Files for Students contain a resume named Consider This Your Turn 1-2 Sample Resume (Word document) or you can use your own resume if requested by your instructor. Be sure to check spelling and grammar before you send the message. Submit your assignment in the format specified by your instructor.

Part 2: ✵ You made several decisions while creating the email message in this assignment. When composing a greeting line to a business to which you are applying, you may want to avoid "To Whom it May Concern" because it sounds very impersonal. What other greeting lines could you use, if you do not know a specific person's name? How can you locate the contact person's name at a business?

3: Sharing Your Research Using an Email Message
Research and Collaboration

Part 1: You have been asked at your new job to speak to your colleagues about the topic, *Email Etiquette at Work*. Handling email professionally provides an all-important competitive edge. Find a partner for this assignment. Each of you should choose which email etiquette topic to research. Share your research by composing an email message that contains your talking points for your presentation. Include the websites you used to cite your research properly. The email message should be addressed to yourself and your partner with a Cc to your instructor. Use the concepts and techniques presented in this chapter to create the email message. Submit your assignment in the format specified by your instructor.

Part 2: ✵ When you represent your business or company through email communication, you convey a positive or negative image to your recipient. What are some common mistakes in professional email messages that convey a poor image of a business? Could a company be liable for what is shared through email? If so, how?

Learn Online

Reinforce what you learned in this chapter with games, exercises, training, and many other online activities and resources.

Student Companion Site Reinforce chapter terms and concepts using review questions, flash cards, practice tests, and interactive learning games, such as a crossword puzzle. These and other online activities and resources are available at no additional cost on www.cengagebrain.com. Visit www.cengage.com/ct/studentdownload for detailed instructions about accessing the resources available at the Student Companion Site.

2 | Managing Calendars with Outlook

Objectives

You will have mastered the material in this chapter when you can:

- Describe the components of the Outlook Calendar
- Add a personal calendar to Outlook
- Add a city to the calendar Weather Bar list
- Navigate the calendar using the Date Navigator
- Display the calendar in various views
- Add national holidays to the default calendar
- Enter, save, move, edit, and delete appointments and events
- Organize your calendar with color categories

- Set the status of and a reminder for an appointment
- Import an iCalendar and view it in overlay mode
- Schedule and modify events
- Schedule meetings
- Respond to meeting requests
- Peek at a calendar
- Print a calendar
- Save and share a calendar

2 | Managing Calendars with Outlook

This introductory chapter covers features and functions common to managing calendars in Outlook 2013.

Roadmap

In this chapter, you will learn how to perform basic calendar tasks. The following roadmap identifies general activities you will perform as you progress through this chapter:

1. CONFIGURE the CALENDAR OPTIONS
2. CREATE AND MANIPULATE APPOINTMENTS
3. SCHEDULE EVENTS
4. SCHEDULE MEETINGS
5. PRINT a CALENDAR
6. SAVE AND SHARE a CALENDAR

At the beginning of step instructions throughout the chapter, you will see an abbreviated form of this roadmap. The abbreviated roadmap uses colors to indicate chapter progress: gray means the chapter is beyond that activity, blue means the task being shown is covered in that activity, and black means that activity is yet to be covered. For example, the following abbreviated roadmap indicates the chapter would be showing a task in the Schedule Meetings activity.

1 CONFIGURE CALENDAR OPTIONS | 2 CREATE & MANIPULATE APPOINTMENTS | 3 SCHEDULE EVENTS

4 SCHEDULE MEETINGS | 5 PRINT CALENDAR | 6 SAVE & SHARE CALENDAR

Use the abbreviated roadmap as a progress guide while you read or step through the instructions in this chapter.

Introduction to the Outlook Calendar

Plan your day, keep track of your deadlines, and increase your daily productivity. Whether you are a student, club organizer, or business professional, you can take advantage of the Outlook Calendar to schedule and manage appointments, events, and meetings. In particular, you can use Calendar to keep track of your class schedule and appointments and to schedule meetings. If you are traveling and do not have electronic access to your calendar, you can print a copy to keep with you. You can use Outlook to view a daily, weekly, or monthly calendar.

In addition to using Calendar in your academic or professional life, you will find it helpful for scheduling personal time. Most people have multiple appointments to keep each day, week, or month. Calendar can organize activity-related information in a structured, readable manner. You can create a calendar folder for a specific project and share it with your friends and co-workers.

Project — Appointments, Events, and Meetings in Calendar

By creating a daily time management schedule, you can stay organized and reduce your stress level. Managing your schedule using a calendar can increase productivity while maximizing free time. Outlook is the perfect tool to maintain both a professional and a personal schedule. The **Calendar** is the Outlook folder that contains your personal schedule of appointments, events, and meetings. In this project, you use the basic features of Calendar to create a calendar for appointments, classes, work schedules, and meetings for a student (Figure 2–1).

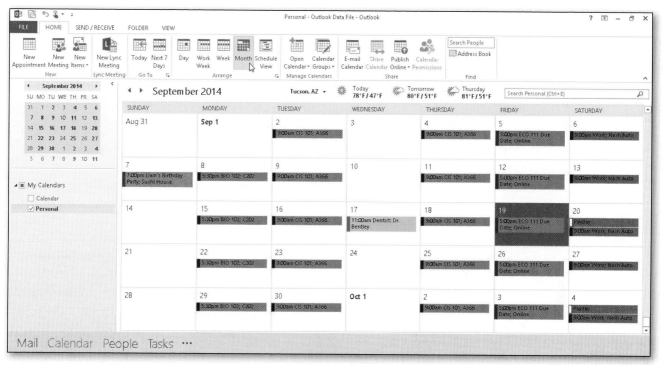

Figure 2–1

People use a calendar to keep track of their schedule and to organize and manage their time. For students, a class list with room numbers and class times would be a good start toward managing their school schedule. For business professionals, the calendar is a dynamic tool that requires frequent updating to keep track of appointments and meetings. You also may want to keep track of personal items, such as doctor appointments, birthdays, and family gatherings.

Configuring the Outlook Calendar

When you start Outlook, the Mail view appears. The Navigation Bar displays four views — Mail, Calendar, People, and Tasks. You changed the Navigation Bar icons to text in Chapter 1. By selecting Calendar, you can create a customized calendar to assist in scheduling your day, week, and month. Before scheduling your first calendar appointment, you can add a personal calendar and customize your settings to fit the way you work. Each day as you check your calendar for the day's events, the Weather Bar displays your local weather so you can plan whether you need an umbrella or not. By adding national holidays to your Outlook calendar, you can make sure these dates are prominent in your calendar.

What advantages does a digital calendar like Outlook provide instead of using a paper planner or wall calendar?

A digital calendar provides access from any location by synching your computer or smartphone with the cloud to view your appointments and meetings. You can view your schedule within an email meeting invitation. You can view more than one calendar at a time, share others' calendars, and overlay calendars to plan a meeting date with colleagues.

For an introduction to Windows 8 and instruction about how to perform basic Windows 8 tasks, read the Office 2013 and Windows 8 chapter at the beginning of this book, where you can learn how to resize windows, change screen resolution, create folders, move and rename files, use Windows Help, and much more.

Calendar Window

The Calendar - Outlook Data File - Microsoft Outlook window shown in Figure 2–2 includes a variety of features to help you work efficiently. It contains many elements similar to the windows in other Office programs, as well as some that are unique to Outlook. The main elements of the Calendar window are the Navigation Pane and the appointment area.

The Navigation Pane includes two panes: the Date Navigator and the My Calendars pane. The **Date Navigator** includes the present month's calendar in Figure 2–2. The calendar displays the current month with a blue box around the current date, scroll arrows to advance from one month to another, and any date on which an item is scheduled in bold. The **My Calendars pane** includes a list of available calendars where you can view a single calendar or view additional calendars side by side. The **appointment area** contains a date banner and a Weather Bar that displays today's weather in the selected city. The appointment area displays one-hour time slots split in half hours by default when viewing Calendar in Day, Work Week, or Week view and is not available in Month view.

Figure 2–2

Calendar Items

An **item** is any element in Outlook that contains information. Examples of calendar items include appointments, events, and meetings. All calendar items start as an appointment. Outlook defines an **appointment**, such as a doctor's appointment, as an activity that does not involve other people or resources, such as conference rooms. Outlook defines an **event**, such as a seminar or vacation, as an activity that occurs at least once and lasts 24 hours or longer. An appointment becomes an event when you schedule it for the entire day. An annual event, such as a birthday, anniversary, or holiday, occurs yearly on a specific date. Events do not occupy time slots in the appointment area and, instead, are displayed in a banner below the day heading when viewing the calendar in Day, Work Week, or Week view. An appointment becomes a **meeting** when people and other resources, such as meeting rooms, are invited.

When you create items on your calendar, it is helpful to show your time using the appointment status information. You set the appointment status for a calendar item using the Show As button, which provides four options for showing your time on the calendar: Free, Tentative, Busy, and Out of Office. For example, if you are studying or working on a project, you might show your time as busy because you are unable to perform other tasks at the same time. On the other hand, a dental appointment or a class would show your time as Out of Office because you need to leave your home or office to attend. Table 2–1 describes the items you can schedule on your calendar and the appointment status option associated with each item. Each calendar item also can be one-time or recurring.

Table 2–1 Calendar Items		
Calendar Item	**Description**	**Show as Default**
One-time appointment	Default calendar item, involves only your schedule and does not invite other attendees or require resources such as a conference room	Busy
Recurring appointment	Occurs at regular intervals, such as weekly, biweekly, monthly, or bimonthly	Busy
One-time event	Occurs at least once and lasts 24 hours or longer, such as a vacation or conference	Free
Recurring event	Occurs at regular intervals, such as weekly, biweekly, monthly, or bimonthly, such as holidays	Free
One-time meeting	Includes people and other resources, such as meeting rooms	Busy
Recurring meeting	Occurs at regular intervals, such as weekly, biweekly, monthly, or bimonthly, such as staff meetings or department meetings	Busy

© 2014 Cengage Learning

To Run Outlook

If you are using a computer to step through the project in this chapter and you want your screens to match the figures in this book, you should change your screen's resolution to 1366 × 768. For information about how to change a computer's resolution, refer to the Office and Windows chapter at the beginning of this book.

The following steps, which assume Windows 8 is running, use the Start screen or search box to run Outlook based on a typical installation. You may need to ask your instructor how to run Outlook on your computer. For a detailed example of the procedure summarized below, refer to the Office and Windows chapter.

For an introduction to Office and instruction about how to perform basic tasks in Office apps, read the Office and Windows chapter at the beginning of this book, where you can learn how to run an application, use the ribbon, save a file, open a file, exit an application, use Help, and much more.

One of the few differences between Windows 7 and Windows 8 occurs in the steps to run Outlook. If you are using Windows 7, click the Start button, type `Outlook` in the `Search programs and files' box, click Outlook 2013, and then, if necessary, maximize the Outlook window. For detailed steps to run Outlook in Windows 7, refer to the Office and Windows chapter at the beginning of this book. For a summary of the steps, refer to the Quick Reference located in the back of this book.

1 Scroll the Start screen for an Outlook tile. If your Start screen contains an Outlook tile, tap or click it to run Outlook and then proceed to Step 5; if the Start screen does not contain the Outlook tile, proceed to the next step to search for the Outlook app.

2 Swipe in from the right edge of the screen or point to the upper-right corner of the screen to display the Charms bar, and then tap or click the Search charm on the Charms bar to display the Search menu.

3 Type `Outlook` as the search text in the Search box and watch the search results appear in the Apps list.

4 Tap or click Outlook 2013 in the search results to run Outlook.

5 If the Outlook window is not maximized, tap or click the Maximize button on its title bar to maximize the window.

To Create a Personal Calendar Folder

1 CONFIGURE CALENDAR OPTIONS | 2 CREATE & MANIPULATE APPOINTMENTS | 3 SCHEDULE EVENTS
4 SCHEDULE MEETINGS | 5 PRINT CALENDAR | 6 SAVE & SHARE CALENDAR

When you schedule an appointment, Outlook adds the appointment to the Calendar folder by default. If you are creating personal, academic, and business items, you may want to create a separate calendar for each group. Users often create multiple calendars to keep personal items separate from academic or business items. As in other Outlook folders, such as the Inbox, you can create multiple folders within the Calendar folder that each contain one or more calendars. The following steps create a calendar to store your personal and school-related information separate from your default Calendar within the same calendar group. *Why? In certain situations, you may need to keep more than one calendar, such as one for business items and another for personal items.*

1
- Tap or click Calendar on the Navigation Bar to display the Outlook Calendar.
- Tap or click FOLDER on the ribbon to display the FOLDER tab (Figure 2–3).

BTW

The Ribbon and Screen Resolution
Outlook may change how the groups and buttons within the groups appear on the ribbon, depending on the computer's screen resolution. Thus, your ribbon may look different from the ones in this book if you are using a screen resolution other than 1366 × 768.

Figure 2–3

2

- Tap or click the New Calendar button (FOLDER tab | New group) to display the Create New Folder dialog box.

- Type `Personal` in the Name text box (Create New Folder dialog box) to enter a name for the new folder.

- If necessary, tap or click the Folder contains arrow button to display a list of items the folder will contain.

- Tap or click Calendar Items to specify what the folder will contain.

- If necessary, tap or click Calendar in the 'Select where to place the folder' list to specify where the folder will be stored (Figure 2–4).

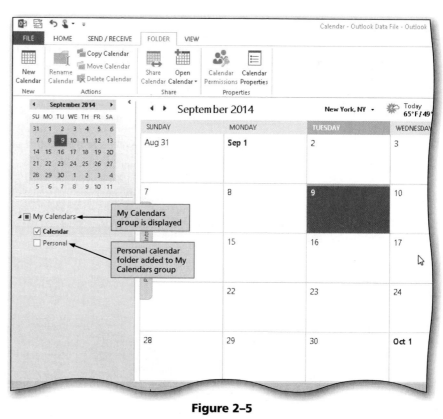

Figure 2–4

3

- Tap or click the OK button to close the Create New Folder dialog box and add the new folder to the My Calendars group (Figure 2–5).

Q&A | Why is the Personal calendar not displayed in the Outlook window? Outlook does not automatically display the newly created calendar until you select it.

Figure 2–5

BTW
Q&As
For a complete list of the Q&As found in many of the step-by-step sequences in this book, visit the Q&A resource on the Student Companion Site located on www.cengagebrain.com. For detailed instructions about accessing available resources, visit www.cengage.com/ct/studentdownload or contact your instructor for information about accessing the required files.

4

- In the My Calendars pane, tap or click Personal to insert a check mark in the check box, so that both the default Calendar and the Personal calendars are selected and displayed in the appointment area of the Outlook window (Figure 2–6).

◀ | Why is the default calendar displayed in a different color from the Personal calendar?
Q&A | Outlook automatically assigns a different color to each new calendar you create to make it easier to distinguish one calendar from the other. Your calendar colors might be different from those shown in Figure 2–6.

Can I select a color for the calendar?
Yes. Tap or click the VIEW tab, tap or click the Color button (VIEW tab | Color group), and then select a color from the Color gallery.

Figure 2–6

5

- Tap or click Calendar in the My Calendars pane to remove the check mark from the Calendar check box so that the default calendar no longer is displayed in the appointment area (Figure 2–7).

◀ | Why does my view look different from what is shown?
Q&A | Figure 2–7 shows Month view, which is the default view for Calendar. If this is not the current view, tap or click the Month button (HOME tab | Arrange group).

What is the purpose of the colored tabs on each side of the appointment area?
The tabs provide navigation to the previous and next appointments.

Figure 2–7

Other Ways

1. Press CTRL+SHIFT+E

To Add a City to the Calendar Weather Bar

Outlook provides a Weather Bar so you can view the current three-day weather forecast when you open the calendar. By default, New York, NY is displayed. You can customize the Weather Bar to display weather symbols such as cloud or snow symbols and today's high and low temperature for your local weather conditions. When you tap or click the forecast, further details appear such as the wind condition, humidity level, precipitation, and a link to a detailed weather forecast online. *Why? Each morning as you view your schedule, the Weather Bar informs you about the day's weather so you can plan your day accordingly.* The following steps add a city to the Personal calendar Weather Bar to display the current forecast.

1

- Tap or click the arrow button to the right of the current city in the Weather Bar to display the Add Location option (Figure 2–8).

Figure 2–8

2

- Tap or click Add Location to display a search text box.

- Type `Tucson` and then press the ENTER key to search for the city location (Figure 2–9).

Q&A Can I search for a city using a postal code?

Yes. Type the postal code to search for the location in the Weather Bar search text box.

Figure 2–9

❸

- Tap or click Tucson, AZ to select the desired location's three-day forecast in the Weather Bar.

- If requested by your instructor, replace Tucson, AZ with your hometown in the Weather Bar (Figure 2–10).

Q&A Why does my Weather Bar display the message 'Weather service is not available'?
Most likely, you are not connected to the Internet. You must have Internet connectivity to display the weather forecast.

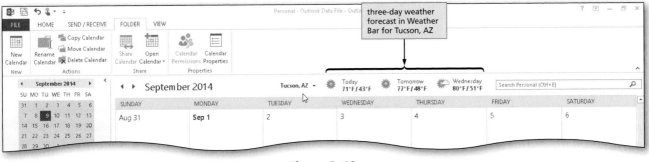

Figure 2–10

BTW

BTWs
For a complete list of the BTWs found in the margins of this book, visit the BTW resource on the Student Companion Site located on www.cengagebrain.com. For detailed instructions about accessing available resources, visit www.cengage.com/ct/studentdownload or contact your instructor for information about accessing the required files.

Navigating the Calendar

Each Microsoft Outlook folder displays the items it contains in a layout called a view. The **calendar view** is the arrangement and format of the folder contents by day, work week, week, month, or schedule, which is a horizontal layout. Recall that the default view of the Calendar folder is Month view. Some people prefer a different view of their calendar, such as weekly or daily. For instance, you might want to view all the items for a day at one time, in which case Day view would work best. Although the Outlook window looks different in each view, you can accomplish the same tasks in each view: you can add, edit, or delete appointments, events, and meetings.

1 CONFIGURE CALENDAR OPTIONS | 2 CREATE & MANIPULATE APPOINTMENTS | 3 SCHEDULE EVENTS
4 SCHEDULE MEETINGS | 5 PRINT CALENDAR | 6 SAVE & SHARE CALENDAR

To Go to a Specific Date

To display a date that is not visible in the current view so that you can view that date in the appointment area, one option is to use the Go to Date Dialog Box Launcher. The following steps display a specific date in the appointment area in a calendar. *Why? Rather than scrolling through your calendars in Outlook to find a specific date, you can quickly find a date in Outlook by using the Go To Date dialog box.*

❶

- Tap or click HOME on the ribbon to display the HOME tab.

- Tap or click the Go to Date Dialog Box Launcher (HOME tab | Go To group) to display the Go To Date dialog box (Figure 2–11).

Figure 2–11

2

- Type 9/3/2014 in the Date text box to enter the date you want to display in the current calendar.

- Tap or click the Show in button, and then select Day Calendar to show the calendar in Day view (Figure 2–12).

Q&A Why did 'Wed' appear next to the date in the Date box?

Outlook automatically includes the day of the week (Wednesday, in this case) when you enter a date in the Date box.

Figure 2–12

3

- Tap or click the OK button to close the Go To Date dialog box and display the selected date in Day view (Figure 2–13).

Figure 2–13

Other Ways

1. Press CTRL+G

To Display the Calendar in Work Week View

1 CONFIGURE CALENDAR OPTIONS | 2 CREATE & MANIPULATE APPOINTMENTS | 3 SCHEDULE EVENTS
4 SCHEDULE MEETINGS | 5 PRINT CALENDAR | 6 SAVE & SHARE CALENDAR

Why? In Outlook, you can display several calendar days at once so that you can see multiple appointments at the same time. **Work Week view** shows five workdays (Monday through Friday) in a columnar style. Hours that are not part of the default workday (8:00 AM – 5:00 PM) appear shaded when viewing the calendar in Day, Work Week, and Week view. The following step displays the calendar in Work Week view.

❶

• Tap or click the Work Week button (HOME tab | Arrange group) to display the work week in the appointment area for the selected date (Figure 2–14).

🔍 **Experiment**

• Scroll up and down in Day view to see how the color changes to reflect hours outside the default workday.

Q&A | Why is Monday through Friday highlighted on the Date Navigator?
The calendar days displayed in the appointment area are highlighted on the Date Navigator.

Figure 2–14

Other Ways

1. Press CTRL+ALT+2

To Display the Calendar in Week View

1 CONFIGURE CALENDAR OPTIONS | 2 CREATE & MANIPULATE APPOINTMENTS | 3 SCHEDULE EVENTS
4 SCHEDULE MEETINGS | 5 PRINT CALENDAR | 6 SAVE & SHARE CALENDAR

Why? *The advantage of displaying a calendar in Week view is to see how many appointments are scheduled for any given week, including weekends.* In **Week view**, the seven days of the selected week appear in the appointment area. The following step displays the calendar in Week view.

❶

• Tap or click the Week button (HOME tab | Arrange group) to display the full week, including weekends, in the appointment area (Figure 2–15).

Figure 2–15

Other Ways

1. Press CTRL+ALT+3

To Display the Calendar in Month View

Month view resembles a standard monthly calendar page and displays a schedule for an entire month. Appointments can be displayed in each date in the calendar. The following step displays the calendar in Month view. *Why? By viewing the entire month without scrolling through individual appointments, you can see when you have an open day.*

1

- Tap or click the Month button (HOME tab | Arrange group) to display one full month in the appointment area (Figure 2–16).

🔍 **Experiment**

- By default, Month view displays dates from the beginning to the end of a calendar month. To select several weeks across two calendar months, tap or click the Date Navigator and then drag to select the weeks you want to view.

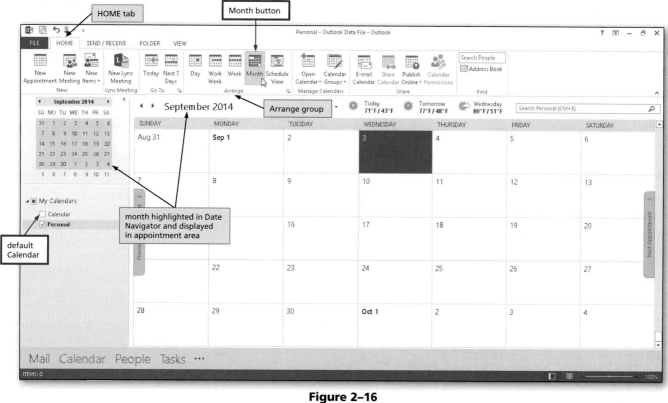

Figure 2–16

Other Ways

1. Press CTRL+ALT+4

To Display the Calendar in Schedule View

The **Schedule View** allows you to view multiple calendars over the course of a single day in a horizontal layout to make scheduling meetings easier. The following steps display the default Calendar and the Personal calendar in Schedule View. *Why? Schedule View is useful when trying to see multiple calendars so that you can check for overlapping items.*

1

- Tap or click Calendar (default Calendar) in the My Calendars pane to insert a check mark in the check box and to display both the default Calendar and the Personal calendar in the appointment area (Figure 2–17).

Q&A | Why are both calendars displayed in Month view?
Outlook uses the view of the existing calendar for a newly displayed calendar. In this case, the Personal calendar was displayed in Month view, so the default Calendar also is displayed in Month view.

Figure 2–17

2

- Tap or click the Schedule View button (HOME tab | Arrange group) to display both calendars in Schedule View (Figure 2–18).

Q&A | Why does Schedule View show a single day instead of multiple days?
Schedule View displays one day at a time.

What does the dark blue shaded area in the calendar represent?
The dark blue shaded area represents the time slot selected in Day view.

Figure 2–18

Other Ways

1. Press CTRL+ALT+5

To Add Holidays to the Default Calendar

Before you add appointments to a calendar, you can mark the standard holidays for one or more countries. You can add holidays to your default calendar folder only, not to a public folder or nondefault calendar such as the Personal calendar. However, you can drag holidays from your default calendar to nondefault calendars. *Why? International businesses should be aware of national holidays within each country where they do business.* The following steps add national holidays to the default calendar.

①

- Tap or click the FILE tab on the ribbon to open the Backstage view (Figure 2–19).

Figure 2–19

②

- Tap or click Options to display the Outlook Options dialog box.

- Tap or click Calendar in the left pane to display the options in the Calendar category (Figure 2–20).

Figure 2–20

3

- Tap or click the Add Holidays button to display the Add Holidays to Calendar dialog box (Figure 2–21).

Q&A

Can I select multiple countries to display more than one set of national holidays?

Yes. You can select the holidays of multiple countries to display in the default calendar.

Figure 2–21

4

- If necessary, tap or click the check box for your country of residence to add that country's national holidays to the default calendar.

- Tap or click the OK button to close the dialog box and display the confirmation message that the holidays were added to your calendar (Figure 2–22).

Figure 2–22

❺

- Tap or click the OK button to close the Microsoft Outlook dialog box.

- Tap or click the OK button to close the Outlook Options dialog box.

- Tap or click the Month button (HOME tab | Arrange group) to display both calendars in Month view in the appointment area (Figure 2–23).

Q&A The national holidays do not appear in the Personal calendar. Where are they displayed?
Holidays are displayed only in the default calendar.

Why are the national holidays on my default calendar different from Figure 2–23?
Your default calendar holiday dates might differ from those shown in Figure 2–23 if you selected a different country.

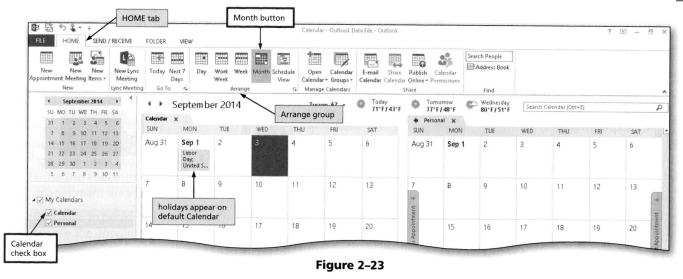

Figure 2–23

❻

- Tap or click Calendar in the My Calendars pane to remove the check mark from the Calendar check box so that the default calendar no longer is displayed in the appointment area.

Creating and Editing Appointments

An appointment is an activity that you schedule in your Outlook calendar that does not require an invitation to others. Recall that every calendar item you schedule in Outlook Calendar begins as an appointment. In Outlook, you easily can change an appointment to an event or a meeting. Scheduling a dental visit, your best friend's birthday, or a class schedule as recurring appointments helps you successfully manage your activities and obligations. To better organize your appointments and meetings in your Outlook calendar, you can add color categories that let you scan and visually associate similar items. For example, you can set the color blue to represent your academic classes and the color green for doctor's appointments.

Creating Appointments in the Appointment Area

A **one-time appointment**, such as a concert event, conference call, or course exam date is an appointment that occurs only once on a calendar. A **recurring appointment**, such as a class throughout an academic course, repeats on the calendar at regular intervals. Appointments can be created in two ways: using the appointment area, where you enter the appointment directly in the appropriate time slot, or using the Untitled – Appointment window, where you can enter more specific details about the appointment such as the location or address of the activity.

BTW
Touch Screen Differences
The Office and Windows interfaces may vary if you are using a touch screen. For this reason, you might notice that the function or appearance of your touch screen differs slightly from this chapter's presentation.

To Add Color Categories

Why? Color categories enable you to easily identify and group associated items in the Outlook Calendar. The following steps add color categories in the calendar.

1

- Tap or click the Categorize button (CALENDAR TOOLS APPOINTMENT tab | Tags group) to display the Categorize list of color categories (Figure 2–28).

Q&A

Can you use color categories for any type of email account?
You should use a Microsoft account as your Outlook email account to take advantage of categories and other special features.

Figure 2–28

2

- Tap or click All Categories to display the Color Categories dialog box (Figure 2–29).

Figure 2–29

3

- Tap or click the Blue Category to select the category.

- Tap or click the Rename button to select the category for renaming.

- Type `Classes` and then press the ENTER key to rename the category (Figure 2–30).

Figure 2–30

4

- Tap or click the Green Category, and then tap or click the Rename button to select the category for renaming.

- Type `Dr. Appointments` and then press the ENTER key to rename the category.

- Tap or click the Orange Category, and then tap or click the Rename button to select the category for renaming.

- Type `Friends & Family` and then press the ENTER key to rename the category.

- Tap or click the Purple Category, and then tap or click the Rename button to select the category for renaming.

- Type `Work` and then press the ENTER key to rename the category (Figure 2–31).

Figure 2–31

Q&A | How many color categories can I set?

You can assign fifteen color categories in Outlook Calendar. Click the New button in the Color Categories dialog box to select colors not shown in the dialog box by default.

5

- Tap or click the OK button to close the Color Categories dialog box.

To Assign a Color Category
to an Appointment

The following steps assign a color category to a calendar appointment. *Why? By color coding your Outlook calendar appointments, you can quickly distinguish among your assigned categories such as class, work, or birthdays.*

1

- If necessary, tap or click the Dentist appointment at 10:00 AM to select the appointment.

- Tap or click the Categorize button (CALENDAR TOOLS APPOINTMENT tab | Tags group) to display the Categorize list of color categories (Figure 2–32).

Figure 2–32

2

- Tap or click the green Dr. Appointments category to display the selected appointment with a medium-green background (Figure 2–33).

Figure 2–33

Creating Appointments Using the Appointment Window

Another way to create an appointment is by using the Appointment window, which provides additional options for entering an appointment, such as the location of the appointment and a recurrence pattern. When you set a **recurrence pattern**, Outlook schedules the appointment on the calendar at regular intervals for a designated period of time, such as a class that you take for an entire semester on Tuesdays and Thursdays.

Outlook also allows you to configure a **reminder**, similar to an alarm clock reminder, which is an alert window that briefly appears on your screen to remind you of an upcoming appointment. You also can set a chime or other sound to play as part of the reminder.

Another option when creating an appointment is to set the **appointment status**, which is how the time for a calendar item is marked on your calendar. The default appointment status setting is Busy, as indicated in the previous steps, but you can change the status to reflect your availability as appropriate.

To Create an Appointment Using the Appointment Window

1 CONFIGURE CALENDAR OPTIONS | 2 CREATE & MANIPULATE APPOINTMENTS | 3 SCHEDULE EVENTS
4 SCHEDULE MEETINGS | 5 PRINT CALENDAR | 6 SAVE & SHARE CALENDAR

Why? Instead of directly entering an appointment in the appointment area, you can specify various details such as the location by using the Appointment window. To schedule an appointment such as a CIS 101 computer class that meets repeatedly over the semester in a particular room on campus, you decide to use the Appointment window. The following steps create an appointment using the Appointment window.

1
- Tap or click HOME on the ribbon to display the HOME tab.

- Tap or click the New Appointment button (HOME tab | New group) to open the Untitled – Appointment window (Figure 2–34).

Figure 2–34

2

• Type CIS 101 in the Subject text box as the appointment subject.

• Press the TAB key to move the insertion point to the Location box.

• Type A366 as the room number of the class (Figure 2–35).

Q&A

Why did the title of the window change from Untitled – Appointment to CIS 101 – Appointment?

The title bar displays the name of the appointment. Because the name of the appointment has changed, the name on the title bar also changes.

Why are the date and time already specified?

When you start to create a new appointment, Outlook sets the start and end times using the time selected in the appointment area.

Figure 2–35

3

• Tap or click the Start time calendar button to display a calendar for the current month (Figure 2–36).

Figure 2–36

4

- Tap or click 2 on the calendar to select the start date of the first CIS 101 class as September 2, 2014.

- Tap or click the Start time box arrow to display a list of time slots (Figure 2–37).

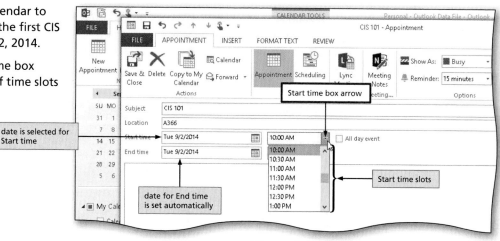

Figure 2–37

5

- Scroll up and then tap or click 9:00 AM to select it as the Start time for the appointment.

- Tap or click the End time box arrow to display a list of time slots (Figure 2–38).

Q&A Why did the End time change to the same date as the Start time?
Outlook automatically sets appointments to occur during a single day.

Why does the second end time list have a duration for each time?
Outlook automatically displays the duration next to the end time to help you set the length of the appointment.

Figure 2–38

6

- Tap or click 10:30 AM (1.5 hours) to select it as the End time for the appointment (Figure 2–39).

Figure 2–39

Other Ways

1. Press CTRL+SHIFT+A

Setting Appointment Options

When creating appointments on the Outlook calendar, you can set a number of options that determine how the appointment is handled. Table 2–2 lists the options available when creating an item on your calendar.

Table 2–2 Calendar Window Options	
Option	**Description**
Show As	Indicates your availability on a specific date and time; if you want to show others your availability when they schedule a meeting with you during a specific time, this must be set accurately
Reminder	Alerts you at a specific time prior to the item's occurrence
Recurrence	If an item on your calendar repeats at regularly scheduled intervals, sets the recurring options so that you only have to enter the item once on your calendar
Time Zone	Shows or hides the time zone controls, which you can use to specify the time zones for the start and end times of the appointment

© 2014 Cengage Learning

Outlook provides five options for indicating your availability on the Calendar, as described in Table 2–3.

Table 2–3 Calendar Item Status Options	
Calendar Item Status Options	**Description**
Free	Shows time with a white bar in Day, Week, Work Week, or Month view
Working Elsewhere	Shows time with a white bar with dots in Day, Week, Work Week, or Month view
Tentative	Shows time with a slashed bar in Day, Week, Work Week, or Month view
Busy	Shows time with a solid bar in Day, Week, Work Week, or Month view
Out of Office	Shows time with a purple bar in Day, Week, Work Week, or Month view

© 2014 Cengage Learning

To Change the Status of an Appointment

1 CONFIGURE CALENDAR OPTIONS | 2 CREATE & MANIPULATE APPOINTMENTS | 3 SCHEDULE EVENTS
4 SCHEDULE MEETINGS | 5 PRINT CALENDAR | 6 SAVE & SHARE CALENDAR

To make sure your time is displayed accurately on the calendar, you can change the appointment status from the default of Busy to Out of Office, meaning you are not in the office during class time while attending CIS 101. The following steps change the status of an appointment. *Why? You can display time indicators such as Busy or Out of Office to show calendar entries that reflect your availability. If you share your calendar, others can see at a glance if you are available.*

1
- Tap or click the Show As box arrow (APPOINTMENT tab | Options group) in the CIS 101 appointment to display the Show As list of appointment status options (Figure 2–40).

Figure 2–40

2

• Tap or click Out of Office to change the appointment status (Figure 2–41).

Figure 2–41

To Set a Reminder for an Appointment

1 CONFIGURE CALENDAR OPTIONS | 2 CREATE & MANIPULATE APPOINTMENTS | 3 SCHEDULE EVENTS
4 SCHEDULE MEETINGS | 5 PRINT CALENDAR | 6 SAVE & SHARE CALENDAR

With the start and end dates and times for the class set and the appointment status selected, you want to schedule a reminder so that you do not forget the class. *Why? Your Outlook Calendar can be your personal alarm clock by displaying reminders of your appointments with options such as snooze and dismiss.* When the reminder is displayed, you can open the appointment for further review. The following steps set a 30-minute reminder for an appointment.

1

- Tap or click the Reminder box arrow (APPOINTMENT tab | Options group) to display the Reminder list of available reminder intervals (Figure 2–42).

Q&A What does the Sound option in the Reminder list do?

In addition to a visual reminder, Outlook allows you to set an auditory alarm, much like an alarm clock.

Figure 2–42

2

- Tap or click 30 minutes to set a reminder for 30 minutes prior to the start time of the appointment (Figure 2–43).

Q&A Why was the reminder time originally scheduled for 15 minutes?

By default, a Reminder is set to occur 15 minutes before the start of an appointment. However, you can increase or decrease the default reminder time.

Figure 2–43

Can you customize the sound that is played when a reminder is displayed?

• When you tap or click the Reminder box arrow (CALENDAR TOOLS APPOINTMENT tab | Options group), tap or click Sound to open the Reminder Sound dialog box.

• Tap or click the Browse button, and then select the sound .wav file that you want played.

• Tap or click the Open button. Tap or click the OK button to select the custom reminder sound.

• A reminder time must be selected before the Sound command appears.

Creating Recurring Appointments

Many appointments are **recurring appointments**, meaning they happen at regular intervals for a designated period of time. The recurring appointment is configured with a recurrence pattern designating the rate of recurrence, for example, weekly, and on what day(s) of the week the appointment occurs.

To Set Recurrence Options for an Appointment

1 CONFIGURE CALENDAR OPTIONS | 2 CREATE & MANIPULATE APPOINTMENTS | 3 SCHEDULE EVENTS
4 SCHEDULE MEETINGS | 5 PRINT CALENDAR | 6 SAVE & SHARE CALENDAR

The CIS 101 class begins on September 2 and is held every Tuesday and Thursday from 9:00 AM to 10:30 AM at regular intervals, making it a recurring appointment. The following steps configure a recurrence pattern for an appointment. *Why? By establishing a recurrence pattern, you do not have to enter each class into the schedule for the entire semester.*

❶

• Tap or click the Recurrence button (APPOINTMENT tab | Options group) to display the Appointment Recurrence dialog box (Figure 2–44).

Q&A Why are the start and end times and the duration already set in the Appointment time area of the Appointment Recurrence dialog box?

Outlook uses the settings you already selected for the appointment.

Figure 2–44

2

- If necessary, in the Recurrence pattern area, tap or click the Weekly option button (Appointment Recurrence dialog box) to set the recurrence pattern.

- If necessary, in the Recur every text box (Appointment Recurrence dialog box), type 1 in the text box to schedule the frequency of the recurrence pattern.

- Tap or click Thursday to insert a check mark in the check box and to schedule the class two times per week (in this case, Tuesday and Thursday) (Figure 2–45).

Q&A

Why is the Tuesday check box already selected in the Recurrence pattern area?

Tuesday is already selected because the class starts on that day of the week.

Why does the Start box in the 'Range of recurrence' area contain a date?

When you display the Appointment Recurrence dialog box, Outlook automatically sets the range of recurrence with the date the appointment starts.

Figure 2–45

3

- In the 'Range of recurrence' area, tap or click the End by option button (Appointment Recurrence dialog box), and then press the TAB key two times to select the End by box.

- Type 12/11/2014 as the day the class ends to replace the displayed end date with a new date (Figure 2–46).

Q&A

What if I do not know the end date, but I know how many times the class meets?

You can tap or click the End after option button and then type the number of times the class meets in the End after text box.

Figure 2–46

4

- Tap or click the OK button to close the Appointment Recurrence dialog box and set the recurrence pattern (Figure 2–47).

Q&A Why did the APPOINTMENT tab change to the APPOINTMENT SERIES tab?

When you set a recurrence pattern, the tab name changes to reflect that you are working with a series.

Figure 2–47

To Save an Appointment

1 CONFIGURE CALENDAR OPTIONS | 2 CREATE & MANIPULATE APPOINTMENTS | 3 SCHEDULE EVENTS
4 SCHEDULE MEETINGS | 5 PRINT CALENDAR | 6 SAVE & SHARE CALENDAR

With the details entered for the CIS 101 class, you can assign the appointment to a color category and then save the appointment. The following steps categorize the appointment, save the appointment series, and close the window. *Why? By changing the color-coded category and saving the appointment, your recurring appointment is scheduled.*

1

- Tap or click the Categorize button (APPOINTMENT SERIES tab | Tags group) to display a list of color-coded categories (Figure 2–48).

Figure 2–48

BTW

Organizing Files and Folders

You should organize and store files in folders so that you easily can find the files later. For example, if you are taking an introductory computer class called CIS 101, a good practice would be to save all Outlook files in an Outlook folder in a CIS 101 folder. For a discussion of folders and detailed examples of creating folders, refer to the Office and Windows chapter at the beginning of this book.

2

- Tap or click the blue Classes category to assign this appointment to a category.

- Tap or click the Save & Close button (APPOINTMENT SERIES tab | Actions group) to save the recurring appointment on the calendar and close the window.

- Tap or click HOME on the ribbon to display the HOME tab.

- Tap or click the Month button (HOME tab | Arrange group) to display the calendar in Month view (Figure 2–49).

Figure 2–49

1 CONFIGURE CALENDAR OPTIONS | 2 CREATE & MANIPULATE APPOINTMENTS | 3 SCHEDULE EVENTS
4 SCHEDULE MEETINGS | 5 PRINT CALENDAR | 6 SAVE & SHARE CALENDAR

To Add More Recurring Appointments

With the CIS 101 class appointment series created, the next step is to create recurring appointments for the remainder of your class and work schedule using the appointment information in Table 2–4. The following steps create the remaining class schedule using the Appointment window. *Why? By adding your full schedule to the Outlook calendar, you will not miss any important appointments.*

Table 2–4 Recurring Appointments

Appoint-ment	Location	Start Date	End Date	Start Time	End Time	Show As	Reminder	Recurrence	Category
BIO 102	C202	9/08/2014	Set in Recurrence	5:30 PM	8:30 PM	Out of Office	30 minutes	Weekly, every Monday; end by Monday, 12/15/2014	Classes
ECO 111 Due Date	Online	9/05/2014	Set in Recurrence	5:00 PM	5:00 PM	Busy	1 hour	Weekly, every Friday; end by Friday, 12/12/2014	Classes
Work	Nash Auto	9/06/2014	Set in Recurrence	9:00 AM	5:00 PM	Busy	15 minutes	Weekly, every Saturday; end by Saturday, 12/13/2014	Work

© 2014 Cengage Learning

1 If necessary, tap or click HOME to display the HOME tab.

2 Tap or click the New Appointment button (HOME tab | New group) to open the Appointment window.

3 Type `BIO 102` as the appointment subject.

4 Type `C202` as the location.

5 Select September 8, 2014 to set the start date.

6 Select the start time as 5:30 PM and the end time as 8:30 PM.

7 Select the Show as box arrow to display the list of appointment status options, and then tap or click the option shown in Table 2–4.

8 Select the Reminder box arrow to display the list of time slots, and then tap or click the option shown in Table 2–4.

9 Tap or click the Recurrence button (APPOINTMENT tab | Options group) and set the recurrence pattern shown in Table 2–4, and then tap or click the OK button to close the Appointment Recurrence window.

10 Tap or click the Categorize button (APPOINTMENT SERIES tab | Tags group) and select the color-coded category shown in Table 2–4.

11 Tap or click the Save & Close button to close the Appointment window.

12 Repeat Steps 1 through 11 to add the information shown in the second and third rows of Table 2–4 (Figure 2–50).

Q&A

Why is the CALENDAR TOOLS APPOINTMENT SERIES tab displayed instead of the CALENDAR TOOLS APPOINTMENT tab?
The CALENDAR TOOLS APPOINTMENT SERIES tab is displayed when you select an appointment that is part of a series. This tab provides tools for working with recurring appointments.

What if I have appointments that recur other than weekly?
You can set daily, weekly, monthly, or yearly recurrence patterns in the Appointment Recurrence dialog box. A recurring appointment can be set to have no end date, to end after a certain number of occurrences, or to end by a certain date.

Figure 2–50

BTW
Outlook Help
At any time while using Outlook, you can find answers to questions and display information about various topics through Outlook Help. Used properly, this form of assistance can increase your productivity and reduce your frustrations by minimizing the time you spend learning how to use Outlook. For instruction about Outlook Help and exercises that will help you gain confidence in using it, read the Office and Windows chapter at the beginning of this book.

Using Natural Language Phrasing

In the previous steps, you entered dates and times in the Appointment window using standard numeric entries, such as 9/08/2014. You also can specify appointment dates and times using natural language. A **natural language phrase** is a phrase closely resembling how people speak during normal conversation. For example, you can type a phrase, such as "next Thursday" or "two weeks from yesterday," or you can type a single word, such as "midnight," and Outlook will calculate the correct date and time relative to the current date and time on the computer's system clock.

Outlook also can convert abbreviations and ordinal numbers into complete words and dates. For example, you can type "Feb" instead of "February" or "the first of May" instead of "5/1". Outlook's Calendar also can convert words such as "yesterday" and "tomorrow" and the names of holidays that occur on the same date each year, such as Valentine's Day. Table 2–5 lists various natural language options.

Table 2–5 Natural Language Options	
Category	**Examples**
Dates Spelled Out	• July twenty-third, March 17th, first of May
	• This Fri, next Sat, two days from now
Times Spelled Out	• Noon, midnight
	• Nine o'clock AM, five-twenty
Descriptions of Times and Dates	• Now
	• Yesterday, today, tomorrow
Holidays	• Cinco de Mayo
	• Christmas Day, Christmas Eve
Formulas for dates and times	3/14/2014 + 12d converts the date to 3/26/2014; use *d* for day, *m* for month, or *y* for year and add that amount of time to any date

© 2014 Cengage Learning

To Create an Appointment Date and Time Using Natural Language Phrases

1 CONFIGURE CALENDAR OPTIONS | **2 CREATE & MANIPULATE APPOINTMENTS** | 3 SCHEDULE EVENTS
4 SCHEDULE MEETINGS | 5 PRINT CALENDAR | 6 SAVE & SHARE CALENDAR

Using a natural language phrase, you can make an appointment for your best friend's birthday party next Monday at 8:00 PM. The following steps create an appointment using natural language phrases for the date and time. *Why? If you are not sure of the exact date for next Tuesday or 36 days from now, you can use a natural language phrase.*

1

• Tap or click the New Appointment button (HOME tab | New group) to open the Untitled – Appointment window.

• Type `Liam's Birthday Party` in the Subject text box, and then press the TAB key to move the insertion point to the Location text box.

• Type `Sushi House` to add the location (Figure 2–51).

Figure 2–51

2

- Press the TAB key to select the first Start time text box, and then type `next sunday` to enter the start date.

- Press the TAB key to convert the phrase to a start date and to select the second Start time text box.

- Type `seven pm` as the time in the second Start time text box to enter the start time (Figure 2–52).

Q&A Do I need to use proper capitalization when entering natural language phrases?
No. Outlook converts the text to the proper date or time, regardless of the capitalization.

Why did the text change to a numeric date when I pressed the TAB key?
If you enter the date using natural language phrasing, Outlook converts typed text to the correct date format when you tap or click to move the insertion point to a different box.

Figure 2–52

3

- Press the TAB key two times to convert the Start time entry to 7:00 PM.

- Type `ten pm` as the time in the second End time box.

- Press the ENTER key to convert the end time text to 10:00 PM.

- Tap or click the Categorize button (APPOINTMENT tab | Tags group) to display the Categorize list.

- Tap or click the orange Friends & Family category to assign this appointment to a category.

- Tap or click the Save & Close button (APPOINTMENT tab | Actions group) to save the appointment and close the window.

- If necessary, scroll to next Sunday's date (Figure 2–53).

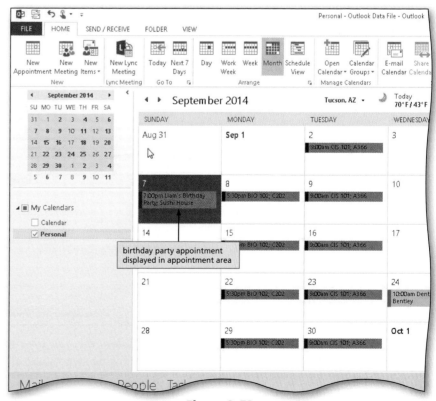

Figure 2–53

Editing Appointments

Schedules often need to be rearranged, so Outlook provides several ways to edit appointments. You can change the subject or location by tapping or clicking the appointment and editing the information directly in the appointment area. You can change the subject, location, date, or time by double-tapping or double-clicking the appointment and making corrections using the Appointment window. You can specify whether all occurrences in a series of recurring appointments need to be changed, or only a single occurrence should be altered.

To Move an Appointment to a Different Time on the Same Day

1 CONFIGURE CALENDAR OPTIONS | 2 CREATE & MANIPULATE APPOINTMENTS | 3 SCHEDULE EVENTS
4 SCHEDULE MEETINGS | 5 PRINT CALENDAR | 6 SAVE & SHARE CALENDAR

Suppose that you cannot attend the Dentist appointment at 10:00 AM on September 24, 2014. The appointment needs to be rescheduled to 11:00 AM for the same amount of time. *Why? Instead of deleting and then retyping the appointment, you can drag it to a new time slot.* The following step moves an appointment to a new time slot.

1

- If necessary, tap or click a scroll arrow on the Calendar in the Navigation Pane until September 2014 is displayed in the calendar on the Date Navigator.

- Tap or click 24 in the September 2014 calendar on the Date Navigator to display the selected date in the appointment area.

- Drag the Dentist appointment from 10:00 AM to the 11:00 AM time slot on the same day to reschedule the appointment (Figure 2–54).

Figure 2–54

Other Ways

1. Double-tap or double-click appointment, change time
2. Press CTRL + O, change time

To Move an Appointment to a Different Date

1 CONFIGURE CALENDAR OPTIONS | 2 CREATE & MANIPULATE APPOINTMENTS | 3 SCHEDULE EVENTS
4 SCHEDULE MEETINGS | 5 PRINT CALENDAR | 6 SAVE & SHARE CALENDAR

Why? If you are moving an appointment to a new date at the same time, you can drag the appointment to the new date on the Date Navigator instead of retyping it. The following step moves an appointment to a new date in the same time slot.

1

- Drag the Dentist appointment on September 24, 2014 to September 17, 2014 on the Date Navigator to move the appointment to a new date (Figure 2–55).

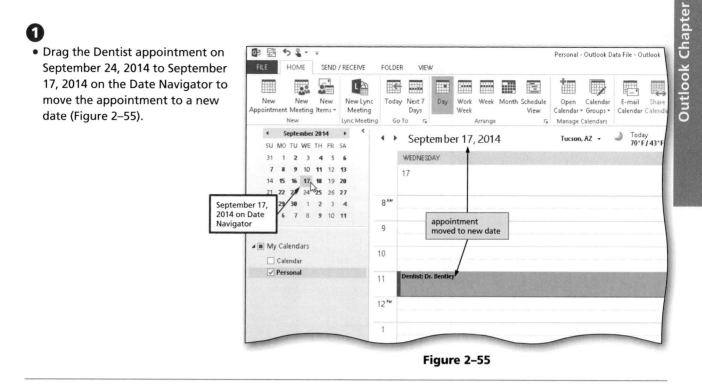

Figure 2–55

To Delete a Single Occurrence of a Recurring Appointment

1 CONFIGURE CALENDAR OPTIONS | 2 CREATE & MANIPULATE APPOINTMENTS | 3 SCHEDULE EVENTS
4 SCHEDULE MEETINGS | 5 PRINT CALENDAR | 6 SAVE & SHARE CALENDAR

Because your school is closed for a Fall Break holiday on October 6, 2014, no classes will meet during that day. The following steps delete a single occurrence of a recurring appointment. *Why? Occasionally, appointments are canceled and must be deleted from the schedule.*

1

- Tap or click the forward navigation arrow in the Date Navigator until October 2014 is displayed.

- Tap or click 6 in the October 2014 calendar on the Date Navigator to display the selected date in the appointment area.

- If necessary, scroll down and tap or click the class, BIO 102, scheduled for October 6, 2014, to select the appointment and display the CALENDAR TOOLS APPOINTMENT SERIES tab (Figure 2–56).

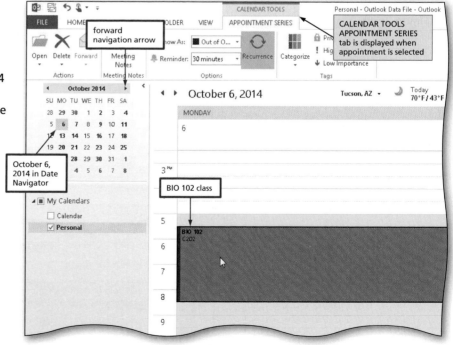

Figure 2–56

2

- Tap or click the Delete button (CALENDAR TOOLS APPOINTMENT SERIES tab | Actions group) to display the Delete list (Figure 2–57).

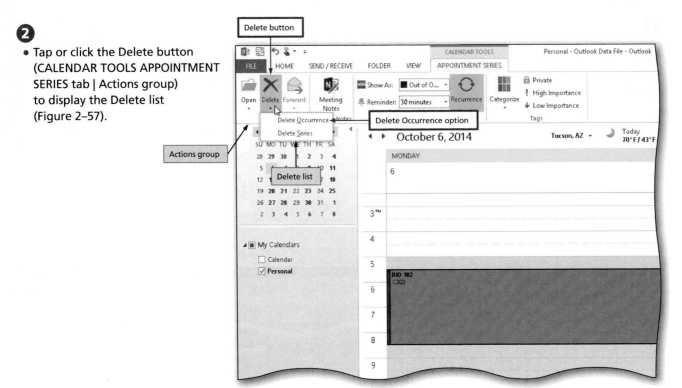

Figure 2–57

3

- Tap or click Delete Occurrence on the Delete list to delete only the selected occurrence (single appointment) from the calendar.

- Tap or click the Month button (HOME tab | Arrange group) to display the Month view (Figure 2–58).

Figure 2–58

Other Ways

1. Tap or click appointment, press DELETE, tap or click Delete Occurrence, tap or click OK

2. Press and hold or right-click appointment, tap or click Delete on shortcut menu, tap or click Delete Occurrence, tap or click OK

Break Point: If you wish to take a break, this is a good place to do so. To resume at a later time, continue to follow the steps from this location forward.

Scheduling Events

Similar to appointments, events are activities that last 24 hours or longer. Examples of events include seminars, vacations, birthdays, and anniversaries. Events can be one-time or recurring, and differ from appointments in one primary way — they do not appear in individual time slots in the appointment area. Instead, the event description appears in a small banner below the day heading. As with an appointment, the event status can be free, busy, tentative, or out of the office and categorized according to the type of event. An all-day appointment displays your time as busy when viewed by other people, but an event or annual event displays your time as free. By default, all-day events occur from midnight to midnight.

To Create a One-Time Event in the Appointment Window

1 CONFIGURE CALENDAR OPTIONS | 2 CREATE & MANIPULATE APPOINTMENTS | 3 SCHEDULE EVENTS
4 SCHEDULE MEETINGS | 5 PRINT CALENDAR | 6 SAVE & SHARE CALENDAR

Why? An event represents an appointment that is scheduled over a period of days such as a conference. A Career Fair is being held at the Chamber of Commerce from November 3, 2014 through November 5, 2014, and you want to attend. Because the Career Fair will last for several days, Outlook will schedule the conference as an event. You are not certain you can attend the fair, so you decide to show your time for the event as Tentative. The following steps create an event on the calendar.

1
- Tap or click the New Items button (HOME tab | New group) to display the New Items list (Figure 2–59).

2
- Tap or click 'All Day Event' to open the Untitled – Event window.

- Type `Career Fair` in the Subject text box, and then press the TAB key to move the insertion point to the Location text box.

- Type `Chamber of Commerce` as the location of the event.

- Tap or click the Start time calendar button to display the Start time calendar.

- Tap or click the forward navigation arrow until the November 2014 calendar is displayed.

- Tap or click 3 in the November 2014 calendar to display Mon 11/3/2014 as the day the Career Fair begins (Figure 2–60).

Q&A Can I create an event by checking the All day event check box in an appointment?
Yes. Tap or click the New Appointment button (HOME tab | New group) and then tap or click 'All day event' to create an event.

Figure 2–59

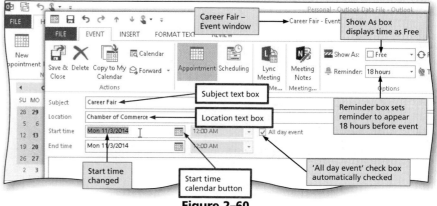

Figure 2–60

❸

- Tap or click the End time calendar button to display the End time calendar.

- Tap or click 5 in the November 2014 calendar to set the end date.

- Tap or click the Show As box arrow (EVENT tab | Options group) to display the Show As list of event status options.

- Tap or click Tentative to set the event status.

- Tap or click the Categorize button (EVENT tab | Tags group) to display the Categorize list of color categories.

- Tap or click Work to assign the event to a category (Figure 2–61).

◄ | Why does the Show As box originally display the time as Free?
Q&A | The default Show As appointment status for events is Free because events do not occupy blocks of time during the
| day on the calendar.

Figure 2–61

❹

- Tap or click the Save & Close button (EVENT tab | Actions group) to save the event and close the window.

- Tap or click 3 in the November 2014 calendar on the Date Navigator to display the selected date in the appointment area (Figure 2–62).

◄ | Why is the Career Fair event displayed at the top of the Day view of the calendar?
Q&A | Events do not occupy time slots on the Day view of the calendar, so they appear as banners at the top of the
| calendar on the day they occur.

| Why is the Appointment area filled with slashed bars?
| The slashed bars identify the time as a tentative event.

Figure 2–62

To Delete a One-Time Event

Why? Because your schedule has changed, you no longer can attend the Career Fair event. The following step deletes an event from your calendar.

1

- If necessary, tap or click the Career Fair event banner in the appointment area of the calendar to select it and to display the CALENDAR TOOLS APPOINTMENT tab on the ribbon.

- Tap or click the Delete button (CALENDAR TOOLS APPOINTMENT tab | Actions group) to delete the Career Fair event from the calendar (Figure 2–63).

Figure 2–63

Other Ways
1. Select event, press DELETE

To Create a Recurring Event Using the Appointment Window

A recurring event is similar to a recurring appointment in that it occurs at regular intervals on your calendar. However, editing a recurring event is slightly different from editing one-time events. You can specify whether all occurrences in a series of recurring events need to be changed or if a single occurrence should be altered.

You want to add your pay schedule to the calendar to keep track of when you receive a paycheck. The following steps create a recurring event for your pay schedule. *Why? To keep up with a periodic event such as your pay date, the recurring event feature gives you a way to remind yourself of important dates.*

1

- Tap or click the New Items button (HOME tab | New group) to display the New Items list.

- Tap or click All Day Event to open the Untitled – Event window.

- In the Subject text box, type `Payday` as the subject.

- In the first Start time text box, type `9/19/2014` as the first payday, and then press the ENTER key (Figure 2–64).

Q&A Do I need to add a location to the Payday event?
No, an event such as a payday, birthday, or anniversary does not have a location.

Figure 2–64

2

- Tap or click the Recurrence button (EVENT tab | Options group) to display the Appointment Recurrence dialog box.

- If necessary, in the Recurrence pattern section, tap or click the Weekly option button to set the Recurrence pattern to Weekly.

- In the Recur every text box, type   2   to have the event appear on the calendar every two weeks.

- If necessary, tap or click the Friday check box to schedule the day for this event.

- If necessary, tap or click any other selected check box in the Recur every section to remove the check marks so that only Friday is selected.

- In the Range of recurrence section, tap or click the 'No end date' option button so that the event remains on the calendar indefinitely (Figure 2–65).

Figure 2–65

❸

- Tap or click the OK button to accept the recurrence settings and close the Appointment Recurrence dialog box.

- Tap or click the Reminder box arrow (RECURRING EVENT tab | Options group) to display the Reminder list of reminder time slots.

- Tap or click None to remove the reminder from the event.

- Tap or click the Categorize button (RECURRING EVENT tab | Tags group) to display the Categorize list of color categories.

- Tap or click the purple Work category to assign the event to a category (Figure 2–66).

Q&A | Why was the reminder removed from the event?
The Payday event does not require a reminder because you do not need to devote time to complete this event.

Figure 2–66

❹

- Tap or click the Save & Close button (RECURRING EVENT tab | Actions group) to save the event and close the window.

- Tap or click the Month button (HOME tab | Arrange group) to view more pay dates on the calendar (Figure 2–67).

Figure 2–67

To Move a Recurring Event to a Different Day

1 CONFIGURE CALENDAR OPTIONS | 2 CREATE & MANIPULATE APPOINTMENTS | 3 SCHEDULE EVENTS
4 SCHEDULE MEETINGS | 5 PRINT CALENDAR | 6 SAVE & SHARE CALENDAR

Why? *A recurring date may change to a different day or duration.* The business you work for is changing its payday from Friday to Saturday. The recurring Payday event must be changed for the entire series. The following steps change the date for all occurrences in a series.

❶

- Tap or click the Day button (HOME tab | Arrange group) to display the Day view.

- Press or click and hold the month name on the Date Navigator to display a list of months with the associated year.

- Tap or click September 2014 on the Date Navigator to display the selected month in the appointment area.

- Tap or click 19 to display September 19, 2014 and the Payday event banner in the appointment area.

- In the appointment area, tap or click the Payday event banner to select it and to display the CALENDAR TOOLS APPOINTMENT SERIES tab (Figure 2–68).

Q&A What does the double arrow symbol on the right side of the event banner represent?

The event appears in the Outlook calendar with a double arrow symbol to show that it is a recurring appointment.

Figure 2–68

2

- Tap or click the Recurrence button (CALENDAR TOOLS APPOINTMENT SERIES tab | Options group) to display the Appointment Recurrence dialog box.

- Tap or click the Saturday check box to place a check mark in the box and to change the recurrence pattern.

- Tap or click the Friday check box to remove the check mark.

- Tap or click the Start box arrow in the Range of Recurrence area, and then click 20 to change the start date to Sat 9/20/2012 (Figure 2–69).

Figure 2–69

3

- Tap or click the OK button to close the Appointment Recurrence dialog box and change the event day.

- Tap or click the Month button (HOME tab | Arrange group) to view the full month calendar (Figure 2–70).

Figure 2–70

Other Ways

1. Double-tap or double-click event, open series, tap or click Recurrence button

2. Tap or click event, press CTRL+O, tap or click Recurrence button

TO DELETE A RECURRING EVENT

Deleting a recurring event is similar to deleting a recurring appointment. If you choose to delete a recurring event, you would use the following steps.

1. Tap or click the scroll arrow on the Date Navigator to display the date of the event.

2. Tap or click the event to display the CALENDAR TOOLS APPOINTMENT SERIES tab.

3. Tap or click the Delete button (CALENDAR TOOLS APPOINTMENT SERIES tab | Actions group) to display the Delete menu.

4. Tap or click Delete Series on the Delete menu to delete the event from the calendar.

If you are using your finger on a touch screen and are having difficulty completing the steps in this chapter, consider using a stylus. Many people find it easier to be precise with a stylus than with a finger. In addition, with a stylus you see the pointer. If you still are having trouble completing the steps with a stylus, try using a mouse.

Scheduling Meetings

As defined earlier, a meeting is an appointment that you invite other people to attend. Each person who is invited can accept, accept as tentative, or decline a meeting request. A meeting also can include resources such as conference rooms. The person who creates the meeting and sends the invitations is known as the **meeting organizer**. The meeting organizer schedules a meeting by creating a **meeting request**, which is an email invitation to the meeting and arrives in each attendee's Inbox. Responses to a meeting request arrive in the Inbox of the meeting organizer. To create a meeting request, you use the Untitled – Meeting request window, which is similar to the Untitled – Appointment window with a few exceptions. The meeting request window includes the To text box, where you enter an email address for **attendees**, who are people invited to the meeting, and the Send button, which sends the invitation for the meeting to the attendees. When a meeting request arrives in the attendee's Inbox, it displays an icon different from an email message icon.

Before you invite others to a meeting, confirm that the meeting date and time are available. Your school or business may have shared calendars that can be downloaded to your Outlook calendar. This shared calendar may be an iCalendar with an .ics file extension. An **iCalendar** represents a universal calendar format used by several email and calendar programs, including Microsoft Outlook, Google Calendar, and Apple iCal. The iCalendar format enables users to publish and share calendar information on the Web and by email.

CONSIDER THIS

Before you send out a meeting request, how can you set the groundwork for an effective meeting?

- Import other calendars to compare everyone's schedule.

- Prepare an agenda stating the purpose of the meeting.

- Be sure you include everyone who needs to attend the meeting. Invite only those people whose attendance is absolutely necessary to ensure that all of the agenda items can be addressed at the meeting.

- Confirm that the location of the meeting is available and that the room is the appropriate size for the number of people invited. Also, make sure the room can accommodate any multimedia equipment that might be needed for the meeting, such as a projector or telephone.

To Import an iCalendar File

1 CONFIGURE CALENDAR OPTIONS | 2 CREATE & MANIPULATE APPOINTMENTS | 3 SCHEDULE EVENTS
4 SCHEDULE MEETINGS | 5 PRINT CALENDAR | 6 SAVE & SHARE CALENDAR

Before scheduling a meeting, you can open your school's calendar to view your availability. Your school has a shared calendar in the iCalendar format that contains the school's master schedule. The following steps import an iCalendar file into Outlook. **Why?** *By importing another calendar, you can compare available dates for a meeting.*

1
- Tap or click the FILE tab on the ribbon to open the Backstage view.

- Tap or click Open & Export to display the Open gallery (Figure 2–71).

Figure 2–71

2

- Tap or click Open Calendar in the Open gallery to display the Open Calendar dialog box.

- Navigate to the mailbox location (in this case, the Chapter 02 folder in the Outlook folder in the Data Files for Students folder) (Figure 2–72).

Figure 2–72

3

- Tap or click School Calendar to select the file, and then tap or click the OK button (Open Calendar dialog box) to open the School Calendar next to the Personal calendar in the appointment area (Figure 2–73).

Why isn't the School Calendar displayed in the My Calendar group?

Outlook organizes multiple calendars in groups. If you frequently work with a set of calendars, you can view them in groups. When you open an iCalendar, it initially might appear in an Other Calendars group.

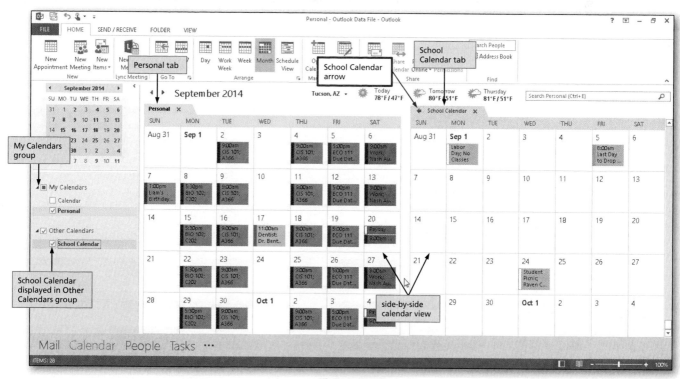

Figure 2–73

To View Calendars in the Overlay Mode

Why? *Before you schedule a meeting on your Personal calendar, you want to review your school's official calendar to avoid scheduling conflicts.* You can view multiple calendars at the same time side-by-side or combined into an overlay view to help you see which dates and times are available in all calendars. The following steps display both calendars in overlay mode and make the Calendar folder the active folder.

1

- Tap or click the School Calendar arrow on the School Calendar tab to view the two calendars in overlay mode (Figure 2–74).

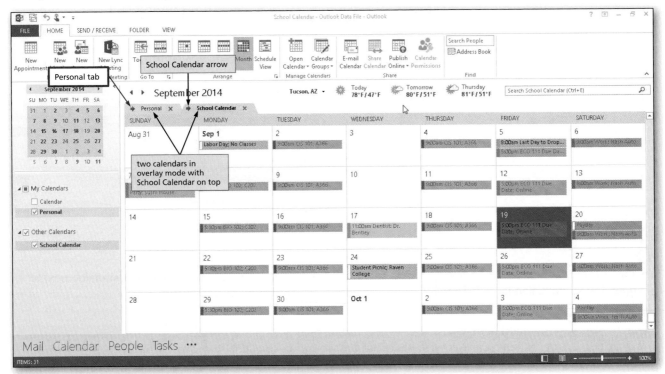

Figure 2–74

2

- Tap or click the Personal tab to display the Personal calendar in front of the School Calendar (Figure 2–75).

Q&A What happens if I click the arrow on the Personal calendar?
Outlook again displays the calendars side by side.

Figure 2–75

To View and Dock the Peek Calendar

The Outlook navigation bar provides a **Peek** feature, a pop-up access to email, calendar, people, and tasks. *Why?* *Using the Peek feature, you can take a quick glance at your schedule without having to rearrange windows or lose your train of thought.* When you hover over Calendar in the Navigation Pane, a Peek calendar of the current month opens and the current date is highlighted with a blue background. The Peek calendar can be docked in the right pane of the calendar. Appointments and meetings scheduled for today appear below the calendar. The following steps view, dock, and remove the Peek calendar.

1

- Tap or click the School Calendar check box in the Navigation Pane to remove the School Calendar from the Outlook window.

- Point to Calendar on the Navigation Bar to display the Peek calendar with today's appointments or meetings (Figure 2–76).

Q&A
Why do I not see any appointments or meetings in the Peek calendar?
If you not have any appointments or meetings today in the default Calendar, the Peek calendar does not display any calendar items.

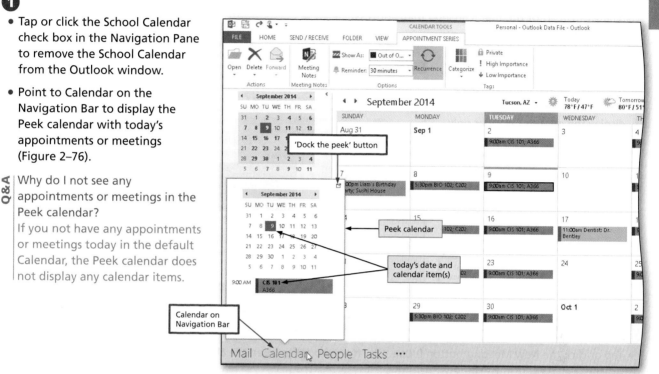

Figure 2–76

2

- Tap or click the 'Dock the peek' button to dock the Peek calendar in the right pane of the Outlook window (Figure 2–77).

3

- Tap or click the 'Remove the peek' button on the docked Peek calendar to remove the Peek calendar.

Figure 2–77

To Change the Time of a Meeting and Send an Update

Your schedule has changed, which means you need to change the time of the meeting with the financial aid office and send an update about the change. Though the invitee can propose a new time, only the originator can change or delete the meeting. **Why?** *You can update any meeting request to add or remove attendees or resources, change the meeting to a recurring series, or move the meeting to a different date or time.* The following steps change the time of the meeting and send an update to the attendee. If you are completing this project on a personal computer, your email account must be set up in Outlook (see Chapter 1) to be able to view the meeting request.

1

- Double-tap or double-click the meeting with the financial aid office (or your instructor) in the default calendar to open the Financial Aid for Next Semester – Meeting window.

- Tap or click the Start time box arrow to display a list of times.

- Tap or click 3:30 PM as the new start time for the meeting (Figure 2–82).

Figure 2–82

2

- Tap or click the Send Update button in the message header to send the new information, close the meeting request, and view the updated meeting in the appointment area (Figure 2–83).

Q&A What if I need to cancel the meeting?
To remove a meeting, tap or click the meeting in the appointment area to display the CALENDAR TOOLS MEETING tab, tap or click the Cancel Meeting button (CALENDAR TOOLS MEETING tab | Actions group), and then tap or click the Send Cancellation button to send the cancellation notice to the attendee and remove the meeting from the calendar.

Figure 2–83

Other Ways

1. Drag meeting to new time, tap or click 'Save changes and send update', tap or click OK, tap or click Send Update

To Reply to a Meeting Request

The financial aid office has received your meeting request in an email message. Outlook allows invitees to choose from four response options: Accept, Tentative, Decline, or Propose New Time. The following steps accept the meeting request. If you have a meeting request in your personal email that is set up using Outlook, substitute your meeting request in the following steps. If you do not have any meeting requests, read these steps without performing them.

1

- Tap or click Mail on the Navigation Bar to display the Inbox folder.

- Double-tap or double-click the email message header to open the meeting invitation (Figure 2–84).

Figure 2–84

2

- Tap or click the Accept button (MEETING tab | Respond group) to display the options for accepting the meeting (Figure 2–85).

3

- Tap or click Send the Response Now to send the accept response and add the meeting to the calendar.

Figure 2–85

Q&A

What happened to the meeting invitation in the Inbox?

When you accept or tentatively accept a meeting request, the invitation is deleted from the Inbox and the meeting is added to your calendar. The meeting response is in the Sent Items folder.

What happens when I decline a meeting request?

When a meeting request is declined, it is removed from your Inbox and the meeting is not added to your calendar. The reply is placed in the Sent Items folder.

To Propose a New Meeting Time

When you receive a meeting invitation, you can propose a new time if the original time is not available in your calendar. When you propose a new time, a proposal is sent to the meeting originator via email, indicating that you tentatively accept the request, but propose the meeting be held at a different time or on a different date. To propose a new time for a meeting, you would perform the following steps.

1. Tap or click the appropriate meeting request to display the CALENDAR TOOLS MEETING OCCURRENCE tab on the ribbon.
2. Tap or click the Propose New Time button (CALENDAR TOOLS MEETING OCCURRENCE tab | Respond group) to display the Occurrence menu.
3. Tap or click the Tentative and Propose New Time option to display the Propose New Time dialog box for the selected meeting.
4. Drag through the time slot that you want to propose, or enter the appropriate information in the Meeting start and Meeting end boxes (Propose New Time dialog box).
5. Tap or click the Propose time button to open the New Time Proposed – Meeting Response window.
6. Tap or click the Send button.

To Cancel a Meeting

To cancel a meeting, you would perform the following steps.

1. Tap or click the meeting request in the appointment area to select the meeting and display the CALENDAR TOOLS MEETING tab on the ribbon.
2. Tap or click the Cancel Meeting button (CALENDAR TOOLS MEETING tab | Actions group) to open the window for the selected meeting.
3. Tap or click the Send Cancellation button in the message header to send the cancellation notice and delete the meeting from your calendar.

Printing Calendars in Different Views

All or part of a calendar can be printed in a number of different views, or **print styles**. You can print a monthly, daily, or weekly view of your calendar and select options such as the date range and fonts to use. You also can view your calendar in a list by changing the current view from Calendar view to List view. Table 2–6 lists the print styles available for printing your calendar from Calendar view.

Table 2–6 Print Styles for Calendar View

Print Style	Description
Daily	Prints a daily appointment schedule for a specific date including one day per page, a daily task list, an area for notes, and a two-month calendar
Weekly Agenda	Prints a seven-day weekly calendar with one week per page and a two-month calendar
Weekly Calendar	Prints a seven-day weekly calendar with one week per page and an hourly schedule, similar to the Daily style
Monthly	Prints five weeks per page of a particular month or date range
Tri-fold	Prints a page for each day, including a daily task list and a weekly schedule
Calendar Details	Prints a list of calendar items and supporting details

© 2014 Cengage Learning

To Print the Calendar in Weekly Calendar Style

1 CONFIGURE CALENDAR OPTIONS | 2 CREATE & MANIPULATE APPOINTMENTS | 3 SCHEDULE EVENTS
4 SCHEDULE MEETINGS | 5 PRINT CALENDAR | 6 SAVE & SHARE CALENDAR

Why? *Printing a calendar enables you to distribute the calendar to others in a form that can be read or viewed, but cannot be edited.* You can print your Personal calendar for a hard copy of your first week of classes. The following steps print a calendar in a weekly calendar style.

1

- If necessary, tap or click Calendar on the Navigation Bar to display the Outlook calendar.

- If necessary, tap or click the Personal check box to display the Personal calendar.

- If necessary, tap or click the other check boxes to close the other calendars.

- Tap or click the Go to Date Dialog Box Launcher (HOME tab | Go To group) to display the Go To Date dialog box.

- Type 9/1/2014 in the Date text box to select that date.

- Tap or click the Show in button, and then tap or click Month Calendar to show the month view in the appointment area.

- Tap or click the OK button to close the Go To Date dialog box (Figure 2–86).

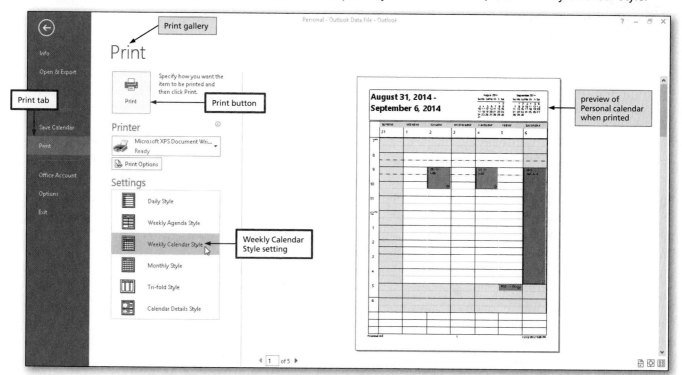

Figure 2–86

2

- Tap or click FILE on the ribbon to open the Backstage view.

- Tap or click the Print tab in the Backstage view to display the Print gallery.

- Tap or click Weekly Calendar Style in the Settings list to preview how the printed calendar will look in Weekly Calendar Style (Figure 2–87).

Experiment

- Tap or click the other settings to preview the different print styles. When finished, select Weekly Calendar Style.

Figure 2–87

❸

- If necessary, tap or click the desired printer to change the currently selected printer.

- Tap or click the Print button in the Print gallery to print the calendar on the currently selected printer (Figure 2–88).

Q&A

How can I print multiple copies of my calendar?

Tap or click the Print Options button to display the Print dialog box, increase the number in the Number of Copies box, and then tap or click the Print button to send the calendar to the printer and return to the calendar.

What if I decide not to print the calendar at this time?

Tap or click FILE on the ribbon to close the Backstage view and return to the calendar window.

Figure 2–88

Other Ways

1. Press CTRL+P, press ENTER

To Change the Calendar View to List View

1 CONFIGURE CALENDAR OPTIONS | 2 CREATE & MANIPULATE APPOINTMENTS | 3 SCHEDULE EVENTS

4 SCHEDULE MEETINGS | 5 PRINT CALENDAR | 6 SAVE & SHARE CALENDAR

By default, the Outlook calendar is displayed in Calendar view, but other options include a List view, which displays the calendar as a table with each row displaying a unique calendar item. *Why? To display all of your calendar appointments, events, and meetings, change the current Calendar view to List view.* The following steps change the view from Calendar view to List view.

❶

- Tap or click VIEW on the ribbon to display the VIEW tab.

- Tap or click the Change View button (VIEW tab | Current View group) to display the Change View gallery (Figure 2–89).

Figure 2–89

2

- Tap or click List in the Change View gallery to display a list of calendar items in the appointment area (Figure 2–90).

Figure 2–90

To Print the Calendar in List View

To print a list of your calendar items in a table, print the List view display. The following steps print the calendar in Table style.

1 Tap or click FILE on the ribbon to open the Backstage view.

2 Tap or click the Print tab in the Backstage view to display the Print gallery.

3 Tap or click the Table Style option in the Settings list to preview the calendar in Table Style.

4 If necessary, tap or click the Printer box to display a list of available printer options, and then tap or click the desired printer to change the selected printer.

5 Tap or click the Print button to send the list of appointments to the selected printer (Figure 2–91).

Q&A When I changed the view from List view to Calendar view, why did the Calendar display the current date and not the date I printed?

The calendar always displays the current date when you change from List view to Calendar view.

BTW

Distributing a Calendar
Instead of printing and distributing a hard copy of a calendar, you can distribute the calendar electronically. Options include sending the calendar via email; posting it on cloud storage (such as SkyDrive) and sharing the file with others; posting it on a social networking site, blog, or other website; and sharing a link associated with an online location of the calendar. You also can create and share a PDF or XPS image of the calendar, so that users can view the file in Acrobat Reader or XPS Viewer instead of in Outlook.

Figure 2–91

Other Ways
1. Press CTRL+P, tap or click Print

Saving and Sharing the Calendar

For security and convenience, you can save your Outlook calendar by backing up your entire Outlook personal folder files (.pst) or an individual calendar (.ics). As a reminder, in Chapter 1 you saved the Outlook .pst file, which contained a backup of your email, calendar, and contacts. Saving your calendar file allows you to back up your appointments, events, and meetings in a single file. You can then move your calendar to another computer, for example, and continue to schedule items there. Besides saving your calendar, you can share it with others, whether they use Outlook or not. Finally, scheduling a meeting with someone who cannot see your calendar can be difficult, so you can share your calendar through email.

With Outlook, each appointment, task, or contact can be saved as a separate iCalendar file or you can save the whole calendar to your local computer or external storage device. An iCalendar file with the .ics file extension can be imported by other programs such as Google Calendar. Instead of emailing an iCalendar file as an attachment to share your calendar, you can share portions of your entire calendar through a built-in function in Outlook.

To Save a Calendar as an iCalendar File

1 CONFIGURE CALENDAR OPTIONS | 2 CREATE & MANIPULATE APPOINTMENTS | 3 SCHEDULE EVENTS
4 SCHEDULE MEETINGS | 5 PRINT CALENDAR | 6 SAVE & SHARE CALENDAR

You have performed many tasks while creating this calendar and do not want to risk losing work completed thus far. Accordingly, you should save the calendar on your hard disk, SkyDrive, or a location that is most appropriate to your situation.

The following steps assume you already have created folders for storing your files, for example, a CIS 101 folder (for your class) that contains an Outlook folder (for your assignments). Thus, these steps save the calendar in the Outlook folder in the CIS 101 folder on your desired save location. For a detailed example of the procedure for saving a file in a folder or saving a file on SkyDrive, refer to the Office and Windows chapter at the beginning of this book.

Why? *By saving a copy of your calendar to an iCalendar format, you can back up or share your calendar with your business colleagues or friends.* The following steps save a calendar. They assume you already have created folders for storing your files, for example, a CIS 101 folder (for your class) that contains an Outlook folder (for your assignments).

1

• Tap or click FILE on the ribbon to display the Backstage view (Figure 2–92).

Figure 2–92

②

- Tap or click the Save Calendar tab to display the Save As dialog box.

- Navigate to the desired save location (in this case, the Outlook folder in the CIS 101 folder or your class folder) (Figure 2–93).

Q&A Where can I find a more detailed example of saving?

For a detailed example of this procedure, refer to Steps 4a and 4b in the "To Save a File in a Folder" section in the Office and Windows chapter at the beginning of this book.

Figure 2–93

③

- Tap or click the More Options button to display the Save As dialog box.

- Tap or click the Date Range arrow to display the Date Range list (Figure 2–94).

④

- If necessary, tap or click Whole calendar on the Date Range list to save the calendar's full details.

- Tap or click the OK button (Save As dialog box) to specify the whole calendar date range.

- Tap or click the Save button to save the calendar as an iCalendar file in the selected location.

Figure 2–94

To Share a Calendar

1 CONFIGURE CALENDAR OPTIONS | 2 CREATE & MANIPULATE APPOINTMENTS | 3 SCHEDULE EVENTS
4 SCHEDULE MEETINGS | 5 PRINT CALENDAR | 6 SAVE & SHARE CALENDAR

Why? *You can send a copy of your calendar in an email message directly from Outlook to inform others when you are available for a meeting.* The following steps share a calendar by forwarding the selected calendar. These steps assume you have an email account set up in Outlook.

①

- Tap or click HOME on the ribbon to display the HOME tab.

- Tap or click the E-mail Calendar button (HOME tab | Share group) to open the Untitled – Message (HTML) window and display the Send a Calendar via E-mail dialog box (Figure 2–95).

Figure 2–95

②

- Tap or click the OK button to attach the Personal calendar to the email message.

- Tap or click the To text box, and then type financialaidhelp@outlook.com (substitute your instructor's email address for the financial aid address) as the recipient's email address (Figure 2–96).

③

- Tap or click the Send button to send your iCalendar to share with the email message recipient.

Q&A When I sent the email with the calendar attachment, an error message opened stating that "No valid email accounts are configured." Why did I get this error message?

You must have an email account set up in Outlook to send the calendar.

Figure 2–96

To Exit Outlook

This project now is complete. The following steps exit Outlook. For a detailed example of the procedure summarized below, refer to the Office 2013 and Windows 8 chapter at the beginning of this book.

1 If you have an email message open, tap or click the Close button on the right side of the title bar to close the message window.

2 Tap or click the Close button on the right side of the title bar to exit Outlook.

BTW
Certification
The Microsoft Office Specialist (MOS) program provides an opportunity for you to obtain a valuable industry credential — proof that you have the Outlook 2013 skills required by employers. For more information, visit the Certification resource on the Student Companion Site located on

www.cengagebrain.com. For detailed instructions about accessing available resources, visit www.cengage.com/ct/studentdownload or contact your instructor for information about accessing the required files.

Chapter Summary

In this chapter, you have learned how to use Outlook to create a personal schedule by entering appointments, creating recurring appointments, moving appointments to new dates, and scheduling events. You also learned how to invite attendees to a meeting, accept a meeting request, and change the time of a meeting. To review your schedule, you learned to view and print your calendar in different views and print styles. Finally, you learned how to save your calendar and share your schedule with others. The items listed below include all the new Outlook skills you have learned in this chapter with the tasks grouped by activity.

Configuring the Outlook Calendar
Create a Personal Calendar Folder (OUT 64)
Add a City to the Calendar Weather Bar (OUT 67)
Go to a Specific Date (OUT 68)
Display the Calendar in Work Week View (OUT 69)
Display the Calendar in Week View (OUT 70)
Display the Calendar in Month View (OUT 71)
Display the Calendar in Schedule View (OUT 71)
Add Holidays to the Default Calendar (OUT 73)

Creating and Editing Appointments
Create a One-Time Appointment Using the Appointment Area (OUT 76)
Add Color Categories (OUT 78)
Assign a Color Category to an Appointment (OUT 80)
Create an Appointment Using the Appointment Window (OUT 81)
Set a Reminder for an Appointment (OUT 85)
Set Recurrence Options for an Appointment (OUT 87)
Save an Appointment (OUT 90)
Create an Appointment Date and Time Using Natural Language Phrases (OUT 92)
Move an Appointment to a Different Time on the Same Day (OUT 94)
Move an Appointment to a Different Date (OUT 94)
Delete a Single Occurrence of a Recurring Appointment (OUT 95)

Scheduling Events
Create a One-Time Event in the Appointment Window (OUT 97)
Delete a One-Time Event (OUT 99)
Create a Recurring Event Using the Appointment Window (OUT 99)
Move a Recurring Event to a Different Day (OUT 101)

Scheduling Meetings
Import an iCalendar File (OUT 104)
View Calendars in the Overlay Mode (OUT 106)
View and Dock the Peek Calendar (OUT 107)
Create and Send a Meeting Request (OUT 108)
Change the Time of a Meeting and Send an Update (OUT 110)
Reply to a Meeting Request (OUT 111)
Propose a New Meeting Time (OUT 112)
Cancel a Meeting (OUT 112)

Printing Calendars in Different Views
Print the Calendar in Weekly Calendar Style (OUT 112)
Change the Calendar View to List View (OUT 114)
Print the Calendar in List View (OUT 115)

Saving and Sharing the Calendar
Save a Calendar as an iCalendar File (OUT 116)
Share a Calendar (OUT 117)

BTW
Quick Reference
For a table that lists how to complete the tasks covered in this book using touch gestures, the mouse, ribbon, shortcut menu, and keyboard, see the Quick Reference Summary at the back of this book, or visit the Quick Reference resource on the Student Companion Site located on www.cengagebrain.com. For detailed instructions about accessing available resources, visit www.cengage.com/ct/studentdownload or contact your instructor for information about accessing the required files.

What decisions will you need to make when configuring the Outlook calendar; scheduling appointments, events, and meetings; printing calendars; and saving and sharing your calendar in the future?

A. Configure the Outlook Calendar:

1. Determine the purpose of your calendar – personal, professional, or for a group.

2. Determine the city displayed on the Weather Bar and if you prefer holidays in your default calendar.

B. Schedule Appointments, Events, and Meetings:

1. Determine if each calendar item is an appointment, event, or a meeting.

2. Determine which appointments and events are one-time or recurring.

3. Plan which color-coded categories would best organize your calendar items.

C. Edit Appointments, Events, and Meetings:

1. Update the details of your calendar items as your schedule changes.

2. Respond to meeting requests.

D. Print Your Calendar:

1. Plan which calendar style would best fit your needs.

E. Save and Share Your Calendar:

1. Plan where your calendar should be stored.

2. Determine how you will share your calendar with friends and colleagues.

How should you submit solutions to questions in the assignments identified with a ✸ symbol?

Every assignment in this book contains one or more questions identified with a ✸ symbol. These questions require you to think beyond the assigned file. Present your solutions to the questions in the format required by your instructor. Possible formats may include one or more of these options: write the answer; create a document that contains the answer; present your answer to the class; discuss your answer in a group; record the answer as audio or video using a webcam, smartphone, or portable media player; or post answers on a blog, wiki, or website.

Apply Your Knowledge

Reinforce the skills and apply the concepts you learned in this chapter.

Updating a Calendar

Note: To complete this assignment, you will be required to use the Data Files for Students. Visit www.cengage.com/ct/studentdownload for detailed instructions or contact your instructor for information about accessing the required files.

Instructions: You are updating the Run for Funds nonprofit fundraising iCalendar named Apply 1-1 Run for Funds Calendar by revising the scheduled activities.

Perform the following tasks:

1. Run Outlook.

2. Open the Apply 1-1 Run for Funds Calendar.ics file from the Data Files for Students.

3. Display only this iCalendar in the Outlook Calendar window. Use Month view to display the calendar for March 2014.

4. Change the Planning Meeting appointment from March 5 to March 12. Move the appointment to one hour later with the same duration.

5. Change the location of the Volunteers Meeting appointment on March 18 to Monte Park.

6. Reschedule the Marketing Meeting from Thursdays starting on March 27 until May 1 to meet at the same time on Tuesdays starting on March 25 until April 29 at the same time.

7. Reschedule a single occurrence of the Marketing Meeting on April 29 to May 1 at the same time.

8. Change the starting and ending time of the race on May 3 to one hour later.

9. If requested by your instructor, change the location of the race from Town Square to your birth city.

10. Save the Calendar as Apply 2-1 Run for Funds Updated and submit the iCalendar in the format specified by your instructor.

11. Print the final calendar in Month view, shown in Figure 2–97, and then submit the printout to your instructor.

12. Delete this calendar from Outlook and exit Outlook.

13. ✳ Most calendar programs save files with the .ics format. Why is it convenient that most calendar programs use the same format?

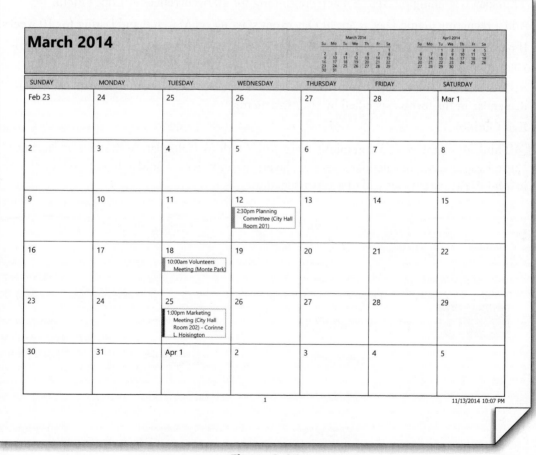

Figure 2–97

Extend Your Knowledge

Extend the skills you learned in this chapter and experiment with new skills. You will use Help to complete the assignment.

Creating and Sharing a Calendar

Instructions: Start Outlook. You are assisting with a local Little League baseball team. Create a new calendar to share the practice and game dates with the team. Use Outlook Help to learn how to create a calendar group, change the color of the calendar, and create a private appointment.

Perform the following tasks:

1. Run Outlook and create a new calendar group called Community Calendars.

2. Create a blank calendar named Tigers Baseball and then move it to the Community Calendars calendar group.

3. Change the color of the entire calendar to the team's color, orange.

4. Create an appointment named Coaches Summit for March 3, 2014 at Lopez Field from 7:00 PM for 2 hours. Mark the appointment as private so that others will not see details of this calendar item.

5. Add a recurring Baseball Practice appointment from 5:00 PM to 6:30 PM on Tuesday and Thursday beginning on March 4 and continuing for 20 occurrences at Lopez Field.

6. Add a recurring Game Day as an All Day event starting on March 8 and lasting for 10 weeks.

7. If requested by your instructor, change the Weather Bar to display weather information for your hometown. The completed calendar is shown in Figure 2–98.

8. Save the Calendar as Extend Your Knowledge 2-1 Tigers Baseball Calendar and submit the iCalendar in the format specified by your instructor.

9. Exit Outlook.

10. ☀ Think about the reason you might share your Outlook Calendar. In the case of sharing a Little League baseball calendar with the players' parents, why would a digital calendar be more helpful to the parents instead of a paper schedule?

Figure 2–98

Analyze, Correct, Improve

Analyze an email message, correct all errors, and improve the design.

Correcting Errors in Calendar Appointments

Note: To complete this assignment, you will be required to use the Data Files for Students. Visit www.cengage.com/ct/studentdownload for detailed instructions or contact your instructor for information about accessing the required files.

Instructions: Start Outlook. Open the Analyze Correct Improve 2-1 file from the Data Files for Students. While reviewing your Outlook calendar, you realize that you created several appointments incorrectly. You will identify and open the incorrect appointments, edit them so that they reflect the correct information, improve the organization by adding categories, and then save all changes.

1. Correct   Display only the Analyze Correct Improve 2-1 Exercise Calendar in the Outlook Calendar window. The Kickboxing class scheduled for Wednesday, October 1, 2014 is a recurring appointment on your calendar. Change the appointment to reflect the Kickboxing class meeting every Thursday starting October 2, 2014 through the end of November from 7:30 PM until 9:00 PM. The class will not meet on Thanksgiving. While adding an appointment for your yearly physical to the Calendar, you inadvertently recorded the appointment time as 3:00 AM instead of 3:00 PM. Edit the appointment on October 7, 2014, and change the Start time to 3:00 PM. The appointment still lasts one hour.

2. Improve   Add reminders 30 minutes before each of the Kickboxing classes. Create a red category for Exercise and a new blue category for Medical. Add the correct category to each of the appointments. If requested by your instructor, add your birthday as an All Day event in 2014. Save the Calendar as Analyze Correct Improve 2-1 Exercise Calendar Updated, as shown in Figure 2–99, and submit the iCalendar in the format specified by your instructor.

3. ✹ When you are reading your email, how can the Peek calendar option be helpful?

Figure 2–99

In the Labs

Use the guidelines, concepts, and skills presented in this chapter to increase your knowledge of Outlook. Labs 1 and 2, which increase in difficulty, require you to create solutions based on what you learned in the chapter; Lab 3 requires you to create a solution, which uses cloud and web technologies, by learning and investigating on your own from general guidance.

Lab 1: Creating Recurring Events

Problem: You would like to set up a calendar to remember your payment schedules for your monthly rent, school loans, car loan, electric bill, mobile phone bill, ISP bill, and yearly bills, as shown in Figure 2–100.

Figure 2–100

Instructions: Perform the following tasks:

1. Create a Calendar named Lab 2-1 Bill Payment Calendar in Outlook.

2. Create the events in the calendar in the year 2014, using the information listed in Table 2–7.

3. For each event, enter the location as Pay online.

Table 2–7 Bill Payment Information			
Payment Type	**Due Date**	**Category**	**Color Code**
Apartment rental	6th day of the month	Living Expense	blue
School loan	25th day of the month	School Expense	green
Car payment	3rd day of the month	Transportation	orange
Electric bill	28th day of the month	Living Expense	blue
Mobile phone bill	12th day of the month	Misc. Expense	purple
ISP bill	Second Monday of each month	Misc. Expense	purple
Tax bill	April 15th	Tax	red
Car inspection	March 30th	Tax	red and orange

4. For each event, show the time as Free.

5. For each event, set the reminder to one day.

6. For each monthly event, set the event to recur every month during 2014.

7. Each event should be an All Day event.

8. If requested by your instructor, add your Mom's birthday with her name as an event in your 2014 Calendar.

9. Save the calendar as an .ics file and submit it in a format specified by your instructor.

10. Print the month of April using the Monthly Style and submit it in a format specified by your instructor.

11. ✴ A calendar can keep you organized. In the case of scheduling your bills, how can a digital calendar assist in increasing your credit score?

Lab 2: **Creating a Calendar**

Problem: You are assisting a local photographer with updating their social media presence, an increasingly vital aspect of marketing. By taking the time to develop a plan for your social media posts, as shown in Figure 2–101, you will remember to keep the online information current.

Figure 2–101

Instructions: Perform the following tasks:

1. Create a calendar named Lab 2-2 Social Media Calendar in Outlook.

2. Create the events in the calendar, using the information listed in Table 2–8.

Table 2–8 Social Media Marketing Events				
Marketing Topic	**Location**	**Posting Date**	**Category**	**Color Code**
20% off sitting fee	facebook.com	September 6, 2014	Facebook	blue
Free 5x7 photo with any purchase	twitter.com	September 12, 2014	Twitter	green
$10 off portrait sitting fee	linkedin.com	September 17, 2014	LinkedIn	red
25% off newborn session fee	plus.google.com	September 17, 2014	Google+	yellow
Three 8x10 portraits for $30	facebook.com	September 22, 2014	Facebook	blue
30% off for Halloween sitting fee	plus.google.com	September 30, 2014	Google+	yellow

© 2014 Cengage Learning

Continued >

In the Labs *continued*

3. For each event in the table, set the reminder as 0 minutes.

4. For each event, show the time as Free.

5. For each Monday and Wednesday throughout the month of September 2014, add a recurring appointment. Enter `Respond to online comments` as the subject. For location, enter `All social media sites`. The appointment should start at 9:00 AM and end one hour later. Add all four color-coded categories and set a 10-minute reminder for each event.

6. Delete the one occurrence of the recurring appointment on September 15.

7. Change your Weather Bar to show the weather for your hometown.

8. If requested by your instructor, add a 10% off portfolio fee on Facebook to celebrate your birthday with a 0-minute reminder. Add this event to the calendar on your birth date in 2014.

9. Save the calendar as an .ics file and submit it in a format specified by your instructor.

10. Print the calendar for the month of September in Monthly style, and then submit the printout in the format specified by your instructor.

11. ✳ What are the advantages of syncing your Outlook Calendar to a mobile phone?

Lab 3: Expand Your World: Cloud and Web Technologies
Opening a Web-Based Calendar in the Outlook Client

Problem: Using the due dates from a CIS class shown in Table 2–9, create an online calendar at Outlook.com using your Microsoft account. Share the online calendar with your instructor. Using Outlook, open the online calendar and print the calendar in the Outlook client. Sharing your calendar in the cloud as a link allows anyone to see your calendar, even if they do not have their own calendar established.

Instructions: Perform the following tasks:

1. If necessary, create a Microsoft account at outlook.com.

2. Open the calendar option at outlook.com and add a calendar named CIS Class Calendar.

3. Open the CIS Class Calendar only and add the following items shown in Table 2–9 to the online calendar.

4. If requested by your instructor, add a Study Session event the day before the test at your home address.

5. Tap or click the Share button to view the sharing options for this calendar. Select the option to send people a view-only link to access this calendar online. Select the ICS option to import into another calendar application to show event details.

Table 2–9 CIS Class Calendar Items			
Description	**Recurrence**	**Due Date**	**Availability**
Outlook Chapter 1 Assignment	None	First Friday in October 2014 at midnight	Free
Outlook Chapter 2 Assignment	None	Second Friday in October 2014 at midnight	Free
Lecture	Every Tuesday	Every Tuesday in October 2014 from 6:00 PM for 3 hours	Busy
Test	None	Last Tuesday at 8:00 PM for one hour	Busy

© 2014 Cengage Learning

6. Submit the outlook.com calendar link in a format specified by your instructor.

7. Select the option to preview the calendar in another calendar application and launch the calendar in Microsoft Outlook. If the online calendar changes, Outlook will automatically update.

8. In the Microsoft Outlook client, print the calendar for the month of October in Monthly style, and then submit the printout in the format specified by your instructor.

9. Exit outlook.com, and then exit Outlook.

10. ✺ In this lab, you shared an online calendar with your instructor and also imported the online calendar to the Outlook client. Name at least 12 calendar functions that outlook.com and the Outlook client have in common.

✺ Consider This: Your Turn

Apply your creative thinking and problem solving skills to design and implement a solution.

1: Creating a Calendar

Personal

Part 1:   You have joined a new local band. One of your responsibilities in the band includes keeping everyone informed of the performance and practice schedule. Create a new calendar of the various appointments and events for summer 2014. Use Table 2–10 to add these items to the calendar named Consider This 2-1 Band Calendar. If requested by your instructor, change the location of the Battle of the Bands to the name of your birth city. Use the concepts and techniques presented in this chapter to create the email message. Submit your assignment in the format specified by your instructor.

Part 2:   ✺ You can publish Outlook calendars to a website to share your calendar. How would publishing a band's performance calendar increase your following? What are the advantages of allowing others to download the performance calendar from the band's website and Facebook?

Table 2–10 Band Schedule						
Description	Location	Date & Time	Show As	Reminder	Recurrence	Category
Band practice	Ryan's house	May 8; 7:00 PM for 3 hours	Busy	1 hour	Weekly until September 4	Practice (yellow)
Peanut Festival	City Park	May 24; 8:00 PM for 2 hours	Busy	1 day	none	Performance (red)
Cascade Resort	Amphitheater	June 14; noon for 2.5 hours	Busy	1 day	none	Performance (red)
Battle of the Bands	Lucas Center	July 18–20	Free	1 day	none	Competition (purple)
Pauley Wedding	Chamber restaurant	August 9; 7:00 PM for 4 hours	Busy	1 week	none	Performance (red)
Fall Festival	City Park	Labor Day; 2:00 PM for 1 hour	Busy	1 day	none	Performance (red)

© 2014 Cengage Learning

Continued >

Consider This: Your Turn *continued*

2: Create Meeting Invitations

Professional

Part 1: Create a calendar for the Roaster's Coffee Shop that sends invitations for upcoming meetings, as shown in Table 2–11. All the meetings are held at Roaster's Coffee Shop. Send a meeting invitation to yourself. If requested by your instructor, add a sixth meeting on June 2nd at 9:00 AM for one hour at the coffee shop to meet with your elementary school for a PTA fund-raiser; include a one-day reminder and show as working elsewhere. Save your calendar as an iCalendar named Consider This 2-2 Roaster's Coffee Shop Calendar. Submit your assignment in the format specified by your instructor.

Table 2–11 Roaster's Coffee Shop Calendar Meetings					
Description	Date	Time	Show As	Reminder	Recurrence
Staff Meeting	Every Thursday in 2014	1:00 PM – 2:00 PM	Out of Office	30 minutes	Weekly
Training for New Staff Meeting	Third day of each month	12:00 PM – 2:00 PM	Tentative	30 minutes	Monthly
Inventory Meeting	April 4, 2014	2:00 PM – 5:00 PM	Busy	45 minutes	None
Performance Meeting	August 15, 2014	All Day Event	Free	1 day	None
Holiday Menu Meeting	December 1, 2014	9:00 AM for 2 hours	Busy	1 day	None

© 2014 Cengage Learning

Part 2: ✷ If you receive a meeting request, you can respond in several ways. What are the four ways to respond to a meeting request? You can add comments with each of these responses. Provide comments to each of the four meeting requests responses explaining why you can or cannot attend the first staff meeting for the coffee shop.

3: Research a Club or Organization's Meeting Schedule

Research and Collaboration

Part 1: To assist a school club or local organization, research their meeting schedule and events. After analyzing each item, determine if the item is an appointment, event, or meeting. Create an iCalendar for the club or organization with at least 15 items throughout the year. Create color-coded categories to assist in organizing the calendar items. Determine the Show As and Reminder settings based on each type of calendar item. Share the calendar with the organization to assist in their planning by sending an email that includes the iCalendar. Use the concepts and techniques presented in this chapter to create the calendar. Submit your assignment in the format specified by your instructor.

Part 2: ✷ A popular calendar website named http://icalshare.com shares useful calendars for holidays, sports teams, astronomy dates, and music events. Write a paragraph about the features of this site in your own words. Include an example of which calendar would be helpful to you.

Learn Online

Reinforce what you learned in this chapter with games, exercises, training, and many other online activities and resources.

Student Companion Site   Reinforce chapter terms and concepts using review questions, flash cards, practice tests, and interactive learning games, such as a crossword puzzle. These and other online activities and resources are available at no additional cost on www.cengagebrain.com. Visit www.cengage.com/ct/studentdownload for detailed instructions about accessing the resources available at the Student Companion Site.

3 Managing Contacts and Personal Contact Information with Outlook

Objectives

You will have mastered the material in this chapter when you can:

- Create a new contact
- Create a contact from an email message
- Modify a contact
- Add a contact photo
- Delete a contact
- Manipulate attachments to contacts
- Display contacts in different views
- Sort a contact list

- Find contacts using complete or partial information
- Find contacts from any Outlook folder
- Create a contact group
- Modify a contact group
- Add and remove names in a contact group
- Preview a contact list
- Print a contact list

3 | Managing Contacts and Personal Contact Information with Outlook

This introductory chapter covers features and functions common to managing contacts in Outlook 2013.

Roadmap

In this chapter, you will learn how to perform basic contact tasks. The following roadmap identifies general activities you will perform as you progress through this chapter:

1. CREATE a NEW CONTACT
2. MODIFY a CONTACT
3. CHANGE the VIEW OF CONTACTS
4. FIND a CONTACT
5. CREATE a CONTACT GROUP
6. PRINT the CONTACT LIST

At the beginning of step instructions throughout the chapter, you will see an abbreviated form of this roadmap. The abbreviated roadmap uses colors to indicate chapter progress: gray means the chapter is beyond that activity, blue means the task being shown is covered in that activity, and black means that activity is yet to be covered. For example, the following abbreviated roadmap indicates the section would be about finding a contact.

1 CREATE NEW CONTACT | 2 MODIFY CONTACT | 3 CHANGE VIEW OF CONTACTS

4 FIND CONTACT | 5 CREATE CONTACT GROUP | 6 PRINT CONTACT LIST

Use the abbreviated roadmap as a progress guide while you read or step through the instructions in this chapter.

Introduction to Outlook Contacts

To keep track of your friends, business partners, family, and others with whom you communicate, you can use Outlook to create contact lists and contact groups. A **contact list** lets you record information about people, such as their email address, phone number, birthday, physical address, and photo. Each person's information is stored in a **contact record** in the contact list. If you have several colleagues at work who you email frequently, you can add them to a **contact group**. You then can send email messages to all of your colleagues using the contact group rather than having to select each contact individually.

Project — Contact List with Groups

People and businesses create contact lists to keep track of people who are important to them or their business. A contact list may contain groups so that several contacts can be identified with a group name rather than individual contact names. Managing your contacts using a contact list can increase productivity greatly.

The project in this chapter follows general guidelines and uses Outlook to create the contact list shown in Figure 3–1. This contact list displays individual contacts and contact groups in a business card layout. In this layout, the individual contacts present essential information such as the name, affiliation, and email address of the contact. A photograph of each contact helps you associate a face to a name. The contact groups display the name of the group, have a group label, and include a different graphic from the individual contacts.

BTW

The Ribbon and Screen Resolution
Outlook may change how the groups and buttons within the groups appear on the ribbon, depending on the computer's screen resolution. Thus, your ribbon may look different from the ones in this book if you are using a screen resolution other than 1366 × 768.

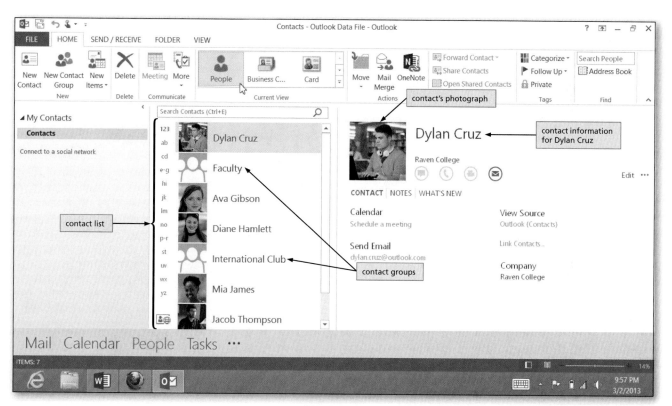

Figure 3–1

Creating a Contact List

The first step in creating a contact list is to enter information such as names, email addresses, and phone numbers for the people you communicate with regularly. After you enter and save contact information, that information is available as you compose email messages. You can type the first few letters of a contact's name into an email message, and Outlook will fill in the rest of the email address for you. If you are working on a mobile device that can make and receive phone calls, you also can use contact information to call someone on your contact list.

For an introduction to Windows 8 and instruction about how to perform basic Windows 8 tasks, read the Office 2013 and Windows 8 chapter at the beginning of this book, where you can learn how to resize windows, change screen resolution, create folders, move and rename files, use Windows Help, and much more.

What advantages does an Outlook contact list provide for marketing a new business such as a restaurant?
Creating a contact list of your customer contacts lets you reach more people who can help your business grow by becoming repeat customers and spreading the word about your business. A restaurant can provide an email sign-up form on its website so that customers can choose to keep up with the latest deals. For example, a restaurant might send monthly email messages to advertise specials such as 20 percent off take-out food on a certain date.

Contacts – Outlook Window

The Contacts – Outlook window shown in Figure 3–2 includes a variety of features to help you work efficiently with a contact list. The Contacts – Outlook window contains many elements similar to the windows in other Office programs, as well as some elements that are unique to Outlook. The main elements of the Contacts window are the My Contacts pane, the contact list, and the People pane.

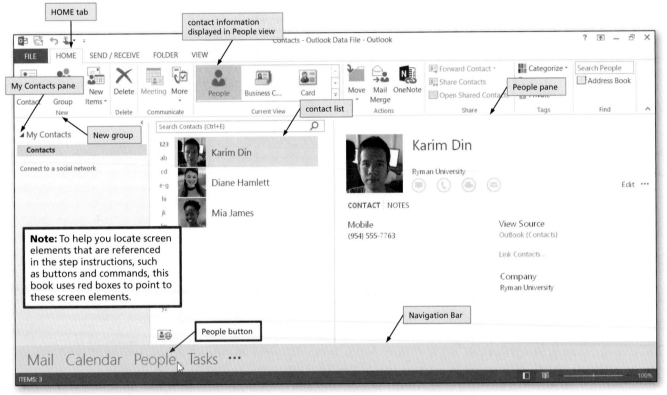

Figure 3–2

BTW
Using More Than One Outlook Data File
If you have multiple email accounts or data files set up in Outlook, you may need to remove the email accounts or data files to practice the steps in this chapter. To remove an account, tap or click the FILE tab, tap or click Account Settings, and then tap or click the Account Settings option. Select the email account and tap or click the Remove button to remove the email account.

To Run Outlook

If you are using a computer to step through the project in this chapter and you want your screens to match the figures in this book, you should change your screen's resolution to 1366 × 768. For information about how to change a computer's resolution, refer to the Office 2013 and Windows 8 chapter at the beginning of this book.

The following steps, which assume Windows 8 is running, use the Search text box to run Outlook based on a typical installation. You may need to ask your instructor how to run Outlook on your computer. For a detailed example of the procedure summarized below, refer to the Office 2013 and Windows 8 chapter.

1 Swipe in from the right edge of the screen or point to the upper-right corner of the screen to display the Charms bar.

2 Tap or click the Search charm on the Charms bar to display the Search menu.

3 Type `Outlook` as the search text in the Search text box and watch the search results appear in the Apps list.

4 Tap or click Outlook 2013 in the search results to run Outlook.

5 If the Outlook window is not maximized, tap or click the Maximize button on its title bar to maximize the window.

To Create a New Contact

To create the contact list in this chapter, you start by adding Dylan Cruz as the first contact. In Chapters 1 and 2, you set up Dylan's email account and calendar in Outlook. When you create or update a contact, you add the contact's name, company name, email address, and other information, such as a Twitter username. The following steps create a new contact in the People view. *Why?* *To organize the contact information of your friends, clients, and colleagues, you should keep an Outlook contact list to communicate efficiently without having to search for information in multiple locations. Dylan is adding himself to his contact list to organize his contact information in a central place.*

1

- Open the Dylan.pst Outlook Data File from the Data Files for Students for Chapter 3.

- Tap or click People (shown in Figure 3–2) on the Navigation Bar to display the Outlook Contacts.

- Tap or click the New Contact button (HOME tab | New group) to display the Untitled – Contact window (Figure 3–3).

Q&A What should I do if I have more than one Outlook data file open in the Navigation Pane?

Open only the Dylan.pst Outlook data file, which appears as Outlook Data File in the Navigation Pane. Close any other Outlook data files open in the Navigation Pane, and then repeat Step 1.

Figure 3–3

2

- Type **Dylan Cruz** in the Full Name text box to enter a name for the contact.

- Type **Raven College** in the Company text box to enter a company (or in this case, a school) for the contact.

- Type **dylan .cruz@outlook .com** in the E-mail text box, and then press the TAB key to enter an email address for the contact (Figure 3–4).

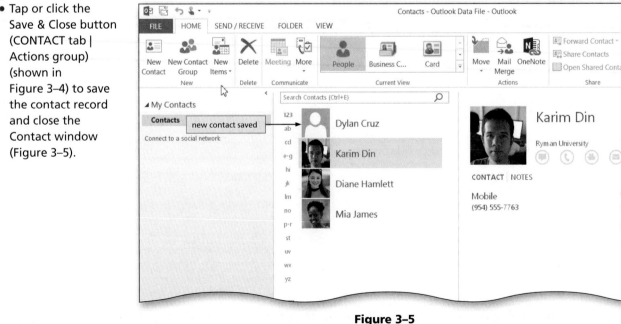

Figure 3–4

Q&A Why did the title of the Contact window change after I entered the name?

As soon as you enter the name, Outlook updates the Contact window title to reflect the information you have entered. Outlook also displays the name in the File as text box. The contact is not saved, however; only the window title and File as text boxes are updated.

Can I add information to other fields for a contact?

Yes. As long as you have the information, you can fill out the fields accordingly. You even can add fields besides those listed by tapping or clicking the All Fields button (CONTACT tab | Show group).

3

- Tap or click the Save & Close button (CONTACT tab | Actions group) (shown in Figure 3–4) to save the contact record and close the Contact window (Figure 3–5).

Figure 3–5

Other Ways

1. Press and hold or right-click contact list, click New Contact   2. Press CTRL+SHIFT+C

To Create Contacts from Email Messages

1 CREATE NEW CONTACT | 2 MODIFY CONTACT | 3 CHANGE VIEW OF CONTACTS
4 FIND CONTACT | 5 CREATE CONTACT GROUP | 6 PRINT CONTACT LIST

Dylan frequently emails Jacob Thompson, an instructor in charge of the Study Abroad program. In addition, as the president of the Student International Club, Dylan contacts Ava Gibson, the club's webmaster. Creating contacts for Jacob and Ava will simplify communications for Dylan. Outlook can create a contact based on the information located within email messages. The following steps create contacts from email messages. *Why? You can quickly add a contact from an email message to better keep track of the sender's information. If you type the first few letters of a contact's name into a new email message, Outlook fills in the email address for you.*

❶

- Tap or click the Mail button in the Navigation Pane to display your mailbox from the Dylan.pst file.

- If necessary, tap or click Inbox in the Navigation Pane to display the Inbox from the Dylan.pst file.

- Tap or click the Jacob Thompson message header to preview the email message in the Reading Pane (Figure 3–6).

Q&A What if I do not have an email message from Jacob Thompson?
If you did not open or import the data file for this chapter, you might not have an email message from Jacob Thompson. In that case, perform these steps using another email message in your mailbox.

Figure 3–6

BTW

Contacts Window

By default, tapping or clicking the People button in the Navigation bar displays the contacts in the Microsoft Outlook window. To display the contacts in a new window, press and hold or right-click the People button in the Navigation bar, and then tap or click Open in New Window on the shortcut menu.

2

• Press and hold or right-click Jacob Thompson's email address (shown in Figure 3–6) in the message header of the Reading Pane to display a shortcut menu (Figure 3–7).

Figure 3–7

3

• Tap or click Add to Outlook Contacts (shown in Figure 3–7) to display the contact window (Figure 3–8).

Q&A Why does the contact window already have Jacob's Thompson's name and email address entered into the Name and Email text boxes?
Outlook automatically detects the name and the email address for the contact from the existing email message.

Figure 3–8

4

- Tap or click the Save button (shown in Figure 3–8) in the contact window to save the contact and open the contact card for Jacob Thompson (Figure 3–9).

Q&A What can you do with the contact card?

The contact card includes shortcuts to tasks typically performed with contacts, such as scheduling a meeting, sending an email message, and editing contact information.

Figure 3–9

5

- Tap or click the Close button (shown in Figure 3–9) in the contact card to close the contact card.
- Tap or click the Ava Gibson message header to preview the email message in the Reading Pane.
- Press and hold or right-click Ava Gibson's email address in the message header of the Reading Pane to display a shortcut menu.
- Tap or click 'Add to Outlook Contacts' to display the contact window.
- Tap or click the Save button in the contact window to save the contact and close the contact window.
- Tap or click the Close button in the contact card to close the contact card.
- Tap or click People in the Navigation Pane to display your contact list, including the new contacts for Jacob Thompson and Ava Gibson (Figure 3–10).

Figure 3–10

Q&A

Can I add more details such as a phone number or work number to the contact window?

You always can add more information such as an another email address or photo to the contact window when you create a contact or later when you have more time.

The two new contact records I added do not appear in the contact list. What should I do?

You probably have another Outlook data file open in Outlook. In the Navigation Pane, note the name of the Dylan.pst data file, such as Contacts – Outlook Data File. Click other items in the Navigation pane to find the one containing the Ava Gibson and Jacob Thompson contact records. Select the Ava Gibson and Jacob Thompson contact records, and then drag them to the Dylan.pst data file, such as the Contacts – Outlook Data File in the Navigation Pane.

CONSIDER THIS

How can I import contacts from an external source such as an iPhone or Android smartphone?

To create a master list of all your contacts in one location in Outlook, you can import your contacts from your smartphone's address book, Internet-based email addresses such as your Gmail contacts, or from within another program such as an Access database. To import your contacts from an external address book:

1. Tap or click Address Book (HOME tab | Find group) to open the Address Book: Contacts dialog box.

2. Tap or click the Address Book arrow to view a list of external address books.

3. Tap or click the external contacts list, such as Contacts (Mobile), to display a list of external contacts.

4. Tap or click the first contact, press the SHIFT key, and tap or click the last contact to select the entire list of contacts.

5. Tap or click File to display the File menu. Tap or click Add to Contacts to add the selected contacts to your Outlook contact list.

6. Tap or click the Close button to close the Address Book: Contacts dialog box.

BTW

Importing Contacts from External Sources

If you need to copy an existing contact list into Outlook, tap or click the FILE tab and then tap or click Open. Next, tap or click Import to open the Import and Export Wizard. Based on the type of contact file, select the import file type and follow the steps for the appropriate import type.

Editing a Contact

After setting up your contact list, you need to keep the information current and add new information, such as a new work phone number, Twitter account username, or picture, to help you interact with your contact. You can attach one or more files to a contact to store documents, tables, pictures, or clip art, for example, along with their contact information. If your colleagues transfer to other companies, remove contact information that you no longer need unless you will continue to interact with them on a regular basis.

To Edit a Contact

1 CREATE NEW CONTACT | 2 MODIFY CONTACT | 3 CHANGE VIEW OF CONTACTS
4 FIND CONTACT | 5 CREATE CONTACT GROUP | 6 PRINT CONTACT LIST

When you created a contact record for Jacob Thompson, it did not include his job title, work phone number, or picture. Mr. Thompson has given you the name of his school, proper title, work phone number, and photo, and you want to edit his contact record to include the new information. In addition, you need to include contact pictures for Dylan and Ava. The following steps edit a contact by entering additional information including pictures. The pictures are available in the Student Data Files for Chapter 3. *Why? The more information you have about a business contact, the better you can provide personalized service. For example, including a business photo of your contact associates a name with a face. A company logo also could be used instead of a professional photo.*

BTW

BTWs

For a complete list of the BTWs found in the margins of this book, visit the BTW resource on the Student Companion Site located on www.cengagebrain.com. For detailed instructions about accessing available resources, visit www.cengage.com/ct/studentdownload or contact your instructor for information about accessing the required files.

1

- Tap or click the Jacob Thompson contact to display Jacob Thompson's contact information in the People pane (Figure 3–11).

Figure 3–11

2

- Tap or click Outlook (Contacts) below the View Source heading (shown in Figure 3–11) to display the Jacob Thompson – Contact window.

- Type **Raven College** in the Company text box to enter a company or school name for the contact.

- Type **(954) 555-3627** in the Business text box, and then press the ENTER key to enter a business phone number for the contact (Figure 3–12).

Figure 3–12

To Add an Attachment to a Contact

Ava Gibson sent you a Word document explaining the Student International College website strategy, and you want to attach the document to her contact record. *Why? Including this document as part of her contact record will help you find the document easily.* Any files you attach to a contact are displayed in the Notes section of the Contact window. You also can insert items such as financial spreadsheets, pictures, and meeting slides to the Notes section. The following steps add an attachment to a contact.

1

- If necessary, tap or click the Ava Gibson contact to display Ava Gibson in the People pane.

- Tap or click Outlook (Contacts) below View Source to display the Ava Gibson – Contact window (Figure 3–17).

Figure 3–17

2

- Tap or click INSERT on the ribbon to display the INSERT tab (Figure 3–18).

Figure 3–18

3

- Tap or click the Attach File button (INSERT tab | Include group) to display the Insert File dialog box.

- Navigate to the file location, in this case, the Chapter 03 folder in the Outlook folder provided with the Data Files for Students.

- Tap or click Website Strategy to select the Word document (Figure 3–19).

Figure 3–19

4

- Tap or click the Insert button (Insert File dialog box) to attach the document to the contact record in the Notes area (Figure 3–20).

Can I add more than one attachment?
Yes; you can add as many attachments as you want.

How do I view an attachment after I have added it?
Open the contact and then double-tap or double-click the attachment to open it.

Figure 3–20

5

- Tap or click CONTACT on the ribbon to display the CONTACT tab.

- Tap or click the Save & Close button (CONTACT tab | Actions group) to save the contact record and close the Contact window (Figure 3–21).

Can I send a meeting request to a contact?
Yes. To send a meeting request to a contact, tap or click the contact to select it, tap or click Meeting (HOME tab | Communicate group), enter the details of the meeting in the Untitled – Meeting window, and then tap or click the Send button.

Figure 3–21

BTW

Changing an Attachment

If you need to change an attachment to another file within a contact, select the original file and then tap or click INSERT on the ribbon. Tap or click Attach File and select the new attachment. Because the original file was selected before attaching the new file, the new file replaces the original file. If the original file were not selected, Outlook would add the new file while keeping the original file.

To Remove an Attachment from a Contact

Sometimes you need to remove attachments that you have added to a contact. Raven College changed its website strategy and Ava Gibson has asked you to delete the original document. You need to remove the attachment from her contact information. *Why? Removing an outdated attachment is important to keep your contact information current.* The following steps remove the attachment from a contact.

1

- If necessary, tap or click the Ava Gibson contact to display Ava Gibson in the People pane.

- Tap or click Outlook (Contacts) below View Source to display the Ava Gibson – Contact window.

- Tap or click the Website Strategy document to select it (Figure 3–22).

Figure 3–22

2

- Press the DELETE key to remove the attachment (Figure 3–23).

3

- Tap or click the Save & Close button (CONTACT tab | Actions group) to save the contact and close the Contact window.

Figure 3–23

Other Ways

1. Click file icon, click Delete (CONTACT tab | Actions group)

Viewing and Sorting a Contact List

Outlook supports several ways for you to view your contact list. **People view** is the default view and shows the People pane. **Business Card view** displays the contacts as if they were business cards, a well-recognized format in business. **Card view** shows the contacts as cards but much smaller than Business Card view, with most information being only partially visible. In **Phone view**, you see the contacts in a list displaying phone information. Finally, in **List view**, the contacts are arranged in a list according to businesses. You also can create custom views to display your contacts in a way that suits a particular purpose.

When working with contacts in any view, you can sort the contacts to display them in a different order. Each view provides different sort options. For example, in Phone view, you can sort the list using any of the column heading buttons that are displayed.

BTW

Filing Contacts
When creating a new contact, Outlook automatically inserts in the File as box the contact's full name, usually in Last Name, First Name format. Outlook sorts contacts on the value stored in the File as box for each contact.

To Change the Current View

1 CREATE NEW CONTACT | 2 MODIFY CONTACT | **3 CHANGE VIEW OF CONTACTS**
4 FIND CONTACT | 5 CREATE CONTACT GROUP | 6 PRINT CONTACT LIST

People view provides useful information, but the other views also can be helpful. Changing the view sometimes can help you find a contact's information more quickly. Use Phone view, for example, when you are looking for a contact's phone number in a long list. *Why? Phone view provides a tabular layout with each contact in one row, and each column containing one contact's information.* The following steps change the current view to Phone view and then to People view to display the contact information on digital business cards.

1

- If necessary, tap or click the More button (HOME tab | Current View group) to display the Phone button.

- Tap or click the Phone button (HOME tab | Current View group) to switch to Phone view (Figure 3–24).

Figure 3–24

2

- If necessary, tap or click the More button (HOME tab | Current View group), and then click Business Card to switch to Business Card view (Figure 3–25).

Q&A What if the More button is not displayed in the Current View group?

You likely are using a lower resolution than 1366 × 768, so the ribbon hides additional buttons. Tap or click the Business Card button in the Current View group to switch to Business Card view.

🔍 **Experiment**

- Tap or click the other views in the Current View group to view the contacts in other arrangements. When you are finished, click Business Card to return to Business Card view.

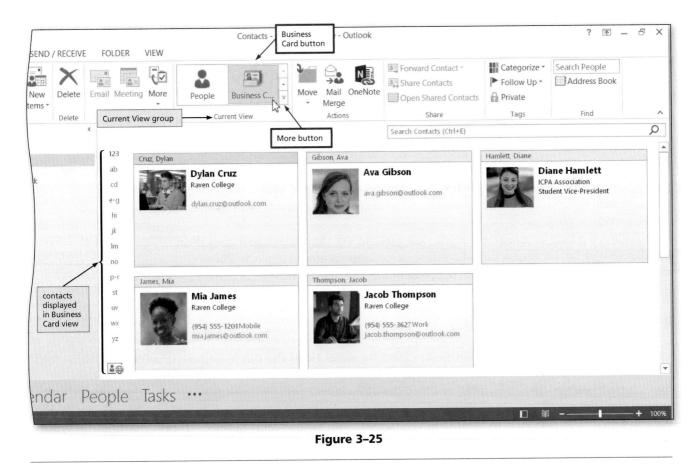

Figure 3–25

To Sort Contacts

Business Card view lists contacts in alphabetical order by default; however, you can sort the contacts to view them in reverse order. *Why? Reverse order is especially helpful if you want to quickly open a record for a contact at the end of a long contact list.* The following steps sort the contact list in reverse order, and then switch back to alphabetical order.

1

- Tap or click VIEW on the ribbon to display the VIEW tab.

- Tap or click the Reverse Sort button (VIEW tab | Arrangement group) to display the contact list in reverse alphabetical order (Figure 3–26).

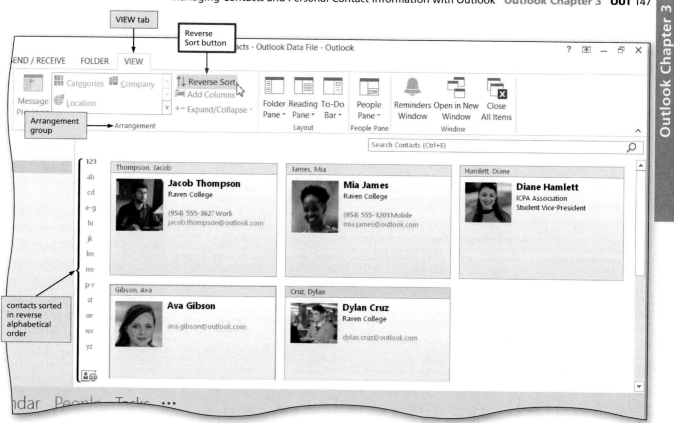

Figure 3–26

2

- Tap or click the Reverse Sort button (VIEW tab | Arrangement group) to display the contact list in the original order (Figure 3–27).

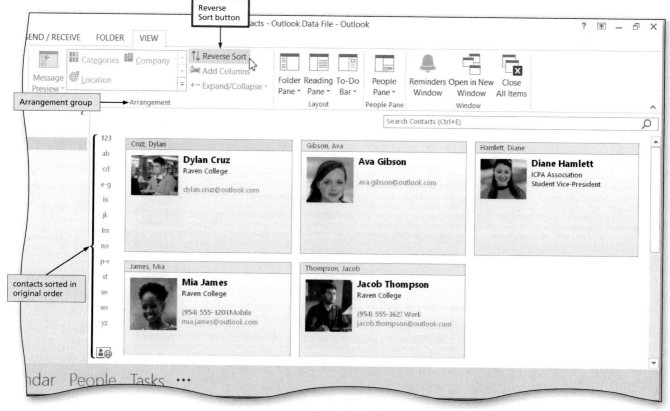

Figure 3–27

Break Point: If you wish to take a break, this is a good place to do so. To resume at a later time, continue to follow the steps from this location forward.

Using Search to Find a Contact

Over time, contact lists can grow quite large, making them difficult to navigate. In addition, you sometimes may not remember details about a contact you want to find. For example, you may remember that someone works for a particular company, but not their name. Alternatively, you may remember a phone number but nothing else. If this happens, you can use the Search Contacts text box to search your contact list.

You also can find contacts using the Search Contacts search box in the Find group on the HOME tab. This works no matter which folder you are using (such as Mail, Calendar, People, or Tasks). This means that anytime you need to find your contacts, you can look them up quickly.

You can maximize your search efforts if you create a list of keywords that you can assign to contacts. The more general the keyword, the more results you will find. Using more specific keywords will reduce the number of results.

To Find a Contact by Searching for Text

1 CREATE NEW CONTACT | 2 MODIFY CONTACT | 3 CHANGE VIEW OF CONTACTS
4 FIND CONTACT | 5 CREATE CONTACT GROUP | 6 PRINT CONTACT LIST

If you only know partial information such as the area code in a phone number, the first word in a school name, or the domain name in an email address, you can use it to find matching contacts. Note that you might find many contacts that contain the text for which you are searching. The text you are using as the search term could be part of an email address, a school name, or a Twitter username, for example. Therefore, you may have to examine the results further. The following steps find all contacts that contain the text, raven. *Why? To save time, you can search for text or tags such as the college name Raven to locate the correct contact(s) quickly.*

1

- Tap or click the Search Contacts text box to display the SEARCH TOOLS SEARCH tab (Figure 3–28).

Q&A | Why is the SEARCH TOOLS SEARCH tab displayed when I click the Search Contacts text box? The SEARCH TOOLS SEARCH tab contains buttons and commands that can help you search contacts.

Figure 3–28

• Type **raven** in the Search Contacts text box to search for all contacts containing the text, raven (Figure 3–29).

Q&A Can I modify a search further after getting the initial results?

Certainly. You can use the SEARCH TOOLS SEARCH tab to refine your search by specifying a name or phone number, for example. You also can expand the search to include all of the Outlook folders.

Figure 3–29

❸

• Tap or click the Close Search button (shown in Figure 3–29) in the Search Contacts text box to close the search and return to the Contacts – Outlook Data File – Outlook window (Figure 3–30).

Figure 3–30

Other Ways

1. Press CTRL+E

To Refine a Search

If you type a full name or email address in the Search Contacts text box, you will find your contact, but the information need not be only in the E-mail field or the Company field. The results might contain contacts where the name or email address is part of the Notes field, for example. In that case, you can find a contact by searching only a particular field. *Why? The results will contain only contacts with the search term in the specified field. No contacts will appear that contain the search term in a different field.*

You want to update the Ava Gibson contact record by searching only the Full Name field. The following steps search for an exact name in a particular field.

1

- Tap or click the Search Contacts text box to display the SEARCH TOOLS SEARCH tab.

- Tap or click the More button (SEARCH TOOLS SEARCH tab | Refine group) to display a list of common properties for refining a search (Figure 3–31).

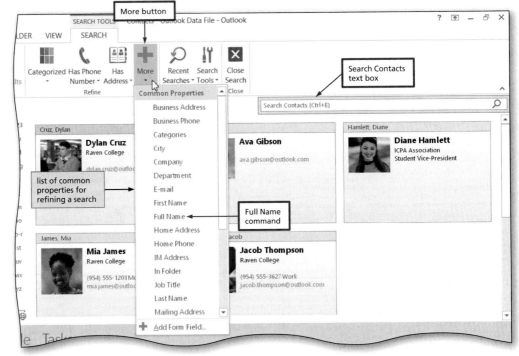

Figure 3–31

2

- Tap or click Full Name (shown in Figure 3–31) to display the Full Name text box below the Search Contacts text box.

- Type **Ava Gibson** in the Full Name text box to search for the Ava Gibson contact (Figure 3–32).

Q&A Why might Outlook display search results that do not seem to contain the search text?

When you perform a search, Outlook searches all specified fields for a match. However, the matching fields might not be displayed in the list of search results, although the contact record does contain the search text.

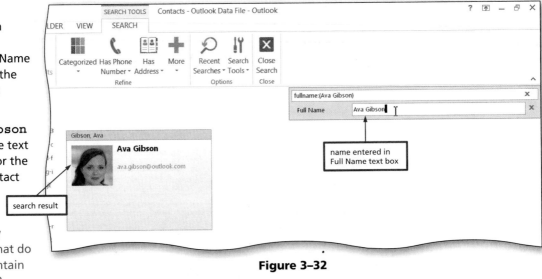

Figure 3–32

❸

- Double-tap or double-click the Ava Gibson contact to open it.

- Type **Manages Student International Club website** in the Notes field to update the contact (Figure 3–33).

❹

- Tap or click the Save & Close button (CONTACT tab | Actions group) (shown in Figure 3–33) to save the contact and close the Contact window.

Figure 3–33

- Tap or click the Close Search button in the Search Contacts text box to close the search and return to the Contacts – Outlook Data File – Outlook window.

To Find a Contact from Any Outlook Window

1 CREATE NEW CONTACT | 2 MODIFY CONTACT | 3 CHANGE VIEW OF CONTACTS
4 FIND CONTACT | 5 CREATE CONTACT GROUP | 6 PRINT CONTACT LIST

You do not have to be working in the Contacts – Outlook window to search for contacts. You can use the Search People text box in the Find group on the HOME tab to search for contacts when you are working with email or performing other Outlook tasks. If what you type in the search box matches a single contact, that entry will be displayed in a contact window. If what you type matches more than one entry, you will be asked to select the contact that you want to view. *Why? For example, if you search for a contact using part of the company name, more than one contact may appear in the search results. You then can select a single contact from the results.*

The following steps search for a contact from the Inbox – Outlook Data File – Outlook window using only part of the company name, college. In this case, you are searching through your college contacts for the information about Mia James.

❶

- Tap or click the Mail button in the Navigation Bar to display the Dylan.pst mailbox (Figure 3–34).

Figure 3–34

2

- Type `college` in the Search People text box (HOME tab | Find group) to search for contacts containing the search text (Figure 3–35).

Q&A
Outlook searched a different Outlook data file instead of the Dylan.pst file. What should I do?
Open only the Dylan.pst Outlook data file, which appears as Outlook Data File in the Navigation Pane. Close any other Outlook data file open in the Navigation Pane, and then repeat the steps.

Figure 3–35

3

- Tap or click Mia James to select the contact and display her contact card (Figure 3–36).

Figure 3–36

4

- Tap or click the Close button to close the window.

- Tap or click the People button in the Navigation Bar to return to the Contacts – Outlook Data File – Outlook window (Figure 3–37).

Figure 3–37

Creating and Editing a Contact Group

When you have several contacts that you frequently email or work with as a group, you can create a contact group and add contacts to it. A **contact group**, also called a **distribution list**, provides a single name for you to use when working with two or more contacts. You are not creating subfolders for contacts, but rather another way to reference multiple contacts at one time. For example, you could create a group called Inner Circle and then add all your closest family and friends to the group. Whenever you want to send an email message to your closest family and friends at one time, you could enter the contact group name, Inner Circle, as the recipient of the email message — and every contact in the group would receive the email message.

To Create a Contact Group from Existing Contacts

1 CREATE NEW CONTACT | 2 MODIFY CONTACT | 3 CHANGE VIEW OF CONTACTS
4 FIND CONTACT | **5 CREATE CONTACT GROUP** | 6 PRINT CONTACT LIST

Why? *A message sent to a contact group goes to all recipients listed in the group. If your contact list gets too cluttered, you can use a contact group to communicate with friends, family, and co-workers more quickly.* When creating contact groups, you choose the name for your contact group and then add the contacts you want to have in the group. To quickly send out an email to all the members of the Student International Club, you want to create a group of all the members who are part of your contact list named International Club. The following steps create a contact group and then add the related contacts to the group.

①

- Tap or click the New Contact Group button (HOME tab | New group) to display the Untitled – Contact Group window (Figure 3–38).

Figure 3–38

②

- Type **International Club** in the Name text box to enter a name for the group (Figure 3–39).

Figure 3–39

③

- Tap or click the Add Members button (CONTACT GROUP tab | Members group) to display the Add Members menu (Figure 3–40).

Figure 3–40

4

- Tap or click From Outlook Contacts to display the Select Members: Contacts dialog box (Figure 3–41).

Figure 3–41

5

- Tap or click the Ava Gibson contact to select it, press and hold the CTRL key, and then click the Mia James contact to select both contacts.

- Tap or click the Members button to move the information to the Members text box (Figure 3–42).

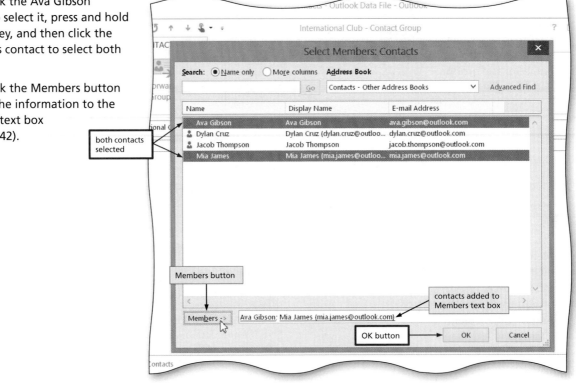

Figure 3–42

6

- Tap or click the OK button to add the contacts to the group (Figure 3–43).

Q&A What if I add the wrong member(s) to the contact group?
In the Contact Group window, select the member you want to remove, and then tap or click the Remove Member button (CONTACT GROUP tab | Members group). Next, repeat Steps 3 – 6 to add any missing members.

Figure 3–43

7

- Tap or click the Save & Close button (CONTACT GROUP tab | Actions group) to save the contact group and close the window (Figure 3–44).

Q&A Why are the contacts and the group displayed in the Contacts window?
You use a contact group to send email messages to a set of contacts using the group name; it does not replace or move the existing contacts.

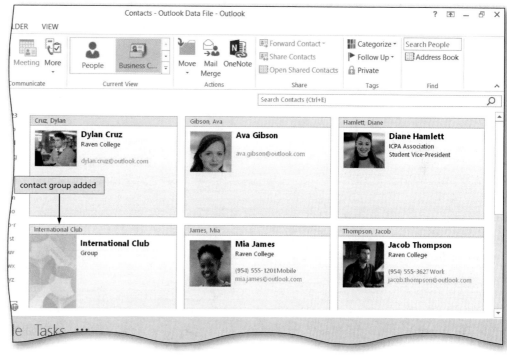

Figure 3–44

To Create a Contact Group from an Existing Email Message

1 CREATE NEW CONTACT | 2 MODIFY CONTACT | 3 CHANGE VIEW OF CONTACTS
4 FIND CONTACT | 5 CREATE CONTACT GROUP | 6 PRINT CONTACT LIST

Outlook allows you to create a group for individuals who are not in your contact list but have sent you an email message. To do this, you copy a name from an email message and then paste the name in the Select Members dialog box when creating the group. The following steps create a contact group named Faculty and then add a member by using information in an email message from Samuel Marks. *Why? You can create a group and add a new contact right after reading an email.*

1

- Tap or click the Mail button on the Navigation Bar to display your mailbox (Figure 3–45).

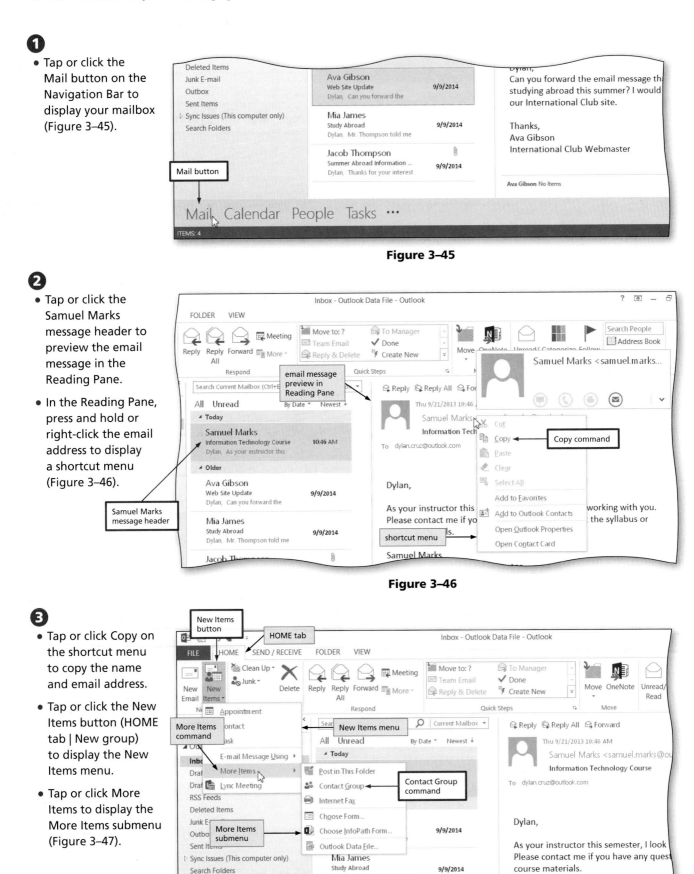

Figure 3–45

2

- Tap or click the Samuel Marks message header to preview the email message in the Reading Pane.

- In the Reading Pane, press and hold or right-click the email address to display a shortcut menu (Figure 3–46).

Figure 3–46

3

- Tap or click Copy on the shortcut menu to copy the name and email address.

- Tap or click the New Items button (HOME tab | New group) to display the New Items menu.

- Tap or click More Items to display the More Items submenu (Figure 3–47).

Figure 3–47

4

- Tap or click Contact Group to display the Untitled – Contact Group window.

- Type **Faculty** in the Name text box to enter a name for the group.

- Tap or click the Add Members button (CONTACT GROUP tab | Members group) to display the Add Members menu.

- Tap or click From Outlook Contacts to display the Select Members: Contacts dialog box (Figure 3–48).

Q&A Why did I tap or click From Outlook Contacts?
You need to display the Select Members dialog box, and you click the From Outlook Contacts menu option to open it. You also could have tapped or clicked From Address Book to display the dialog box.

Figure 3–48

5

- Press and hold or right-click the Members text box to display a shortcut menu.

- Tap or click Paste on the shortcut menu to paste the copied name and email address (Figure 3–49).

Figure 3–49

6

- Tap or click the OK button to add the contact to the group.

- Tap or click the Save & Close button (CONTACT GROUP tab | Actions group) to save the contact and close the window.

- Tap or click People in the Navigation Bar to display your contacts (Figure 3–50).

Q&A

Can I forward a contact group to someone else?

Yes. You can forward a contact group by selecting the contact group, tapping or clicking Forward Contact (HOME tab | Share group), and then selecting the option you want to use to forward the contact group.

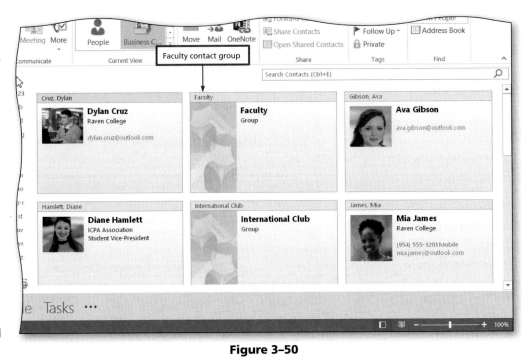

Figure 3–50

To Add a Name to a Contact Group

1 CREATE NEW CONTACT | 2 MODIFY CONTACT | 3 CHANGE VIEW OF CONTACTS
4 FIND CONTACT | 5 CREATE CONTACT GROUP | 6 PRINT CONTACT LIST

As you meet and work with people, you can add them to one or more contact groups. You have been contacting the instructor Jacob Thompson about the Study Abroad program and you want to add him to the Faculty contact group. *Why? By adding people to a group, you can send email messages and meeting invitations to groups of people that you contact frequently without having to enter each individual email address.* The following steps add a new contact to the Faculty contact group.

1

- Double-tap or double-click the Faculty contact group to display the Faculty – Contact Group window (Figure 3–51).

Figure 3–51

- Tap or click the Add Members button (CONTACT GROUP tab | Members group) to display the Add Members menu.

- Tap or click From Outlook Contacts to display the Select Members dialog box.

- Tap or click Jacob Thompson to select his contact record.

- Tap or click the Members button to add Jacob Thompson to the Members text box (Figure 3–52).

3

- Tap or click the OK button to add Jacob Thompson to the contact group.

- Tap or click the Save & Close button (CONTACT GROUP tab | Actions group) to save the contact and close the Faculty – Contact Group window.

Figure 3–52

To Add Notes to a Contact Group

1 CREATE NEW CONTACT | 2 MODIFY CONTACT | 3 CHANGE VIEW OF CONTACTS
4 FIND CONTACT | 5 CREATE CONTACT GROUP | 6 PRINT CONTACT LIST

You can add reminder notes to a contact group. *Why? As you create groups, you may have trouble remembering who is part of the group and why.* The contact group notes are only displayed in the Contacts list when Card view is selected. You would like to add a note to the International Club contact group to remind you that the club officer's term expires in May. The following steps add a note to a contact group and display the note in the Card view.

1

- Double-tap or double-click the International Club contact group to display the International Club – Contact Group window (Figure 3–53).

Figure 3–53

2

• Tap or click the Notes button (CONTACT GROUP tab | Show group) to display the Notes page.

• Type **The International Club officer's term expires on May 3.** in the Notes page to create a reminder (Figure 3–54).

Figure 3–54

3

• Tap or click the Save & Close button on the Notes page to close the International Club – Contact Group window.

• Tap or click the Card button (HOME tab | Current View group) to display the contact list in Card view, which in this case includes the contact group note for the International Club (Figure 3–55).

Figure 3–55

To Remove a Name from a Contact Group

1 CREATE NEW CONTACT | 2 MODIFY CONTACT | 3 CHANGE VIEW OF CONTACTS
4 FIND CONTACT | 5 CREATE CONTACT GROUP | 6 PRINT CONTACT LIST

Why? Periodically, you may need to remove someone from a contact group. For example, contacts may switch jobs or ask to be removed from your list because they no longer are working on or participating in a club or project. Mia James is graduating from college and will no longer be participating in the Student International Club. You have decided to remove her from the International Club contact group so that she will not receive email messages sent to the group. The following steps remove a contact from a group.

1

- If necessary, scroll in the Contacts window until the International Club contact group is visible.

- Double-tap or double-click the International Club contact group to display the International Club – Contact Group window (Figure 3–56).

Figure 3–56

International Group – Contact Group window

Mia James contact

2

- Tap or click the Mia James member to select it.

- Tap or click the Remove Member button (CONTACT GROUP tab | Members group) to remove Mia James from the contact group (Figure 3–57).

Save & Close button

CONTACT GROUP tab

Remove Member button

Members group

Mia James contact removed from group

Figure 3–57

3

- Tap or click the Save & Close button (CONTACT GROUP tab | Actions group) to save the changes to the contact group and close the window.

- Tap or click the People button (HOME tab | Current View group) to display the Contact list (Figure 3–58).

People button

Current View group

contact list displayed in People view

Figure 3–58

Q&A When you remove a contact from a contact group, does it also remove the contact from Outlook?
No. The contact remains in Outlook, even after removing it from a contact group.

How can I delete a contact group?
To delete a contact group, select the contact group to delete, and then tap or click Delete (HOME tab | Delete group).

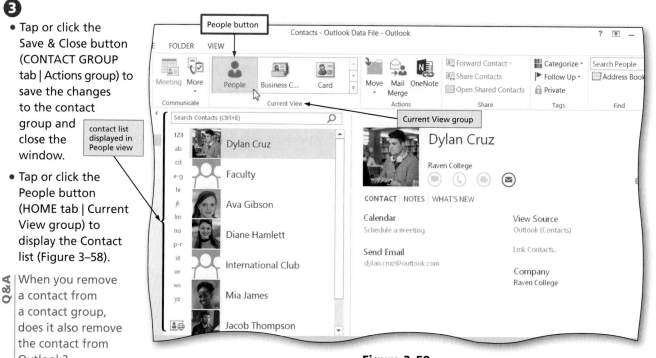

BTW
Q&As
For a complete list of the
Q&As found in many of
the step-by-step sequences
in this book, visit the Q&A
resource on the Student
Companion Site located on
www.cengagebrain.com. For
detailed instructions about
accessing available resources,
visit www.cengage.com/ct/
studentdownload or
contact your instructor for
information about accessing
the required files.

Printing Your Contacts

All or part of your contacts can be printed in a number of different views, or **print styles.** You can distribute a printed contact or contact list to others in a form that can be read or viewed, but cannot be edited. You can choose to print only one contact or the entire list. To print only part of your contacts, select one or more contacts and then change the print options so that you print your selection. This section previews the entire contact list and then prints the selected contacts in Card style. Table 3–1 lists the print styles available for printing your contacts from Contact view.

Table 3–1 Print Styles for Contact View	
Print Style	**Description**
Card	Prints a list of contacts separated by alphabetic dividers and provides a sheet for adding more contact information
Small Booklet	Prints a list of contacts similar to Card style but designed so that it can be folded into a small booklet
Medium Booklet	Prints a list of contacts similar to Card style but designed so that it can be folded into a medium-sized booklet
Memo	Prints a page for each contact, each page formatted to look like a memo
Phone Directory	Prints a list of contacts showing phone numbers only

© 2014 Cengage Learning

To Preview a Contact List

1 CREATE NEW CONTACT | 2 MODIFY CONTACT | 3 CHANGE VIEW OF CONTACTS
4 FIND CONTACT | 5 CREATE CONTACT GROUP | **6 PRINT CONTACT LIST**

You can print preview a single contact or multiple pages of contacts displayed as cards or in phone lists. The following steps preview the contact list in various print styles. *Why? Unless you change the print options, you will see all your contacts when you preview the list before printing.*

1
- In the Contacts window, select the Ava Gibson and Jacob Thompson contacts (Figure 3–59).

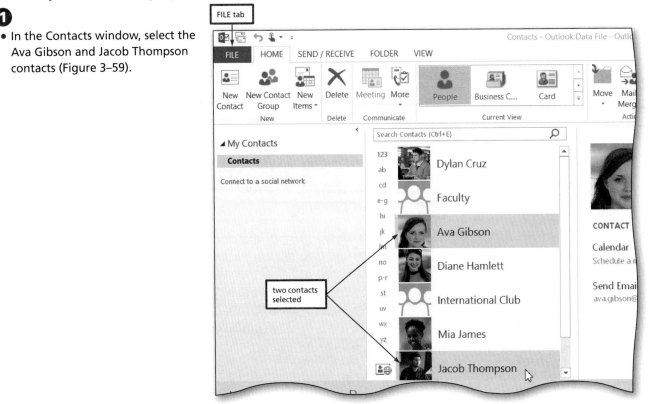

Figure 3–59

2

- Tap or click FILE on the ribbon (shown in Figure 3–59) to open the Backstage view.

- Tap or click the Print tab in the Backstage view to display the Print gallery (Figure 3–60).

Q&A Why are all the contacts displayed when I selected only two contacts?

By default, the print range is set for all items to display and print. You can change the Print Options to print only the selected items.

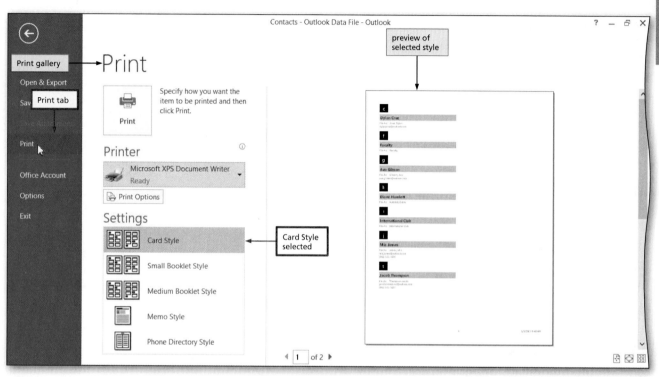

Figure 3–60

3

- Tap or click Medium Booklet Style in the Settings area to change the print style (Figure 3–61).

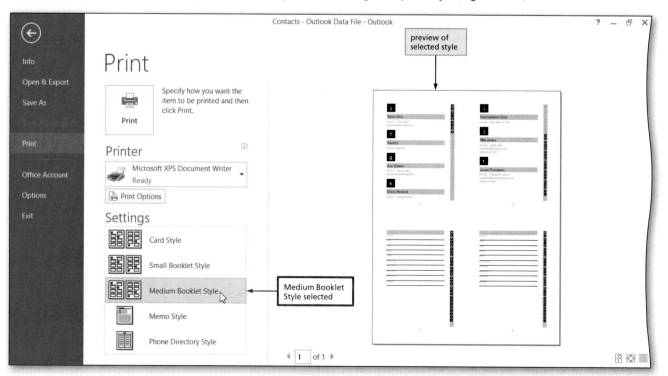

Figure 3–61

4

• Tap or click Phone Directory Style in the Settings area to change to Phone Directory Style (Figure 3–62).

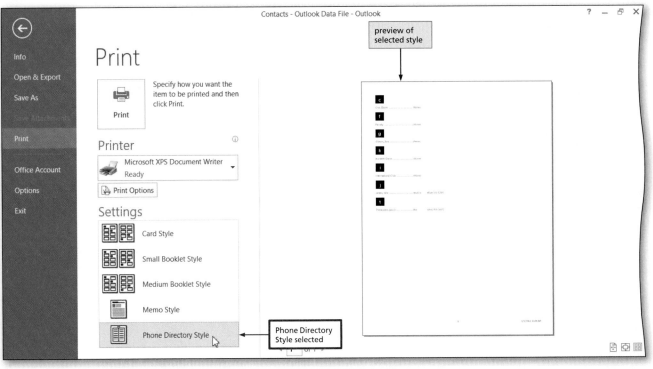

Figure 3–62

5

• Tap or click Card Style in the Settings area to change to Card Style (Figure 3–63).

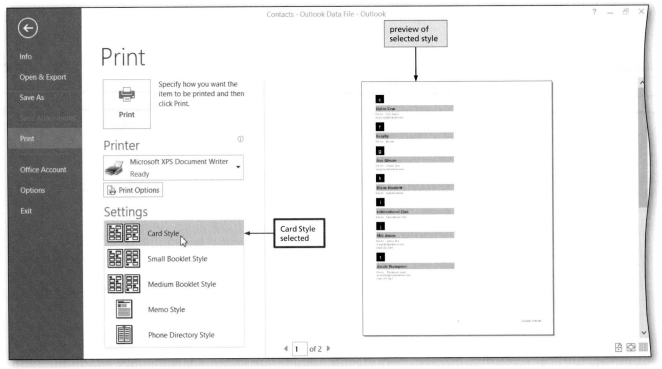

Figure 3–63

6

- Tap or click the Print Options button to display the Print dialog box (Figure 3–64).

Figure 3–64

7

- Tap or click the 'Only selected items' option button (Print dialog box) to preview only the selected contacts (Figure 3–65).

Figure 3–65

❽

• Tap or click the Preview button (Print dialog box) to close the dialog box and preview only the selected contacts.

• Tap or click the print preview to zoom in to view the selected contacts (Figure 3–66).

Q&A If I click the other styles, will they only show selected contacts?
No. If you change the style, the preview returns to showing all contacts. To see the selected contacts in a particular style, you select the style and then change the print options.

Figure 3–66

To Print a Contact List

1 CREATE NEW CONTACT | 2 MODIFY CONTACT | 3 CHANGE VIEW OF CONTACTS
4 FIND CONTACT | 5 CREATE CONTACT GROUP | **6 PRINT CONTACT LIST**

Why? *Before heading to a meeting, you may want a printed list of contacts for reference.* The following step prints the selected contacts in Card style.

❶

• Tap or click the Print button to print the selected contacts (Figure 3–67).

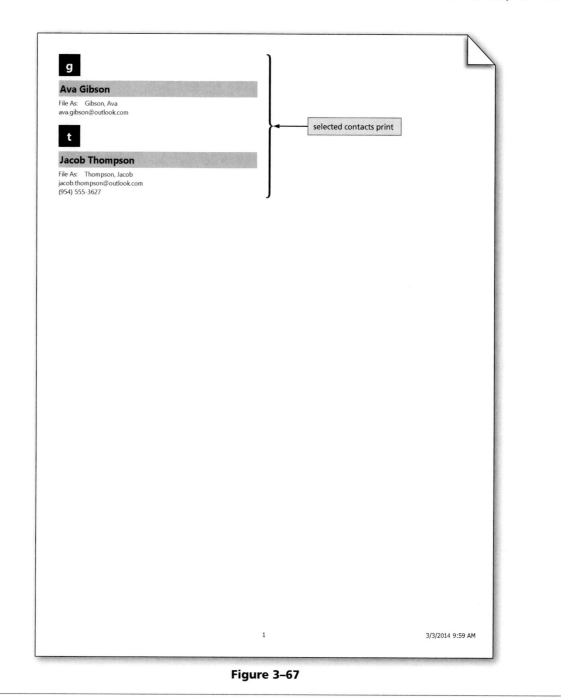

Figure 3–67

To Exit Outlook

This project now is complete. The following steps exit Outlook. For a detailed example of the procedure summarized below, refer to the Office 2013 and Windows 8 chapter at the beginning of this book.

1 If you have a contact open, tap or click the Close button on the right side of the title bar to close the Contact window.

2 Tap or click the Close button on the right side of the title bar to exit Outlook.

Chapter Summary

In this chapter, you have learned how to use Outlook to create a contact list, view and sort contacts, search for contacts, create and edit a contact group, and print contacts. The items listed below include all the new Outlook skills you have learned in this chapter with the tasks grouped by activity.

Creating a Contact List
Create a New Contact (OUT 133)
Create Contacts from Email Messages (OUT 135)

Editing a Contact
Edit a Contact (OUT 138)
Delete a Contact (OUT 141)
Add an Attachment to a Contact (OUT 142)
Remove an Attachment from a Contact (OUT 144)

Viewing and Sorting a Contact List
Change the Current View (OUT 145)
Sort Contacts (OUT 146)

Using Search to a Find a Contact
Find a Contact by Searching for Text (OUT 148)

Refine a Search (OUT 150)
Find a Contact from Any Outlook Window (OUT 151)

Creating and Editing a Contact Group
Create a Contact Group from Existing Contacts (OUT 153)
Create a Contact Group from an Existing Email Message (OUT 155)
Add a Name to a Contact Group (OUT 158)
Add Notes to a Contact Group (OUT 159)
Remove a Name from a Contact Group (OUT 160)

Printing your Contacts
Preview a Contact List (OUT 162)
Print a Contact List (OUT 166)

CONSIDER THIS

Consider This: Plan Ahead

What decisions will you need to make when creating contacts from friends, family, and co-workers, editing contacts, creating a contact group, and printing contacts in the future?

A. Create Contacts:

1. Determine the people with whom you plan to interact on a regular basis, such as your friends, family, and co-workers. Adding too many contacts can make it difficult to manage your contact list.
2. Determine the information that would be most helpful about each of your contacts.

B. Edit Contacts:

1. Determine if any additional contact information should be added to a contact.
2. Determine which contacts should be deleted, such as those with whom you no longer have regular communication.
3. Request pictures of your contacts to add to their contact information.
4. Add file attachments as needed to contacts.

C. View and Sort Contact Lists:

1. Select a view that displays the information you need in a contact list.
2. Switch views as necessary to have quick access to people's information.
3. Create a custom view if none of the built-in views is suitable for you.
4. Sort contacts to display them in a different order.

D. Use Search to Find Contacts:

1. Determine the preferred way to view the contacts to find the information you are seeking.
2. Determine the sort order to use for your contacts, considering what information you are trying to find.

E. Create and Edit Contact Groups:

1. Plan the relationship of the contacts that are organized under the group name.
2. Consider a good name for a contact group that will make it easier for you to remember the purpose of the group.

F. Print your Contacts:

1. Plan how best to display your contacts.

BTW
Quick Reference
For a table that lists how to complete the tasks covered in this book using touch gestures, the mouse, ribbon, shortcut menu, and keyboard, see the Quick Reference Summary at the back of this book, or visit the Quick Reference resource on the Student Companion Site located on www.cengagebrain.com. For detailed instructions about accessing available resources, visit www.cengage.com/ct/studentdownload or contact your instructor for information about accessing the required files.

CONSIDER THIS

How should you submit solutions to questions in the assignments identified with a ✳ symbol?

Every assignment in this book contains one or more questions identified with a ✳ symbol. These questions require you to think beyond the assigned file. Present your solutions to the questions in the format required by your instructor. Possible formats may include one or more of these options: write the answer; create a document that contains the answer; present your answer to the class; discuss your answer in a group; record the answer as audio or video using a webcam, smartphone, or portable media player; or post answers on a blog, wiki, or website.

Apply Your Knowledge

Reinforce the skills and apply the concepts you learned in this chapter.

Editing a Contact List

Note: To complete this assignment, you will be required to use the Data Files for Students. Visit www.cengage.com/ct/studentdownload for detailed instructions or contact your instructor for information about accessing the required files.

Instructions: Start Outlook. Edit the contact list provided in the file called Apply Your Knowledge 3–1 Contacts, located on the Data Files for Students. The Apply Your Knowledge 3–1 Contacts file contains four contacts and a contact group. Many of the contacts have changed and some are incomplete. You now need to revise these contacts and print them in Card view (Figure 3–68).

Perform the following tasks:

1. Import the Apply Your Knowledge 3–1 Contacts file into Outlook.

2. Change Mary Jayden's company to **Valencia College**. Move Mary's Work phone number to the Mobile phone number text box. Change her job title to **Advisor**.

3. Change Lukas Johnson's company to **Seminole State**. Type **LJohnson .SCC@email.com** as his new email address, and change his phone number to **555-0110**.

4. Change Lauren Mariel's email address to **LMariel@valenciacollege.edu**. Add the following as her Web page address: **http://www.valenciacollege.edu/ lmariel**. Add a Home phone of **555-7341**.

5. Change the job title for Sean Roberts to **Senior Instructor**.

6. Change the Valencia College contact group name to Valencia. Add the Mary Jayden contact to the contact group and remove the Lukas Johnson contact from the contact group.

c

Dylan Cruz
File As: Cruz, Dylan
dylan.cruz@outlook.com

j

Mary Jayden
File As: Jayden, Mary
Mary.Jayden@email.com
555-0520

Lukas Johnson
File As: Johnson, Lukas
LJohnson.SCC@email.com
555-0110

m

Lauren Mariel
File As: Mariel, Lauren
LMariel@valenciacollege.edu
555-7341
555-0419

r

Sean Roberts
File As: Roberts, Sean
Sean.Roberts@email.com
555-0401

v

Valencia
File As: Valencia

Steven Freund   1   4/25/2013 2:10 PM

Figure 3–68

Continued >

Apply Your Knowledge *continued*

7. Add a new contact using your name and email address.

8. Print the final contact list in Card Style, as shown in Figure 3–68, and then submit the printout to your instructor.

9. Export the Apply Your Knowledge 3–1 Contacts file to a USB flash drive, and then delete the file from the hard disk.

10. Outlook can display your contacts in a variety of views. Which view do you prefer, and why?

Extend Your Knowledge

Extend the skills you learned in this chapter and experiment with new skills. You may need to use Help to complete the assignment.

Creating a Contact Folder

Note: To complete this assignment, you will be required to use the Data Files for Students. Visit www.cengage.com/ct/studentdownload for detailed instructions or contact your instructor for information about accessing the required files.

Instructions: Start Outlook. The Extend Your Knowledge 3–1 Contacts file located on the Data Files for Students has no contacts. You will create a new contacts folder, add contacts to the new contacts folder, and print the contact list (Figure 3–69). You also will share the contact folder with others.

Perform the following tasks:

1. Use Help to learn about creating a contacts folder and sharing a contact list.

2. Start Outlook and create a new contacts folder named Marketing Department.

3. Create the contacts displayed in Table 3–2.

4. Create a contact group called Everyone. Add all of the contacts to this group.

5. Create a contact group called Research Group. Add all the employees with Research as their job title to this group.

6. Create a contact using your mother's name and email address. If you do not want to disclose your mother's email address or if she does not have one, replace it with your email address.

7. Print the contact list in Phone Directory view, as shown in Figure 3–69, and then submit the printout to your instructor.

Figure 3–69

Table 3–2 Marketing Department Information

Full Name	Company	Job Title	Email Address	Business Phone
Ariel Miranda	Video Solutions	Advertising	miranda@videosolutions.com	555-1278
Cindy Vindo	Video Solutions	Research	vindo@videosolutions.com	555-1290
Kaitlyn Wells	Video Solutions	Planning	wells@videosolutions.com	555-1358
Tami Townsend	Video Solutions	Purchasing	townsend@videosolutions.com	555-2751
Victoria Wickers	Video Solutions	Research	wickers@videosolutions.com	555-2776
David Sanders	Video Solutions	Research	sanders@videosolutions.com	555-2689

© 2014 Cengage Learning

8. Use the Share Contacts button (HOME tab | Share group) to email the contact list to your instructor.

9. ✸ Why might it be advantageous to create separate folders within your contacts?

Analyze, Correct, Improve

Analyze contacts and correct all errors and/or improve the contact records.

Correcting Contacts and Contact Groups

Note: To complete this assignment, you will be required to use the Data Files for Students. Visit www.cengage.com/ct/studentdownload for detailed instructions or contact your instructor for information about accessing the required files.

Instructions: Start Outlook. Import the Analyze 3–1 Contacts file in the Data Files for Students folder into Outlook. While reviewing your Outlook contacts, you realize that you made several mistakes. You will identify and open the incorrect contacts, edit them so that they reflect the correct information, add the missing contact, edit the contact group, and then save all changes. You also will print the contacts in Small Booklet style (Figure 3–70).

Figure 3–70

Continued >

Analyze, Correct, Improve *continued*

Perform the following tasks:

1. Correct While creating your contacts in Outlook, you inadvertently transposed everyone's first and last names and forgot to add area codes to the phone numbers you entered. In your Contacts list, correct the entries by switching the last and first names, and then adding the area code, 555, to each phone number.

2. Improve Add other information for each contact, including a second phone number, company, and job title. Be sure that at least two of the contacts are with the same company, and then add a contact group using the company's name as the contact group name. Add all contacts from that company to the contact group.

3. ✸ When might you want to file your contacts in first name, last name format as opposed to last name, first name format?

In the Labs

Design, create, modify, and/or use contacts using the guidelines, concepts, and skills presented in this chapter. Labs are listed in order of increasing difficulty.

Lab 1: **Creating Departmental Contacts**

Problem: You are a graduate assistant for the provost at North Loomsberg State College (NLSC) and have been asked to create a contact list of the departmental offices on campus. Each department now has an email address, so that email messages can be sent there and then forwarded by the dean of each department as necessary. Table 3–3 lists each department's contact information. Enter the contacts into the contacts list. The contact list you create will look like that in Figure 3–71.

Perform the following tasks:

1. Create the contacts in the Contacts window, using the information listed in Table 3–3.

2. For each contact, list the full name using the department name.

3. For each contact, list the company as NLSC.

Dylan Cruz

Full Name:	Information Technology
Last Name:	Technology
First Name:	Information
Company:	NLSC
Business Address:	8817 NLSC Lane, Wastion, AZ 48971
Business:	555-8419
Business Fax:	555-8513
E-mail:	info_tech@nlsc.edu
E-mail Display As:	Information Technology (info_tech@nlsc.edu)
Web Page:	http://www.nlsc.edu

1

Figure 3–71

Table 3–3 Departmental Information			
Department	**Email Address**	**Business**	**Fax**
Information Technology	info_tech@nlsc.edu	555-8419	555-8513
Social Sciences	social_sciences@nlsc.edu	555-8428	555-8529
Humanities	humanities@nlsc.edu	555-8478	555-8578
Business	business@nlsc.edu	555-8420	555-8525
Language Arts	language@nlsc.edu	555-8452	555-8554
Mathematics	math@nlsc.edu	555-8490	555-8593

© 2014 Cengage Learning

4. For each contact, list the webpage address as http://www.nlsc.edu.

5. For each contact, list the business address as 8817 NLSC Lane, Wastion, AZ 48971.

6. Print the contacts list using Memo style, and submit it in a format specified by your instructor.

7. ✹ What other information might be useful to include in the contact information for the various departments at your institution?

Lab 2: Creating an Employee Contact List

Problem: You are the owner of Blue Pool, a small pool supply store. Your store has decided to email reminders to employees such as weekly schedules, store specials to memorize, and other information. You have two shifts in your store, morning and afternoon. You need to create a list of all your contacts, and add contact groups, so that you send specific information just to the morning and afternoon employees (Figure 3–72).

Figure 3–72

Perform the following tasks:

1. Create two contact groups called Morning and Afternoon.

2. Enter the contacts in the Contacts list, using the information listed in Table 3–4. Do not add the shift information to the contacts. Use the shift information to determine in which contact group you should place the contacts. Add the contacts to the appropriate contact group.

Continued >

In the Labs *continued*

Table 3–4 Blue Pool Store Employee Information				
Full Name	**Email Address**	**Home Phone**	**Mobile Phone**	**Shift**
Victoria Anne	victoria.anne@email.com	555-7394		Morning
Dennis Camello	dencam@email.com	555-1826	555-9478	Morning
Emma Fox	emma0909@email.com		555-6483	Afternoon
Madelyn Cecilo	maddysworld@email.com	555-7128	555-8652	Afternoon

3. Print the contacts list in Small Booklet style, and then submit it in the format specified by your instructor.

4. ✳ What additional information about your employees might be useful to add to your contacts folder?

Lab 3: Expand Your World: Cloud and Web Technologies
The Outlook Social Connector

Problem: The Outlook Social Connector allows you to merge information about your friends or connections on an online social network, such as Facebook or LinkedIn, with your Outlook contacts. In addition, information your contacts might change in their social networking profile will be updated in your contact list automatically. In this assignment, you will set up the Social Connector in Outlook.

Perform the following tasks:

1. If necessary, start Outlook.

2. Choose at least three friends or connections from a Facebook or LinkedIn account and add them to Outlook as contacts. The names and email addresses you enter in Outlook should match exactly the names and email addresses used in their profile on the online social network. If you do not have a social network account, create one on a social networking website such as Facebook or LinkedIn.

3. Tap or click VIEW on the ribbon to display the VIEW tab.

4. Tap or click the People Pane button (VIEW tab | People Pane group) to display the People Pane menu.

5. Tap or click Account Settings on the People Pane menu.

6. In the Microsoft Office dialog box, tap or click the check box(es) next to the social networking accounts you want to add to Outlook (Figure 3–73).

Figure 3–73

7. Enter your username and password for the social networking account you want to add to Outlook, and then click the Connect button. Repeat this step if you want to add other social networking accounts to Outlook.

8. When you are finished adding accounts, click the Finish button.

9. Tap or click the Close button.

10. View your contact list and take note of the additional information included from your social network account.

11. Submit your contact list in the format specified by your instructor.

✳ Consider This: Your Turn

Apply your creative thinking and problem solving skills to design and implement a solution.

Note: To complete this assignment, you will be required to use the Data Files for Students. Visit www.cengage.com/ct/studentdownload for detailed instructions or contact your instructor for information about accessing the required files.

1: Create a Study Group List
Academic

Part 1:   Use the concepts and techniques presented in this chapter to create contacts for a study group at Biostent University using the information in Table 3–5. Use Biostent University as the company name. You should create the first contact and then create the rest as contacts from the same company. Add other information for each contact, and then add two or more contact groups in a way that logically organizes the contacts. Each contact should belong to at least one contact group, but no contact group should contain all contacts. Print the list in Card style and in Phone Directory style. Submit it in the format specified by your instructor.

Table 3-5 Study Group Contacts			
Full Name	**Email Address**	**Home Phone**	**Mobile Phone**
Marge Jones	mjones@live.com	555-7812	
Juan Escobar	gocanatel@hotmail.com	555-8772	555-9871
April Kent	April.Kent@live.com		555-2145
Addison Hu	addison9871@live.com		555-8912
Larry Honda	SuperHonda@hotmail.com	555-7728	555-3476
Kim Young	Kim.Young@live.com	555-5874	

© 2014 Cengage Learning

Part 2:   ✳ You made several decisions while creating the contact list in this assignment, such as what information to add to the contacts and how to separate contacts into contact groups. What was the rationale behind each of these decisions?

2: Create a Team List
Professional

Part 1:   At Hannah's Handbaskets, you are in charge of scheduling your team of employees. The business is located at 9821 South End Dr., Tarnnel, IN 33389. Whenever you create a schedule, you need to email it to your entire team. You also use email to send your team important information they should know. Using the contacts and techniques presented in this chapter, create contacts for each member of your team using the information in Table 3–6. Add other information you feel is

Continued >

Consider This: Your Turn *continued*

Table 3-6 Team List Contacts		
Full Name	**Email Address**	**Home Phone**
Carla Angel	angel@hannashandbaskets.com	555-1278
Angel Esposita	esposita@hannashandbaskets.com	555-8221
Abigail Shin	shin@hannashandbaskets.com	555-9856
Nina Montgomery	montgomery@hannashandbaskets.com	555-3846
Stan Applebaum	applebaum@hannashandbaskets.com	555-2877
Josiah Bell	bell@hannashandbaskets.com	555-8745

© 2014 Cengage Learning

necessary to store for each contact. Create a contact group called Team and add the contacts to the group. Print the contact list in Card style and submit it in the format specified by your instructor.

Part 2: ✳ You made several decisions while creating the contact list in this assignment, such as what information to add to the contacts. What was the rationale behind each of these decisions?

3: Outlook Contact Best Practices
Research and Collaboration

Part 1: Your consulting team has been hired by a new company, HiTech Toolworks, to provide suggestions about how to use Microsoft Outlook to store contact information. The company currently stores employee information in an Excel spreadsheet, and thinks it might be easiest to somehow import the information to Outlook. The spreadsheet also includes confidential information, so HiTech Toolworks is looking for you to provide guidance about what types of information it should not store in Outlook.

Form a team of three people and use the concepts and techniques presented in this chapter to provide HiTech Toolworks the following information: (1) instructions about how to import data from an Excel spreadsheet into Outlook, (2) examples of information HiTech Toolworks should not store for each contact, and (3) how employees can share contacts with one another so that each employee does not have to maintain their own separate contact list. Submit your assignment in a format specified by your instructor.

Part 2: You made several decisions while compiling the information about Microsoft Outlook for HiTech Toolworks in this assignment, such as how to go about importing information from an external file, recommending types of data not to store about a contact in Outlook, and the best way to share contacts in Outlook. Should everyone in the company have access to all contact information, or should access to some information be restricted? What was the rationale behind each of these decisions and suggestions? Where did you obtain your information?

Learn Online

Reinforce what you learned in this chapter with games, exercises, training, and many other online activities and resources.

Student Companion Site   Reinforce chapter terms and concepts using review questions, flash cards, practice tests, and interactive learning games, such as a crossword puzzle. These and other online activities and resources are available at no additional cost on www.cengagebrain.com. Visit www.cengage.com/ct/studentdownload for detailed instructions about accessing the resources available at the Student Companion Site.

4 | Creating and Managing Tasks with Outlook

Objectives

You will have mastered the material in this chapter when you can:

- Create a new task
- Create a task with a status
- Create a task with a priority
- Create a task with a reminder
- Create a recurring task
- Categorize a task
- Configure Quick Clicks
- Categorize email messages

- Update a task
- Attach a file to a task
- Assign a task
- Forward a task
- Send a status report
- Print tasks
- Create a note
- Change the view of notes

4 | Creating and Managing Tasks with Outlook

This introductory chapter covers features and functions common to creating and managing tasks in Outlook 2013.

Roadmap

In this chapter, you will learn how to perform basic contact tasks. The following roadmap identifies general activities you will perform as you progress through this chapter:

1. CREATE a NEW TASK
2. CATEGORIZE a TASK
3. CATEGORIZE an EMAIL MESSAGE
4. ASSIGN a TASK
5. PRINT a TASK
6. CREATE AND USE NOTES

At the beginning of step instructions throughout the chapter, you will see an abbreviated form of this roadmap. The abbreviated roadmap uses colors to indicate chapter progress: gray means the chapter is beyond that activity, blue means the task being shown is covered in that activity, and black means that activity is yet to be covered. For example, the following abbreviated roadmap indicates the section would be about assigning a task.

1 CREATE NEW TASK | 2 CATEGORIZE TASK | 3 CATEGORIZE EMAIL MESSAGE
4 ASSIGN TASK | 5 PRINT TASK | 6 CREATE AND USE NOTES

Use the abbreviated roadmap as a progress guide while you read or step through the instructions in this chapter.

Introduction to Outlook Tasks

Whether you are keeping track of your school assignments that are due next week or the action items that your boss needs completed as soon as possible, you can use Outlook tasks to manage your to-do list by generating a checklist and tracking activities. Instead of keeping a paper list of the things you need to do, you can use Outlook to combine your various tasks into one list that has reminders and tracking. A **task** is an item that you create in Outlook to track until its completion. A **to-do item** is any Outlook item such as a task, an email message, or a contact that has been flagged for follow-up later.

Creating and managing tasks in Outlook allows you to keep track of projects, which might include school assignments, work responsibilities, or personal activities. Using a task, you can record information about a project such as start date, due date, status, priority, and percent complete. Outlook also can remind you about the task so that you do not forget to complete it. If you are managing a project, for example, you can assign tasks to people so that everyone can complete their portion of the project.

Project — Managing Tasks

People and businesses create tasks to keep track of projects that are important to them or their organizations. Tasks can be categorized and monitored to ensure that all projects are completed in a timely fashion. You can track one-time tasks as well as tasks that recur over a period of time. You also can prioritize tasks so that you can decide which ones must be completed first.

The project in this chapter follows general guidelines and uses Outlook to create the task list shown in Figure 4–1. The task list in the Dylan Chapter 4 mailbox includes tasks that are organized using class, personal, and project team categories.

Figure 4–1

Creating a Task

The first step in creating a task for your to-do list is to open the Tasks category in Outlook. After you create a list of tasks, you can sync your tasks across multiple devices such as your smartphone and laptop, staying up to date and improving your productivity.

What advantages does an Outlook task list provide beyond a basic to-do list?

Many business employees use an Outlook task list to detail their hours, business expenses, and mileage. Instead of jotting down how many hours you worked on Thursday to report later, remembering the tolls paid on a business trip, or how many miles you must list on your expense report, you can store this information in a task. When it is time to turn in your work hours or expense report, you can easily retrieve the details from your task list.

For an introduction to Windows 8 and instruction about how to perform basic Windows 8 tasks, read the Office 2013 and Windows 8 chapter at the beginning of this book, where you can learn how to resize windows, change screen resolution, create folders, move and rename files, use Windows Help, and much more.

To-Do List Window

The To-Do List – Outlook Data File window shown in Figure 4–2 includes a variety of features to help you manage your tasks. It contains many elements similar to the windows in other Office programs, as well as some that are unique to Outlook. The main elements of the To-Do List window are the Navigation Pane, the To-Do list pane, and the Preview pane. The My Tasks folder in the Navigation Pane displays the To-Do list link and Tasks folder. Clicking the To-Do list link displays the tasks in the To-Do list view, and tapping or clicking Tasks displays the tasks in the task folder in Simple List view.

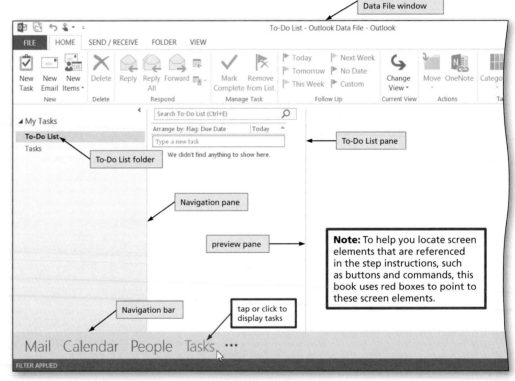

Figure 4–2

One of the few differences between Windows 7 and Windows 8 occurs in the steps to run Outlook. If you are using Windows 7, click the Start button, type Outlook in the 'Search programs and files' box, click Outlook 2013, and then, if necessary, maximize the Outlook window.

To Run Outlook

If you are using a computer to step through the project in this chapter and you want your screens to match the figures in this book, you should change your screen's resolution to 1366 × 768. For information about how to change a computer's resolution, refer to the Office and Windows chapter at the beginning of this book.

The following steps, which assume Windows is running, use the Search text box to run Outlook based on a typical installation. You may need to ask your instructor how to run Outlook on your computer. For a detailed example of the procedure summarized below, refer to the Office 2013 and Windows 8 chapter.

1 Swipe in from the right edge of the screen or point to the upper-right corner of the screen to display the Charms bar.

2 Tap or click the Search charm on the Charms bar to display the Search menu.

3 Type `Outlook` as the search text in the Search text box and watch the search results appear in the Apps list.

4 Tap or click Outlook 2013 in the search results to run Outlook.

5 If the Outlook window is not maximized, tap or click the Maximize button on its title bar to maximize the window.

Creating a To-Do List

The first step in creating a To-Do list is to select a folder for storing your tasks. By default, Outlook stores tasks in the Tasks folder, but you also can create a personal folder in which to store your tasks, using the technique presented in Chapter 2. In this chapter, you will create tasks in the Tasks folder.

To Create a New Task

1 CREATE NEW TASK | 2 CATEGORIZE TASK | 3 CATEGORIZE EMAIL MESSAGE
4 ASSIGN TASK | 5 PRINT TASK | 6 CREATE AND USE NOTES

Dylan Cruz, the student president of the International Club, would like to create a task list to keep track of what is going on in the club and in his own classes. To start, Dylan plans to create the first task, which is to contact a speaker for the club in October at least a month before the meeting so that he does not forget to complete the task. The following steps create a new task. *Why? To stay organized, you should keep Outlook tasks to make sure you complete all the items on your to-do list.*

1

• Open the Dylan Chapter 4.pst Outlook Data File from the Data Files for Students for Chapter 4.

• Tap or click Tasks (shown in Figure 4–2) on the Navigation Bar to display the Outlook Tasks.

• Tap or click the New Task button (HOME tab | New group) to display the Untitled – Task window (Figure 4–3).

Figure 4–3

Q&A Why is my screen different? My Untitled – Task window does not have the two buttons named Assign Task and Send Status Report in the Manage Task group as shown in Figure 4–3.
If you do not have an email account connected to Outlook (covered in Chapter 1), you will not have these two buttons.

The New Task button does not appear on the HOME tab. What should I do?
Click the New Items button (HOME tab | New group), and then click Task. Now the New Task button should appear on the HOME tab.

2

- Type **Contact a Speaker** in the Subject text box to enter a subject for the task.

- Type **Study Abroad program speaker for the October meeting** in the task body area to enter a description for the task (Figure 4–4).

Q&A Why did the title of the Task window change after I entered the subject?

As soon as you enter the subject, Outlook updates the Task window title to reflect the information you entered. The task is not saved, however; only the window title is updated.

Figure 4–4

3

- Tap or click the Start date Calendar button to display a calendar for the current month (Figure 4–5).

Q&A Why does my calendar display a different month?

Depending on the actual calendar month, your current month may be different.

Figure 4–5

4

- If necessary, tap or click the next month arrow or previous month arrow an appropriate number of times to advance to September 2014.

- Tap or click 5 to select Fri 9/5/2014 as the start date (Figure 4–6).

Q&A Why did the due date change?
If you enter a start date, the due date automatically changes to match the start date. You can change the due date if needed.

Can I just type the date?
Yes, you can type the date. Using the calendar allows you to avoid potential errors due to typing mistakes.

What if September 2014 is in the past?
If September 2014 is in the past, tap or click the previous month arrow an appropriate number of times until you reach September 2014.

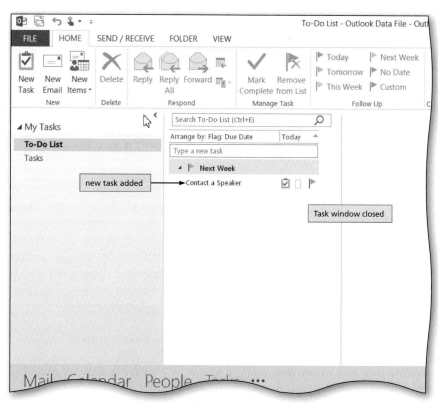

Figure 4–6

5

- Tap or click the Save & Close button (TASK tab | Actions group) (shown in Figure 4–6) to save the task and close the Task window (Figure 4–7).

Q&A My tasks are displayed in an arrangement different from the one in Figure 4–7. What should I do?
Tap or click the Change View button or the More button (HOME tab | Current View group), and then click To-Do List.

Figure 4–7

Other Ways

1. Press CTRL+N

To Create a Task with a Due Date

When you create the first task, the due date is set automatically after you enter the start date. If you have a specific due date, you can enter it when you create a task. Dylan needs to create a meeting agenda before the October meeting on October 2. The following steps create a task with a due date. *Why? You can quickly add a specific due date to set a deadline for a task. You also can sort by the due date, placing the most urgent tasks at the top of your list.*

1

- Tap or click the New Task button (HOME tab | New group) to display the Untitled – Task window.

- Type **Create an Agenda** in the Subject text box to enter a subject for the task (Figure 4–8).

Figure 4–8

2

- Tap or click the Due date Calendar button to display a calendar for the current month.

- Tap or click the next month arrow button an appropriate number of times to advance to October 2014.

- Tap or click 2 to select Thu 10/2/2014 as the due date (Figure 4–9).

Figure 4–9

3

- Tap or click the Save & Close button (TASK tab | Actions group) to save the task and close the Task window (Figure 4–10).

Figure 4–10

To Create a Task with a Status

1 CREATE NEW TASK | 2 CATEGORIZE TASK | 3 CATEGORIZE EMAIL MESSAGE
4 ASSIGN TASK | 5 PRINT TASK | 6 CREATE AND USE NOTES

Dylan is planning a fundraising project for the International Club that will be presented at the November meeting on 11/6/2014. Outlook allows you to assign a status to any task you create. You can assign one of five status indicators: Not Started, In Progress, Completed, Waiting on someone else, and Deferred. Dylan has already started working on the fundraising project ideas, so the task status should be set to In Progress. The following steps create a task with a status. *Why? You can reflect your current progress by changing the status of a task.*

1

- Tap or click the New Task button (HOME tab | New group) to display the Untitled – Task window.

- Type **Fundraising Project** in the Subject text box to enter a subject for the task.

- Tap or click the Due date Calendar button to display a calendar for the current month.

- Tap or click the next month arrow button an appropriate number of times to advance to November 2014.

- Tap or click 6 to select Thu 11/6/2014 as the due date (Figure 4–11).

Figure 4–11

2

- Tap or click the Status box arrow to display the status options (Figure 4–12).

Figure 4–12

3

- Tap or click In Progress to change the status of the task (Figure 4–13).

Figure 4–13

4

- Tap or click the Save & Close button (TASK tab | Actions group) to save the task and close the Task window (Figure 4–14).

new task added to Later group (the name of your group may differ)

Figure 4–14

To Create a Task with a Priority

1 CREATE NEW TASK | 2 CATEGORIZE TASK | 3 CATEGORIZE EMAIL MESSAGE
4 ASSIGN TASK | 5 PRINT TASK | 6 CREATE AND USE NOTES

As you itemize your work, Outlook can organize each task by setting priorities to reflect its importance. Dylan is hosting an International Food Festival on October 19 and needs to confirm the catering details at least five days in advance. As you enter the task in Outlook, you should set a high priority for this event as appropriate. Outlook allows for three priority levels: Low, Normal, and High. The following steps set the priority of a task. **Why?** *Using the built-in priority feature, you can later sort according to the importance of the task so you can determine how best to focus your time.*

1

- Tap or click the New Task button (HOME tab | New group) to display the Untitled – Task window.

- Type **Confirm Caterer for International Food Festival** in the Subject text box to enter a subject for the task.

- Tap or click the Due date Calendar button to display a calendar for the current month.

- Tap or click the next month arrow button an appropriate number of times to advance to October 2014.

- Tap or click 14 to select Tue 10/14/2014 as the due date (Figure 4–15).

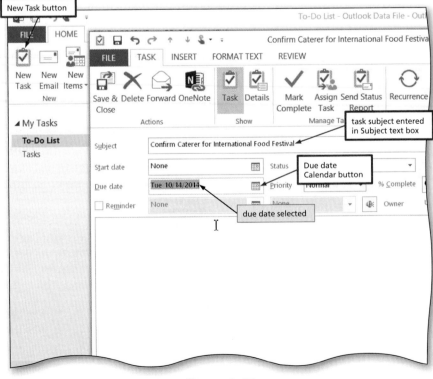

Figure 4–15

2

- Tap or click the Priority box arrow to display the priority options (Figure 4–16).

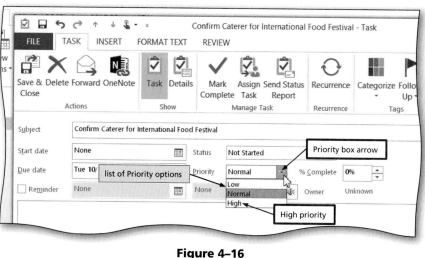

Figure 4–16

3

- Tap or click High to set the priority (Figure 4–17).

4

- Tap or click the Save & Close button (TASK tab | Actions group) to save the task and close the Task window.

Figure 4–17

To Create a Task with a Reminder

1 CREATE NEW TASK | 2 CATEGORIZE TASK | 3 CATEGORIZE EMAIL MESSAGE
4 ASSIGN TASK | 5 PRINT TASK | 6 CREATE AND USE NOTES

When you are busy with classes, a task reminder is helpful to ensure that you complete a project. Mr. Thompson, the faculty advisor, has asked Dylan to send the October meeting agenda to him by the end of September. *Why? By adding a reminder to a task, Outlook can remind you about the task automatically.* Reminders can be set before the task is actually due so you will have enough time to complete the task. The following steps add a task and set the reminder option for a week before the task is due.

1

- Tap or click the New Task button (HOME tab | New group) to display the Untitled – Task window.

- Type **Send Meeting Agenda to Mr. Thompson** in the Subject text box to enter a subject for the task.

- Type **October International Club agenda** in the task body area to enter a description for the task.

- Tap or click the Due date Calendar button to display a calendar for the current month.

- Tap or click the next month arrow an appropriate number of times to advance to September 2014.

- Tap or click 30 to select Tue 9/30/2014 as the due date (Figure 4–18).

Figure 4–18

2

- Tap or click the Reminder check box to insert a check mark, enable the Reminder boxes, and configure Outlook to display a reminder (Figure 4–19).

Figure 4–19

3

- Tap or click the Reminder Calendar button to display a calendar for September.

- Tap or click 23 to select Tue 9/23/2014 as the Reminder date (Figure 4–20).

Q&A

Can I change the time that Outlook displays the reminder?

Yes. When you set a reminder, Outlook automatically sets the time for the reminder to 8:00 AM. You can change the time by tapping or clicking the Reminder box arrow and then selecting a time. You also can use the Outlook Options dialog box to change the default time to whatever time you desire.

Figure 4–20

❹

- Tap or click the Save & Close button (TASK tab | Actions group) to save the task and close the Task window (Figure 4–21).

Q&A How does Outlook remind me of a task?

If you selected a reminder for a task, Outlook displays the Task window for the task at the specified time. If you used the Sound icon to set an alarm for the reminder, Outlook also plays the sound when it displays the Task window.

new task added to Next Month group (your group may differ)

Figure 4–21

To Create More Tasks

1 CREATE NEW TASK | 2 CATEGORIZE TASK | 3 CATEGORIZE EMAIL MESSAGE
4 ASSIGN TASK | 5 PRINT TASK | 6 CREATE AND USE NOTES

Dylan has additional tasks related to his studies. These include three tasks regarding a project in his business course to develop a business plan. The first task is to research the information for the business plan. An additional task is to write the business plan document. He also needs a task for editing and posting the business plan assignment.

Table 4–1 displays the business plan tasks with their due dates. The following step creates these remaining tasks in the Task window. *Why? By adding academic tasks to your list, an item that requires attention will not be overlooked.*

Table 4–1 Additional Tasks

Subject	Due Date
Research the Information for the Business Plan	10/1/2014
Write the Business Plan	10/8/2014
Edit and Post the Business Plan	10/15/2014

© 2014 Cengage Learning

❶

- Tap or click the New Task button (HOME tab | New group) to display the Untitled – Task window.

- Enter the subject in the Subject text box for the first task in Table 4–1.

- Tap or click the Due date Calendar button to display a calendar for the current month, and then select the due date for the task as shown in Table 4–1.

- Tap or click the Save & Close button (TASK tab | Actions group) to save the task and close the Task window.

- Repeat the actions in bullets 1 through 4 for the two remaining tasks in Table 4–1 (Figure 4–22).

New Task button

new tasks added

Figure 4–22

To Create a Recurring Task

So far, the tasks you created had a specific date for completion. Sometimes, a task occurs repeatedly until the due date. For example, Dylan has a weekly assignment due in his Global Business course on Mondays from September 8 until December 1. The task will be considered complete on December 1, but it occurs every week until then.

When you create a task, Outlook allows you to specify if it is a recurring task. You can select whether the task recurs daily, weekly, monthly, or yearly. For each of those options, you can provide specifics. For example, if it is a monthly task, you can specify the day of the month it occurs. You also can choose to have a task automatically regenerate itself to keep the task from ending. If you know the ending date, you can specify the exact end date.

The following steps add a recurring weekly task. *Why? When you have a task that occurs at regular intervals, you should set a recurring task to keep you informed.*

❶

- Tap or click the New Task button (HOME tab | New group) to display the Untitled – Task window.

- Type **Global Business Course Assignment** in the Subject text box to enter a subject for the task.

- Type **Submit assignment online** in the task body area to enter a description for the task.

- Tap or click the Start date Calendar button to display a calendar for the current month.

- Tap or click the next month arrow button an appropriate number of times to advance to September 2014.

- Tap or click 8 to select Mon 9/8/2014 as the start date (Figure 4–23).

Figure 4–23

❷

- Tap or click the Recurrence button (TASK tab | Recurrence group) to display the Task Recurrence dialog box (Figure 4–24).

Figure 4–24

3

- Tap or click the End by option button to select it.

- Tap or click the End by box arrow to display a calendar.

- If necessary, tap or click the next month arrow button an appropriate number of times to advance to December 2014.

- Tap or click 1 to select Mon 12/1/2014 as the End by date (Figure 4–25).

Figure 4–25

4

- Tap or click the OK button (Task Recurrence dialog box) to accept the recurrence settings (Figure 4–26).

5

- Tap or click the Save & Close button (TASK tab | Actions group) to save the task and close the Task window.

Figure 4–26

To Create Another Recurring Task

As part of Dylan's role as the president of the International Club, a recurring task is necessary for collecting the donations for the International Red Cross. He and his team plan to collect the donations from the donation bins placed around campus every Saturday from October 4 until November 22.

The following step adds another recurring task. **Why?** *When you have a task that occurs at regular intervals, you should add it as a recurring task to keep you informed.*

❶

- Tap or click the New Task button (HOME tab | New group) to display the Untitled – Task window.

- Type `Collect Donations` in the Subject text box to enter a subject for the task.

- Tap or click the Start date Calendar button to display a calendar for the current month.

- Tap or click the next month arrow button an appropriate number of times to advance to October 2014.

- Tap or click 4 to select Sat 10/4/2014 as the start date.

- Tap or click the Recurrence button (TASK tab | Recurrence group) to display the Task Recurrence dialog box.

- Tap or click the End by option button to select it.

- Tap or click the End by box arrow to display a calendar.

Figure 4–27

- Tap or click the previous month arrow button an appropriate number of times to return to November 2014.

- Tap or click 22 to select Sat 11/22/2014 as the End by date.

- Tap or click the OK button to accept the recurrence settings.

- Tap or click the Save & Close button (TASK tab | Actions group) to save the task and close the Task window (Figure 4–27).

BTW

Task Options
You can modify options for tasks, such as changing the default reminder time for tasks with due dates, changing default colors for overdue and completed tasks, and setting the Quick Click flag. To access task options, open the Backstage view, click Options, and then click Tasks.

TO ADD A TASK USING THE TO-DO LIST PANE

You sometimes need to add a task quickly. You can do this using the To-Do List Pane. The To-Do List Pane lets you create quick tasks that normally are due the day you add them. If you wanted to add a task using the To-Do List Pane, you would use the following steps.

1. Tap or click the 'Type a new task' box to select the text box.

2. Type a description to enter a description of the task.

3. Press the ENTER key to finish adding the task and display it in the To-Do list with the current date.

Categorizing Tasks

Outlook allows you to categorize email messages, contacts, tasks, and calendar items so that you can identify which ones are related to each other as well as quickly identify the items by their color. In Chapter 2 of this text, color categories were used to organize calendar items. In the same way, you can color-categorize tasks to organize and manage different types of tasks.

Six color categories are available by default, but you also can create your own categories and select one of 25 colors to associate with them. After you create a category, you can set it as a Quick Click. The **Quick Click** category is the category applied by default when you tap or click an item's category column in the To-Do list pane. For example, the default Quick Click category is the red category. If you tapped or clicked a task's category column in the To-Do list pane, the red category automatically is assigned to it.

To Create a New Category

1 CREATE NEW TASK | 2 CATEGORIZE TASK | 3 CATEGORIZE EMAIL MESSAGE
4 ASSIGN TASK | 5 PRINT TASK | 6 CREATE AND USE NOTES

Why? *Custom categories can organize tasks listed in Outlook.* The first category you want to create is for International Club tasks. You intend to use the International Club category for all tasks that are related to the International Club at Raven College. To create a category, select a task and then create the category. Outlook applies the category to the selected task. After you create a category, apply it to other tasks as necessary. The following steps create a color category and apply it to a task.

1

- Tap or click the Contact a Speaker task to select it.

- Tap or click the Categorize button (HOME tab | Tags group) to display the Categorize menu (Figure 4–28).

Q&A Why do I have to select the Contact a Speaker task?
To activate the Categorize button, you first need to select a task or group of tasks.

Figure 4–28

BTW

Q&As

For a complete list of the Q&As found in many of the step-by-step sequences in this book, visit the Q&A resource on the Student Companion Site located on www.cengagebrain.com. For detailed instructions about accessing available resources, visit www.cengage.com/ct/studentdownload or contact your instructor for information about accessing the required files.

2

- Tap or click All Categories to display the Color Categories dialog box (Figure 4–29).

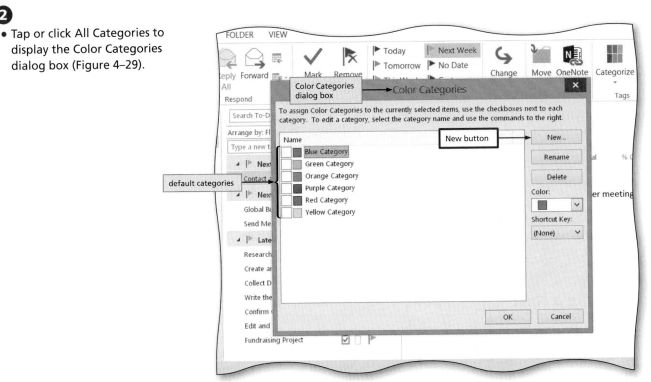

Figure 4–29

3

- Tap or click the New button (Color Categories dialog box) to display the Add New Category dialog box (Figure 4–30).

Figure 4–30

4

- Type **International Club** in the Name text box to enter a name for the category.

- Tap or click the Color box arrow to display a list of colors (Figure 4–31).

Figure 4–31

5

- Tap or click the Dark Teal square (column 1, row 5) to select a category color.

- Tap or click the OK button (Add New Category dialog box) to create the new category and display it in the Color Categories dialog box (Figure 4–32).

Figure 4–32

6

- Tap or click the OK button (Color Categories dialog box) to assign the Contact a Speaker task to the International Club category (Figure 4–33).

Figure 4–33

BTW

BTWs

For a complete list of the BTWs found in the margins of this book, visit the BTW resource on the Student Companion Site located on www.cengagebrain.com. For detailed instructions about accessing available resources, visit www.cengage.com/ct/studentdownload or contact your instructor for information about accessing the required files.

To Categorize a Task

After creating a category, you can apply other tasks that are related to that category. *Why? You can easily identify all the tasks for a specific category by using color categories.* The following steps assign a task to an existing color category.

1
- Tap or click the Create an Agenda task to select it.
- Tap or click the Categorize button (HOME tab | Tags group) to display the Categorize menu (Figure 4–34).

Figure 4–34

2
- Tap or click International Club to assign the Create an Agenda task to that category (Figure 4–35).

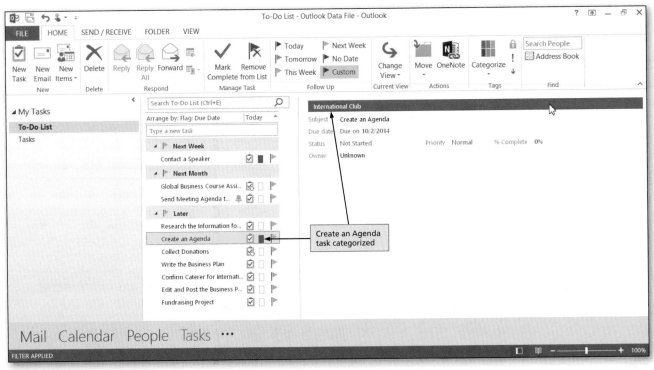

Figure 4–35

To Categorize Multiple Tasks

Outlook allows you to categorize multiple tasks at the same time. All of the course-related tasks can be assigned to a new category called Course Work. The tasks to assign to the Course Work category include the three business plan assignments and the Global Business course tasks.

The following steps create the Course Work category and apply it to the course-related tasks. *Why? As a student, you can view a single category to locate all of your assignments.*

1

- Select the Research the Information for the Business Plan, Write the Business Plan, Edit and Post the Business Plan, and the Global Business Course Assignment tasks.

- Tap or click the Categorize button (HOME tab | Tags group) to display the Categorize menu (Figure 4–36).

Q&A How do I select more than one task?
Tap or click the first task, press and hold the CTRL key, and then tap or click the other tasks to select them.

Figure 4–36

2

- Tap or click All Categories to display the Color Categories dialog box.

- Tap or click the New button (Color Categories dialog box) to display the Add New Category dialog box (Figure 4–37).

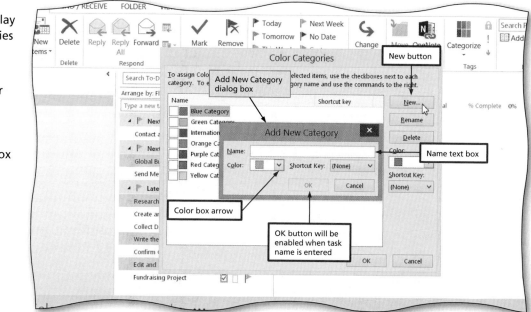

Figure 4–37

3

- Type **Course Work** in the Name text box to enter a name for the category.
- Tap or click the Color box arrow to display a list of colors.
- Click the Dark Red square (column 1, row 4) to select the category color.
- Tap or click the OK button (Add New Category dialog box) to create the Course Work category (Figure 4–38).

Figure 4–38

4

- Tap or click the OK button (Color Categories dialog box) to assign the selected tasks to a category (Figure 4–39).

Figure 4–39

To Categorize Remaining Tasks

Now that you know how to categorize multiple tasks at once, you decide to categorize the remaining tasks by assigning them to the International Club category. The following steps categorize the remaining tasks. *Why? When you sort by category, you will be able to view at a glance what tasks need completion in each of the facets of your life.*

1

- Select the Create an Agenda, Collect Donations, Fundraising Project, Confirm Caterer for International Food Festival, and Send Meeting Agenda to Mr. Thompson tasks.

- Tap or click the Categorize button (HOME tab | Tags group) to display the Categorize menu.

- Tap or click International Club to categorize the selected tasks (Figure 4–40).

Figure 4–40

To Rename a Category

After categorizing the project tasks, Dylan decides to change the name of the International Club category to the Student International Club category. The following steps rename a color category. *Why? By renaming the color categories, you can assign names that are meaningful to you.*

1

- Tap or click the Categorize button (HOME tab | Tags group) to display the Categorize menu.

- Tap or click All Categories to display the Color Categories dialog box (Figure 4–41).

Q&A

Do the category tasks have to be selected before renaming the category?

No, any task can be selected. When you change the name, Outlook will update every task in that category.

Figure 4–41

2

- Tap or click the International Club category to select it.

- Tap or click the Rename button (Color Categories dialog box) to select the category name for editing.

- Type **Student International Club** and then press the ENTER key to change the category name (Figure 4–42).

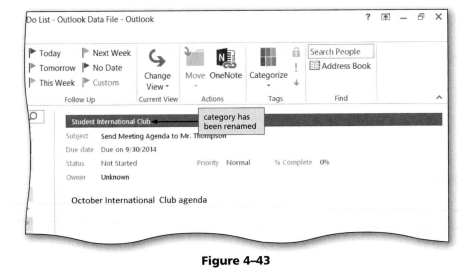

Figure 4–42

3

- Tap or click the OK button (Color Categories dialog box) to apply the changes (Figure 4–43).

Figure 4–43

1 CREATE NEW TASK | 2 CATEGORIZE TASK | 3 CATEGORIZE EMAIL MESSAGE
4 ASSIGN TASK | 5 PRINT TASK | 6 CREATE AND USE NOTES

To Set a Quick Click

So far, you have been categorizing tasks using the Categorize menu options. You could assign a task to a category by tapping or clicking the category box next to each task in the To-Do list pane. If you tap or click the category box, the default category is applied.

If you have a particular category that you know you will use frequently, you can set it as the default category. Outlook allows you to do this by setting the category as a Quick Click.

Dylan realizes that most of his tasks are related to the International Club, so he decides to set the default category as the Student International Club category. The following steps assign the default category using a Quick Click. *Why? You can assign a frequently used color category (Quick Click category) by selecting it as your default color category.*

• Tap or click the Categorize button (HOME tab | Tags group) to display the Categorize menu (Figure 4–44).

Figure 4–44

• Tap or click Set Quick Click to display the Set Quick Click dialog box.

• Tap or click the category button to display the list of categories (Figure 4–45).

Figure 4–45

• Tap or click Student International Club to set it as the Quick Click category (Figure 4–46).

• Tap or click the OK button (Set Quick Click dialog box) to apply the changes.

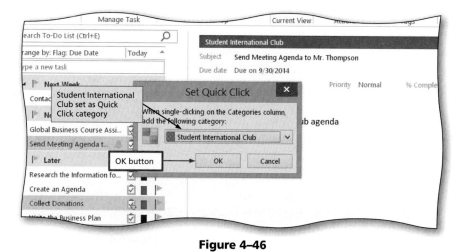

Figure 4–46

Break Point: If you wish to take a break, this is a good place to do so. To resume at a later time, continue to follow the steps from this location forward.

BTW
**Copying and
Moving Tasks**
If you want to move or copy an existing task to another folder, select the task, and then click the Move button (HOME tab | Move group). Click the Other Folder command if you want to move the task, or click the Copy to Folder command if you want to copy the task. Next, select the folder to which you want to move or copy the task, and then click the OK button.

Categorizing Email Messages

Recall that you can use categories with email messages, contacts, tasks, and calendar items. Any category you create for a task then can be used for your email messages. Categorizing your email messages allows you to create a link between them and other related items in Outlook. By looking at the category, you quickly can tell which Outlook items go together.

1 CREATE NEW TASK | 2 CATEGORIZE TASK | 3 CATEGORIZE EMAIL MESSAGE
4 ASSIGN TASK | 5 PRINT TASK | 6 CREATE AND USE NOTES

To Categorize an Email Message

Dylan received a couple of email messages from members of the International Club. These email messages can be assigned to the Student International Club category. The following steps categorize email messages. *Why? Color categories can be assigned to email messages, enabling you to quickly identify them and associate them with related tasks.*

1
- Tap or click the Mail button in the Navigation Pane to switch to your Inbox.
- Select the Ava Gibson and Mia James email messages.
- Tap or click the Categorize button (HOME tab | Tags group) to display the Categorize menu (Figure 4–47).

Q&A | What should I do if my Inbox is not displayed?
Tap or click the Inbox folder in the Navigation Pane to view the mailbox.

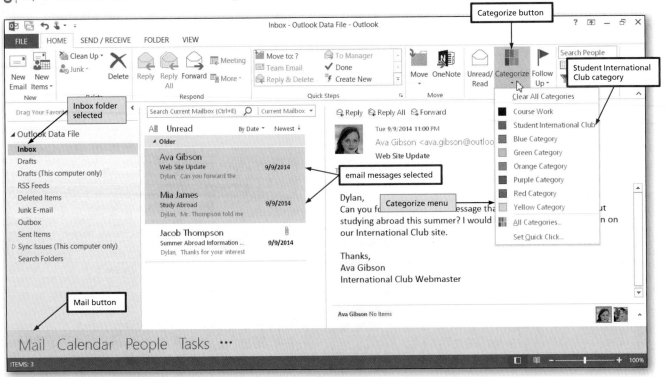

Figure 4–47

❷

- Tap or click Student International Club to assign the selected email messages to the Student International Club category (Figure 4–48).

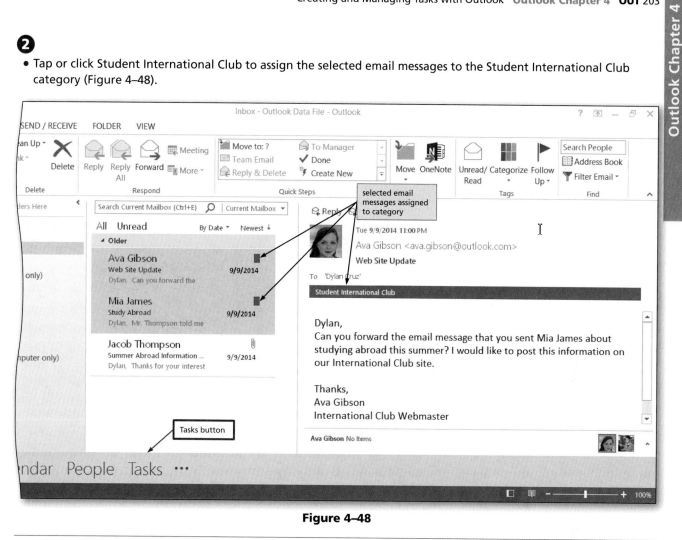

Figure 4–48

Managing Tasks

After creating one or more tasks in your To-Do list, you can perform maintenance on your tasks to manage them. Maintenance can include marking tasks complete when you finish them, updating them, assigning some of them to other people, adding attachments to them, and even removing them. Outlook allows you to manage your tasks and modify them as necessary while you are tracking them.

People sometimes create a To-Do list and never look at it again. To make the best use of your To-Do list, you should review it often to identify tasks that can be marked as complete, removed, or updated. For example, when you email the agenda for the meeting to Mr. Thompson, mark the task as complete. That way, you will not have to remember later whether you completed the assignment.

When you are working on a project with others, you sometimes may want to assign tasks to them. Outlook allows you to assign tasks to other people and still monitor the tasks. When a task has been assigned to another person, that person can accept or reject the task. If the task is rejected, it comes back to you. If it is accepted, the task belongs to that person to complete. When you assign a nonrecurring task, you can retain a copy and request a status report when the task is completed. If the task is a recurring task, you cannot retain a copy, but can request a status report when the task is completed.

BTW

Outlook Help
At any time while using Outlook, you can find answers to questions and display information about various topics through Outlook Help. Used properly, this form of assistance can increase your productivity and reduce your frustrations by minimizing the time you spend learning how to use Outlook. For instruction about Outlook Help and exercises that will help you gain confidence in using it, read the Office and Windows chapter at the beginning of this book.

Can you assign tasks to others within a business or club setting?

In the professional world, you typically work on projects as a member of a group or team. As you organize the large and small tasks required to complete the project, you can assign each task to members of your team and track the progress of the entire project.

To Update a Task

1 CREATE NEW TASK | 2 CATEGORIZE TASK | 3 CATEGORIZE EMAIL MESSAGE
4 ASSIGN TASK | 5 PRINT TASK | 6 CREATE AND USE NOTES

The November International Club meeting has been moved so the fundraising project task is due on November 13 instead of on November 6. The following steps change the due date for a task. *Why? As tasks change, be sure to update the due dates of your tasks.*

1

- Tap or click the Tasks button in the Navigation Pane (shown in Figure 4–48) to display the To-Do list.

- Double-tap or double-click the Fundraising Project task to display the Fundraising Project – Task window (Figure 4–49).

Figure 4–49

2

- Tap or click the Due date Calendar button to display a calendar for November.

- Tap or click 13 to select Thu 11/13/2014 as the due date.

- Tap or click Save & Close (TASK tab | Actions group) to save the changes (Figure 4–50).

Q&A How do I change the task name only?

Tap or click the task name in the task list to select it, and then tap or click it again to edit the name.

Figure 4–50

To Attach a File to a Task

Outlook allows you to attach a file to a task. *Why? This is helpful if you want quick access to information when you are looking at a task.* Jacob Thompson has emailed you a Study Abroad flyer, which you already have saved to your computer. You decide that you should attach it to the Contact a Speaker task so that you can share the flyer with the speaker. The following steps attach a document to a task.

1

- Double-tap or double-click the Contact a Speaker task (shown in Figure 4–50) to display the Contact a Speaker - Task window.

- Tap or click INSERT on the ribbon to display the INSERT tab (Figure 4–51).

Figure 4–51

2

- Tap or click the Attach File button (INSERT tab | Include group) to display the Insert File dialog box.

- If necessary, navigate to the folder containing the data files for this chapter (in this case, the Chapter 04 folder in the Outlook folder in the Data Files for Students folder).

- Tap or click Study Abroad (Word document) to select the file to attach (Figure 4–52).

Figure 4–52

3

- Tap or click the Insert button (Insert File dialog box) to attach the file (Figure 4–53).

Figure 4–53

4

- Tap or click TASK on the ribbon to display the TASK tab.

- Tap or click Save & Close (TASK tab | Actions group) to save the changes (Figure 4–54).

Figure 4–54

1 CREATE NEW TASK | 2 CATEGORIZE TASK | 3 CATEGORIZE EMAIL MESSAGE
4 ASSIGN TASK | 5 PRINT TASK | 6 CREATE AND USE NOTES

To Assign a Task

In addition to creating your own tasks, you can create tasks to assign to others. Ava Gibson has volunteered to collect the International Red Cross donations. To assign a task, you first create the task, and then send it as a task request to someone. **Why?** *You can assign a task to someone else while ensuring that you retain a copy of the task and receive a status report once the task is completed.* The following steps assign a task.

1

- Double-tap or double-click the Collect Donations task (shown in Figure 4–54) to display the Collect Donations - Task window (Figure 4–55).

Figure 4–55

2

- Tap or click the Assign Task button (TASK tab | Manage Task group) to display the Assign Task options (Figure 4–56).

Q&A Why is my window missing the Assign Task button?
To follow the steps in the Assign Tasks section of this chapter, you need to set up an email account in Outlook as shown in Chapter 1.

Figure 4–56

3

- Type **ava. gibson@ outlook.com** in the To text box to enter a recipient (Figure 4–57).

Figure 4–57

4

- Tap or click the Send button (shown in Figure 4–57) to send the task to Ava Gibson (Figure 4–58).

Figure 4–58

To Forward a Task

1 CREATE NEW TASK | 2 CATEGORIZE TASK | 3 CATEGORIZE EMAIL MESSAGE
4 ASSIGN TASK | 5 PRINT TASK | 6 CREATE AND USE NOTES

In addition to assigning a task to a person, you can forward a task to a person. *Why? When you forward a task, you are forwarding a copy of the task to the person who can add it to their To-Do list for tracking.* Mia James has agreed to assist you in creating the agenda for the October meeting task. By forwarding the task to Mia, the task appears on her to-do list and she can track it on her own. The following steps forward a task.

1

- Double-tap or double-click the Create an Agenda task (shown in Figure 4–58) to display the Create an Agenda – Task window (Figure 4–59).

Figure 4–59

2

• Tap or click the Forward button (TASK tab | Actions group) to display the FW: Create an Agenda – Message (HTML) window (Figure 4–60).

Figure 4–60

3

• Type `mia.james@outlook.com` in the To text box to enter a recipient.

• Type **Attached is the agenda task for you to add to your to-do list.** in the message body area to enter a message.

• Press the ENTER key two times and then type **Dylan** to complete the message (Figure 4–61).

Figure 4–61

4

- Tap or click the Send button to forward the task to Mia James (Figure 4–62).

Figure 4–62

To Send a Status Report

1 CREATE NEW TASK | 2 CATEGORIZE TASK | 3 CATEGORIZE EMAIL MESSAGE
4 ASSIGN TASK | 5 PRINT TASK | 6 CREATE AND USE NOTES

While a task is in progress, you can send status reports to other people. The status reports indicate the status and completion percentage of the task. Mr. Jacob Thompson has requested that he be kept informed about the agenda for the October meeting. Dylan has completed 25 percent of the work and wants to inform him that the task is in progress. The following steps create and send a status report. *Why? If you have been assigned a task, you can submit a status report at some point prior to completion of the task. This could be used to detail why the task has not been completed or why the task needs to be amended.*

1

- Double-tap or double-click the Create an Agenda task to display the Create an Agenda - Task window.

- Tap or click the Status box arrow to display a status list.

- Tap or click In Progress to change the status of the task (Figure 4–63).

Figure 4–63

2

- Tap or click the Up arrow to change the % Complete to 25% (Figure 4–64).

Figure 4–64

3

- Tap or click the Send Status Report button (TASK tab | Manage Task group) to display the Task Status Report: Create an Agenda - Message (Rich Text) window.

- Type `jacob.thompson@outlook.com` in the To text box to enter a recipient.

- Type `Mr. Thompson,` and then press the ENTER key two times in the message body area to enter the greeting line of the message.

- Type `Here is my first update on this task.` in the message.

- Press the ENTER key two times, and then type `Dylan` to complete the message (Figure 4–65).

Figure 4–65

4

- Tap or click the Send button to send the status report to Jacob Thompson.

- Tap or click the Save & Close button (TASK tab | Actions group) to save the changes to the task (Figure 4–66).

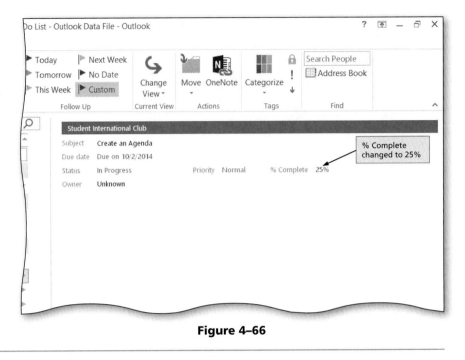

Figure 4–66

To Mark a Task Complete

1 CREATE NEW TASK | 2 CATEGORIZE TASK | 3 CATEGORIZE EMAIL MESSAGE
4 ASSIGN TASK | 5 PRINT TASK | 6 CREATE AND USE NOTES

When you accomplish a task, you should mark it as complete so that you know it is finished. You have just completed the research for the business plan. *Why?* *You can mark a task as complete so that you no longer have to worry about it.* The following steps mark a task as complete.

1

- Tap or click the Research the Information for the Business Plan task to select it (Figure 4–67).

Figure 4–67

❷

- Tap or click the Mark Complete button (HOME tab | Manage Task group) to mark the Research the Information for the Business Plan task as completed (Figure 4–68).

Why was the Research the Information for the Business Plan task removed from the To-Do list? Once you mark a task as complete, Outlook removes it from the To-Do list and places it in the Completed list. You can see the Completed list by changing your view to Completed using the Change View button (HOME tab | Current View group).

Figure 4–68

To Remove a Task

You sometimes may need to remove a task. **Why?** *When you remove a task, it no longer is displayed in your To-Do List.* For example, the Student International Club has decided to remove the Fundraising Project task until the club has time to promote the project. The following steps remove a task.

❶

- Tap or click the Fundraising Project task to select it (Figure 4–69).

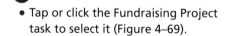

Figure 4–69

2

• Tap or click the Remove from List button (HOME tab | Manage Task group) to remove the task (Figure 4–70).

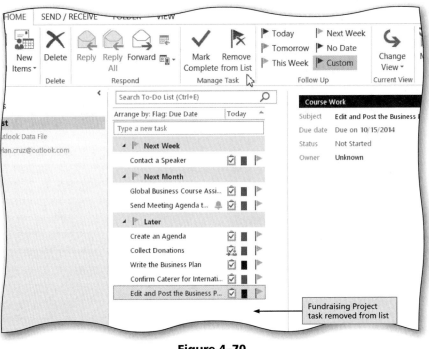

Figure 4–70

1 CREATE NEW TASK | 2 CATEGORIZE TASK | 3 CATEGORIZE EMAIL MESSAGE
4 ASSIGN TASK | 5 PRINT TASK | 6 CREATE AND USE NOTES

TO DELETE A CATEGORY

When you no longer need a category, you can delete it. Deleting a category removes the category from the category list but not from the tasks that already have been assigned to it. If you wanted to delete a category, you would use the following steps.

1. Tap or click a task within the category that you would like to delete.

2. Tap or click the Categorize button (HOME tab | Tags group) to display the Categorize menu.

3. Tap or click All Categories to display the Color Categories dialog box.

4. Tap or click the category that you want to delete to select it.

5. Tap or click the Delete button (Color Categories dialog box) to delete the color category.

6. Tap or click the Yes button (Microsoft Outlook dialog box) to confirm the deletion.

7. Tap or click the OK button (Color Categories dialog box) to close the dialog box.

BTW
Touch Screen
Differences
The Office and Windows interfaces may vary if you are using a touch screen. For this reason, you might notice that the function or appearance of your touch screen differs slightly from this chapter's presentation.

Choosing Display and Print Views

When working with tasks, you can change the view to see your tasks better. For instance, you can view your tasks as a detailed list, simple list, priority list, or a complete list. Change the view of your tasks to fit your current needs. For example, if you want to see tasks listed according to their priority (High, Normal, or Low), you can display the tasks in the Prioritized view. You also can print tasks in a summarized list or include the details for each task.

To Change the Task View

Tasks can be displayed in different customized view layouts. *Why?* *If you would like to see the total picture of what you have to accomplish, the Detailed view provides all the task details, including task subject, status, due date, and categories. By displaying tasks in Detailed view, you can view all tasks, including completed tasks.* The following steps change the view to Detailed view.

1

- Tap or click the Change View button (HOME tab | Current View group) to display the Change View gallery (Figure 4–71).

Q&A

The Change View button does not appear on my HOME tab. What should I do?
Tap or click the More button (HOME tab | Current View group) to display the Change View gallery.

Figure 4–71

2

- Tap or click Detailed to change the view (Figure 4–72).

Experiment

- Tap or click the other views in the Current View gallery to view the tasks in other arrangements. When you are finished, tap or click Detailed to return to Detailed view.

Figure 4–72

To Print Tasks

If you need to print your tasks, Outlook provides printing options based upon the view and tasks you have selected. For example, in the To-Do List view, you can select a single task and print in Table Style or Menu Style. In Detailed view, which is the current view, you can print only in Table Style. The following steps print the tasks using Table Style. *Why? Sometimes it is easier to print a To-Do list to view at any time when you are not working at your computer.*

1

- Tap or click FILE on the ribbon to open the Backstage view.
- Tap or click the Print tab in the Backstage view to display the Print gallery (Figure 4–73).

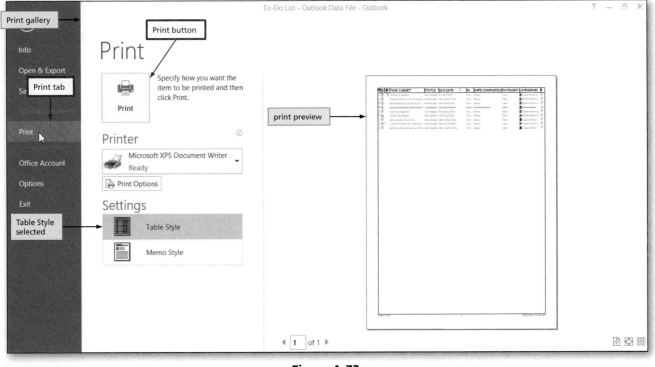

Figure 4–73

2

- If necessary, tap or click Table Style in the Settings section to select a print format.
- Tap or click the Print button to print the tasks in Table Style (Figure 4–74).

Figure 4–74

Using Notes

Outlook allows you to create the equivalent of paper notes using the Notes feature. Use notes to record ideas, spur-of-the-moment questions, and even words that you would like to recall or use at a later time. You can leave notes open on the screen while you continue using Outlook, or you can close them and view them in the Notes window. The Notes window contains the Navigation Pane and Notes Pane.

CONSIDER THIS

Can I use the Outlook Notes as sticky notes?

Notes are the electronic equivalent of yellow paper sticky notes. You can jot down notes for the directions that you find online to your interview, for example, or write questions that you want to remember to ask.

1 CREATE NEW TASK | 2 CATEGORIZE TASK | 3 CATEGORIZE EMAIL MESSAGE

4 ASSIGN TASK | 5 PRINT TASK | 6 CREATE AND USE NOTES

To Create a Note

Why? *A note can save a reminder from a phone conversation, information you find online for future reference, or even a grocery list.* As Dylan was surfing the web, he came across some information that he would like to share at the next club meeting. When text is entered into a note, it is saved automatically with the last modified date shown at the bottom of the note; therefore, you do not have to tap or click a Save button. The following steps create a note reminder.

1

- Tap or click the Navigation Options button (three dots) on the Navigation bar to display the Navigation Options menu (Figure 4–75).

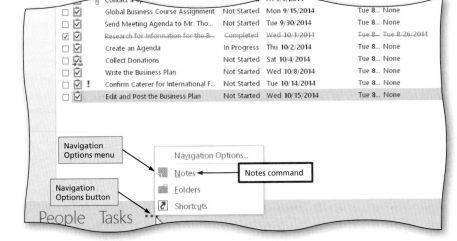

Figure 4–75

2

- Tap or click Notes to open the Notes – Outlook Data File – Outlook window.

- Tap or click the New Note button (HOME tab | New group) to display a new blank note (Figure 4–76).

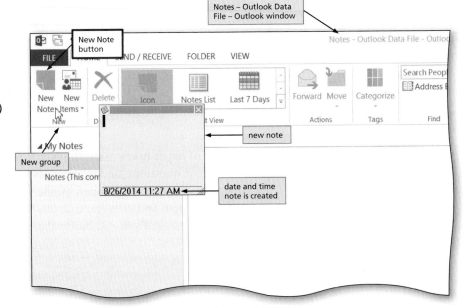

Figure 4–76

3

- Type `82% of those that studied abroad acquired skill sets that influenced their career path` as the note text to enter a note (Figure 4–77).

Figure 4–77

4

- Tap or click the Close button to save and close the note (Figure 4–78).

Q&A

Why is my Notes view different from Figure 4–78?

There are three basic Notes views: Icon, Notes List, and Last 7 Days. In Figure 4–78, the note is displayed in Icon view. To switch to Icon view, tap or click the Icon button (HOME tab | Current View group).

Can I print notes?

Yes. First, select the note(s) you want to print. To select multiple notes, hold the CTRL key while tapping or clicking the notes to print. Next, tap or click the FILE tab to open the Backstage view, tap or click the Print tab, and then tap or click the Print button.

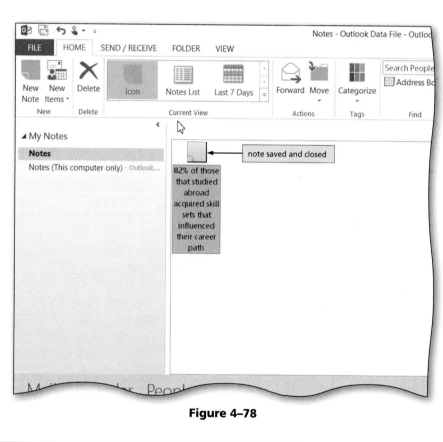

Figure 4–78

Other Ways

1. Press CTRL+SHIFT+N

To Change the Notes View

1 CREATE NEW TASK | 2 CATEGORIZE TASK | 3 CATEGORIZE EMAIL MESSAGE

4 ASSIGN TASK | 5 PRINT TASK | **6 CREATE AND USE NOTES**

Why? *You would like to display your notes as a list instead in the sticky note layout.* As with tasks, you can change the view of your notes. You decide to change your notes view to Notes List. The following step changes the view to Notes List view.

1

- Tap or click the Notes List button (HOME tab | Current View group) to change the view to Notes List (Figure 4–79).

Experiment

- Tap or click the other views in the Current View group to view the notes in other arrangements. When you are finished, tap or click Notes List to return to Notes List view.

Figure 4–79

To Delete a Note

1 CREATE NEW TASK | 2 CATEGORIZE TASK | 3 CATEGORIZE EMAIL MESSAGE
4 ASSIGN TASK | 5 PRINT TASK | **6 CREATE AND USE NOTES**

Why? *When you no longer need a note, you should delete it.* After sharing the note about studying abroad at the club meeting, you decide to delete the note because you no longer need it. The following step deletes a note.

1

- If necessary, tap or click the note about studying abroad to select it.
- Tap or click the Delete button (HOME tab | Delete group) to delete the note (Figure 4–80).

Figure 4–80

To Exit Outlook

This project now is complete. The following steps exit Outlook. For a detailed example of the procedure summarized below, refer to the Office 2013 and Windows 8 chapter at the beginning of this book.

 If you have a note or task open, tap or click the Close button on the right side of the title bar to close the window.

 Tap or click the Close button on the right side of the title bar to exit Outlook.

Chapter Summary

In this chapter, you have learned how to use Outlook to create a task, categorize tasks, categorize email messages, manage tasks, print tasks, create notes, and print notes. The items listed below include all the new Outlook skills you have learned in this chapter with the tasks grouped by activity.

Creating a Task
Create a New Task (OUT 181)
Create a Task with a Due Date (OUT 184)
Create a Task with a Status (OUT 185)
Create a Task with a Priority (OUT 186)
Create a Task with a Reminder (OUT 187)
Create More Tasks (OUT 189)
Create a Recurring Task (OUT 190)
Create Another Recurring Task (OUT 192)

Categorizing Tasks
Create a New Category (OUT 193)
Categorize a Task (OUT 196)
Categorize Multiple Tasks (OUT 197)
Categorize Remaining Tasks (OUT 199)
Rename a Category (OUT 199)
Set a Quick Click (OUT 200)

Categorizing Email Messages
Categorize an Email Message (OUT 202)

Managing Tasks
Update a Task (OUT 204)
Attach a File to a Task (OUT 205)
Assign a Task (OUT 206)
Forward a Task (OUT 208)
Send a Status Report (OUT 210)
Mark a Task Complete (OUT 212)
Remove a Task (OUT 213)

Choosing Display and Print Views
Change the Task View (OUT 215)
Print Tasks (OUT 216)

Using Notes
Create a Note (OUT 218)
Change the Notes View (OUT 219)
Delete a Note (OUT 220)

Consider This: Plan Ahead

What decisions will you need to make when creating tasks, categorizing email messages, choosing views, and using notes in the future?

A. Create Tasks:

1. Determine what projects you want to track. People use tasks to keep track of the projects that are most important to them.

2. Determine the information you want to store for a task. For any task, you can store basic information, add attachments, and add detailed instructions.

B. Categorize Tasks and Email Messages:

1. Plan categories for tasks. To identify and group tasks and other Outlook items easily, assign the items to categories.

2. Assign emails to the same categories as tasks.

C. Manage Tasks:

1. Determine which tasks may need to be assigned to others.

D. Choose Display and Print Views:

1. Determine the preferred way to view the tasks to find the information you are seeking.

2. Determine how you want to view your tasks.

E. Use Notes:

1. Determine what reminder notes would assist you.

CONSIDER THIS

BTW

Quick Reference

For a table that lists how to complete the tasks covered in this book using touch gestures, the mouse, ribbon, shortcut menu, and keyboard, see the Quick Reference Summary at the back of this book, or visit the Quick Reference resource on the Student Companion Site located on www.cengagebrain.com. For detailed instructions about accessing available resources, visit www.cengage.com/ct/studentdownload or contact your instructor for information about accessing the required files.

How should you submit solutions to questions in the assignments identified with a ✳ symbol?

Every assignment in this book contains one or more questions identified with a ✳ symbol. These questions require you to think beyond the assigned file. Present your solutions to the questions in the format required by your instructor. Possible formats may include one or more of these options: write the answer; create a document that contains the answer; present your answer to the class; discuss your answer in a group; record the answer as audio or video using a webcam, smartphone, or portable media player; or post answers on a blog, wiki, or website.

Apply Your Knowledge

Reinforce the skills and apply the concepts you learned in this chapter.

Editing a Task List

Note: To complete this assignment, you will be required to use the Data Files for Students. Visit www.cengage.com/ct/studentdownload for detailed instructions or contact your instructor for information about accessing the required files.

Instructions: Start Outlook. Import the Apply Your Knowledge 4–1 Tasks file from the Data Files for Students folder into Outlook. The Apply Your Knowledge 4–1 Tasks file contains tasks for Dr. Tom Nodori. Many of the tasks have changed and some are incomplete. You need to revise the tasks and then create categories for them. Then, you will print the resulting task list (Figure 4–81).

☐	✔	SUBJECT	DUE DATE	CATEGORIES	⟨⟩
	☐	CIS 101	Mon 1/5/2015	Spring Classes	⚑
	☐	CIS 202	Tue 1/6/2015	Spring Classes	⚑
	☐	CIS 201	Wed 1/7/2015	Spring Classes	⚑
	☐	Microsoft Office 2013 Seminar	Thu 2/19/2015	Seminars	⚑
	☐	Seminar Banquet	Fri 2/20/2015	Seminars	⚑

Figure 4–81

Perform the following tasks:

1. Display the Apply Your Knowledge 4–1 Tasks folder in the Outlook To-Do List window.

2. Change the due date of the Microsoft Office 2013 Seminar task to February 19, 2015.

3. Change the due date of the Seminar Banquet task to February 20, 2015. In the Task body, type **Closing banquet for all speakers and attendees.**

4. Change the task name of CIS 315 to CIS 202. Configure the task as a recurring task that occurs every Tuesday and Thursday from January 6, 2015 until April 30, 2015.

5. Make CIS 201 a recurring task that occurs every Wednesday from January 7, 2015 until April 29, 2015.

6. Make CIS 101 a recurring task that occurs every Monday, Wednesday, and Saturday from January 5, 2015 until May 2, 2015.

7. Create two color categories. Name the first one Spring Classes and the second one Seminars. Use the colors of your choice.

8. Categorize CIS 101, CIS 201, and CIS 202 using the Spring Classes category. Categorize the Microsoft Office 2013 Seminar and Seminar Banquet tasks using the Seminars category.

9. Print the final task list, as shown in Figure 4–81, and then submit it in the format specified by your instructor.

10. Export the Apply Your Knowledge 4–1 Tasks folder to a USB flash drive and then delete the folder from the hard disk.

11. ✹ What task categories would you create to categorize the tasks in your personal life?

Extend Your Knowledge

Extend the skills you learned in this chapter and experiment with new skills. You may need to use Help to complete the assignment.

Creating Notes

Note: To complete this assignment, you will be required to use the Data Files for Students. Visit www.cengage.com/ct/studentdownload for detailed instructions or contact your instructor for information about accessing the required files.

Instructions: Start Outlook. Import the Extend Your Knowledge 4–1 Notes file from the Data Files for Students folder into Outlook. The Extend Your Knowledge 4–1 Notes file has no notes. You will create new notes, categorize the notes, and then print the notes.

Perform the following tasks:

1. Use Help to learn about customizing notes.

2. Display the Extend Your Knowledge 4–1 Notes folder in the Outlook Notes window.

3. Create the following notes:
   - Send an email message to Dr. Johnson about upcoming appointment
   - Remember to review new website design
   - Apply for passport
   - Review newsletter
   - Ask supervisor for website content
   - Set up secondary email account to handle work email messages

4. Select the Apply for passport note, and then create a color category named Critical. Use a color of your choosing.

Continued >

STUDENT ASSIGNMENTS

Extend Your Knowledge *continued*

5. Categorize the notes about the website using a new "Website" category. Use a color of your choosing.

6. Categorize the remaining notes using a new "Upcoming" category. Use a color of your choosing.

7. Replace "Dr. Johnson" in the "Send an email message to Dr. Johnson about upcoming appointment" note with the name of your favorite teacher.

8. Change the view to Notes List. Print the notes in Table Style, as shown in Figure 4–82, and then submit them in the format specified by your instructor.

9. Export the Extend Your Knowledge 4–1 Notes folder to a USB flash drive and then delete the folder from the hard disk.

10. ✳ When is it appropriate to create a note instead of creating a task?

SUBJECT	CREATED	CATEGORIES
Set up secondary email account to handle work email messages	Sat 4/6/2015 11:01 AM	Upcoming
Ask supervisor for website content	Sat 4/6/2015 11:00 AM	Website
Review newsletter	Sat 4/6/2015 11:00 AM	Upcoming
Apply for passport	Sat 4/6/2015 11:00 AM	Critical
Remember to review new website design	Sat 4/6/2015 11:00 AM	Website
Send an email message to Dr. West about upcoming appointment	Sat 4/6/2015 11:00 AM	Upcoming

1

Figure 4–82

Analyze, Correct, Improve

Analyze tasks and correct all errors and/or improve tasks.

Correcting Tasks and Task Groups

Note: To complete this assignment, you will be required to use the Data Files for Students. Visit www.cengage.com/ct/studentdownload for detailed instructions or contact your instructor for information about accessing the required files.

Instructions: Start Outlook. Import the Analyze 4–1 Tasks file from the Data Files for Students folder into Outlook. While reviewing your Outlook tasks, you realize that you created several tasks incorrectly, failed to add a task, and categorized some tasks inappropriately. You will identify and open the incorrect tasks, edit them so that they reflect the correct information, add the missing task, apply the right categories, and then save all changes. You also will print the tasks (Figure 4–83).

☐	☑ SUBJECT	DUE DATE	CATEGORIES	�۴
	☐ Paint House	Fri 1/16/2015	House	▶
	☐ Take car for 30,000 service	Sat 2/7/2015	Automobile	▶
	☐ Fertilize lawn	Sat 3/14/2015	House	▶
	☐ Add pool chemicals	Wed 4/1/2015	House	▶

1

Figure 4–83

Continued >

Analyze, correct, improve *continued*

Perform the following tasks:

1. Correct While creating your tasks in Outlook, you inadvertently specified the incorrect year for the due date of each task. In your task list, change the due date for each task so that the year is 2015 instead of 2014.

2. Improve Add other information to each task, including an appropriate start date, category, status, reminder, and priority.

3. ✳ When might you want to set a priority for your tasks?

In the Labs

Design, create, modify, and/or use tasks and notes using the guidelines, concepts, and skills presented in this chapter. Labs are listed in order of increasing difficulty.

Lab 1: **Creating Departmental Tasks**

Problem: You are an assistant for the Information Technology (IT) department at Cometins Pharmaceuticals. Your team is working on upgrading staff computers and will use Microsoft Outlook to keep track of all tasks. Table 4–2 lists the regular tasks and Table 4–3 lists the recurring tasks for the IT department. Enter the tasks into the To-Do list. The task list you create will look like the one in Figure 4–84.

Perform the following tasks:
1. Create a Tasks folder named Lab 4–1 Tasks.
2. Create the regular tasks in the Lab 4–1 Tasks folder using the information listed in Table 4–2.

Table 4–2 Information Technology Tasks

Task	Start Date	Due Date	Status	Priority
Back up data	3/6/2015	3/13/2015	In Progress	Normal
Remove old computers	3/13/2015	3/27/2015		Normal
Install new computers	3/27/2015	4/17/2015		High
Test new computers	4/17/2015	4/24/2015		High
Restore backed up data	4/24/2015	5/8/2015		Normal

© 2014 Cengage Learning

3. Create the recurring tasks in the Lab 4–1 Tasks folder using the information listed in Table 4–3.

Table 4–3 Information Technology Recurring Tasks

Task	Start Date	Due Date	Recurrence
Perform software updates	5/12/2015	5/9/2017	Monthly, second Tuesday
Perform virus scans	5/8/2015	5/19/2017	Weekly, Fridays

© 2014 Cengage Learning

4. Create a color category called Maintenance, using a color of your choice. Classify the Perform software updates and Perform virus scans tasks using the Maintenance category.

5. Create a color category called Computer Upgrades, using a color of your choice. Categorize all tasks with this category.

6. Print the Lab 4–1 Tasks list in Table Style, and then submit it in a format specified by your instructor (Figure 4–84).

7. Export the Lab 4–1 Tasks folder to your USB flash drive and then delete the folder from the hard disk.

8. ✳ Why is it a good idea to include as much detail as possible in each task?

☑ SUBJECT	DUE DATE	CATEGORIES
☐ Back up data	Fri 3/13/2015	Computer Upgrades
☐ Remove old computers	Fri 3/27/2015	Computer Upgrades
☐ Install new computers	Fri 4/17/2015	Computer Upgrades
☐ Test new computers	Fri 4/24/2015	Computer Upgrades
☐ Restore backed up data	Fri 5/8/2015	Computer Upgrades
☐ Perform software updates	Tue 5/9/2017	Computer Upgrades, ...
☐ Perform virus scans	Fri 5/19/2017	Computer Upgrades, ...

1

Figure 4–84

Continued >

In the Labs *continued*

Part 1 Perform the following tasks:

1. Start your web browser and navigate to outlook.com.

2. Sign in to outlook.com. If necessary, sign up for a new account.

3. View the calendar.

4. Create the tasks shown in Table 4–6.

Table 4–6 Johnston Hills Photography Tasks

Event	Due Date	Time	Reminder Type	Reminder Time	Priority
Tagleo Wedding	May 2, 2015	6:00PM	Email	2 weeks before	High
Lipton Bar Mitzvah	May 9, 2015	12:00PM	Email	2 weeks before	High
A-1 Electronics Annual Dinner	May 15, 2015	7:00PM	Email	1 week before	Normal
Jacobs Birthday Party	May 16, 2015	3:00PM	Email	2 days before	Low
East Ridge Class Reunion	May 30, 2015	6:30PM	Email	1 week before	Normal

© 2014 Cengage Learning

5. When you have finished adding the tasks, share the calendar with your instructor. Your instructor should be able to view the details on your calendar, but should not be able to edit anything. If you have additional items on your calendar that you do not want to share with your instructor, contact your instructor and determine an alternate way to submit this assignment.

6. ✳ When would you want to add your tasks to Outlook.com instead of using Microsoft Outlook? Is there a way to automatically get your tasks in Microsoft Outlook to appear in your Outlook.com account?

✳ Consider This: Your Turn

Apply your creative thinking and problem solving skills to design and implement a solution.

Note: To complete this assignment, you will be required to use the Data Files for Students. Visit www.cengage.com/ct/studentdownload for detailed instructions or contact your instructor for information about accessing the required files.

1: Create Study Group Tasks

Academic

Part 1: Use the concepts and techniques presented in this chapter to create tasks for a study group using the information in Table 4–7. You are in charge of your study group, which consists of students who are taking Introduction to Computer Information Systems (CIS 114) and Computers in Society (CIS 211) classes. You are charged with creating tasks for the major tests in each class. Using Table 4–7, create the tasks as shown. Categorize the tasks based upon the Class column. Print the final list of tasks, and then submit it in the format specified by your instructor.

Table 4–7 Study Group Tasks			
Class	**Deliverable Name**	**Due Date**	**Chapters Covered**
CIS 101	Assignment 1	9/18/2015	1–4
CIS 101	Assignment 2	11/6/2015	5–8
CIS 101	Assignment 3	12/11/2015	6–12
CIS 114	Semester Project	12/15/2015	1–12
CIS 211	Exam 1	9/14/2015	1–5
CIS 211	Exam 2	10/26/2015	6–10
CIS 211	Final Exam	12/21/2015	1–10

© 2014 Cengage Learning

Part 2: ☀ You made several decisions when creating the task list in this assignment, such as how to store the information about each task. What was the rationale behind each of these decisions?

2: Create a Team List

Professional

Part 1: After attending a professional development event, you now have several bits of information that you would like to create as notes in Outlook, so that later on you can use the ideas from the event with the rest of your managers and staff. You have created a list of items you want to use as your notes, which is shown in Table 4–8. You indicate which notes will be used for managers and which notes will be used for staff members in the Audience column. Create the notes and categorize them appropriately. Print the notes list and submit it in the format specified by your instructor.

Table 4–8 Event Notes	
Note	**Audience**
Motivate employees	Managers
Customers are always right	Staff
Everyone shares responsibility	Managers
Document customer purchasing habits	Managers
Maintain a positive attitude at all times	Managers, Staff
Develop relationships with customers	Staff

© 2014 Cengage Learning

Part 2: ☀ You made several decisions when creating the notes in this assignment, such as what to type for each note and how to categorize the notes. What was the rationale behind each of these decisions?

3: Creating and Assigning Tasks

Research and Collaboration

Part 1: Your Introduction to Computer Information Systems instructor has assigned a term paper to be completed by a team of three people. Each person in the team is responsible for researching one computer manufacturer and writing about the company's history, products currently offered, and a roadmap for the future. After each team member performs adequate research and writes his or her part of the paper, he or she will send it to another team member for a peer review. After all team members have performed a peer review, they will finalize their content and send it to you to compile into one document and prepare it for submission. Using Outlook, each team member should create tasks for the work they will have to perform on the term paper (for example, research, writing the first draft, sending for peer review, performing a peer review, finalizing content,

Continued >

Consider This: Your Turn *continued*

compiling into one master document, preparing for submission, and submitting the paper). Add as much information to the tasks as possible, such as the start date, due date, priority, status, and percent complete. Categorize the tasks appropriately. Then, assign the peer review task to the team member who will be performing a review on your content. Finally, send a status report to all team members showing how much of each task you currently have completed. Submit the task list in a format specified by your instructor.

Part 2: ✺ You have made several decisions while creating the task list in this assignment, such as which tasks to create, what details to add to each task, and how to categorize each task. What was the rationale behind each of these decisions?

Learn Online

Reinforce what you learned in this chapter with games, exercises, training, and many other online activities and resources.

Student Companion Site Reinforce chapter terms and concepts using review questions, flash cards, practice tests, and interactive learning games, such as a crossword puzzle. These and other online activities and resources are available at no additional cost on www.cengagebrain.com. Visit www.cengage.com/ct/studentdownload for detailed instructions about accessing the resources available at the Student Companion Site.

5 | Customizing Outlook

Objectives

You will have mastered the material in this chapter when you can:

- Add another email account
- Insert Quick Parts in email messages
- Insert hyperlinks in email messages
- Insert images in email messages
- Create a search folder
- Set the default message format
- Create an email signature
- Format a signature

- Assign signatures
- Customize personal stationery
- Configure junk email options
- Create rules
- Configure AutoArchive settings
- Adjust calendar settings
- Subscribe to a news feed

5 | Customizing Outlook

This chapter covers features and functions common to customizing Outlook 2013.

Roadmap

In this chapter, you will learn how to perform basic customizing tasks. The following roadmap identifies general activities you will perform as you progress through this chapter:

1. CUSTOMIZE EMAIL MESSAGES
2. CUSTOMIZE SIGNATURES and STATIONERY
3. MANAGE JUNK EMAIL FILTERS
4. CONFIGURE RULES
5. CHANGE CALENDAR OPTIONS
6. ADD a NEWS FEED

At the beginning of step instructions throughout the chapter, you will see an abbreviated form of this roadmap. The abbreviated roadmap uses colors to indicate chapter progress: gray means the chapter is beyond that activity, blue means the task being shown is covered in that activity, and black means that activity is yet to be covered. For example, the following abbreviated roadmap indicates the section would be about configuring rules.

1 CUSTOMIZE EMAIL MESSAGES | 2 CUSTOMIZE SIGNATURES & STATIONERY | 3 MANAGE JUNK EMAIL FILTERS

4 CONFIGURE RULES | 5 CHANGE CALENDAR OPTIONS | 6 ADD NEWS FEED

Use the abbreviated roadmap as a progress guide while you read or step through the instructions in this chapter.

Introduction to Customizing Outlook

Outlook provides many options for customizing your experience when working with email messages, calendars, and other items. From creating custom email signatures to adjusting how the workweek is displayed in your calendar, you can make Outlook fit your requirements so that you can use it more efficiently. For example, a rule is a command that tells Outlook how to process an email message. Using rules, you quickly can categorize or flag your email messages as they arrive so that you can identify at a glance which ones you first want to address. You can change the fonts and colors that are used by default as well. Outlook's customization options can help you become more productive.

Project — Adding a New Email Account and Customizing Options

People often have more than one email account. In fact, some people have more than they can remember. Outlook allows you to manage multiple email accounts. That way, you can read your email messages from all accounts without needing to use several email programs such as one for a Microsoft email account, another for a Gmail account, and a third for a school email account.

The project in this chapter follows general guidelines and uses Outlook to add a new email account and customize Outlook options, as shown in Figure 5–1.

(a) New email account

(b) Signature and stationery

(c) Outlook options

(d) Customized calendar

Photo courtesy of Corinne Hoisington

Figure 5–1

Adding New Email Accounts

As you learned in Chapter 1, when setting up an email account, you need to know basic information such as the email address and password. For example, in Figure 5–2, the first mailbox is displayed as Outlook Data File (Dylan Chapter 5.pst). The second mailbox displayed in Figure 5–2 is an additional Internet-based email account named dylancruz95@live.com.

Figure 5–2

After you install Outlook, the Auto Account Setup feature runs and helps you to set up the first email account that Outlook manages. You can add another account and then use Outlook to manage two or more mailboxes.

Depending on your instructor's preferences and your email services, you can perform the steps in this chapter by opening an Outlook data file provided with the book and by adding a new email account to Outlook. Before you can add a new email account in Outlook, you must have an account set up with an email service provider that is different from any other account already set up in Outlook. For example, you might have a Microsoft account that provides email service. If you have not configured this account in Outlook, you can complete the steps in this chapter to do so.

To add a new account, you use the Add Account option in the Backstage view, which lets you add an account using the Add Account dialog box. If you want to add an account and change advanced settings, you should use the Account Settings dialog box instead.

My work email address requires additional information to set up my account. Where do I place this server information?

For the work email account you plan to add, make sure you know the account properties and settings before you start to add the account. Gather the following information: type of account, such as email, text messaging, or fax mail; your name, email address, and password; server information, including account type and the addresses of incoming and outgoing mail servers. You typically receive the server information from the IT staff at your place of employment. If additional server information is needed, tap or click Manual setup or additional server types when you create an account to add this information.

To Run Outlook

If you are using a computer to step through the project in this chapter and you want your screens to match the figures in this book, you should change your screen's resolution to 1366 × 768. For information about how to change a computer's resolution, refer to the Office 2013 and Windows 8 chapter at the beginning of this book.

The following steps, which assume Windows 8 is running, use the Search text box to run Outlook based on a typical installation. You may need to ask your instructor how to run Outlook on your computer. For a detailed example of the procedure summarized below, refer to the Office 2013 and Windows 8 chapter.

1 Swipe in from the right edge of the screen or point to the upper-right corner of the screen to display the Charms bar.

2 Tap or click the Search charm on the Charms bar to display the Search menu.

3 Type `Outlook` as the search text in the Search text box and watch the search results appear in the Apps list.

4 Tap or click Outlook 2013 in the search results to run Outlook.

5 If the Outlook window is not maximized, tap or click the Maximize button on its title bar to maximize the window.

One of the few differences between Windows 7 and Windows 8 occurs in the steps to run Outlook. If you are using Windows 7, click the Start button, type Outlook in the `Search programs and files` box, click Outlook 2013, and then, if necessary, maximize the Outlook window. For a summary of the steps to run Outlook in Windows 7, refer to the Quick Reference located at the back of this book.

TO ADD AN EMAIL ACCOUNT

Dylan has a second email address that he dedicates to mailing lists. Dylan uses a second email account (dylancruz95@live.com) within Outlook so that he can manage both his primary and secondary email accounts. To follow all the steps within this chapter, an additional email account is necessary.

If you choose to add an email account to Outlook, you would use the following steps. If you are performing these steps on your computer, enter the name, email address, and password for an email account you own but have not yet added to Outlook.

1. Tap or click the FILE tab and then tap or click Add Account.
2. Tap or click the Your Name text box and then type your first and last name to associate your name with the account.
3. Tap or click the E-mail Address text box and then type your full email address to associate your email address with the account.
4. Tap or click the Password text box and then type your password to verify the password to your email account.
5. Tap or click the Retype Password text box and then type your password again to confirm your password.
6. Tap or click the Next button to configure your account settings and sign in to your mail server.
7. Tap or click the Finish button to add the secondary email account.
8. Tap or click the new email account to select it.

For an introduction to Office and instruction about how to perform basic tasks in Office apps, read the Office and Windows chapter at the beginning of this book, where you can learn how to run an application, use the ribbon, save a file, open a file, exit an application, use Help, and much more.

BTW

Multiple Email Accounts

If you have multiple email accounts configured in Outlook, you can decide which email account to use each time you compose and send a new email message. To select the account from which to send the email message, click the From button in the Untitled – Message window, and then click the desired email account.

BTW
Touch Screen
Differences
The Office and Windows interfaces may vary if you are using a touch screen. For this reason, you might notice that the function or appearance of your touch screen differs slightly from this chapter's presentation.

Customizing Email Messages

No matter what type of message you are composing in Outlook, whether business or personal, you always can find a way to add your unique style. With a variety of features such as background colors, graphics, designs, hyperlinks, and custom signatures, your email message starts as a blank, generic canvas and becomes an attractive, memorable communication.

To Add a Hyperlink to an Email Message

1 CUSTOMIZE EMAIL MESSAGES | 2 CUSTOMIZE SIGNATURES & STATIONERY | 3 MANAGE JUNK EMAIL FILTERS
4 CONFIGURE RULES | 5 CHANGE CALENDAR OPTIONS | 6 ADD NEWS FEED

Mia James asked Dylan to send her the web address of the travel advisory page that the U.S. Department of State maintains. Mia is planning to study abroad this summer, and wants to check the web page for advice about locations she will visit. Dylan can send her the web address as a hyperlink in an email message. *Why? Outlook automatically formats hyperlinks so that recipients can use them to access a website directly.* To follow the link, the recipient can double-tap or hold down the CTRL key and click the hyperlink, which is formatted as blue, underlined text by default. The following steps add a hyperlink within an email message.

1

- If the Dylan Chapter 5.pst Outlook Data File is not open in Outlook, click Outlook Data File in the Navigation Pane to display its contents.

- Tap or click the New Email button (HOME tab | New group) to open the Untitled – Message (HTML) window.

- Type **mia.james@outlook.com** in the To text box to enter the email address of the recipient.

- Tap or click the Subject text box, and then type **Travel Alert** to enter the subject line.

- Press the TAB key to move the insertion point into the message area (Figure 5–3).

Figure 5–3

2

- Type **Mia,** as the greeting line and then press the ENTER key twice to insert a blank line between the greeting line and the message text.

- Type **Per your request, the U.S. Travel Alert site can be found at** and then press the SPACEBAR to enter the message text.

- Tap or click INSERT on the ribbon to display the INSERT tab (Figure 5–4).

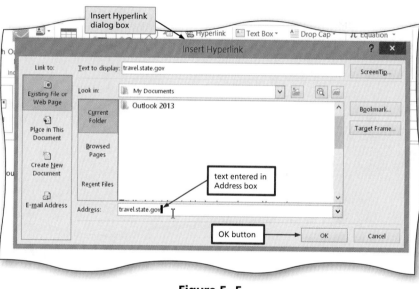

Figure 5–4

3

- Tap or click the Hyperlink button (INSERT tab | Links group) to open the Insert Hyperlink dialog box.

- In the Address box, type **travel.state.gov** to enter a hyperlink to a web address (Figure 5–5).

Q&A Why do I not have to type the http:// part of the web address?
When you insert a hyperlink, Outlook does not require the hypertext transfer protocol (http) portion of the address.

Figure 5–5

4

- Tap or click the OK button to insert the hyperlink in the message body (Figure 5–6).

Figure 5–6

Other Ways

1. Press CTRL+K

To Create and Insert Quick Parts

How often do you include the same snippet or phrase in your correspondence, such as directions to your home, answers to frequently answered questions, or even the full name of a school or business? To assist you in these situations, Outlook includes **Quick Parts**, common building blocks that can be recycled and used again within your email messages. The first step in creating a Quick Part is to select the content that you want to reuse. After naming the contents and saving them to the Quick Part gallery, you can use the Quick Parts whenever you need to repeat that phrase. *Why? Quick Parts allow you to save pieces of content to reuse them easily within your email messages.* Several students have requested that Dylan send them the link to the travel alert website in the past month. The following steps save a phrase to the Quick Parts gallery.

1
- Select the phrase 'Per your request, the U.S. Travel Alert site can be found at travel.state.gov'.
- Tap or click the Quick Parts button (INSERT tab | Text group) to display the Quick Parts list of options (Figure 5–7).

Figure 5–7

2
- Tap or click 'Save Selection to Quick Part Gallery' to display the Create New Building Block dialog box.
- Replace the text in the Name text box by typing **Travel Alert** to change the name of the new building block (Figure 5–8).

Figure 5–8

❸

- Tap or click the OK button (Create New Building Block dialog box) to add the Travel Alert Building Block to the Quick Parts gallery (Figure 5–9).

🔎 **Experiment**

- Tap or click the Quick Parts button (INSERT tab | Text group) to display a list of Quick Parts options. Tap or click Travel Alert to insert the building block into the email message. When you are finished, tap or click the Undo button on the Quick Access Toolbar to remove the travel alert text.

Figure 5–9

To Insert an Image into an Email Message

1 CUSTOMIZE EMAIL MESSAGES | 2 CUSTOMIZE SIGNATURES & STATIONERY | 3 MANAGE JUNK EMAIL FILTERS
4 CONFIGURE RULES | 5 CHANGE CALENDAR OPTIONS | 6 ADD NEWS FEED

As you learned in Chapter 1, you can attach files to an email message, including image files. Outlook also provides the ability to insert an image directly within the message body of an email message. *Why? The recipient can quickly view the image without downloading an attachment or saving the picture on their computer.* Dylan would like to add a recent picture from his study abroad experience in Japan. The picture is available with the Data Files for Students for Chapter 05. The following steps insert an image into an email message.

❶

- Tap or click after the travel.state.gov web address, and then press the ENTER key twice to move the insertion point to a new line.

- Tap or click the Pictures button (INSERT tab | Illustrations group) to display the Insert Picture dialog box.

- Navigate to the file location, in this case, the Chapter 05 folder in the Outlook folder provided with the Data Files for Students.

- Tap or click Japan to select the photo of Japan (Figure 5–10).

Figure 5–10

2

- Tap or click the Insert button (shown in Figure 5–10) to add an image to the message body (Figure 5–11).

3

- Tap or click the Save button on the Quick Access Toolbar to save the email message in the Drafts folder.

- Close the Travel Alert – Message (HTML) window.

Figure 5–11

Photo courtesy of Corinne Hoisington

Can I use Outlook to allow a message recipient to vote, such as when I want to poll club members for their preferred speaker for our next event?

When composing a message, you can configure voting options by using the Properties dialog box. For example, you can choose to use voting buttons as well as request delivery and read receipts. To configure voting options:

1. While composing a message, tap or click OPTIONS on the ribbon to display the OPTIONS tab.

2. Tap or click the Use Voting Buttons button (OPTIONS tab | Tracking group) to display a list of options.

3. Tap or click Custom to display the Properties dialog box.

4. Select voting options in the Voting and Tracking options area.

5. Tap or click the Close button to close the Properties dialog box.

To Search Using Advanced Find

**1 CUSTOMIZE EMAIL MESSAGES | 2 CUSTOMIZE SIGNATURES & STATIONERY | 3 MANAGE JUNK EMAIL FILTERS
4 CONFIGURE RULES | 5 CHANGE CALENDAR OPTIONS | 6 ADD NEWS FEED**

At the top of the message pane is the **Instant Search** text box, which displays search results based on any matching words in your email messages. You can use the options on the SEARCH TOOLS SEARCH tab to broaden or narrow the scope of your search using the Advanced Find features. For example, Dylan would like to search for messages that have attachments. The following steps use instant search with Advanced Find features to locate email messages with attachments. **Why?** *Using Advanced Find, you can quickly search for an email with an attachment.*

①

- If necessary, select your Inbox, and then tap or click the Instant Search text box to display the SEARCH TOOLS SEARCH tab (Figure 5–12).

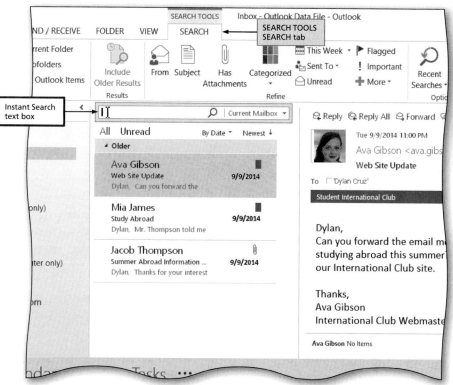

Figure 5–12

②

- Tap or click the Has Attachments button (SEARCH TOOLS SEARCH tab | Refine group) to display email messages with attachments (Figure 5–13).

③

- Tap or click the Close Search button (shown in Figure 5–13) to display the Inbox messages without the search criteria.

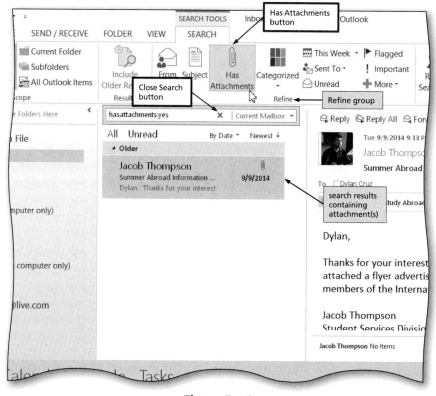

Figure 5–13

To Create a New Search Folder

Use search folders to gather email messages and other items into a folder based on search criteria. For example, Dylan wants to place messages with attachments into a separate search folder. You might want to create other search folders to view all messages that you have not read yet or to combine messages from a specific person. The following steps create a new search folder for email messages with attachments. *Why? By using search folders, you can better manage large amounts of email.*

1

- Tap or click FOLDER on the ribbon to display the FOLDER tab.

- Tap or click the New Search Folder button (FOLDER tab | New group) to display the New Search Folder dialog box (Figure 5–14).

Figure 5–14

2

- Scroll down to view the Organizing Mail category.

- Tap or click 'Mail with attachments' (New Search Folder dialog box) to select the type of email to store in a search folder (Figure 5–15).

Figure 5–15

❸

- Tap or click the OK button (New Search Folder dialog box) to create a new search folder that searches for and collects email messages with attachments (Figure 5–16).

Figure 5–16

To Display Outlook Options

1 CUSTOMIZE EMAIL MESSAGES | 2 CUSTOMIZE SIGNATURES & STATIONERY | 3 MANAGE JUNK EMAIL FILTERS
4 CONFIGURE RULES | 5 CHANGE CALENDAR OPTIONS | 6 ADD NEWS FEED

Why? *To customize your Outlook email with default settings such as the message format, you use the Outlook Options dialog box.* The following step displays the Outlook Options dialog box.

❶

- Tap or click FILE on the ribbon to open the Backstage view.

- Tap or click the Options tab in the Backstage view to display the Outlook Options dialog box (Figure 5–17).

Q&A What options can I set in the General category?
The General category allows you to customize the user interface by enabling the Mini Toolbar and Live Preview, and changing the ScreenTip style and Theme. You also can personalize Microsoft Outlook by specifying your user name and initials. The Start up options allow you to specify whether Outlook should be the default program for email, contacts, and calendar.

Figure 5–17

To Set the Message Format

Email messages can be formatted as HTML, Plain Text, or Rich Text. As you learned in Chapter 1, you can format an individual email message using one of these message formats. To make sure that all your email messages use the HTML format by default, set the message format in the Outlook Options dialog box. The HTML message format allows the most flexibility when composing email messages. The following steps set the default message format to HTML. *Why? Instead of changing each email message to a different format, you can set a default in the Outlook options. All new messages display the default format.*

1
- Tap or click Mail in the Category list to display the Mail options (Figure 5–18).

Figure 5–18

2
- Tap or click the 'Compose messages in this format' box arrow to display a list of formatting options (Figure 5–19).

Figure 5–19

❸

- If necessary, tap or click HTML to set the default message format to HTML (Figure 5–20).

What if HTML already is selected as the default message format? Depending on who set up Outlook, the default message format already might be HTML. In that case, you can skip Step 3.

What if I want to choose a different format? When you display the available message formats, choose the type you want to use. For example, if you want all new email messages to be in the Plain Text format, tap or click the Plain Text option.

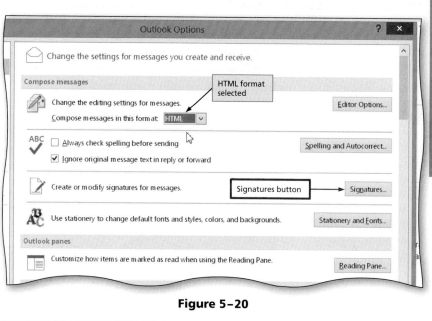

Figure 5–20

Can I sort my email messages by conversation instead of by date, which is the default setting?

Yes, you can sort by conversation if you prefer to sort your email messages by their subject field grouped by conversation. To sort by conversation:

1. Tap or click VIEW on the ribbon to display the VIEW tab.

2. Tap or click the Show as Conversations (VIEW tab | Messages group) to select Show as Conversations.

Your Inbox is re-sorted, linking email messages in the same conversation together. Individual messages that do not belong to a conversation will look the same as before, while those involved in conversations will have a white triangle on the upper-left part of the message header.

Creating Signatures and Stationery

You can configure Outlook to add signatures to your email messages automatically. A **signature** is similar to a closing set of lines in a formal letter. It can include your full name, job title, email address, phone number, company information, and logo. You even can include business cards in your signature.

If you have more than one email account, you need to select the account for which you want to create the signature. You can create the signature while you are creating an email message or you can use the Outlook Options dialog box at any other time. If you create the signature while writing an email message, you have to apply the signature to the email message, because Outlook will not insert it automatically. If you create a signature using the Outlook Options dialog box, it is added automatically to all subsequent messages.

Besides adding signatures to your email messages, you can customize the **stationery**, which determines the appearance of your email messages, including background, fonts, and colors. You can pick fonts to use in the email message text, or you can select a theme or stationery design and apply that to your email messages.

To Create an Email Signature

An email signature provides a consistent closing to every email message without requiring you to retype signature lines repeatedly. Dylan would like to create an email signature named School that includes his name, title, and email address. The following steps create an email signature. **Why?** *An email signature provides your contact information in a condensed format, typically two to four lines.*

1

- Tap or click the Signatures button (Outlook Options dialog box) (shown in Figure 5–20) to display the Signatures and Stationery dialog box (Figure 5–21).

Figure 5–21

2

- Tap or click the New button (Signatures and Stationery dialog box) to display the New Signature dialog box (Figure 5–22).

Figure 5–22

❸

- Type `School` in the 'Type a name for this signature' text box to enter a name for the signature.

- Tap or click the OK button (shown in Figure 5–22) to name the signature (Figure 5–23).

Figure 5–23

To Format an Email Signature

1 CUSTOMIZE EMAIL MESSAGES | 2 CUSTOMIZE SIGNATURES & STATIONERY | 3 MANAGE JUNK EMAIL FILTERS
4 CONFIGURE RULES | 5 CHANGE CALENDAR OPTIONS | 6 ADD NEWS FEED

The email message signature will include Dylan's name, title, and email address. In addition, he wants to use a format that suits him. The format of the signature should be attractive, but maintain a professional, clean appearance. The following steps format and add the text for the signature. *Why? An email signature should convey the impression you are trying to make. A company might require employees to use a certain email signature when communicating with customers to create a consistent look.*

❶

- Tap or click the Font box arrow (Signatures and Stationery dialog box) to display a list of fonts (Figure 5–24).

Figure 5–24

2

- Scroll down until Rockwell is visible, and then tap or click Rockwell to select the font.

- Tap or click the Font Size box arrow to display a list of font sizes (Figure 5–25).

Figure 5–25

3

- Tap or click 14 to change the font size.

- Tap or click the Font Color box arrow to display a list of colors (Figure 5–26).

Figure 5–26

4

- Tap or click Blue, Accent 5 (first row, ninth column) to change the font color.

- Type **Dylan Cruz** in the signature body to enter the first line of the signature.

- Tap or click the Font Color box arrow to display a list of colors.

- Tap or click Automatic to change the font color to automatic, which is black (Figure 5–27).

Figure 5–27

5

- Press the ENTER key and then tap or click the Font Size box arrow to display a list of font sizes.

- Tap or click 12 to change the font size.

- Type **President of the Student International Club at Raven College** in the signature body to enter the second line of the signature.

Figure 5–28

- Press the ENTER key and then type **dylan.cruz@outlook.com** in the signature body to enter the third line of the signature (Figure 5–28).

To Add an Image to an Email Signature

1 CUSTOMIZE EMAIL MESSAGES | 2 CUSTOMIZE SIGNATURES & STATIONERY | 3 MANAGE JUNK EMAIL FILTERS
4 CONFIGURE RULES | 5 CHANGE CALENDAR OPTIONS | 6 ADD NEWS FEED

You can add an image such as a photo or logo to your signature to create visual appeal. Dylan would like to add the Student International Club logo in the signature. The picture is available in the Data Files for Students for Chapter 5. The following steps add a logo image to a signature and save the changes. *Why? Adding a logo can promote brand or organization identity.*

①

- Move the insertion point to the beginning of the first line of the signature text.

- Tap or click the Insert Picture button (Signatures and Stationery dialog box) to display the Insert Picture dialog box.

- Navigate to the file location, in this case, the Chapter 05 folder in the Outlook folder provided with the Data Files for Students.

- Tap or click Globe to select the Globe logo (Figure 5–29).

Figure 5–29

②

- Tap or click the Insert button (Insert Picture dialog box) (shown in Figure 5–29) to insert the image into the signature (Figure 5–30).

Figure 5–30

③

- Tap or click the Save button (Signatures and Stationery dialog box) to save the changes to the signature (Figure 5–31).

Figure 5–31

To Configure Signature Options

After creating a signature, you need to assign it to an email account. You can associate the signature with as many accounts as you want. When working with an account, you can set two default signatures: one for new messages and one for replies and forwards. Dylan wants to apply his signature for new messages to his email account named dylancruz95@live.com (select your own account). The following steps set the default signature for new messages. If you are completing these steps on a personal computer, your email account must be set up in Outlook (see Chapter 1) to be able to select an email account to apply the signature. *Why? By associating a signature with a particular email account, your signature automatically appears at the bottom of new messages.*

1

- Tap or click the E-mail account box arrow to display a list of accounts.

- Tap or click your email account, in this case dylancruz95@live.com, to select the email account (Figure 5–32).

Figure 5–32

2

- Tap or click the New messages box arrow to display a list of signatures.

- Tap or click School to make it the default signature for new messages (Figure 5–33).

Q&A
How do I place a signature in all messages including replies and forwards?
Tap or click the Replies/forwards box arrow and then tap or click School to make it the default signature for all message replies and forwards.

Figure 5–33

3

- Tap or click the OK button (Signatures and Stationery dialog box) to save the changes to the signature settings, close the Signatures and Stationery dialog box, and return to the Outlook Options dialog box (Figure 5–34).

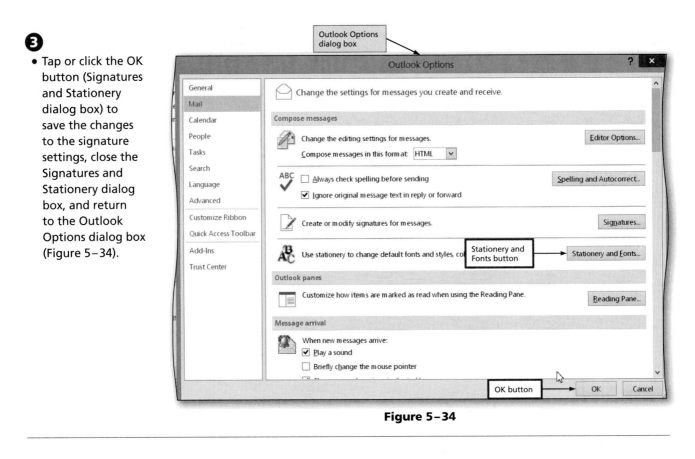

Figure 5–34

To Customize Stationery

1 CUSTOMIZE EMAIL MESSAGES | 2 CUSTOMIZE SIGNATURES & STATIONERY | 3 MANAGE JUNK EMAIL FILTERS
4 CONFIGURE RULES | 5 CHANGE CALENDAR OPTIONS | 6 ADD NEWS FEED

Outlook provides backgrounds and patterns for email message stationery and offers themes, which are sets of unified design elements, such as fonts, bullets, colors, and effects that you can apply to messages. Dylan decides to use a stationery named Compass, which fits with his international interests. The following steps customize the email message stationery. *Why? Stationery provides a distinctive look for your email messages.*

1

- Tap or click the Stationery and Fonts button (Outlook Options dialog box) to display the Signatures and Stationery dialog box (Figure 5–35).

Figure 5–35

2

• Tap or click the Theme button (Signatures and Stationery dialog box) to display the Theme or Stationery dialog box (Figure 5–36).

Figure 5–36

3

• Tap or click Compass to select it and display a preview of its formats (Figure 5–37).

Figure 5–37

4

- Tap or click the OK button (Theme or Stationery dialog box) to apply the theme to the stationery (Figure 5–38).

Figure 5–38

5

- Tap or click the OK button (Signatures and Stationery dialog box) to save the theme settings and return to the Outlook Options dialog box.

- Tap or click the OK button (Outlook Options dialog box) (shown in Figure 5–34 on page OUT 254) to close the Outlook Options dialog box.

To Preview Message Changes

1 CUSTOMIZE EMAIL MESSAGES | 2 CUSTOMIZE SIGNATURES & STATIONERY | 3 MANAGE JUNK EMAIL FILTERS
4 CONFIGURE RULES | 5 CHANGE CALENDAR OPTIONS | 6 ADD NEWS FEED

Why? *You want to preview the changes you made to your email signature and stationery and see how they look in an email message.* The following steps display a new email message without sending it.

1

- Tap or click the New Email button (HOME tab | New group) to create a new email message (Figure 5–39).

2

- Close the email message without sending it.

Figure 5–39

To Assign Signatures to a Single Email Message

1 CUSTOMIZE EMAIL MESSAGES | 2 CUSTOMIZE SIGNATURES & STATIONERY | 3 MANAGE JUNK EMAIL FILTERS
4 CONFIGURE RULES | 5 CHANGE CALENDAR OPTIONS | 6 ADD NEWS FEED

If you use multiple email accounts, you can set a signature for each account or you can apply a signature to an individual email message. Dylan still needs to send the email about the travel alert to Mia and wants to apply the School signature to that message, which is now stored in the Drafts folder. *Why? Instead of assigning your email address to one signature, you may want to create different signatures and apply a signature to individual emails before you send them.* The following steps assign a signature to a single email message.

1

- Tap or click the Drafts folder in the Navigation Pane to display the message header for the Travel Alert email message in the message list.

- Double-tap or double-click the Travel Alert message header in the messages pane to open the Travel Alert – Message (HTML) window (Figure 5–40).

Figure 5–40

Photo courtesy of Corinne Hoisington

2

- Place the insertion point to the right of the Japan image and then press the ENTER key to move to the next line.

- Tap or click INSERT on the ribbon to display the INSERT tab.

- Tap or click the Signature button (INSERT tab | Include group) to display a list of signatures (Figure 5–41).

Figure 5–41

3

- Tap or click School to add the School signature to the email message body (Figure 5–42).

4

- Tap or click the Save button on the Quick Access Toolbar to save the email message in the Drafts folder.

- Tap or click the Close button to close the email message.

Figure 5–42

Break Point: If you wish to take a break, this is a good place to do so. To resume at a later time, continue to follow the steps from this location forward.

Managing Junk Email Options

As you learned in Chapter 1, junk email is bulk email, spam, or other unwanted email messages. Outlook uses a filter to control the amount of junk email you receive. The junk email filter evaluates incoming messages and sends to the Junk E-mail folder those messages that meet the criteria for junk email. You can use the Junk button in the Delete group on the HOME tab to override the default criteria when viewing email messages by deciding to block the sender, never block the sender, never block the sender's domain, or never block a group or mailing list.

Using the Junk E-mail Options dialog box, you can change even more settings (Figure 5–43). Table 5–1 describes the options you can adjust using the Junk E-mail Options dialog box.

Figure 5–43

Table 5–1 Junk Email Options	
Tab	**Description**
Options	Allows you to choose the level of protection (No Automatic Filtering, Low, High, Safe Lists Only), as well as set whether junk email is deleted, links are disabled in phishing messages, and warnings are provided for suspicious domain names.
Safe Senders	Permits the specification of safe e-mail addresses and domains. Email messages from the listed email addresses and domains will not be treated as junk email.
Safe Recipients	Specifies that email messages sent to email addresses or domains in the safe recipient list will not be treated as junk email.
Blocked Senders	Allows you to manage your list of blocked email addresses and domains.
International	Manages which domains and encodings you would like to block based on languages used.

BTW

Junk Email
It usually is a good idea to check your Junk E-mail folder regularly to make sure no items are labeled as junk inadvertently. If, after clicking the Junk E-mail folder, you find an email message that is not junk, select the email message, click the Junk button (HOME tab | Delete group), click Not Junk, and then click the OK button.

© 2014 Cengage Learning

To Add a Domain to the Safe Senders List

The junk email filter in Outlook is turned on by default, providing a protection level that is set to Low. This level is designed to catch only the most obvious junk email messages. Dylan feels that too many incoming messages from Microsoft are being sent to his Junk E-mail folder. Microsoft.com can be added to the Safe Sender list, which adjusts the filter sensitivity of Outlook, so the messages are sent to the Inbox instead of the Junk E-mail Folder. If you are completing these steps on a personal computer, your email account must be set up in Outlook (see Chapter 1) to be able to select an email account to configure the junk email options. The following steps configure the junk email options for an email account. *Why? The Junk E-mail Folder helps to sort out relevant email messages from junk mail.*

1

- Tap or click your personal email account (in this case, dylancruz95@live.com) in the Navigation Pane to select the mailbox (Figure 5–44).

Q&A Why did I have to select the email account?

To change junk email options for an account, the account first should be selected. If you selected a different mailbox, you would have changed junk email settings for that account.

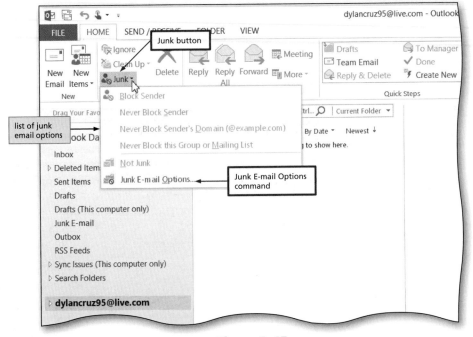

Figure 5–44

2

- Tap or click the Junk button (HOME tab | Delete group) to display the Junk options (Figure 5–45).

Figure 5–45

3

- Tap or click Junk E-mail Options to display the Junk E-mail Options dialog box (Figure 5–46).

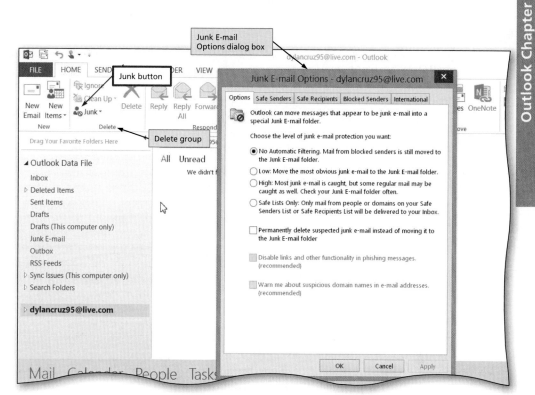

Figure 5–46

4

- Tap or click the Safe Senders tab (Junk E-mail Options dialog box) to display the Safe Senders options (Figure 5–47).

Figure 5–47

5

- Tap or click the Add button (Junk E-mail Options dialog box) to display the 'Add address or domain' dialog box (Figure 5–48).

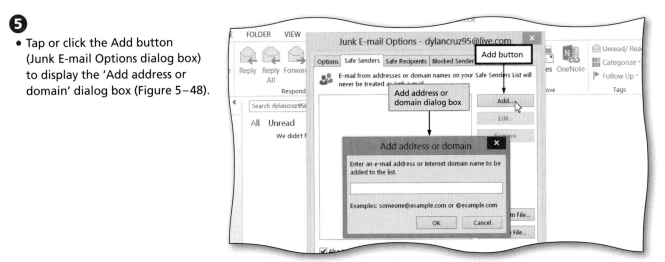

Figure 5–48

6

- Type **@Microsoft.com** in the text box to enter a domain name to add to the Safe Sender's list (Figure 5–49).

Q&A

Do I have to type the @ symbol?
Although Outlook recommends that you type the @ symbol to indicate a domain name, you can omit the symbol. In that case, you leave it up to Outlook to determine if your entry is a domain name or email address. Most of the time, Outlook interprets the entry correctly; however, to be certain, type the @ symbol.

Figure 5–49

7

- Tap or click the OK button (Add address or domain dialog box) to add the domain to the Safe Senders List (Figure 5–50).

Figure 5–50

To Block a Specific Email Address

Why? You may want to block a specific email address or domain to prevent people or companies from sending you messages you do not want to receive. Dylan has received multiple unwanted emails from the following email address: getrich2@live.com. He considers these messages as junk email. The following steps block a specific email address using the junk filters.

1

- Tap or click the Blocked Senders tab (Junk E-mail Options dialog box) to display the Blocked Senders options.

- Tap or click the Add button (Junk E-mail Options dialog box) to display the 'Add address or domain' dialog box.

- Type `getrich2@live .com` in the text box to enter the domain name to add to the Blocked Sender's list (Figure 5–51).

2

- Tap or click the OK button (Add address or domain dialog box) to add the domain to the Blocked Senders List.

- Tap or click the OK button (Junk E-mail Options dialog box) to close the Junk E-mail Options dialog box.

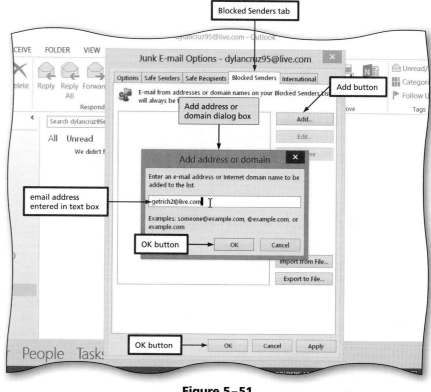

Figure 5–51

Working with Rules

To further automate the processing of email messages in Outlook, you can create rules. A **rule** is a set of instructions that tells Outlook how to handle email messages in your mailbox. You can create rules that apply to email messages you have received and those you send. For example, you can specify that email messages from a particular user be categorized automatically or placed in a specified folder. You can create rules from a template or from scratch based on conditions you specify. Rules apply to an email account, not a single folder or file. If you are working with a data file instead of an email account, you cannot create rules.

To simplify the process of creating rules, Outlook provides a Rules Wizard, which presents a list of conditions for selecting an email message and then lists actions to take with messages that meet the conditions. If necessary, you also can specify exceptions to the rule. For example, you can move certain messages to a specified folder unless they are sent with high importance.

To Create a New Rule

Dylan would like to create a rule to flag all email messages from your faculty advisor, Jacob Thompson, for follow-up. This way, he easily can remember to follow up with Mr. Thompson on important tasks. If you are completing these steps on a personal computer, your email account must be set up in Outlook so that you can select an email account to create a rule. The following steps create a rule that automatically flags email messages. *Why? Rules help you file and follow up on email messages. For example, your instructor can create a rule for messages from a specific course section, such as CIS 101. You can set CIS 101 in the Subject line to be flagged for follow-up and moved to a folder named Literacy.*

❶
- Tap or click the Outlook Data File Inbox to display the Inbox messages.
- Tap or click the Jacob Thompson email message to select it (Figure 5–52).

Figure 5–52

❷
- Tap or click the Rules button (HOME tab | Move group) to display a list of rule options (Figure 5–53).

Figure 5–53

❸

• Tap or click the Create Rule command to display the Create Rule dialog box (Figure 5–54).

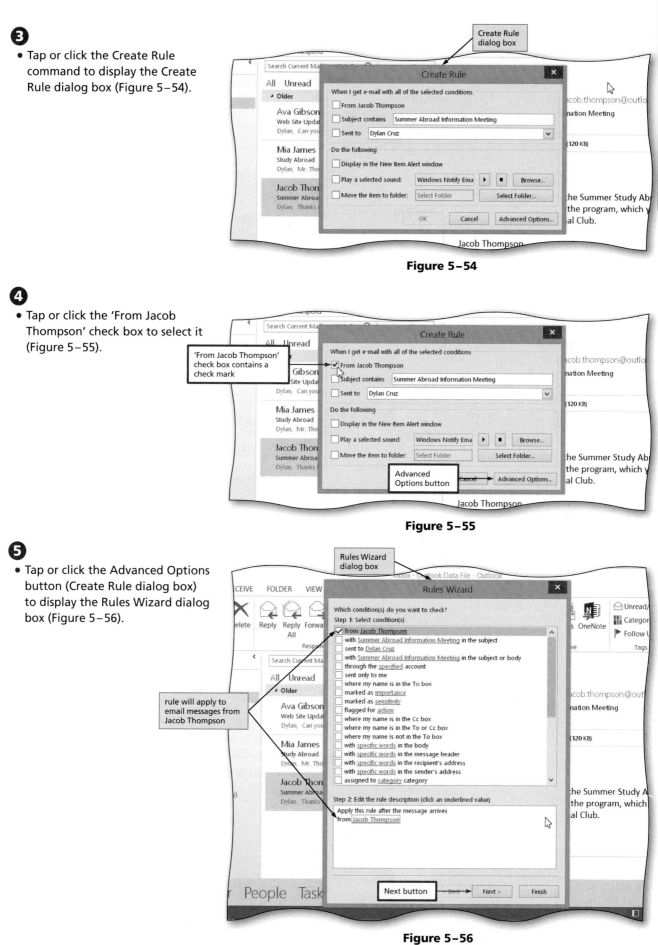

Figure 5–54

❹

• Tap or click the 'From Jacob Thompson' check box to select it (Figure 5–55).

Figure 5–55

❺

• Tap or click the Advanced Options button (Create Rule dialog box) to display the Rules Wizard dialog box (Figure 5–56).

Figure 5–56

6

- Tap or click the Next button (Rules Wizard dialog box) to continue to the next step, where you specify one or more actions to take with a selected message (Figure 5–57).

Figure 5–57

7

- Tap or click the 'flag message for follow up at this time' check box to select it.

- If necessary, tap or click the Yes button if a dialog box opens informing you that the rule you are creating can never be edited in previous versions of Outlook (Figure 5–58).

Q&A What is the effect of selecting the 'flag message for follow up at this time' check box? Messages that meet the conditions you specify, in this case, messages from Jacob Thompson, appear in the message list with a flag icon to indicate they need to be followed up.

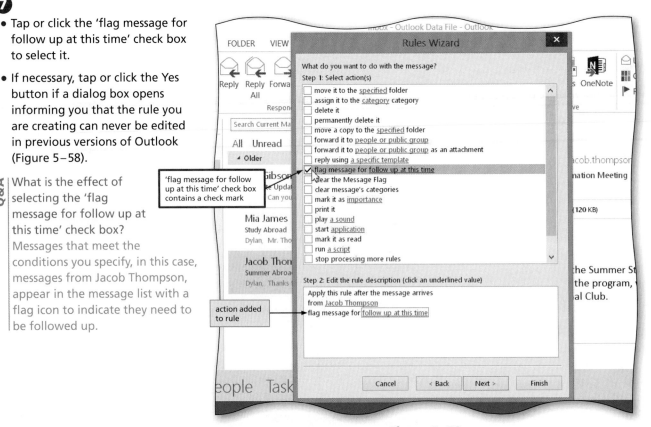

Figure 5–58

8

• Tap or click the 'follow up at this time' link in the Step 2 area to display the Flag Message dialog box (Figure 5–59).

Q&A
For what purposes can I use the Flag Message dialog box?
You can flag a message for follow up (the default) or for other options, including For Your Information, No Response Necessary, and Reply. You also can specify when to follow up: Today (the default), Tomorrow, This Week, Next Week, No Date, or Complete.

Figure 5–59

9

• Tap or click the OK button (Flag Message dialog box) to accept the default settings and return to the Rules Wizard dialog box (Figure 5–60).

10

• Tap or click the Finish button (Rules Wizard dialog box) to save the rule.

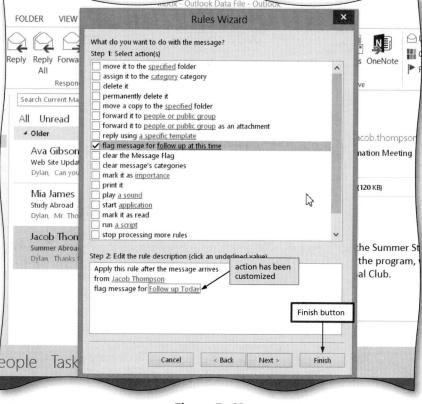

Figure 5–60

To Run Rules

Rules that you create run for all incoming email messages received after you create the rule. *Why? If you want to apply rules to email messages that you already received, you use the Rules and Alerts dialog box.* The following steps run the newly created rule.

1

• Tap or click the Rules button (HOME tab | Move group) to display a list of rule options (Figure 5–61).

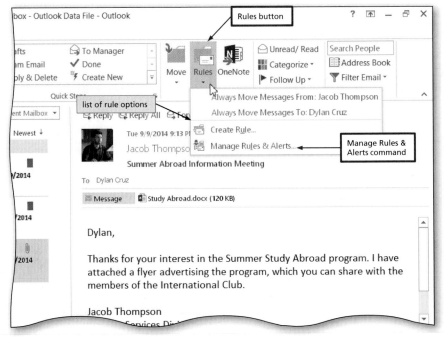

Figure 5–61

2

• Tap or click the Manage Rules & Alerts command to display the Rules and Alerts dialog box (Figure 5–62).

Q&A After I create a rule, can I modify it?

Yes. To modify an existing rule, select the rule you want to modify, tap or click the Change Rule button, and then tap or click the Edit Rule Settings command. Next, make the desired changes in the Rules Wizard. Tap or click the Finish button after making all necessary changes.

Figure 5–62

3

- Tap or click the Run Rules Now button (Rules and Alerts dialog box) to display the Run Rules Now dialog box.

- Tap or click the Jacob Thompson check box to select it and specify the rule that will run.

- Tap or click the Run Now button (Run Rules Now dialog box) to run the rule (Figure 5–63).

Figure 5–63

4

- Tap or click the Close button (Run Rules Now dialog box) to close the Run Rules Now dialog box.

- Tap or click the OK button (Rules and Alerts dialog box) (shown in Figure 5–62) to close the Rules and Alerts dialog box (Figure 5–64).

Figure 5–64

To Delete a Rule

Why? When you no longer need a rule, you should delete it. After further consideration, you decide that you do not need to flag all email messages from your faculty advisor; therefore, you decide to delete the rule. The following steps delete a rule.

1

- Tap or click the Rules button (HOME tab | Move group) (shown in Figure 5–64) to display a list of rule options.

- Tap or click the Manage Rules & Alerts command to display the Rules and Alerts dialog box (Figure 5–65).

Figure 5–65

2

- Tap or click the Delete button (Rules and Alerts dialog box) to display the Microsoft Outlook dialog box (Figure 5–66).

Figure 5–66

3

- Tap or click the Yes button (Microsoft Outlook dialog box) to delete the Jacob Thompson rule (Figure 5–67).

4

- Tap or click the OK button (Rules and Alerts dialog box) to close the Rules and Alerts dialog box.

Figure 5–67

TO SET UP AUTOMATIC REPLIES

Outlook provides a quick way to set up automatic replies for when you may be away from your email account, such as when you are out of the office; however, your email account must support automatic replies using Microsoft Exchange. If you wanted to set up automatic replies, you would use the following steps.

1. Tap or click the FILE tab to display the Backstage view.

2. If necessary, tap or click Info in the Backstage view to display account information.

3. Tap or click Automatic Replies to display the Automatic Replies dialog box.

4. Tap or click 'Send automatic replies' to turn on automatic replies.

5. Change the Start time to select the day and time for the automatic replies to start.

6. Change the End time to select the day and time for the automatic replies to stop.

7. Select Inside My Organization and enter an email message for email messages to be sent inside your organization.

8. Select Outside My Organization and enter an email message for email messages to be sent outside your organization.

9. Tap or click OK to save the rule for automatic replies.

BTW

Cleanup Tools
In addition to archiving email messages, Outlook provides cleanup tools to help control the size of your mailbox. To access the various cleanup tools, display the Backstage view, click the Info tab, if necessary, click the Cleanup Tools button, and then click the desired cleanup tool you want to access.

To Set AutoArchive Settings

1 CUSTOMIZE EMAIL MESSAGES | 2 CUSTOMIZE SIGNATURES & STATIONERY | 3 MANAGE JUNK EMAIL FILTERS
4 CONFIGURE RULES | 5 CHANGE CALENDAR OPTIONS | 6 ADD NEWS FEED

Why? *You can have old items in Outlook automatically transferred to a storage file. Items are only considered old after a certain number of days that you specify.* Dylan decides that he should back up the email messages in his email account. By default, when AutoArchive is turned on, Outlook archives messages every 14 days. The following steps turn on AutoArchive.

1

- Tap or click the FILE tab to display the Backstage view.

- Tap or click Options in the Backstage view to display the Outlook Options dialog box.

- Tap or click Advanced in the Category list to display the Advanced options (Figure 5–68).

Figure 5–68

2

- Tap or click the AutoArchive Settings button (Outlook Options dialog box) to display the AutoArchive dialog box (Figure 5–69).

Figure 5–69

❸

- Tap or click the 'Run AutoArchive every' check box to select it and enable AutoArchive (Figure 5–70).

❹

- Tap or click the OK button (AutoArchive dialog box) to close the AutoArchive dialog box.

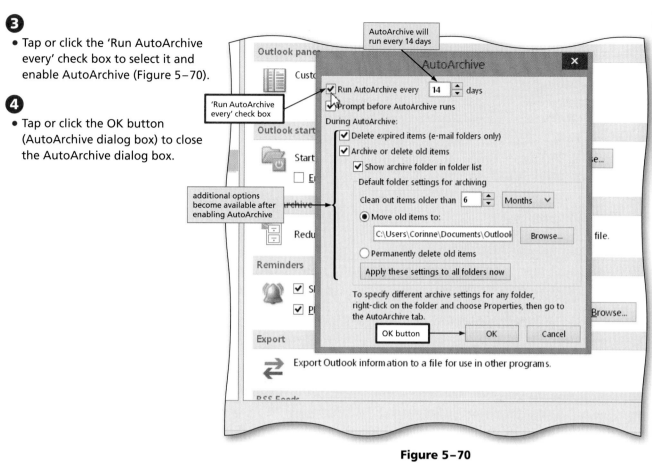

Figure 5–70

Customizing the Calendar

You can customize the Calendar to better suit your needs. For example, you can select the days of your workweek and set the displayed time range to reflect the start and end times of your workday. You also can change the default reminder time from 15 minutes to any other interval, such as five minutes or a half-hour. Other Calendar options you can customize include the calendar font and current time zone.

BTW
Advanced Options
In addition to the various Outlook options presented in this chapter, Outlook allows users to view and change advanced options. To access the advanced options, open the Outlook Options dialog box and then click Advanced in the Category list.

To Change the Work Time on the Calendar

Dylan would like to customize the work time on the Calendar so that it reflects his work schedule. He normally works from 8:30 AM to 5:00 PM on Mondays, Wednesdays, Fridays, and Saturdays. The following steps change the Calendar settings to match the work schedule and make Monday the first day of the week. *Why? By default, the Calendar Work Week is set for Monday through Friday, but you can select which days comprise your workweek.*

1

- Tap or click Calendar in the Category list in the Outlook Options dialog box to display the Calendar options (Figure 5–71).

Figure 5–71

2

- Tap or click the Start time box arrow to display a list of start times.

- Select 8:30 AM to change the start time.

- Tap or click the End time box arrow to display a list of end times.

- Select 4:30 PM to change the end time (Figure 5–72).

Figure 5–72

3

- Tap or click the Tue check box to deselect it.

- Tap or click the Thu check box to deselect it.

- Tap or click the Sat check box to select it (Figure 5–73).

Figure 5–73

4

- Tap or click the 'First day of week' box arrow to display a list of days.

- Tap or click Monday to change the first day of the week to Monday (Figure 5–74).

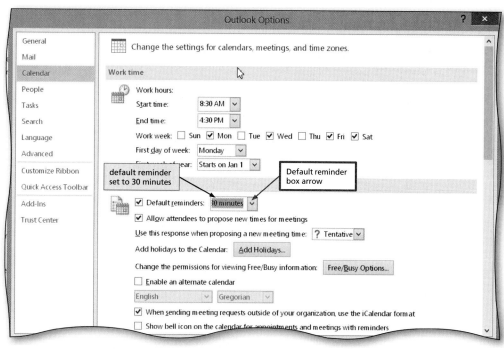

Figure 5–74

To Change the Time for Calendar Reminders

To further customize the Outlook calendar, Dylan would like to increase the time for reminders to 30 minutes. The following step changes the time for reminders. *Why? By default, the Calendar reminders are set for 15 minutes prior to an appointment or meeting.*

1

- Tap or click the Default reminders box arrow to display a list of times.

- Tap or click 30 minutes to select it as the default time for reminders (Figure 5–75).

Figure 5–75

To Change the Time Zone Setting

Why? *When you travel, your time zone may change and your calendar should be updated. If you change the time zone setting in Calendar, Outlook updates your appointments to display the new time zone when you arrive.* Dylan is participating in the Study Abroad program this summer in Madrid, Spain, and needs to change the time zones accordingly. The following steps change the time zone.

1
- Scroll down until the Time zones settings are visible in the Outlook Options dialog box (Figure 5–76).

Figure 5–76

2
- Tap or click the Time zone box arrow to display a list of time zones (Figure 5–77).

Figure 5–77

3

- Slide or scroll and then tap or click (UTC+01:00) Brussels, Copenhagen, Madrid, Paris to select the time zone (Figure 5–78).

Figure 5–78

4

- Tap or click the OK button (Outlook Options dialog box) to close the Outlook Options dialog box.
- Tap or click the Calendar button in the Navigation Pane to display the Calendar to view the changes (Figure 5–79).

Figure 5–79

Working with RSS Feeds

Really Simple Syndication (RSS) is a way for content publishers to make news, blogs, and other content available to subscribers. RSS feeds typically are found on news websites, political discussion boards, educational blogs, and other sites that frequently update their content. For example, the CNN website contains two RSS feeds that allow people to view top stories and recent stories in one convenient location. If you frequently visit websites that offer RSS feeds, you quickly can review the feed content of all the websites in a simple list in your browser by subscribing to their RSS feeds, without having to first navigate to each individual site.

If you want to use Outlook to read the feed, you can add the RSS feed to your account using the Account Settings dialog box. Outlook creates an easy way to manage and work with your RSS feed. Some accounts let you access the feeds from your web browser if they are using a common feeds folder; however, not all accounts allow for this.

To Subscribe to an RSS Feed

1 CUSTOMIZE EMAIL MESSAGES | 2 CUSTOMIZE SIGNATURES & STATIONERY | 3 MANAGE JUNK EMAIL FILTERS
4 CONFIGURE RULES | 5 CHANGE CALENDAR OPTIONS | **6 ADD NEWS FEED**

Dylan subscribes to several RSS feeds in his web browser. To view the feed using Outlook, he needs to set up an RSS feed called Life Rocks 2.0 from http://www. nirmaltv.com/feed/. The following steps subscribe to an RSS feed and display the messages. *Why? The benefit of displaying an RSS feed in Outlook is the ability to combine feeds from multiple web sources in one place. You no longer have to visit different websites for news, weather, blogs, and other information.*

- Tap or click the Mail button in the Navigation bar to display the mailboxes in the Navigation Pane.

- Press and hold or right-click the RSS Feeds folder in the Navigation Pane to display a shortcut menu (Figure 5–80).

Q&A What should I do if an RSS Feeds folder does not appear in Dylan's mailbox?
Press and hold or right-click the RSS Feeds folder in a different mailbox on your computer.

Figure 5–80

2

- Tap or click the Add a New RSS Feed command to display the New RSS Feed dialog box (Figure 5–81).

Figure 5–81

3

- Type **http://www .nirmaltv.com/feed/** in the text box to enter the address of an RSS feed (Figure 5–82).

Figure 5–82

4

- Tap or click the Add button (New RSS Feed dialog box) to add the RSS feed to the RSS Feeds folder.

- Tap or click the Yes button (Microsoft Outlook dialog box) to confirm you want to add the RSS feed (Figure 5–83).

Experiment

- Tap or click the different messages to see what has been posted in the RSS Feeds folder.

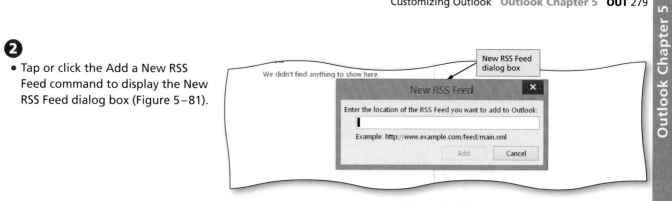

Figure 5–83

To Delete an RSS Feed

Why? When you no longer need to use an RSS feed, you should delete it so that you do not have unwanted messages in your account. The following steps delete an RSS feed.

1

- Press and hold or right-click the Untitled folder below the RSS Feeds folder in the Navigation Pane to display a shortcut menu (Figure 5–84).

Figure 5–84

2

- Tap or click the Delete Folder command to display the Microsoft Outlook dialog box (Figure 5–85).

Figure 5–85

3

- Tap or click the Yes button (Microsoft Outlook dialog box) to delete the RSS Feed (Figure 5–86).

Figure 5–86

To Reset the Time Zone Setting

Why? You should change the time zone back to your original time zone before quitting Outlook. The following steps reset the time zone.

1 If necessary, tap or click the FILE tab to open the Backstage view, and then tap or click Options to display the Outlook Options dialog box.

2 Tap or click Calendar, and then scroll down until the Time zones settings are visible in the Outlook Options dialog box.

3 Tap or click the Time zone box arrow to display a list of time zones.

4 Tap or click your time zone to select the time zone.

To Exit Outlook

This project now is complete. The following steps exit Outlook. For a detailed example of the procedure summarized below, refer to the Office 2013 and Windows 8 chapter at the beginning of this book.

1 If you have an appointment open, tap or click the Close button on the right side of the title bar to close the Contact window.

2 Tap or click the Close button on the right side of the title bar to exit Outlook.

BTW
Quick Reference
For a table that lists how to complete the tasks covered in this book using touch gestures, the mouse, ribbon, shortcut menu, and keyboard, see the Quick Reference Summary at the back of this book, or visit the Quick Reference resource on the Student Companion Site located on www.cengagebrain.com. For detailed instructions about accessing available resources, visit www.cengage.com/ct/ studentdownload or see the inside back cover of this book.

Chapter Summary

In this chapter, you have learned how to add another email account, customize Outlook options, add signatures and stationery, manage the junk email filter, create rules, customize calendar options, and add RSS Feeds. The items listed below include all the new Outlook skills you have learned in this chapter with the tasks grouped by activity.

What decisions will you need to make when customizing email messages, adding signatures and stationery, managing junk email options, working with rules, customizing the calendar, and adding RSS feeds in the future?

A. Customize Email Messages:

1. Determine which options you want to customize.

2. Determine the information to include in your signature.

3. Determine the layout that you would like for stationery.

B. Managing Junk Email Options:

1. Determine which domains should be placed on the Safe Senders list.

2. Determine which specific email addresses should be placed on the Blocked Senders list.

C. Working with Rules:

1. Plan rules to use with your email messages.

2. Determine how you would like your email messages to be processed.

D. Customizing the Calendar:

1. Determine the calendar settings you need.

E. Adding RSS Feeds:

1. Determine what news feeds you would like to use.

How should you submit solutions to questions in the assignments identified with a ❈ symbol?

Every assignment in this book contains one or more questions identified with a ❈ symbol. These questions require you to think beyond the assigned file. Present your solutions to the questions in the format required by your instructor. Possible formats may include one or more of these options: write the answer; create a document that contains the answer; present your answer to the class; discuss your answer in a group; record the answer as audio or video using a webcam, smartphone, or portable media player; or post answers on a blog, wiki, or website.

Apply Your Knowledge

Reinforce the skills and apply the concepts you learned in this chapter.

Creating a Signature

Instructions: Start Outlook. You will be using the Signatures and Stationery dialog box (Figure 5–87) to create a signature to use when you send email messages to others.

Figure 5–87

Perform the following tasks:

1. Display the Outlook Options dialog box. Tap or click Mail and then tap or click the Signatures button to display the Signatures and Stationery dialog box.

2. Tap or click the New button to create a signature. Type `standard` as the name of the signature.

3. Change the font to Times New Roman and the font size to 12.

4. On three lines, enter the following information: your name, your email address, and your major.

5. Set the signature to apply to new messages, replies, and forwards.

6. Tap or click the Personal Stationery tab and then tap or click the Theme button.

7. Select the Ice theme as your stationery.

8. Accept the changes in the dialog boxes and then create a new email message addressed to your instructor to display your new signature and stationery.

9. Submit the email message in the format specified by your instructor.

10. ✦ Why is it a good idea to configure Outlook to include a signature in outgoing email messages?

Extend Your Knowledge

Extend the skills you learned in this chapter and experiment with new skills. You may need to use Help to complete the assignment.

Adding a Second Email Account to Microsoft Outlook

Instructions: You are going to add a second email account to Microsoft Outlook so that you can send and receive email messages from two accounts. If you do not already have another email account to add to Microsoft Outlook, sign up for a free account using a service such as Outlook. com, Gmail, or Yahoo!. Once you create the account, you will add the email account to Outlook using the Add Account Wizard shown in Figure 5–88, and then send an email to your instructor.

Figure 5–88

Continued >

Extend Your Knowledge *continued*

Perform the following tasks:

1. If necessary, navigate to a free email service and sign up for a free email account.

2. Start Outlook and display the Backstage view.

3. If necessary, tap or click the Info tab to display the Info gallery.

4. Tap or click the Add Account button to display the first dialog box in the Add Account Wizard.

5. Enter the desired information for the email account you are adding, including your name, email address, and password.

6. Tap or click the Next button to instruct Outlook to automatically configure the account. If Outlook is unable to configure the account automatically, you may need to manually configure the account settings.

7. When the account has been configured successfully, tap or click the Finish button.

8. Open a new email message addressed to your instructor stating that you have configured a new email account in Outlook. Send the email message to your instructor using the account you have just configured.

9. ✸ In what circumstances is it helpful to have multiple email accounts configured in Microsoft Outlook?

Analyze, Correct, Improve

Analyze the Outlook configuration and correct all errors and/or improve the configuration.

Copying and Modifying a Signature

Instructions: Start Outlook. Your boss has informed you that it is not acceptable to send business-related email messages without an approved company signature and an appropriate theme. Figure 5–89 shows an example of an email signature used by one of your coworkers. You will modify the signature to reflect your information and then change the default theme for your email messages.

Figure 5–89

Perform the following tasks:

1. Correct Review the signature used in Figure 5–89. Change the name in the signature to reflect your name, update the title to one of your choosing, and change the phone number to your phone number (you may use a fictitious phone number if you are not comfortable including yours). Save the signature and configure it to be included with all new email messages, as well as forwarded messages and replies.

2. Improve Change the color, font, and font size of your name in the signature so that it stands out from the other information in the signature. Next, choose an appropriate theme for your email messages. If necessary, make additional changes to the font color you used in the signature to make sure it is readable with the new theme.

3. ✲ Why might businesses want all employees to use consistent signatures? Have you ever received an email message without sufficient contact information in the signature? If so, how did you obtain the information you needed?

In the Labs

Design, create, modify, and/or use signatures and rules using the guidelines, concepts, and skills presented in this chapter. Labs are listed in order of increasing difficulty.

Lab 1: **Creating Custom Signatures**

Problem: You communicate with both professors and other students via email. Your professors ask students to clearly identify themselves in email messages, but you do not want to include the same information in email messages you send to your friends. Instead, you want to include your nickname and cell phone number in your email signature. You will create two signatures: one to use when you send email messages to your professors, and another for email messages you send to friends. You will use the Signatures and Stationery dialog box to create the signatures (Figure 5–90).

Figure 5–90

Continued >

In the Labs *continued*

Perform the following tasks:

1. Display the Outlook Options dialog box. Tap or click Mail and then tap or click the Signatures button to display the Signatures and Stationery dialog box.

2. Tap or click the New button to create a signature. Type `Academic` as the name of the signature.

3. Change the font to Arial and the font size to 14.

4. On three lines, enter the following information: your name, the name of your school, the classes in which you are enrolled, and your email address.

5. Using the Academic signature, send an email message to your instructor. The email message should specify that the signature is the Academic signature.

6. Display the Outlook Options dialog box. Tap or click Mail and then tap or click the Signatures button to display the Signatures and Stationery dialog box.

7. Tap or click the New button to create a signature. Type `Personal` as the name of the signature.

8. Change the font to Comic Sans MS, the font size to 16, and the font color to one of your choosing.

9. On three lines, enter the following information: your name, your phone number, and your email address.

10. Using the Personal signature, send an email message to a friend. The email message should specify that the signature is the Personal signature.

11. ✹ Do you think it is easier to switch back and forth between different signatures or manually type signature information individually into each email message? Why?

Lab 2: **Configuring Junk Email**

Problem: You occasionally find email messages you want to read in the Junk E-mail folder for your Outlook email account. You also receive spam from a certain email address. You want to use the Junk E-mail Options dialog box (Figure 5–91) to make sure you receive email messages from some senders, while blocking email messages from another sender.

Perform the following tasks:

1. In Outlook, display the Junk E-mail Options dialog box.

2. Tap or click the Safe Senders tab.

3. Add CNN.com to the Safe Senders list. Write down what is displayed in the Safe Senders list.

4. Tap or click the Safe Recipients tab. Add ewhite173@gmail.com to the Safe Recipients list. Write down what is displayed in the Safe Recipients list.

Figure 5–91

5. Tap or click the Blocked Senders tab. Add @crazyedigames.com to the Blocked Senders list. Write down what is displayed in the Blocked Senders list.

6. Submit what you have recorded in the format specified by your instructor.

7. ✸ What other domains and email addresses might you add to the Safe Senders list? What are some examples of other domains and email addresses you might add to the Blocked Senders list?

Lab 3: Expand Your World: Cloud and Web Technologies

Problem: RSS feeds are web technologies that can deliver up-to-date content directly to Outlook. You want to add an RSS feed from CNN.com so that you can view technology news in Outlook (Figure 5–92).

Figure 5–92

Perform the following tasks:

1. Run your browser and navigate to CNN.com.

2. Navigate to the page on the CNN.com website that displays the list of available RSS feeds.

3. Select and copy the web address for the Technology RSS feed.

4. In Outlook, press and hold or right-click the RSS Feeds folder (or the feeds folder for your email account) and then display the New RSS Feed dialog box.

5. Paste the web address from Step 3 into the text box.

6. Add the feed to Outlook.

7. Open the first RSS message.

8. Print the message and then submit it in the format specified by your instructor.

9. ✸ What other RSS feeds might you find useful to include in Microsoft Outlook?

Consider This: Your Turn

Apply your creative thinking and problem solving skills to design and implement a solution.

1: Create Rules

Academic

Part 1: For three of the classes you are currently taking, create email folders for each class. Create rules to move messages related to the classes to the appropriate class email folder. Write a rule for one class that flags messages for follow-up the following week. Write down the rules and then submit your work in the format specified by your instructor.

Part 2: ✸ You made several decisions when creating the rules in this exercise, such as which folders to create and how to set up the rule to identify to which class an email message belongs. What was the rationale behind each of these decisions?

2: Create a Company Signature

Professional

Part 1: Your supervisor has asked you to create an email signature to be used in all outgoing email communication from company employees. He has not given you specifics about what should be in the signature, but you do know that it is important to provide useful information. Create a new signature in Outlook that will be used as the company's standard signature, and determine which information to include in the signature, how it should be formatted, and how the items in the signature should be arranged. Then, send an email to your instructor that contains the signature.

Part 2: ✸ You made several decisions when creating the signature in this exercise, such as what information to include, how to format the signature, and how to arrange the items in the signature. What was the rationale behind each of these decisions?

3: Subscribe to Feeds

Research and Collaboration

Part 1: Your instructor has assigned teams of three people to search for and identify websites that contain RSS feeds. Your team should search for RSS feeds providing useful information that you want to display in Microsoft Outlook. Each team member should locate an RSS feed from at least five different websites and record the name and web address of the site containing the RSS feed, the information the RSS feed contains, and how often the RSS feed is updated. Compare the list with the lists from your teammates. Were any RSS feeds or types of RSS feeds similar? If so, which ones? Do you find value in the RSS feeds your teammates identified?

Part 2: ✸ You made several decisions when searching for RSS feeds in this exercise, such as where to search for the RSS feeds and which types of RSS feeds would be useful to include in Outlook. What was the rationale behind each of these decisions?

Learn Online

Reinforce what you learned in this chapter with games, exercises, training, and many other online activities and resources.

Student Companion Site Reinforce chapter terms and concepts using review questions, flash cards, practice tests, and interactive learning games, such as a crossword puzzle. These and other online activities and resources are available at no additional cost on www.cengagebrain.com. Visit www.cengage.com/ct/studentdownload for detailed instructions about accessing the resources available at the Student Companion Site.

Index

Note: **Boldfaced** page numbers indicate key terms.

Quick Reference Summary

Microsoft Office Outlook 2013 Quick Reference Summary

Task	Page Number	Touch Gesture	Ribbon	Other On-Screen Area	Shortcut Menu	Keyboard Shortcut
Add Attachment to Contact	OUT 142		Attach File button (INSERT tab | Include group), select file, click Insert			
Add Email Account	OUT 237		FILE tab | click Add Account button			
Add Image to Email Signature	OUT 251			Insert Picture button (Signatures and Stationery dialog box)		
Add Name to Contact Group	OUT 149		Add Members button (CONTACT GROUP tab | Add Members group)			
Add RSS Feed	OUT 278	Press and hold RSS Feeds folder, tap Add a New RSS Feed			Right-click RSS Feeds folder, click Add a New RSS Feed	
Appointment, Change Date for	OUT 95			Double-tap or double-click appointment, change date or Drag appointment to different date in Date Navigator		CTRL+O, change date
Appointment, Change Time for	OUT 94			Double-tap or double-click appointment, change time or Drag appointment to a different time slot in appointment area		CTRL+O, change time
Appointment, Create in Appointment Area	OUT 76			Tap or click date, type appointment title or Drag to select time slots, type appointment title		
Appointment, Create Using Appointment Window	OUT 81		New Appointment button (HOME tab | New group)			CTRL+ SHIFT+A

Microsoft Office Outlook 2013 Quick Reference Summary *(continued)*

Task	Page Number	Touch Gesture	Ribbon	Other On-Screen Area	Shortcut Menu	Keyboard Shortcut
Appointment, Delete	OUT 96		Delete button (CALENDAR TOOLS APPOINTMENT tab | Actions group)		Delete	DELETE
Appointment, Save	OUT 89		Save button (Quick Access Toolbar)			CTRL+S
Appointment, Save & Close	OUT 89		Save & Close button (APPOINTMENT tab | Actions group)	Close button, Yes to save changes		
Appointment, Set Reminder for	OUT 85		Reminder box arrow (APPOINTMENT tab | Options group)			
Appointment, Set Status for	OUT 84		Show As box arrow (APPOINTMENT tab | Options group)			
Assign Task	OUT 206		Assign Task button (TASK tab | Manage Task group)			
Assign Theme to Stationery	OUT 255			Stationery and Fonts button (Outlook Options dialog box), Theme button (Signatures and Stationery dialog box)		
Attach Outlook Item to Task	OUT 205		Outlook Item button (INSERT tab | Include group)			
Attachment, Open	OUT 22			Double-tap or double-click attachment in message header		
Attachment, Preview	OUT 20			Tap or click attachment in message header		
Attachment, Save	OUT 20		Save As button (ATTACHMENT TOOLS ATTACHMENTS tab | Actions group)		Save As	
Attachment, Add to Contact	OUT 142		Attach File button (INSERT tab | Include group), select file, click Insert			
Attachment, Add to Task	OUT 203		Attach File button (INSERT tab | Include group)			
Attachment to Contact, Change	OUT 143		Attach File button (INSERT tab | Include group), select file, click Insert	Double-click contact, click attachment, click Attach File button (INSERT tab | Include group), select file, click Insert		
Attachment to Contact, Remove	OUT 144		Click file icon, click Delete (CONTACT tab | Actions group)	Double-click contact, click attachment, press DELETE		DELETE
AutoArchive Settings, Configure	OUT 271		FILE tab | Options tab, Advanced category, click AutoArchive Settings button (Outlook Options dialog box)			

Microsoft Office Outlook 2013 Quick Reference Summary (continued)

Task	Page Number	Touch Gesture	Ribbon	Other On-Screen Area	Shortcut Menu	Keyboard Shortcut
Automatic Replies, Set Up	OUT 271		FILE tab | Info tab, click Automatic Replies			
Calendar, Delete Personal Calendar	OUT 108		Delete Calendar button (FOLDER tab | Actions group)		Delete Calendar	
Calendar, Display Day View	OUT 69		Day button (HOME tab | Arrange group)			CTRL+ALT+1
Calendar, Display List View	OUT 115		Change View button (VIEW tab | Current View group), List button			
Calendar, Display Month View	OUT 71		Month button (HOME tab | Arrange group)			CTRL+ALT+4
Calendar, Display Personal	OUT 64			Tap or click folder check box		
Calendar, Display Schedule View	OUT 71		Schedule View button (HOME tab | Arrange group)			CTRL+ALT+5
Calendar, Display Week View	OUT 70		Week button (HOME tab | Arrange group)			CTRL+ALT+4
Calendar, Display Work Week View	OUT 69		Work Week button (HOME tab | Arrange group)			CTRL+ALT+2
Calendar, Email	OUT 118		E-mail Calendar button (HOME tab | Share group)			
Calendar, Go To a Specific Date	OUT 68		Dialog Box Launcher (HOME tab | Go To group)			CTRL+G
Calendar, Overlay Mode	OUT 106			Tap or click arrow on displayed calendar		
Calendar, Print Weekly Style	OUT 112		Weekly Calendar Style (FILE tab | Print tab), Print button			CTRL+P
Calendar, Recurrence Options, Set for Appointment	OUT 87		Recurrence button (APPOINTMENT tab | Options group)			
Calendar, Reminder, Set for Appointment	OUT 85		Reminder button (APPOINTMENT tab | Options group)			
Calendar, Remove Default Calendar from Appointment Area	OUT 66			Tap or click Calendar check box to remove the check mark in My Calendars pane		
Calendar, Save as iCalendar File	OUT 116		Save button (FILE tab | Save Calendar tab)			
Calendar, Change Time Zone for	OUT 276		FILE tab | Options tab, Calendar category, Time zone box arrow (Outlook Options dialog box)			

Microsoft Office Outlook 2013 Quick Reference Summary *(continued)*

Task	Page Number	Touch Gesture	Ribbon	Other On-Screen Area	Shortcut Menu	Keyboard Shortcut
Calendar Options, Set	OUT 273		FILE tab | Options tab, Calendar category (Outlook Options dialog box)			
Categorize Contact	OUT 145		Categorize or Follow Up button (CONTACT tab | Tags group)			
Categorize Email Message	OUT 202	Press and hold email message's category column, tap category	Categorize button (HOME tab | Tags group)		Right-click email message's category column, click category	
Categorize Multiple Tasks	OUT 197		Select tasks, click Categorize button (HOME tab | Tags group)		Select tasks, right-click one task's category column, click All Categories	
Categorize Task	OUT 196		Click task, click Categorize button (HOME tab | Tags group)		Right-click task's category column, click All Categories	
Category, Create	OUT 193		Categorize button (HOME tab | Tags group)			
Category, Delete	OUT 214			Delete button (Color Categories dialog box)		
Category, Rename	OUT 199		Click Categorize button (HOME tab | Tags group), click All Categories, click category, click Rename		Right-click task's category column, click All Categories, select category, click Rename button	
Change Attachment to Contact	OUT 134		Attach File button (INSERT tab | Include group), select file, click Insert	Double-click contact, click attachment, click Attach File button (INSERT tab | Include group), select file, click Insert		
Change Notes View	OUT 220		Notes List (HOME tab | Current View group)			
Change Task View	OUT 216		Change View button (HOME tab | Current View group)			

Microsoft Office Outlook 2013 Quick Reference Summary *(continued)*

Task	Page Number	Touch Gesture	Ribbon	Other On-Screen Area	Shortcut Menu	Keyboard Shortcut
Change Work Time on Calendar	OUT 273		FILE tab | Options tab | Calendar category, options in Work time area (Outlook Options dialog box)			
Color Categories, Add to Calendar	OUT 78		Categorize button (CALENDAR TOOLS APPOINTMENT tab | Tags group), All Categories			
Color Category, Assign to Appointment	OUT 80		Categorize button (CALENDAR TOOLS APPOINTMENT tab | Tags group), category			
Configure Junk Email Options	OUT 259		Junk button (HOME tab | Delete group)			
Contact, Create	OUT 133		New Contact button (HOME tab | New group)			CTRL+ SHIFT+C
Contact, Create from Email Message	OUT 135	Press and hold email address in message, tap Add to Outlook Contacts			Right-click email address in message, click Add to Outlook Contacts	
Contact, Create from Existing Contact	OUT 129		New Items button (HOME tab | New group), click Contact from the Same Company			
Contact, Delete	OUT 141	Tap contact, press DELETE	Delete button (HOME tab | Delete group)	Click contact, press DELETE	Right-click contact, click Delete	DELETE
Contact, Edit	OUT 138	Tap contact, tap Outlook (Contacts)		Click contact, click Outlook (Contacts)		
Contact, Find by Searching for Text	OUT 148			Click Search Contacts text box, type search text		CTRL+E
Contact, Find from Any Outlook Window	OUT 151			Click button in Navigation bar, type search text in Find a Contact search box (HOME tab | Find group)		
Contact Group, Add Name to	OUT 158		Open contact group, click Add Members button (CONTACT GROUP tab | Members group)			
Contact Group, Add Notes to	OUT 159		Open contact group, click Notes button (CONTACT GROUP tab | Show group)			

Microsoft Office Outlook 2013 Quick Reference Summary *(continued)*

Task	Page Number	Touch Gesture	Ribbon	Other On-Screen Area	Shortcut Menu	Keyboard Shortcut
Contact Group, Create from Email Message	OUT 152, OUT 155	Press and hold contact group name in To or Cc box, select Add to Outlook Contacts	New Items button (HOME tab | New group), click More Items, click Contact Group, enter name, click Add Members button (CONTACT GROUP tab | Add Members group), click Members text box, enter email address	Right-click contact group name in To or Cc box, select Add to Outlook Contacts		
Contact Group, Create from Existing Contacts	OUT 153		New Contact Group button (HOME tab | New group), enter name, click Add Members button (CONTACT GROUP tab | Members group)			
Contact Group, Delete	OUT 161		Select contact group, click Delete (HOME tab | Delete group)			
Contact Group, Remove Name from	OUT 160		Open contact group, click member, click Remove Member button (CONTACT GROUP tab | Members group)			
Contact List, Preview	OUT 162		FILE tab | Print tab, select print style			
Contact List, Print	OUT 166		FILE tab | Print tab, click Print button			
Contact List, Print Only Selected Items	OUT 164		FILE tab | Print tab | click Print Options button, click Only selected items option button, click Print button			
Contact List, Select Style	OUT 163		FILE tab | Print			
Contact View, Change	OUT 145		More button (HOME tab | Current View group), click view			
Contacts, Sort	OUT 138		Reverse Sort button (VIEW tab | Arrangement group)			
Create Category	OUT 186		Categorize button (HOME tab | Tags group)			
Create Contact	OUT 133		New Contact button (HOME tab | New group)			CTRL+ SHIFT+C
Create Contact from Email Message	OUT 135	Press and hold email address in message, tap Add to Outlook Contacts			Right-click email address in message, click Add to Outlook Contacts	

Microsoft Office Outlook 2013 Quick Reference Summary *(continued)*

Task	Page Number	Touch Gesture	Ribbon	Other On-Screen Area	Shortcut Menu	Keyboard Shortcut
Create Contact from Existing Contact	OUT 129		New Items button (HOME tab | New group), click Contact from the Same Company			
Create Contact Group Create from Email Message	OUT 146		Copy email address, click New Items button (HOME tab | New group), click More Items, click Contact Group, enter name, click Add Members button (CONTACT GROUP tab | Add Members group), click Members text box, paste email address			
Create Contact Group from Existing Contacts	OUT 144		New Contact Group button (HOME tab | New group), enter name, click Add Members button (CONTACT GROUP tab | Members group)			
Create Email Signature	OUT 248		FILE tab | Options tab| Mail category | click Signatures button (Outlook Options dialog box)			
Create Note	OUT 218		New Note (HOME tab | New group)			CTRL+N
Create Recurring Task	OUT 183		New Task button (HOME tab | New group), click Recurrence button (TASK tab | Recurrence group)			
Create Rule	OUT 265		Rules button (HOME tab | Move group)			
Create Task	OUT 173		New Task button (HOME tab | New group)			
Create Task with Due Date	OUT 176		New Task button (HOME tab | New group), click Due date box arrow			
Create Task with Priority	OUT 179		New Task button (HOME tab | New group), click Priority box arrow			
Create Task with Reminder	OUT 180		New Task button (HOME tab | New group), click Reminder check box, click Reminder date box arrow			

Microsoft Office Outlook 2013 Quick Reference Summary *(continued)*

Task	Page Number	Touch Gesture	Ribbon	Other On-Screen Area	Shortcut Menu	Keyboard Shortcut
Create Task with Status	OUT 177		New Task button (HOME tab | New group), click Status box arrow			
Current View, Change for Contacts	OUT 137		More button (HOME tab | Current View group), click view			
Custom Date, Flag Email Message with	OUT 199		Follow Up button (HOME tab | Tags group), click Custom		Right-click email's flag column, click Custom	
Customize Stationery	OUT 254		FILE tab | Options tab, Mail category, click Stationery and Fonts button (Outlook Options dialog box)			
Default Message Format, Set	OUT 246		FILE tab | Options tab, Mail category, click Compose messages in this format box arrow (Outlook Options dialog box)			
Delete Category	OUT 213			Delete button (Color Categories dialog box)		
Delete Note	OUT 221		Delete button (HOME tab | Delete group)			
Delete Rule	OUT 270		Rules button (HOME tab | Move group), click Manage Rules and Alerts, click Delete button (Rules and Alerts dialog box)			
Delete Task	OUT 212		Remove from List button (HOME tab | Manage Task group) or Display task, click Delete button (HOME tab | Delete group)		Right-click task, click Delete	DELETE
Display Outlook Options	OUT 245		FILE tab | Options tab			
Dock the Peek Calendar, View	OUT 107			'Dock the peek' button on calendar		
Due Date, Create Task with	OUT 176		New Task button (HOME tab | New group), click Due date box arrow			
Edit Contact	OUT 130			Double-click contact		
Email Account, Add	OUT 6		Add Account button (FILE tab | Info)			
Email Account, Remove	OUT 6		Account Settings button (FILE tab | Info tab)			
Email Account, Add	OUT 237		FILE tab | Add Account			

Outlook Quick Reference

Microsoft Office Outlook 2013 Quick Reference Summary (continued)

Task	Page Number	Touch Gesture	Ribbon	Other On-Screen Area	Shortcut Menu	Keyboard Shortcut
Email Address, Block	OUT 263		Blocked Senders tab (Junk E-mail Options dialog box), click Add button			
Email Message, Attach File to	OUT 37		Attach File button (MESSAGE tab | Include group) or INSERT tab	Include group	Drag file to message		
Email Message, Change Message Format	OUT 31		Plain Text button (FORMAT TEXT tab | Format group)			
Email Message, Check Spelling	OUT 32		Spelling & Grammar button (REVIEW tab | Proofing group)			F7
Email Message, Close	OUT 35			Close button		
Email Message, Compose New	OUT 12		New Email button (HOME tab | New group)			CTRL+SHIFT+M; in Inbox folder, CTRL+N
Email Message, Delete	OUT 46		Delete button (HOME tab | Delete group)	Delete icon on message or Drag to Deleted Items folder	Delete	DELETE
Email Message, Forward	OUT 39		Forward button (HOME tab | Respond group)		Forward	CTRL+F
Email Message, Mark as Read	OUT 19				Mark as Read	
Email Message, Open	OUT 19			Double-tap or double-click message header		CTRL+O
Email Message, Print	OUT 22		Print button (FILE tab | Print)		Quick Print	CTRL+P
Email Message, Reply	OUT 28		Reply button (HOME tab | Respond group)	Reply in Reading Pane	Reply	CTRL+R
Email Message, Reply All	OUT 28		Reply All button (HOME tab | Respond group)	Reply all in Reading Pane	Reply All	CTRL+SHIFT+R
Email Message, Save without Sending	OUT 35		Save button (Quick Access Toolbar)			CTRL+S
Email Message, Send	OUT 16			Send button in message header		ALT+S or CTRL+ENTER
Email Message, Set High Importance for	OUT 38		High Importance button (MESSAGE tab | Tags group)			
Email Message, Set Importance	OUT 38		High Importance button or Low Importance button (MESSAGE tab | Tags group)			
Email Message, View in Reading Pane	OUT 18			Tap or click message header in message list		

Microsoft Office Outlook 2013 Quick Reference Summary *(continued)*

Task	Page Number	Touch Gesture	Ribbon	Other On-Screen Area	Shortcut Menu	Keyboard Shortcut
Email Message, Categorize	OUT 202		Categorize button (HOME tab | Tags group)		Right-click email message's category column, click category	
Email Message, Categorize Using OUT Quick Click	OUT 198			Click category column for email message		
Email Message, Flag for Follow-Up	OUT 198		Follow Up button (HOME tab | Tags group)		Right-click email's flag column, click option	
Email Message, Flag with Custom Date	OUT 199		Follow Up button (HOME tab | Tags group), click Custom		Right-click email's flag column, click Custom	
Email Signature, Create	OUT 248		FILE tab | Options tab, Mail category, Signatures button (Outlook Options dialog box)			
Email Signature, Format	OUT 249			Formatting options (Signatures and Stationery dialog box)		
Event, Create	OUT 97		New Items button (HOME tab | New group), All Day Event		New All Day Event	CTRL+ SHIFT+A, click All day event check box
Event, Delete	OUT 99		Delete button (CALENDAR TOOLS APPOINTMENT tab | Actions group)			DELETE
Event, Save	OUT 99		Quick Access Toolbar, Save button			CTRL+S
Event, Save & Close	OUT 99		Save & Close button (EVENT tab | Actions group)			
Event, Set as Recurring	OUT 99		Recurrence button (EVENT tab | Options group)			
Exit Outlook	OUT 49			Close button		ALT+F4
File, Attach to Contact	OUT 131		Attach File button (INSERT tab | Include group), select file, click Insert			
File, Attach to Task	OUT 203		Attach File button (INSERT tab | Include group)			
File Attached to Contact, Remove	OUT 135			Double-click contact, click attachment, press DELETE		DELETE

Microsoft Office Outlook 2013 Quick Reference Summary *(continued)*

Task	Page Number	Touch Gesture	Ribbon	Other On-Screen Area	Shortcut Menu	Keyboard Shortcut
Find Contact by Searching for Email Address	OUT 139			Click Search Contacts text box, type search text		CTRL+E
Find Contact from Any Outlook Folder	OUT 142			Click folder in Navigation Pane, type search text in Find a Contact search box (HOME tab | Find group)		
Flag Email Message for Follow-Up	OUT 198	Press and hold email's flag column, tap option	Follow Up button (HOME tab | Tags group)		Right-click email's flag column, click option	
Flag Email Message with Custom Date	OUT 199	Press and hold email's flag column, tap Custom	Follow Up button (HOME tab | Tags group), click Custom		Right-click email's flag column, click Custom	
Folder, Create Personal Calendar Folder	OUT 64		New Calendar button (FOLDER tab | New group)		New Folder	
Folder, Move Email Message to	OUT 43		Move button (HOME tab | Move group)	Drag to folder	Move, folder name	
Format Email Signature	OUT 249			Formatting options (Signatures and Stationery dialog box)		
Forward Task	OUT 208		Forward button (TASK tab | Actions group)			CTRL+F
Holidays, Add to Default Calendar	OUT 73		Add Holidays button (FILE tab | Options tab, Calendar category)			
Hyperlink, Add to Email Message	OUT 238		Select text, click Hyperlink button (INSERT tab | Links group)			CTRL+K
iCalendar File, Import	OUT 104		Open Calendar (FILE tab | Open & Export tab)			
Image, Add to Email Message	OUT 241		Pictures button (INSERT tab | Illustrations group)			
Image, Add to Email Signature	OUT 252			Insert Picture button (Signatures and Stationery dialog box)		
Item, Attach to Task	OUT 205		Outlook Item button (INSERT tab | Include group)			
Junk Email Options, Configure	OUT 259		Junk button (HOME tab | Delete group)			
Language Preferences, Set	OUT 9		FILE tab | Options tab, Language category			
Mailbox Size, View	OUT 47		Folder Properties button (FOLDER tab | Properties group), Folder Size button			

Microsoft Office Outlook 2013 Quick Reference Summary *(continued)*

Task	Page Number	Touch Gesture	Ribbon	Other On-Screen Area	Shortcut Menu	Keyboard Shortcut
Mark Task as Complete	OUT 211		Mark Complete button (HOME tab | Manage Task group)		Right-click task, click Mark Complete	
Meeting, Cancel Meeting	OUT 112		Cancel Meeting button (CALENDAR TOOLS MEETING tab | Actions group)			
Meeting, Change Meeting Time	OUT 110			Double-tap or double-click meeting, change details or Drag meeting to new time		
Meeting, Create Meeting Request	OUT 108		New Meeting button (HOME tab | New group)			CTRL+SHIFT+Q
Meeting, Propose New Time	OUT 112		Propose New Time button (CALENDAR TOOLS MEETING tab | Respond group)			
Meeting, Reply to Meeting Request	OUT 111		Accept button (MEETING tab | Respond group)			
Meeting, Send Meeting Request	OUT 108			Send button in Meeting window		ALT+S
Meeting, Update Changed Meeting	OUT 110		Send Update button (MEETING tab | Show group)	Send Update button in Meeting window		
Member, Add to Contact Group	OUT 149		Add Members button (CONTACT GROUP tab | Add Members group)			
Message Format, Set Default	OUT 246		FILE tab | Options tab, Mail category, click Compose messages in this format box arrow			
Multiple Tasks, Categorize	OUT 190		Select tasks, click Categorize button (HOME tab | Tags group)		Select tasks, right-click one task's category column, click All Categories	
Name, Add to Contact Group	OUT 149		Add Members button (CONTACT GROUP tab | Add Members group)			
Name, Remove from Contact Group	OUT 150		Remove Member button (CONTACT GROUP tab | Members group)			
Natural Language Phrasing	OUT 92			Message window, type phrase		
Navigation Bar Options, Change	OUT 6			Navigation Options button on Navigation bar		
Note, Create	OUT 218		New Note (HOME tab | New group)			CTRL+SHIFT+N

Microsoft Office Outlook 2013 Quick Reference Summary *(continued)*

Task	Page Number	Touch Gesture	Ribbon	Other On-Screen Area	Shortcut Menu	Keyboard Shortcut
Note, Delete	OUT 220		Delete button (HOME tab | Delete group)			
Notes View, Change	OUT 219		Notes List button (HOME tab | Current View group)			
Options for Junk Email, Configure	OUT 259		Junk button (HOME tab | Delete group)			
Outlook Data File, Open	OUT 8		Open Outlook Data File (FILE tab | Open & Export tab)			
Outlook Item, Attach to Task	OUT 205		Outlook Item button (INSERT tab | Include group)			
Outlook Options, Display	OUT 245		FILE tab | Options tab			
People Pane, Change View	OUT 24		People Pane button (VIEW tab | People Pane group)	Expand/Collapse arrow on People Pane		
Personal Calendar Folder, Create	OUT 64		New Calendar button (FOLDER tab | New group)			CTRL+ SHIFT+E
Preview Contact List	OUT 152		FILE tab | Print tab			
Print Contact List	OUT 156		FILE tab | Print tab, click Print button			
Print Only Selected Items in Contact List	OUT 154		FILE tab | Print tab, click Print Options button, click Only selected items option button, click Print button			
Print Tasks	OUT 217		FILE tab | Print tab, click Print button			
Priority, Create Task with	OUT 179		New Task button (HOME tab | New group), click Priority box arrow			
Quick Click, Set	OUT200		Categorize button (HOME tab | Tags group), click Set Quick Click		Right-click task's category column, click Set Quick Click	
Quick Click, Use to Categorize Email Message	OUT 198			Click category column for email message		
Quick Parts, Create	OUT 240		Quick Parts button (INSERT tab | Text group)			
Reading Pane, Reposition	OUT 26		Reading Pane button (VIEW tab | Layout group)			

Microsoft Office Outlook 2013 Quick Reference Summary *(continued)*

Task	Page Number	Touch Gesture	Ribbon	Other On-Screen Area	Shortcut Menu	Keyboard Shortcut
Recurring Task, Create	OUT 183		New Task button (HOME tab | New group), click Recurrence button (TASK tab | Recurrence group)			
Refine Search	OUT 141		Click Search Contacts text box, click More button (Search Tools Search tab | Refine group), click property			CTRL+E
Reminder, Create Task with	OUT 180		New Task button (HOME tab | New group), click Reminder check box, click Reminder date box arrow			
Remove Attachment to Contact	OUT 135			Double-click contact, click attachment, press delete		DELETE
Remove Name from Contact Group	OUT 150		Remove Member button (CONTACT GROUP tab | Members group)			
Remove Task	OUT 212		Remove from List button (HOME tab | Manage Task group) or Display task, click Delete button (HOME tab | Delete group)		Right-click task, click Delete	DELETE
Rename Category	OUT 193		Click Categorize button (HOME tab | Tags group), click All Categories, click category, click Rename		Right-click task's category column, click All Categories, select category, click Rename button	
RSS Feed, Delete	OUT 280	Press and hold RSS feed, tap Delete Folder			Right-click RSS feed, click Delete Folder	
RSS Feed, Subscribe to	OUT 278	Press and hold RSS Feeds folder, tap Add a New RSS Feed			Right-click RSS Feeds folder, click Add a New RSS Feed	
Rule, Create	OUT 264		Rules button (HOME tab | Move group), click Create Rule			

Task	Page Number	Touch Gesture	Ribbon	Other On-Screen Area	Shortcut Menu	Keyboard Shortcut
Rule, Delete	OUT 270		Rules button (HOME tab | Move group), click Manage Rules and Alerts, click Delete button (Rules and Alerts dialog box)			
Rule, Run	OUT 268		Rules button (HOME tab | Move group), click Manage Rules and Alerts, click Run Rules Now button (Rules and Alerts dialog box)			
Run Rule	OUT 268		Rules button (HOME tab | Move group), click Manage Rules and Alerts, click Run Rules Now button (Rules and Alerts dialog box)			
Safe Senders List, Add Domain to	OUT 260		Junk button (HOME tab | Delete group), click Junk E-mail Options, click Safe Senders tab, click Add button			
Search, Refine	OUT 150, OUT 243		Click Search Contacts text box, click More button (SEARCH TOOLS SEARCH tab | Refine group), click property			CTRL+E
Search, Use Instant Search	OUT 243	Tap Instant Search text box		Click Instant Search text box		
Search Folder, Create	OUT 244		New Search Folder button (FOLDER tab | New group)			
Select Style for Contact List	OUT 153		FILE tab | Print tab			
Send Status Report	OUT 209		Send Status Report button (TASK tab | Manage Task group)			
Sensitivity Level, Set for All New Messages	OUT 10		FILE tab | Options tab, Mail category			
Set Default Message Format	OUT 246		FILE tab | Options tab, Mail category, Compose messages in this format box arrow (Outlook Options dialog box)			
Set Junk Email Options	OUT 259		Junk button (HOME tab | Delete group)			

Microsoft Office Outlook 2013 Quick Reference Summary *(continued)*						
Task	**Page Number**	**Touch Gesture**	**Ribbon**	**Other On-Screen Area**	**Shortcut Menu**	**Keyboard Shortcut**
Set Quick Click	OUT 195		Categorize button (HOME tab | Tags group), click Set Quick Click		Right-click task's category column, click Set Quick Click	
Signature, Add Image to	OUT 251			Insert Picture button (Signatures and Stationery dialog box)		
Signature, Assign to Single Email Message	OUT 252		Open message, click Signature button (INSERT tab | Include group)			
Signature, Create for Email	OUT 248		FILE tab | Options tab, Mail category, click Signatures button (Outlook Options dialog box)			
Signature, Format	OUT 249			Font box arrow (Signatures and Stationery dialog box)		
Signature Options, Set	OUT 253			Select settings (Signatures and Stationery dialog box)		
Sort Contacts	OUT 146		Reverse Sort button (VIEW tab | Arrangement group)			
Stationery, Assign Theme to	OUT 255			Stationery and Fonts button (Outlook Options dialog box), Theme button (Signatures and Stationery dialog box)		
Stationery, Customize	OUT 254		FILE tab | Options tab, Mail category, click Stationery and Fonts button (Outlook Options dialog box)			
Status, Create Task with	OUT 177		New Task button (HOME tab | New group), click Status box arrow			
Status Report, Send	OUT 210		Send Status Report button (TASK tab | Manage Task group)			
Subscribe to RSS Feed	OUT 278	Press and hold RSS Feeds folder, tap Add a New RSS Feed			Right-click RSS Feeds folder, click Add a New RSS Feed	
Task, Add with To-Do List Pane	OUT 192	Tap 'Type a new task' box, enter description		Click 'Type a new task' box, enter description		

Microsoft Office Outlook 2013 Quick Reference Summary *(continued)*

Task	Page Number	Touch Gesture	Ribbon	Other On-Screen Area	Shortcut Menu	Keyboard Shortcut
Task, Assign	OUT 206		Assign Task button (TASK tab | Manage Task group)			
Task, Attach File to	OUT 205		Attach File button (INSERT tab | Include group)			
Task, Categorize	OUT 196		Click task, click Categorize button (HOME tab | Tags group)		Right-click task's category column, click All Categories	
Task, Create	OUT 181		New Task button (HOME tab | New group)			
Task, Create Recurring	OUT 190		New Task button (HOME tab | New group), Recurrence button (TASK tab | Recurrence group)			
Task, Create with Due Date	OUT 184		New Task button (HOME tab | New group), click Due date box arrow			
Task, Create with Priority	OUT 186		New Task button (HOME tab | New group), click Priority box arrow			
Task, Create with Reminder	OUT 187		New Task button (HOME tab | New group), click Reminder check box, click Reminder date box arrow			
Task, Create with Status	OUT 185		New Task button (HOME tab | New group), click Status box arrow			
Task, Forward	OUT 208		Forward button (TASK tab | Actions group)			CTRL+F
Task, Mark Complete	OUT 212		Mark Complete button (HOME tab | Manage Task group)		Right-click task, click Mark Complete	
Task, Print	OUT 216		FILE tab	Print tab, select style, click Print button			
Task, Remove	OUT 213		Remove from List button (HOME tab | Manage Task group) or Display task, click Delete button (HOME tab | Delete group)		Right-click task, click Delete	DELETE

Microsoft Office Outlook 2013 Quick Reference Summary *(continued)*

Task	Page Number	Touch Gesture	Ribbon	Other On-Screen Area	Shortcut Menu	Keyboard Shortcut
Task, Send Status Report for	OUT 209		Send Status Report button (TASK tab | Manage Task group)			
Task, Update	OUT 204	Double-tap task		Double-click task		
Task View, Change	OUT 215		Change View button (HOME tab | Current View group)			
Tasks, Print	OUT 217		FILE tab | Print tab, click Print button			
Theme, Apply to Email Message	OUT 15		Themes button (OPTIONS tab | Themes group)			
Theme, Save	OUT 16		Themes button (OPTIONS tab | Themes group), Save Current Theme			
Theme, Assign to Stationery	OUT 255			Stationery and Fonts button (Outlook Options dialog box), Theme button (Signatures and Stationery dialog box)		
Time Zone, Change in Calendar	OUT 276		FILE tab | Options tab, Calendar category, click Time zone box arrow (Outlook Options dialog box)			
Update Task	OUT 202			Double-click task		
View, Change	OUT 145		More button (HOME tab | Current View group), click view			
Weather Bar, Add City to	OUT 67			Arrow button for current city, Add Location		
Work Time, Change on Calendar	OUT 273		FILE tab | Options tab, Calendar category (Outlook Options dialog box)			

Important Notes for Windows 7 Users

The screen shots in this book show Microsoft Office 2013 running in Windows 8. If you are using Microsoft Windows 7, however, you still can use this book because Office 2013 runs virtually the same way on both platforms. You will encounter only minor differences if you are using Windows 7. Read this section to understand the differences.

Dialog Boxes

If you are a Windows 7 user, the dialog boxes shown in this book will look slightly different than what you see on your screen. Dialog boxes for Windows 8 have a title bar with a solid color, and the dialog box name is centered on the title bar. Beyond these superficial differences in appearance, however, the options in the dialog boxes across both platforms are the same. For instance, Figures 1 and 2 show the Font dialog box in Windows 7 and the Font dialog box in Windows 8.

Figure 1 Font Dialog Box in Windows 7

Figure 2 Font Dialog Box in Windows 8

Alternate Steps for Running an App in Windows 7

Nearly all of the steps in this book work exactly the same way for Windows 7 users; however, running an app (or program/application) requires different steps for Windows 7. The following steps show how to run an app in Windows 7.

Running an App (or Program/Application) Using Windows 7

1. Click the Start button on the taskbar to display the Start menu.
2. Click All Programs and then click the Microsoft Office 2013 folder (Figure 3).
3. If necessary, click the name of the folder containing the app you want to run.
4. Click the name of the app you want to run (such as Excel 2013).

Figure 3   Running an App Using the Windows 7 Start Menu